ISLAM
A LIVING FAITH

NATANA J. DELONG-BAS

ANSELM
A C A D E M I C

DEDICATION

For John L. Esposito and John O. Voll,
finest of mentors and dearest of friends,
for teaching me everything I know about Islam

Created by the publishing team of Anselm Academic.

Cover image: © LeoPatrizi / istock.com

Printed in the United States of America

7083

ISBN 987-1-59982-865-7

DeLong-Bas provides an excellent introduction to Islam for twenty-first century readers, introducing the major themes of the faith tradition and providing engaging portraits of historic and contemporary Muslims. One among the book's many strengths is its presentation of topics of contemporary interest within the historical framework of the Islamic faith tradition. Her model analysis of the politics and theologies of gender examines historical developments and current controversies. Coverage of the history and evolution of Muslim-Christian relations from the time of Muhammad to the present contributes importantly to scholarship as well as adds a dimension not usually covered in books introducing Islam.

—John Voll, Georgetown University

In this book, De-Long Bas writes about Islam not just eruditely—but engagingly and accessibly as well. The result is a broad-ranging discussion of many key issues that skillfully lays bare the diversity and complexity of the Islamic tradition. Highly recommended for all those who have been waiting for such a lucid introduction to what has been described as "the fastest-growing religion" in the world today.

—Asma Afsaruddin, Indiana University

DeLong-Bas's *Islam: A Living Faith* is a must read. This exceptionally well-written, informative, and engaging introduction to Islam and Christian-Muslim relations will be welcomed by teachers, students, religious leaders, and the general public.

—John L. Esposito, Georgetown University

DeLong-Bas has drawn upon her rich experiences as a teacher and scholar to produce an outstanding textbook on Islam. This accessible and well-written work is informed by current scholarship and includes many features that make it an attractive resource for the classroom. In particular, the study questions and recommended readings and films provide opportunities to further explore the many important issues that are addressed in each chapter. Its title *Islam: A Living Faith* captures well one of the great strengths of this book—it both introduces the reader to the rich history and traditions of Islam and explains how that heritage is being expressed and lived out by Muslims today.

—John Kaltner, Rhodes College

Islam: A Living Faith is *the* go-to primer for those interested in understanding the fastest-growing religion on earth. DeLong-Bas gives a thorough presentation of Islam's core beliefs, practices, and historical development in an accessible narrative. The text pays particular attention to issues of contemporary concern: the difference between Sunnis and Shia Muslims; the nature of the caliphate; Sharia and Islamic law; the status of women and non-Muslims; Sufism, Islamic spirituality, and mysticism; the nature of jihad; terrorism; and Islamic ideals of governance and international relations. With reviews, discussion questions, and suggestions for further resources in every chapter, I highly recommend it for teachers as well as students.

—Tamara Sonn, Georgetown University

Author Acknowledgments

I would like to express my deepest appreciation to Anselm Academic for the pleasure of working on this book together. It has been an incredible experience of teamwork, bringing together many minds, visions, and ideas. Special thanks are due to the following:

Brad Harmon for initiating a conversation about this book, recognizing a gap in substantive, informed publications on Islam by a Catholic press and seeing an opportunity for greater understanding between Christianity and Islam.

Kathleen Walsh for superb questions, comments, and editing—and for being such a joy to work with. Her perspective as a teacher of world religions courses and her insights on what material would be most helpful and informative to students was infinitely helpful to me in mapping the content of this book.

The anonymous reviewers who graciously offered valuable and thoughtful feedback and questions on different chapters, suggesting critical additions and clarifications and calling for the addition of a chapter on Muslim-Christian relations. I have done my best to respond to their recommendations and hope I have done them justice. This book is much stronger for their careful attention.

Annie Belt for her sharp eye for detail and for thinking about the impact of the presentation of the material and how it might be perceived or read. She sent me back to the drawing board numerous times, pushing for greater clarity and accessibility for a nonspecialist audience—and made this book better in the process.

Maura Hagarty for prompt and efficient project management and for always being responsive, keeping me informed of schedules and deadlines, and offering encouragement along the way.

The image researchers for finding a stunning cover picture and other illustrations.

My father, Rev. James A. DeLong, for reading through the entire manuscript, offering feedback, and engaging in deep discussions of biblical and Qur'anic material. I hope there are no remaining split infinitives.

And, as always, to my husband, Christophe, and children, Aurora and Gabriel, for their support throughout the process of envisioning, researching, writing, and revising this book, particularly as we juggled challenging medical issues. Their patience, humor, and unending belief in what I was trying to accomplish made all the difference.

Publisher Acknowledgments

Thank you to the following individuals who reviewed this work in progress:

Rita George-Tvrtković, *Benedictine University, Lisle, Illinois*
Marcia Hermansen, *Loyola University of Chicago*
Frances Leap, *Seton Hill University, Greensburg, Pennsylvania*

Contents

INTRODUCTION

As the faith tradition of 1.6 billion people globally, Islam is the second largest and fastest-growing of the world's religions and is expected to be the world's largest religion by the end of the twenty-first century.[1] Islam represents about 23% of the global population today, so that one out of almost every four people on this planet identifies as Muslim. That percentage is expected to grow to nearly 30% by 2050.

Numbers alone suggest the need for accurate information about Islam as a religion, about how Muslims live out that faith in their daily lives, and how this belief system impacts systems of government and law, women's and minority rights, and international relations. Many in the West question Islam's compatibility with the core concepts of Western civilization—democracy, human rights, and secular law—and ask whether Muslims can fully integrate into non-Muslim societies.[2]

These are important questions. Finding answers will require looking beyond stereotypes and popular, but often inaccurate, perceptions to facts and allowing Muslim voices and actions to define their faith as they live and know it. Although the stereotypical image of a Muslim is one of an Arab man with either a beard or a turban or an Arab woman covered from head to toe in black, only about 20% of the world's Muslims are Arab and live in the Middle East. Most of the world's Muslims (62%) live in the Asia-Pacific region. The largest Muslim populations today are found in Indonesia, India, Pakistan, Bangladesh, and Nigeria, not the Middle East. India's population is growing the fastest and is expected to overtake Indonesia's

---

1. Statistics are from *www.pewresearch.org/fact-tank/2016/07/22/muslims-and-islam-key-findings-in-the-u-s-and-around-the-world/*.

2. For one of the most influential analyses of this type, see Samuel P. Huntington, *The Clash of Civilizations and the Remaking of World Order* (New York: Simon and Schuster, 2011). Although ultimately calling for an international order based on the recognition of and cooperation between civilizations, Huntington's thesis has been challenged for its insistence on civilizational difference and for Othering, which result in claims of Western superiority.

claim as home to the world's largest Muslim population by 2050. Yet Muslims are currently a minority population in India at just under 15% of the total population.[3]

By contrast, Muslims constitute less than 1% of the American population and 6% of the European population. Although the Muslim population is growing at a rate of about 1% per decade in Europe, it is expected to remain a minority.[4] Similarly, the American Muslim population is expected to grow minimally by 2050 to about 2% of the population. About half of the growth of the American Muslim population between 2010 and 2015 was due to immigration. The other half was due to natural increase. There has been little net change due to religious conversion.[5]

The small number of Muslims in the United States, in particular, means that most Americans do not personally know and have never interacted with a Muslim. A 2015 YouGov poll in the United States found that 74% of respondents did not personally work with a Muslim, 68% did not have a friend who was Muslim, and 87% had never been inside a mosque. Yet, despite that lack of personal experience and encounter, fully 40% said they supported the creation of a national database to track Muslims. This suggests that Americans' lack of exposure to and knowledge of Muslims may promote fear of them as the Other.[6] This is particularly true when that Other is often seen engaged in violence, whether in news coverage or other media

---

3. Statistics are from *www.pewresearch.org/fact-tank/2015/04/21/by-2050-india-to-have-worlds-largest-populations-of-hindus-and-muslims/*.

4. Statistics are from *www.pewresearch.org/fact-tank/2016/07/19/5-facts-about-the-muslim-population-in-europe/*.

5. Statistics are from *www.pewresearch.org/fact-tank/2016/01/06/a-new-estimate-of-the-u-s-muslim-population-/*.

6. Mona Chalabi, "How Anti-Muslim Are Americans? Data Points to Extent of Islamophobia," *The Guardian*, December 8, 2015. On the question of whether Muslims are truly different from non-Muslims, including with respect to fusing religious and political authority and being prone to mass political violence, see the social scientific analysis by M. Steven Fish, *Are Muslims Distinctive? A Look at the Evidence* (New York: Oxford University Press, 2011). Fish finds, e.g., that although Islamists are responsible for a disproportionate share of terrorist bombings in the contemporary world, a large portion of those attacks occur in seven countries, none of which are in the West and most of which occurs in the context of larger conflicts, such as civil wars or insurgencies. See Fish, "Large-Scale Political Violence and Terrorism," chapter 5 in *Are Muslims Distinctive?*, 133–71, esp. 170–71.

portrayals that tend to focus on exceptional stories of tragedy and terror, rather than normal, everyday life.[7]

Such images are powerful, particularly when combined with ongoing terrorist attacks and violence targeting Europe and the United States. Yet such images can also be misleading in portraying what appears to be a pervasive and exclusive "radical Islamic threat" to Western public safety. The reality is that, between 2008 and 2016, there were twice as many terrorism incidents in the United States perpetrated by right-wing extremists, often white supremacists, than by those claiming inspiration from a radical interpretation of Islam, such as that espoused by ISIS.[8] More Muslims than Americans or Europeans have been killed in terrorist attacks.[9] Most terrorist attacks do not occur on American or European soil, but in Muslim countries—60% in Iraq, Afghanistan, and Pakistan alone between 2004 and 2013.[10] Terrorist attacks by Muslims account for less than 0.33% of all murders in the United States: a total of 54 in 2016,

---

7. While the media should report terrorist incidents, some question why incidents perpetrated by Muslims seem to be automatically labeled as terrorist, while descriptions of other terrorist cases pay more attention to the personal psychology and history of the attacker, who may be described as "deranged" or a "mass murderer" rather than as a "terrorist." See, e.g., the report by Erin M. Kearns, Allison Betus, and Anthony Lemieux, "Why Do Some Terrorist Attacks Receive More Media Attention than Others?" March 5, 2017, *https://papers.ssrn.com/sol3/papers.cfm?abstract_id=2928138*. For a broad analysis of religiously inspired terrorism and cultures of violence, see Mark Juergensmeyer, *Terror in the Mind of God* (Oakland: University of California Press, 2017). For an analysis of negative media portrayals of Arabs in particular and their impact on perceptions and policies, see Jack G. Shaheen, *Guilty: Hollywood's Verdict on Arabs after 9/11* (Northampton, MA: Olive Branch, 2008).

8. A breakdown of the 201 designated terrorism incidents can be found at *http://www.theinvestigativefund.org/investigation/2017/06/22/home-hate/*. Of these incidents, 115 were perpetrated by right-wing extremists, compared to 63 by "Islamist domestic terrorism." Most of these 115 incidents—76%—were foiled, meaning that no attack took place, as compared with only 35% of those involving right-wing extremists. Though there were more attacks by right-wing extremists that produced fatalities (about 33%) than by those claiming Islamic inspiration (13%), the total number of fatalities was slightly higher for those claiming Islamic inspiration (90) than for right-wing extremists (79).

9. Official statistics indicate Muslim casualties accounted for 82% to 97% of total casualties between 2007 and 2012, according to the *National Counterterrorism Center Report on Terrorism, 2011* (Washington, DC: National Counterterrorism Center, 2012), *https://fas.org/irp/threat/nctc2011.pdf*.

10. Ruth Alexander and Hannah Moor, "Are Most Victims of Terrorism Muslim?" *BBC News Magazine,* January 20, 2015, *http://www.bbc.com/news/magazine-30883058*.

as compared with 11,000 Americans killed by other individuals or groups that year from gun homicides alone. Since the tragedy of 9/11, a total of 123 fatalities have been caused by Muslim-American extremists, as compared with 240,000 murders by other individuals or groups over the same time period.[11]

While these tragedies should not be underplayed, the statistics raise serious questions as to whether Muslim Americans as such constitute a genuine threat to American public safety, particularly given their long history in the United States.[12] They also suggest that allowing a minority of dangerous and violent individuals and organizations to speak for an entire faith tradition with a 1,400-year-long history is a slippery slope. While the forty-six Muslim Americans who were linked to violent extremism at home or abroad in 2016 should be regarded as a security concern, that concern should not be applied wholesale and without justification to the entire population of 3.3 million Muslim Americans, many of whom are highly educated professionals, making valuable contributions to society as doctors, computer scientists, engineers, technicians, and researchers and professors, among other fields.[13] For many, these contributions reflect their devotion to Islam as a living faith.

Many polls have found the overwhelming majority of the world's Muslims reject terrorism and extremism.[14] Instead, they

---

11. Of those 123, 49 occurred at a single event—the Pulse nightclub shooting in Orlando, Florida in 2016. See Charles Kurzman, "Muslim-American Involvement with Violent Extremism, 2015," Triangle Center on Terrorism and Homeland Security, Duke University, February 2, 2016, at *https://kurzman.unc.edu/files/2016/02/Kurzman_Muslim-American_Involvement_in_Violent_Extremism_2015.pdf.*

12. For a history of Muslims in the United States dating to the sixteenth century and including immigrants, beginning with slaves and native-born populations, see Edward E. Curtis, *Muslims in America: A Short History* (New York: Oxford University Press, 2009).

13. Muslim Americans have the second-highest education levels among major religious groups in the United States. "Muslims in the United States," Council on Foreign Relations, September 19, 2011, at *www.cfr.org/united-states/muslims-united-states/p25927.*

14. For general Muslim views on terrorism and extremism, see, e.g., John L. Esposito and Dalia Mogahed, *Who Speaks for Islam? What a Billion Muslims Really Think* (New York: Gallup, 2008.) For specific Muslim views on ISIS, which are overwhelmingly negative, see *www.pewresearch.org/fact-tank/2015/11/17/in-nations-with-significant-muslim-populations-much-disdain-for-isis/.*

seek constructive channels for living out their faith—prayer, charitable giving, disaster relief, community activism, care for the poor and marginalized, and, not least, dialogue—dialogue between individuals, between countries, and between religions. Through dialogue, community programs, billboard campaigns,[15] op-ed pieces, books, articles, and social media efforts such as Muslims Against ISIS,[16] #NotInMyName,[17] #MuslimsAreSpeakingOut,[18] and MyJihadInc@ MyJihadOrg,[19] Muslims hope to reclaim their own voices and speak for themselves, rather than having extremists claim media headlines and airwaves, claiming to speak for them.

This book aims to contribute to constructive dialogue, to explore Islam as a living practice, not just a belief system, of individuals and communities. Chapter 1 introduces the Five Pillars, which all Muslims are expected to fulfill throughout their lives. Chapter 2 offers the life and legacy of Muhammad. The Qur'an and its role in the lives of Muslims is explored in chapter 3. Next, some of the tougher issues that have led to unrest, such as the development of sectarian identities (Sunnis and Shia) are considered in chapter 4; Shariah and Islamic law, which are implemented in different ways across time and space, are presented in chapter 5; chapter 6 examines the mystical tradition of Sufism as both protest and inner spirituality; and chapter 7 considers competing visions of jihad as personal discipline and nonviolent struggle for change versus militancy. The final chapters turn to the meaning of Islam for Muslim women and state policies related to gender in chapter 8 and the history Muslim-Christian encounters in chapter 9. The goal is to help twenty-first-century readers place contemporary events in a broad context, to encounter Islam as a faith tradition that both holds certain core beliefs and values as eternal and yet remains a living faith that requires reinterpretation in changing contexts and circumstances. It is hoped a critical approach to these topics will provide a more nuanced foundation for

---

15. See the "ISIS Sucks" campaign begun by SoundVision at *https://www.sound vision.com/isis_sucks*.

16. See *https://www.facebook.com/Muslims-Against-ISIS-1444672609121662/*.

17. See *http://isisnotinmyname.com*.

18. See *http://www.ffeu.org/muslimsarespeakingout/*.

19. See *https://twitter.com/MyJihadOrg*.

policy considerations, domestic and international, as well as for individual encounters in an era of interfaith and intercultural dialogue.

If there is ever to be global peace, understanding, and cooperative coexistence, it must begin with knowledge, rather than fear, of the religious Other. It is in that spirit that this book was written. Readers are encouraged to set aside the fearful headlines and consider Islam in its entirety as a living faith.

The Five Pillars
Living Islam as an Individual and as a Community

As a living faith, Islam is more than a belief system; it is a "path" for living a righteous life centered on love of God and love of neighbor.[1] This "path" is marked by the Five Pillars—a common set of practices that unite the faith community (*ummah*). Muslims of every time and place, women and men, are expected to fulfill the Five Pillars, which give practitioners a strong sense of individual and communal identity. While local practices may vary in the specifics, the Five Pillars are always central to Muslim life and faith. They also keep Islam solidly grounded as a faith focused on orthopraxy (correct behavior), not just orthodoxy (correct belief).

Although the Five Pillars are a starting point for understanding Islam, they do not hold all of Muslim belief and practice.[2] All Muslims respect and are expected to adhere to the Five Pillars, but some Muslims are more dedicated to their complete fulfillment than others. Yet, even when Muslims fall short, there remains a sense that the Five Pillars represent the ideal Muslims should strive to achieve.

---

1. As stated in "A Common Word," a 2007 letter signed by 138 Muslim leaders and scholars and sent to Christian religious leaders as an invitation to dialogue between Islam and Christianity. See *http://www.acommonword.com* and chapter 9 in this book for more information.

2. For concerns on the use of the Five Pillars in a reductive way that risks neglecting other important aspects of Islam, as well as for variations in the Five Pillars across time and space, see Daniel Varisco, "Islam Obscured: The Rhetoric of Anthropological Representation," in *The Anthropology of Islam Reader*, ed. Jens Kreinath (London: Routledge, 2012), 322–43, esp. 325.

A Brief History of the Pillars

The Five Pillars are

1. *Shahadah*—declaration of faith
2. *Salat*—five daily prayers
3. *Zakat*—charitable giving
4. *Sawm*—fasting during the month of Ramadan
5. *Hajj*—pilgrimage to Mecca

These are the core expressions of Islam, practices that have been central to Muslim identity and practice since the lifetime of Muhammad. Note that jihad is *not* one of the Five Pillars, however much some extremists today may try to make it one.[3]

Although the Five Pillars are all mentioned in the Qur'an, they do not appear together in a single verse. Qur'an 4:162 specifies belief in God, the Last Day, and Muhammad's revelation, prayers, and *zakat*. Fasting during Ramadan is specified in Q 2:183–85, and Hajj is required in Q 2:196. All of the pillars are believed to have been implemented in their current form during Muhammad's life and appear in the earliest hadith collections (accounts of Muhammad's sayings and deeds) as essential obligations. They were placed together in a famous hadith declaring, "Islam is built upon five pillars."

The Qur'an describes the pillars as a framework for worship and a commitment to faith (responsibilities to God) and moral responsibility (responsibilities to other people), rather than as a formal, systematic statement of faith or creed. The mechanics and meanings of the pillars are discussed extensively in legal and theological writings and play an important role in popular piety.

Key to the practice of the pillars is the worldwide Muslim faith community, or *ummah*. Although it is up to the individual to carry out the pillars, this is done as a member of a broader community. Qur'an 2:143 teaches that God has established the *ummah* for its members to serve as witnesses of God's guidance to all people. The *ummah* is intended as the chief source of identity and belonging for the Muslim; it transcends all other identities—tribal, ethnic, or

---

3. This topic will be addressed in chapter 7, "Jihad: The Struggle to Live Islam and Its Teachings."

national—and is inclusive and diverse by nature. In Q 9:71, God specifically commands members of the *ummah* to protect one another, call each other to good and forbid what is evil, observe regular prayers, regularly give alms, and obey God and God's Messenger. In return, God promises to shower the *ummah* with God's mercy. This indicates God had a specific purpose in forming the *ummah* as a community, rather than simply creating individuals. This *ummah* is intended to live in relationship—with God and with each other.

Practically speaking, membership in the *ummah* indicates an acceptance of God's sovereignty and of the prophethood and leadership of Muhammad as key parts of Muslim identity. Muslims often refer to the *ummah* in everyday speech to foster a sense of connection to other Muslims that transcends geographic, ethnic, and other boundaries. This concept became particularly important in the European colonial era (the nineteenth and twentieth centuries), when Muslims sought ways to draw together to keep their identity, particularly when competing with European concepts such as nationalism and state borders. Islamic resistance movements called for the *ummah* to defend itself against European intrusions, invoking the *ummah* to reinvigorate Islamic solidarity. The concept was so powerful even secular nationalists tapped into it for nation-building after the colonial era.

Today most Muslims think of membership in the *ummah* as a social identity that fosters a sense of connection to other Muslims. This is particularly the case when Muslims appear to be suffering injustice or oppression, with Muslims in Chechnya, Bosnia, Kosovo, Palestine, Afghanistan, Iraq, and Syria being the most frequently cited cases. Nevertheless, a minority of extremists, such as ISIS, project a vision of the *ummah* as a political rather than a social identity for Muslims. Their goal is to assert leadership of a global caliphate that eliminates borders between countries and "reunites" the *ummah* under a single leader. They claim this represents a "return" to the past; however, as will be discussed later, this idealized vision of the past has little grounding in history.[4]

---

4. Details can be found in chapter 4, "Sunnis and Shia: The Origins and Evolutions of Sectarianism in Islam." Briefly, most of the world's Muslims—the Sunnis—often look to the Abbasid Empire (750–1258 CE) as a golden age in Islamic history, a time when all Muslims were united under a single leader. However, the historical record is far more complex, with rival caliphates and leaders in different places at different times; indeed, memories of this "unity" might be best described as invented memories.

The sense of community fostered by membership in the *ummah* has been critical to the development of Islam as a global religion that transcends time and space. This sense of community is also reflected in the focus of each of the Five Pillars.

Shahadah: The Declaration of Faith and Membership in the *Ummah*

"*Ashhadu 'an la illahah illa Allah wa ashhadu 'anna Muhammad rasul Allah*"

"I witness that there is no god but The God and I witness that Muhammad is God's Messenger."

Proclaiming this statement, or witnessing, is the first of the Five Pillars and marks an individual's entry into the broader Muslim faith community.[5] The statement consists of two phrases—the first focused on God and the second confirming Muhammad's role as the bearer of God's message to humanity. This makes two things clear. First, God is the only God—a statement of God's uniqueness known as *tawhid*; nothing and no one are to be associated with God. Second, Muhammad is neither God nor a divine figure; he is simply a man who carried a divine message. Just as the Ten Commandments in Christianity and Judaism assert the believer's obligations to God first and to the community second, so the order of the phrases of the *shahadah* indicate the primary importance of God followed by membership in the *ummah*.

Although declaring the *shahadah* marks the moment of one's conversion to Islam, the *shahadah* is not a one-time declaration or event. Rather, it begins an ongoing attestation of faith throughout a Muslim's life. The *shahadah* is proclaimed during prayer, community

---

5. In this sense, it can be compared to the Christian sacrament of baptism, when *baptism* is defined as entry into the faith community (church) with the intent of pursuing a lifelong relationship with God and the church. Similar to evangelical understandings of baptism as the declaration of a personal decision to accept God/Jesus into their lives, declaration of the *shahadah* expresses belief in God. However, the similarities end there. The *shahadah* is not associated with the concept of sin in Islam, whereas Roman Catholic and many mainstream Protestant Christians believe baptism is necessary for forgiveness of original sin, passed down from Adam and Eve. Muslims do not believe in original sin, so have no theological need for baptism.

events and gatherings, and often as part of the repetitive phrases used by Sufis in their devotional practices. The first half can also be used as a response to surprising, shocking, or tragic news or as a means of greeting others. The *shahadah* is a frequent subject of calligraphy, used in artwork ranging from simple pen and ink to more elaborate illuminations, from carved wood to marble, as sculptures or as adornment for mosques, homes, and other buildings. Keeping the *shahadah* central to daily life is a means of assuring daily attention to God and remembering the main tenets of the faith.

For those born into the faith, the *shahadah* is simply a part of normal worship and cultural practice. Those who convert to Islam must make a formal, public declaration in the presence of two adult witnesses. This shows the decision is not simply a private one about personal spiritual matters but also one that carries a sense of social responsibility to the community.

People living in non-Muslim majority countries seeking to convert to Islam sometimes find it hard to find a local mosque or local Muslims in order to make a formal conversion.[6] The Internet has come to the rescue with sites like IslamiCity.com offering to arrange multiparty phone calls for witnessing purposes. Many sites offer additional services to create the sense of being part of the online *ummah*, bringing an ancient concept into virtual reality.[7]

Salat: Prayer and Remembrance of God Five Times per Day

"*Allahu akbar! Allahu akbar!*"—"God is the Greatest! God is the Greatest!" Five times per day, this call to prayer (*adhan*) is issued from minarets and sound systems of mosques around the world, inviting the faithful to pause amid the busyness of daily life to remember the Divine.

Like many faith traditions, prayer is central to Islamic worship. Prayer is an opportunity to regularly remember God's power, presence, majesty, and mercy, as well as to re-center one's life on

---

6. Today, there are apps such as Near Mosques Finder that can help locate mosques.

7. For more on Islamic uses of cyberspace, see Gary R. Bunt, *iMuslims: Rewiring the House of Islam* (Chapel Hill: University of North Carolina Press, 2009).

God. Muslims are supposed to pray five times per day—at sunrise, noon, mid-afternoon, sunset, and evening. The exact times vary daily, based on the rising and setting of the sun, which changes paths throughout the year. In the past, people had to rely on personal observation or wait for the calls to prayer, which marked the appropriate times. Today, believers can find daily times for prayer listed online, based on their country of location, as well as apps and special alarms that can be set through computers, watches, mobile phones, and other devices.[8]

While five daily prayers may sound like a huge time commitment, prayers generally last only ten to fifteen minutes.[9] In addition, because people are sometimes unable to complete five separate prayer sessions, such as while traveling, it is possible to consolidate the prayer times into three sessions.[10] A famous hadith records Muhammad saying that Islam did not come to be a burden to people, but a blessing. Thus, rather than a list of obligations to check off on a daily basis, the five daily prayers are designed to encourage believers to begin and end their days with remembrance of God and to remember God at different moments throughout the day. In other words, rather than relegating God to a once-a-week formal worship service, prayer incorporates remembrance of God into the daily routine, making God a real presence in the believer's life.

Islamic prayer is a spiritual and physical endeavor that combines meditation, devotion, and physical exercise. While it can be performed individually, Muslims prefer to pray in groups, again

---

8. Examples include iPray Lite, which keeps track of prayer times and also offers options from the sound of clicking prayer beads to the turning wheel of a handheld metal counter to keep track of prayer repetitions.

9. The exception is the Friday noon prayer, which takes longer because of the inclusion of a sermon/homily (*khutbah*). Friday prayers can last from twenty minutes to an hour, depending on the length of the sermon.

10. In practice, many Muslims find the demands of daily life, particularly in the workplace, can make five daily prayers challenging. Some make accommodations, including by routinely praying during three occasions during the day, such as first thing in the morning, during lunch breaks, and before bed at night. Many Shia routinely pray during three occasions per day, combining the noon and mid-afternoon and then the sunset and evening prayers. They nevertheless pray five sets of prayers. Moojan Momen, *An Introduction to Shi'i Islam: The History and Doctrines of Twelver Shi'ism* (New Haven: Yale University Press, 1987), 178.

emphasizing the importance of community. Once a week, for the Friday "noon" prayer, Muslim men must attend communal prayers (*jumaa*) in the mosque.[11] Although women are not required to attend the mosque, they did so during Muhammad's lifetime and many increasingly choose to do so today to express their devotion to God and to be part of the community of faith.[12] The Friday service at the mosque includes a sermon/homily (*khutbah*) by the prayer leader (*imam*) that relates the teachings of the Qur'an to contemporary issues and circumstances faced by the local community.

Traditionally, the prayer leader was the person recognized as the most pious and knowledgeable among those gathered. While this still happens in some places today, particularly in informal gatherings, many mosques have one or several people specifically hired to fulfill this position. In many places, a full-time *imam* is also expected to provide counseling and guidance outside of prayer times, as well as to oversee other mosque activities, such as education and community outreach.[13] Although the *imam* is typically a man, women are permitted to lead other women in prayer, and there are some women-only mosques.[14] Some Muslim women, particularly in the West, have called for women to lead mixed-gender prayer services to better reflect the face of the Muslim community. In support, they cite Muhammad's appointment of a woman, Umm

---

11. Although called the "noon" prayer, the service typically takes place closer to 1 or 1:30 pm. Some Shia hold communal prayer on Thursday night, rather than Friday noon, to distinguish themselves from Sunnis.

12. There are some mosques that do not admit women worshipers, making access to the mosque a central focus for activists concerned about Muslim women's rights.

13. Unlike Christianity, Islam has no ordained clergy, in part because there are no sacraments in Islam. (See the section on "Pillars versus Sacraments" at the end of this chapter.) Nevertheless, throughout Islamic history, there has been a need for faith community leaders with a greater depth of knowledge in scripture, history, ritual, law, and so on. Although there is no ordained clergy in Islam, imams often fulfill comparable roles to Christian priests and pastors, serving as leaders of their congregations and surrounding communities, particularly in the West.

14. Examples include China's Muslims, who have a history of women-only mosques in the Henan, Shanxi, and Hebei provinces dating to the seventeenth century, and, more recently, the founding of the first American women-only mosque in Los Angeles, California, in 2015. Women-only mosques can also be found in Uzbekistan, Afghanistan, the Maldives, Indonesia, Lebanon, the Sudan, Northern Somalia, Germany, and the Netherlands.

Waraqa, to serve as the prayer leader for her household, which included women and men.[15]

Preparation for prayer involves cleaning body and mind from the "dirt" of the outside world. Muslims leave their shoes at the entrance to the mosque, so as not to track dirt into sacred space. They perform ablutions[16] before prayer, beginning with cleansing the heart and mind from worldly thoughts and concerns and proceeding to literally washing away the physical dirt of the world from the hands, face, arms up to the elbows, and feet, all with the intent of focusing exclusively on God. Many mosques have fountains or other water-access points to facilitate this process.[17] When water is not available, sand may be used. The focus is more on the symbolism of the ablutions—that cleanliness is preparation for godliness—than the mechanics.

Muhammad said the entire earth should be considered a mosque, reminding Muslims of the sacredness of the earth itself as God's creation. Practically speaking, this means prayer need not be confined to a particular building; rather believers can engage in prayer wherever they are at the appointed time. Prayer is supposed to be made in a clean space. Muslims typically use prayer carpets to create that clean space at their convenience. Some Muslims keep a carpet in their briefcase or desk drawer at work. Foldable carpets that fit inside a wallet also exist for ease of transportation.

Muslims always pray facing Mecca, no matter where on earth—or off the earth—they are. This practice provides a central focus for the faith community and symbolizes global unity as Muslims throughout the world all face the same location. As home to

---

15. Despite significant opposition by conservatives and traditionalists to women fulfilling this position in a mixed-gender setting—ranging from criticism to death threats—some women have publicly led Friday prayers, beginning with Amina Wadud. See her biography in chapter 8 on women and gender.

16. There are two kinds of ablutions that may be performed. Major ablutions (*ghusl*) of the entire body and hair must be performed after sex, menstruation, or childbirth. Minor ablutions (*wudu'*) are described above and would also be required before touching or reading the Qur'an.

17. A Malaysian company, AACE Technologies, has invented an Automatic Wudu Washer to help save water, given that many Muslim-majority countries face chronic water shortages. See *https://www.youtube.com/watch?v=s557KuEZttk*. The device also plays recorded Qur'an verses.

A Muslim child at prayer on a prayer rug with an open Qur'an and prayer beads. Open hands for *du'a* (prayers of personal petition) symbolize humility before God in asking for help and openness to God's presence and blessings.

the Grand Mosque, believed to house the original altar built to the One God by Abraham and Ismail (Ishmael), Mecca is considered the holiest city in Islam.[18] So vital is this concept that Muslims are buried facing Mecca to symbolize ongoing prayer.

Inside a mosque, the direction of Mecca is indicated by a special marker called a *mihrab*, typically a niche or brick or stone of a different color on a main wall. If the structure was originally built as a mosque, the building is oriented to position believers in the correct direction for prayer. Sometimes, this creates unusual placement for the building when seen from the outside. If the structure was not originally built as a mosque, the interior is laid out to position worshippers in the direction of Mecca, even though the orientation inside the building may seem odd. The presence of a *minbar*, the pulpit from which the Friday sermon is given, also indicates the location of the *mihrab*. Many hotels in the Muslim world have a *mihrab*

---

18. The second holiest city is Medina, the birthplace of the *ummah* and where Muhammad died. The third is Jerusalem, which was the original direction for prayer. According to Muslim tradition, God changed the direction of prayer during Muhammad's Night Journey, reflecting Islam's shared origin as an Abrahamic faith and the particularity of Islam. See Omid Safi, *Memories of Muhammad: Why the Prophet Matters* (New York: HarperOne, 2009), 169.

HRH Prince Sultan bin Salman bin Abdulaziz Al Saud (b. 1956)

The first Muslim and Arab astronaut, HRH Prince Sultan bin Salman bin Abdulaziz Al Saud flew as a payload specialist with the STS-51-G Space Shuttle *Discovery* in 1985. Born in Riyadh, Saudi Arabia, he completed his undergraduate education in mass communications at the University of Denver and holds a master's degree in social and political science from Syracuse University. Prince Sultan's time in outer space raised some challenging questions with respect to the five daily prayers: how to calculate prayer times, how to determine the direction of Mecca from outer space, and how to prostrate in zero gravity. Solutions for these challenges required blending ancient ritual with modern technology. Because calculating prayer times requires a location on earth to track the relative position of the sun, it was decided that prayer times would be based on the location of takeoff. Traveling meant the five prayers could be consolidated into three time slots.

Prince Sultan, seated right foreground, is an accomplished pilot and a scientist. While in space, he conducted experiments on the effects of zero gravity on the separation of different types of oil from water in order to combat oil spills on water.

To find Mecca, the prince simply looked out the window and calculated the position of Mecca from there. Prostration proved the greatest challenge. Special shoes were built and anchored to the floor to provide a stable position. The prince was then assisted by other astronauts in the physical challenge of prostration in zero gravity. Prince Sultan reportedly recited the entire Qur'an in outer space and provided the first live Arabic commentary for viewers. In sharing his experiences, he hopes to revive Islam's long heritage of exploration of science and technology.

marker inside individual rooms to help believers find the appropriate direction for prayer. There are also a variety of online and phone apps, keyrings, and prayer rugs that include compasses always pointing to Mecca.[19]

Prayer is the ultimate expression of the word *Islam*, which means "submission." During prayer, Muslims repeatedly prostrate, taking a kneeling position and touching their foreheads to the ground. Some Muslims make so many prostrations over a lifetime, they form a callus on their foreheads.[20] Prostration is a position of supreme ultimate vulnerability, as it exposes the back of the neck—the area where the spine meets the skull. In many past civilizations, a subject was expected to prostrate before a ruler when making a request, particularly when asking pardon for a crime. This symbolized the powerlessness of the one making the request and their absolute submission to the power of the ruler. If the request was granted, the ruler would invite the subject to rise. If not, the subject was already in position for punishment. Transferring this position to prayer signifies the believer's unbounded submission to the will of God, expressing hope of receiving mercy but acknowledging that only God can and will judge and that punishment might be deserved.

During prayer, believers are expected to stand in straight lines, shoulder to shoulder. This highlights that prayer is a collective and unified activity and symbolizes the equality of all those gathered to pray, with no distinctions based on race, tribe, socioeconomic status, and so on. Although the prayer leader (*imam*) is respected for knowledge and piety, even the prayer leader is considered equal to everyone else and stands in line.

Men and women stand in separate locations during prayer. In most places, men are in the front lines and women are in the back. This is supposed to protect the modesty of women, so that men do not look at them inappropriately during prayer. In other locations,

---

19. Sites facilitating this include *http://www.qibla.com.br*, *http://qib.la* and *http://www.al-habib.info/qibla-pointer/*. There are also apps such as Find Mecca, which is a digital GPS that works with iPads and iPhones.

20. Muslims who are public figures trying to present themselves as particularly pious may seek to draw attention to such calluses. One example is former Egyptian President Anwar al-Sadat, who sought to portray himself as the "Believer President," in part by the prominence of his callus.

men gather on one side of the room and women on the other, similar to an Eastern Orthodox Church or an Orthodox synagogue. This allows for a sense of gender equality while respecting the tradition of gender separation. In still other places, women pray behind a barrier or even in a separate room or balcony. Some Muslim women today consider this last arrangement objectionable, because they do not have direct access to the *imam* and the full prayer experience, particularly when sound systems are subpar or live-screen broadcasts are not available. Equal access to the mosque and prayer space is a frequent focus of Muslim women's rights activists.

Prayer begins standing upright, raising the hands, and declaring *"Allahu Akbar!"* "God is the Greatest!" The worshipper then either folds their hands over their stomach or chest or leaves their arms at their side and recites the opening chapter of the Qur'an and another verse of personal choice. This is followed by bending at the waist with their back and neck straight, while making additional proclamations of God's greatness. The worshipper then again stands upright, declaring praise to God, before prostrating and proclaiming God's glory three times. Following that, the worshipper sits back on their heels, asking for forgiveness and proclaiming God's greatness. This full cycle is called a *raka*. The number of *rakas*, which varies between two and four, depends on the time of day. The prayer ends with the invocation of peace, with each worshipper turning their head right and left to greet the angels believed to be sitting on each shoulder. After completing these obligatory prayers, worshippers may then make prayers of personal petitions (*du'a*), such as those for health, safety, or help with personal matters such as upcoming exams, having a child, or finding a marriage partner.

Muslims in the West often find the Friday noon prayers the most challenging to attend because they fall in the middle of the workday. Some companies offer a designated space to Muslim employees to accommodate this religious requirement. Muslims who have the option often use their lunch breaks to attend prayers at a mosque, provided there is one close enough. This explains why many people show up for Friday prayers at staggered times and dressed for work. Joining communal prayer already in progress is not considered disruptive. Each person simply completes the required prayers on their own to catch up with the group.

Zakat: Charitable Giving and Charitable Living

Charity is an important obligation in Islam and is an expected way of life. Muslims believe all things, including wealth, belong to God; thus human beings must use wealth entrusted to them for the benefit of the community, not just themselves. Regular giving to charity is intended to keep the giver detached from wealth as a personal possession and to view it, instead, as an opportunity for community cohesion. Both the Qur'an and Muhammad's example insist on charity as an obligatory act of faith. Charity takes place on two levels: *zakat* as obligatory charity and *sadaqah* as voluntary charity.

As a pillar, *zakat* requires once a year the distribution of 2.5 percent, or 1/40, of a believer's entire wealth to the less fortunate members of the community. Although many Muslims prefer to pay *zakat* during the month of Ramadan, this is not required. *Zakat* can be paid any time of the year.

Calculating *zakat* follows specific guidelines outlined in the hadith and includes not only income and revenues, but all of a believer's assets, including real estate, investments, stocks and bonds, livestock, gold, currencies, jewelry, and other commodities. Because of the breadth and complexity of *zakat* calculations, legal and theological commentaries give much attention to what is and is not included, based on amounts and methods of calculation set in Medina in Muhammad's lifetime. Today, Muslims can find *zakat* calculators online as well as apps to determine what they owe.

Because charity is intended for the less fortunate, Muslims whose financial assets do not reach a certain level are not obliged to pay *zakat*. Just as the five daily prayers are not designed to burden the individual believer, so *zakat* is not intended to bankrupt those already struggling to get by. Although there is no shame associated with being the recipient of charity, in practice, often even the poorest of the poor will make some contribution to *zakat* in recognition that there is always someone worse off and to keep focused on caring for others, rather than only oneself.

Annual payment of *zakat* works to redistribute wealth within the Muslim community. Symbolically, *zakat* is intended to solidify a sense of community that goes beyond one's immediate family. Many

Muslims prefer to give their contribution to a specific organization or family. Today, some countries, including Saudi Arabia, require payment of *zakat* through an authorized mosque to prevent money laundering or charitable contributions ending up in the hands of extremist organizations.

In addition, *sadaqah*, or voluntary charity, is strongly encouraged, although not obligatory. *Sadaqah* does not have a set amount or number of times it must be paid during the year. Parallel to the Jewish custom of *tzedakah*, it is considered a righteous act and is left to the individual's conscience.

Sawm: Fasting during Ramadan as Piety and Remembrance of the Less Favored

Just as charitable giving highlights awareness of the less fortunate, fasting during the month of Ramadan keeps Muslims mindful of those who regularly go without food or access to a clean, safe water supply. This yearly experience of hunger and thirst are intended to create a sense of empathy within the Muslim, which he or she is then expected to direct outward, for example, in charitable contributions to alleviate poverty.

Many religious traditions use fasting to encourage a spiritual connection between the believer and the Divine. Lack of caloric intake can lead to an altered state of mind and greater spiritual openness, as the believer sets aside physical, bodily needs in favor of personal discipline. Fasting reminds believers of their ultimate dependence on God for their needs. Among acts of worship, God places the highest importance on fasting. The eleventh-century scholar al-Ghazali (d. 1111) described fasting as half of the patient forbearance (*sabr*) Muslims are expected to demonstrate as part of their faith.[21]

Ramadan is the ninth month of the lunar calendar. During this month, Muhammad received the first revelation of the Qur'an. Unlike the solar calendar used in the West, which marks months according to particular seasons, the shorter lunar calendar's months

---

21. The other half is gratitude (*shukr*), according to the hadith.

rotate throughout the seasons. Thus, in some years, Ramadan falls in winter; in others, it falls in summer. While fasting from sunrise to sunset is never "easy," Muslims find the shorter, cooler days of winter less demanding than the long, hot days of summer, particularly in desert countries where temperatures have reached as high as 129 degrees Fahrenheit.[22]

The Ramadan fast requires abstaining from food, drink, sexual activity, impure thoughts, and smoking from sunrise to sunset. Traditionally, dawn is considered to have arrived when one can distinguish between a white thread and a black thread with the naked eye. From this time until sunset, all those physically able observe the fast. As with the other pillars, even the fast of Ramadan is not intended as a burden. Young children and the elderly are not expected to fast, though many choose to participate, if only for a short time, to be part of the collective experience. Young children grow into fasting as they mature, beginning with short fasts and gradually building up to the full fast. Those with medical conditions that require regular intakes of food, such as diabetics who must regulate their blood sugar or pregnant or nursing mothers, are exempt from the fast, either temporarily until the condition has resolved or permanently in the case of a permanent condition or illness. Those with temporary conditions can make up the fast at a later time. Those unable to fast or who do not wish to make it up at a later time can fulfill the obligation by providing meals to two hungry people for each day of the fast. This assures that the symbolism of Ramadan remains intact, keeping the focus on hunger and poverty, while not overburdening the individual.

In Muslim-majority countries, following the fast is eased by the sense of social solidarity that comes when everyone around you is doing the same thing. In some countries, day and night are essentially reversed during Ramadan because most people are fasting. Particularly in the Gulf countries, many people sleep during the day and are awake at night to eat, visit with friends and, sometimes, work. School can be challenging for both students and teachers, as lack of food, water, and sleep can be detrimental to a person's ability to

---

22. See *https://www.washingtonpost.com/news/capital-weather-gang/wp/2016/07 /22/two-middle-east-locations-hit-129-degrees-hottest-ever-in-eastern-hemisphere -maybe-the-world/?utm_term=.4b06d09ba00e.*

concentrate and retain information. Muslims may find fasting more challenging in a non-Muslim-majority setting, such as the West, where an individual Muslim may be the only person observing it. The realities of work, school, and even sports have made questions about fasting popular topics of discussion among Muslims, in the real world and online. Some athletes, such as Hakeem Olajuwon, have become famous for their dedication to fasting, even in the midst of NBA playoffs. Others have chosen to postpone fasting out of respect for their team or once-in-a-lifetime events, such as the Olympics.[23]

Traditionally, Ramadan begins with the sighting of the new moon. Families and communities often gather together to look for this sign, although they still depend on a religious official to make the formal declaration. Planning to take time off from work at the end of Ramadan can prove challenging, as one can only predict when Ramadan will begin and end generally, rather than knowing precisely in advance.

Muslims rise early in the morning during Ramadan to eat a hearty breakfast, called *suhur*, to get them through the day. When the sun has set, a light meal called *iftar* breaks the fast. *Iftar* traditionally begins with a glass of water and some dates, in accordance with Muhammad's example, followed by prayer. This tradition has some medical benefit because it marks a small introduction of hydration and sugar back into the body, allowing the digestive juices to start flowing, followed by a break before a larger late evening meal is eaten. Family and friends typically gather together for the evening meal, continuing the strong sense of family and community. Food for the meal is prepared during the day, making fasting an even greater challenge to those in charge of the cooking. Special acts of piety during Ramadan include extra prayers at the mosque and recitation of the entire Qur'an.

The celebration of Eid al-Fitr, or the feast of the breaking of the fast, marks the end of Ramadan. The three days of Eid are a

---

23. Fasting became a particular concern during the 2012 Summer Olympics in London. Athletes had to choose whether to fast or postpone the fast until after their competition. Choices varied with some fasting and others choosing to make it up later. The issue was covered by the media with comparisons to Christian and Jewish athletes when qualifying events or events have taken place on days of worship. In the Muslim case, the challenge was more extensive not only because of abstention from food and water but also because the issue lasted longer than one day.

celebration comparable to Christmas, with special foods and sweets unique to this time of year, visits from family and friends, and gift giving. In Muslim-majority countries, Eid is a national holiday. In keeping with the community spirit of the pillars, Eid often marks a time for repairing broken relationships, including amnesty for prisoners and debtors.

Hajj: Pilgrimage of a Lifetime

Once in his or her life, every Muslim, woman and man, who is physically and financially able, is expected to make the pilgrimage to Mecca. The Hajj is the largest annual religious gathering in the world with about two million participants every year. Muslims look forward to and often save for a lifetime to make this pilgrimage. Officials in charge of administrating the Hajj have described the logistics as comparable to planning for thirty Super Bowls, with the main difference being that everyone who comes expects to play the game.

The Hajj is the ultimate expression of community, with Muslims from throughout the world gathered in Mecca at the same time to engage in the same rituals together. It visibly demonstrates the unity found within the diversity of global Islam, as Muslims of all different ethnic, racial, and national backgrounds travel, stand, walk, and pray together in a massive worship session.

The Hajj takes place between the eighth and twelfth or thirteenth days of the last month of the Islamic calendar, Dhu al-Hijjah. Although one can certainly travel to Mecca and participate in the same rituals outside of this time frame, such a pilgrimage would count as an *umrah*, or lesser pilgrimage, rather than as the Hajj itself.[24] Limiting proper Hajj to the last month of the year follows the example set in Muhammad's lifetime. It also symbolically marks the culmination of the religious experience by drawing Muslims together in what is often described as a dress rehearsal for Judgment Day in which one is stripped bare of worldly trappings and concerns and stands in God's presence to answer for how one's time on earth was spent and to repent and ask for forgiveness for those times when one did not behave as one

---

24. Muslims are encouraged to go on *umrah* as an expression of piety, but it does not replace the religious obligation of Hajj.

should have. Many Muslims describe Hajj as a life-changing moment of rededication to living a more righteous existence. Some deliberately delay going on Hajj until they feel spiritually worthy.

Ideally, the Hajj serves as the great equalizer among Muslims. Believers enter a state of ritual purity called *ihram* on Hajj, setting aside worldly concerns and preoccupations to focus on the Divine and the eternal. Pilgrims are expected to be patient and to help each other, even in the midst of the most grueling and dangerous rituals. Loss of temper, rudeness, refusal to help someone in need, or selfish behavior could invalidate one's entire Hajj experience in God's eyes.

To symbolize the absolute equality of all pilgrims and utter humility before God, pilgrims wear simple clothing, also called *ihram*. For men, this consists of two seamless pieces of white cloth, one wrapped around the waist and the other across the chest. Women do not have a specific dress code in terms of color or design but are expected to wear simple, modest, flowing garments that cover the body and hair and leave the face and hands visible. The simple clothing emphasizes setting aside worldly concerns and socioeconomic status symbols as a reminder that the only "adornment" God cares about is piety (Q 7:26). Regardless of whether a believer is rich or poor, black or white, male or female, God cares about what is in the heart, not appearance, personal wealth, or social status. Grooming, such as trimming one's nails or wearing jewelry or perfume, is forbidden during the Hajj, as is sexual activity or hunting. Pilgrims are expected to maintain ritual purity in body and heart, focusing exclusively on worshipping God. Many pilgrims save their Hajj garments for burial.

Hajj rituals are complex and exacting. Knowing what to do and say and when requires study and preparation in advance. Because pilgrims are required to go on Hajj in groups, many will gather together beforehand to prepare.

Pilgrims begin by approaching Mecca[25] and declaring their arrival to God. They enter Mecca and go to the Grand Mosque, home to the Kaaba, which contains the Black Stone that Muslims believe Abraham and Ismail used to build the first altar to God. Many pilgrims try to get close enough to the stone to kiss it, although this is impractical and dangerous given the sheer number of pilgrims.

---

25. Mecca is located in Saudi Arabia. Access to Mecca is restricted to Muslims to maintain its sanctity.

Muslims circumambulate the Kaaba, covered with a black silk cloth embroidered with verses from the Qur'an. Some worshippers, dressed in *ihram*, are observing the lesser pilgrimage for *umrah*, while others, in everyday clothing, are present simply for prayer.

The Kaaba is the focal point of Muslim prayer and enjoys pride of place in the Hajj. In imitation of the angels circumambulating God's throne in heaven, pilgrims move in circles around the Kaaba seven times to symbolize their entry into God's presence.

Many of the Hajj rituals recall events in the life of Abraham, particularly related to his two sons, Ismail (Ishmael) and Isaac. Muslims consider Abraham the first monotheist and the common faith ancestor of Muslims, Jews, and Christians alike. Interestingly, much of the textual material related to these rituals does not appear in the Qur'an, but in the Old Testament. Hajj rituals include running between the hills of Safa and Marwa in imitation of Hagar's[26] desperate search for water after Abraham abandoned her and their son, Ismail, in the desert. Hagar's search ended when, after crying out to God for help, God sent the angel Gabriel, who struck the ground with his wing, sending

---

26. Although the book of Genesis in the Bible describes Hagar as a slave in Abraham's home, Muslims consider her a wife. Abraham's other wife, Sarah, was long unable to bear children. When she was finally given a son, Isaac, Sarah insisted on banishing Hagar and Ismail. This history is replayed during these rituals.

forth water. Muslims still drink from this well, known as Zamzam, as part of the Hajj ritual. Many believe this water contains special curative powers, so they bottle it and take it back home.

Another important ritual that recalls Abraham's life is the ritual stoning of the devil. Pilgrims throw stones at three stone pillars that represent the devil/temptation. Abraham is said to have thrown stones at the devil to drive him away when he tried to tempt Abraham away from God. Pilgrims today use the stoning ritual to not only drive away evil but also throw sin, temptation, and negative thoughts out of their lives. This ritual is often the most dangerous moment of the Hajj because pilgrims throw stones and other objects, such as shoes, from all directions.

Most pilgrims agree, the most important moment of the Hajj is the day of reckoning on the Plain of Arafat, where Muhammad gave his Farewell Sermon shortly before his death. Here, in preparation for Judgment Day, believers stand before God, pray, repent for their sins, and ask for forgiveness. Many pilgrims reflect back on this as the moment when they felt closest to God. It is common to make personal requests, such as healing for family members or for courage to change what they feel is wrong in their lives or to persevere amid hardship.

Following completion of the Hajj rituals, Muslims celebrate the second major Islamic holy day, the Eid al-Adha, or Feast of the Sacrifice,[27] which again commemorates an event in the life of Abraham: the near sacrifice of his son in obedience to God's command. Muslims believe this son was Ismail, rather than Isaac as in the Old Testament, but the story still ends with God's replacement of the intended son with a ram. In commemoration of this event, pilgrims pay to have an animal slaughtered, ranging from a sheep to a camel, depending on their financial means and whether they pay individually or in a group. Men also either shave their heads or have a symbolic tuft of hair cut off after the sacrifice, before the three days of Eid festivities begin.

The symbolism of the sacrifice is twofold. First, it shows that Hajj pilgrims, like Abraham, obey God's commands and hold nothing dearer than God. In a desert environment, livestock represented wealth and survival, so sacrificing an animal represented a significant loss to the family. Secondly, unlike Old Testament sacrifices in which the meat from the animal was either burned or reserved

---

27. This holiday is celebrated by all Muslims, regardless of whether they are on Hajj.

for consumption by high priests and their families, the meat from animals sacrificed after Hajj is redistributed to poor people, again emphasizing Islam's commitment to community.[28]

Completion of the Hajj entitles the pilgrim to use the honorific title Hajji for men and Hajja for women. Many pilgrims visit the Prophet's Mosque and tomb in Medina[29] before returning home.

At a time when the global Muslim population tops 1.6 billion, some question the viability of maintaining traditional Hajj rituals in the future. Already, the Saudi government uses a quota system to limit the number of pilgrims who can attend annually from each country because of the sheer logistical challenges of such enormous numbers and the accompanying safety issues. The Saudi government has spent billions of dollars expanding the spaces where rituals take place, including the construction of a "pedestrian superhighway" to facilitate travel between locations, but, every year, some pilgrims are trampled to death or are injured or die from being struck with objects flying during the ritual stonings. Fireproof tents have helped reduce fire hazards in pilgrim lodging areas. Despite the dangers, Muslims take the obligation to undergo Hajj seriously, meaning that demand for access rises with each passing year. Some have suggested using modern technology to provide other means of fulfilling Hajj obligations, such as by going on a "virtual Hajj" online,[30] but most cling to the ideal of the genuine physical experience.

Pillars versus Sacraments

On many levels, the Five Pillars fulfill functions similar to the sacraments in the Christian tradition: they bring believers into the faith

---

28. In the past, because of the intense heat and lack of refrigeration, distribution of meat could occur only within a limited geographic range. Today, however, the Saudi government, which oversees the Hajj, maintains a fleet of airplanes that can deliver the meat anywhere in the world, giving global significance to this ancient ritual.

29. Literally "the city of the Prophet," Medina is about 200 miles north of Mecca.

30. Examples include the video game Second Life, which allows you to create an avatar to go on virtual Hajj and the app Mecca 3D: An Interactive Journey to Islam. These simulated experiences do not "count" as the official Hajj, but can provide a sense of walking through the rituals that many might not experience physically; but they cannot capture the full experience, particularly the sense of community and solidarity that many Muslims describe after making the physical Hajj.

community, encourage an ongoing relationship with the community of believers, call believers to live moral and ethical lives and avoid sin and temptation, and draw them closer to God. However, Islam does not have sacraments in the complete Christian sense of the word. Christians view their sacraments as rituals that channel God's grace to all who receive them with the proper disposition. They are often associated with particular life events, such as birth, marriage, and death, and represent moments of grace throughout a person's life.[31] They may also fulfill an important theological purpose, such as forgiveness of original sin[32] through baptism or taking holy orders in ordination. The Pillars, on the other hand, are not specific to any particular life event or moment. They do not provide forgiveness of sins[33] or commemorate the lifetime of any individual or significant moments in anyone's ministry. They do not establish a particular group of leaders within the faith community. Instead, the Five Pillars emphasize individual accountability—the idea that a person can only be responsible for their own actions, not those of another. Not only do Muslims believe each believer will be judged individually by God but also that each person can personally and directly engage with God through prayer. There is no need for intermediaries.[34]

---

31. Roman Catholics believe in seven such sacraments, instituted by Jesus and entrusted to the Church: three sacraments of initiation: baptism, the Eucharist, and confirmation; two sacraments of healing: Penance and reconciliation, and anointing of the sick or extreme unction; and two sacraments of service: matrimony and holy orders. Protestants define as a sacrament only those rituals instituted by Jesus: baptism and Holy Communion. Protestants believe that the other five do not have sufficient biblical evidence to be considered sacraments, although they still have symbolic value.

32. Original sin is the Christian belief that the sin committed by Adam and Eve in the Garden of Eden has been passed down to all human beings, requiring God's forgiveness, which is given through baptism.

33. Although Muslims ask for forgiveness while carrying out certain pillars, such as the Hajj and prayer, they recognize that whether or not to forgive is entirely God's choice. Consequently, the focus is more on what Muslims owe to God than it is on what they hope to gain.

34. This differs from Roman Catholic belief in the role of priests and saints as intermediaries between believers and God. It is closer to Protestant belief in the need for clergy as leaders and administrators of sacraments, but not intermediaries. In the Islamic tradition, only Muhammad is believed to serve as an intermediary, based on a hadith, but even then only with God's approval. Sufis are an exception to this belief, as they consider those recognized as "saints" to serve as intermediaries. See chapter 6, "Sufis: Saints and Subversives in the Quest for the Divine," for details.

Review Questions

1. Identify and discuss the significance of each of the Five Pillars. What overall vision do they provide of Islam as a faith tradition? Are there any important aspects of religious faith or observance that are missing from the Five Pillars?
2. How do the Five Pillars contribute to building a sense of community (*ummah*) among Muslims? What rights and responsibilities does membership in the Muslim community bring?
3. How do the Five Pillars help Muslims set priorities in personal, family, and community life? What do they indicate about the importance and prioritization of a believer's relationship with God compared to relationships with other people?
4. What purposes does prayer fulfill in Islam?
5. Discuss the impact of science and technology on the practice of the Five Pillars. Does the use of science and technology enhance or detract from the experience? Why?

Discussion Questions

1. What do the Five Pillars indicate about the importance of belief versus practice in Islam? Is it possible to live as a faithful Muslim if faith is kept as a strictly private belief system?
2. What impact do the Five Pillars have on Muslim identity as individuals and as part of a community of believers?
3. What role might the Five Pillars play with respect to citizenship and community involvement for Muslims? Is it possible to live as both a faithful Muslim and a fully participating member of a non-Muslim society? Why or why not?

For Further Study

Readings

Bianchi, Robert R. *Guests of God: Pilgrimage and Politics in the Islamic World.* Oxford: Oxford University Press, 2008.

Bowen, John R. *A New Anthropology of Islam*. New York: Cambridge University Press, 2012.

Cornell, Vincent. "Fruit of the Tree of Knowledge: The Relationship between Faith and Practice in Islam." In *The Oxford History of Islam*, edited by John L. Esposito, (63–106). New York: Oxford University Press, 1999.

Hussain, Musharraf. *The Five Pillars of Islam: Laying the Foundations of Divine Love and Service to Humanity*. Leicestershire: Kube Publishing, 2012.

Kreinath, Jens, ed. *The Anthropology of Islam Reader*. London: Routledge, 2012.

Films

Inside Mecca. Films for the Humanities and Sciences (Firm), Films Media Group, and National Geographic Television and Film. New York: Films Media Group, 2010.

Accompanies three pilgrims—two men and one woman from Malaysia, South Africa, and the United States—through their pre-Hajj, Hajj, and post-Hajj experiences and their personal meanings.

Ramadan Mubarak. Islamic Circle of North America. Chicago: Sound Vision, 1997.

A Muslim children's program made by Pakistani American Muslims designed to introduce various practices for Ramadan from around the world, using puppets, music, cartoons, and humor. Available at *https://www.youtube.com/watch?v=3Hv95fGrUZo*.

Nawaz, Zarqa, and Joe MacDonald. *Me and the Mosque*. [Montreal]: National Film Board of Canada, 2010.

Addresses issues related to mosque access for women in Canada and the United States. Written and directed by a Canadian Muslim woman who was also the creative inspiration for the popular Canadian Broadcasting Corporation television series *Little Mosque on the Prairie*. Available at *https://www.youtube.com /watch?v=sder6fD_Kp8*.

Links

Islam for Catholics 101, *https://www.youtube.com/watch?v=Kh_QiAp ASRQ*—Features the author's discussion of the Five Pillars and their role in the lives of Muslims.

IslamiCity, *IslamiCity.com*—Offers a variety of services related to the Five Pillars and beyond to the creation of a virtual *ummah*.

IslamicFinder, *islamicfinder.org*—Provides a daily and monthly schedule for the five daily prayers by geographic location.

Mecca 3D: An Interactive Journey to Islam, *mecca3d.net*—App designed to allow for a virtual 3D Hajj.

Muslim Aid America, *muslimaidusa.org*—Provides both a *zakat* calculator and options for donation geared toward development projects.

Muhammad
Biography and Legacy of the Prophet

Although Islam is an adamantly monotheistic faith that worships only God, the Prophet Muhammad is a pivotal human figure, serving as the ideal role model of a person of faith, family member, friend, and leader.[1] For Muslims, Muhammad is the one who demonstrates perfectly how to live the teachings of the Qur'an and submit to God. Thus his example, or Sunna, provides a practical demonstration of how Muslims are to live, both with God and with other people.[2]

The Pre-Islamic Context

Islam did not arise in a religious vacuum. It arose in something more like a religious vortex in which multiple faith traditions competed in the religious marketplace. That marketplace offered choices in

---

1. This emphasis on Muhammad's humanity means that Muslims neither worship nor pray to Muhammad and do not consider Muhammad to be a savior. Muhammad's role in Islam is thus comparable to Jesus' role in Christianity only as a role model to follow, not as a divine figure. Though Christians consider Jesus to be divine and human and the embodiment of God's Word, Muslims respect and revere Jesus as a prophet (someone who receives a divine revelation intended to warn people) and a Messenger (a prophet guaranteed the success of the message); however, Muslims believe that Jesus, like Muhammad, is strictly a human being.

2. Though there are some in the West who try to understand Islam through the Qur'an alone, Muslims insist on the importance of knowing and understanding Muhammad's example as a guide for interpreting and understanding the Qur'an. For an example of a scholarly attempt to read the Qur'an without reference to Muhammad's life story, see Gabriel Said Reynolds, *The Qur'an and Its Biblical Subtext* (London: Routledge, 2010).

religious rhetoric and formal confessions of faith, including Judaism and Christianity. The majority of pre-Islamic Arabs were polytheists, but monotheism was also strongly present. Different approaches to religion attracted different people for different reasons. Polytheism was attractive because it was personalized and local. Local holy men, local deities, local shrines, local stories, and local religious practices formed the center of small-scale community life. Monotheism, on the other hand, offered a larger-scale vision of unity based on dedication to a single, universal deity, albeit one that was less personalized and often represented by relatively remote priests and temples. The array of religious beliefs reflected the range of views, needs, and ideas of the people they served. They also formed the context in which Muhammad delivered his message.[3]

Some people were satisfied with the religious status quo, finding meaning, purpose, and even social, political, or economic status and power within their faith tradition. Others felt marginalized and dissatisfied with ongoing tribal warfare, poverty, and injustice. These different objectives and perceptions guided expectations not only for religious leadership but also for the broader faith community. It was into this context that Muhammad was born.

Muhammad's Life Story

Early Life

According to Islamic tradition, Muhammad was born in 570 CE in what is today Mecca, Saudi Arabia. He belonged to the prominent tribe of Quraysh,[4] which should have assured him of a certain social status. However, the death of his father before he was born introduced a level of instability and insecurity that marked his early life and helped shape his character. Muhammad's personal

---

3. For background on the pre-Islamic religious environment, see F. E. Peters, *The Hajj: The Muslim Pilgrimage to Mecca and the Holy Places* (Princeton: Princeton University Press, 1995), 3–37.

4. The Quraysh were in charge of the Kaaba, the central shrine in Mecca, which, at that time, contained representations of a reported 360 different gods and goddesses. As a central religious "way station," the Kaaba was an important site of pilgrimage and, thus, of commercial and financial interests. The livelihood of the Quraysh was inextricably tied to control over the Kaaba.

experience of marginalization created empathy in him for others in similar situations of social injustice; this empathy became a hallmark of his preaching and ministry. It also made him a relatable figure to those outside of the power structures of society or even within their own families.

Like many infants at the time, Muhammad was sent to a wet nurse in the desert when he was eight days old. She cared for him until he turned two. This practice was believed to strengthen children for the tough environment of the desert and served to establish a "milk relationship" between the nursing woman and the child that created a legal, lifelong kinship with her and her family. Although Muhammad was returned to his mother, she died when he was only six years old. His grandfather, Abd al-Muttalib, then took him in, but two years later, when his grandfather died, Muhammad went to live with his uncle, Abu Talib. The loss of so many close family members and protectors in his early years left Muhammad with a keen sense of the fragility of life and the vulnerability of those who had not obtained legal majority and were unable to care or fend for themselves. He always reminded followers to care for their parents, who are children's protectors, especially their mothers, as noted in the famous hadith, "Paradise lies at the feet of the mothers."

Other than these losses, little is known of the historical Muhammad before his call to prophethood and ministry, except for what can be gleaned from hagiographical stories.[5] Largely miracle accounts, these stories are best understood as having devotional and spiritual value rather than providing factual evidence.[6]

---

5. The earliest biography of Muhammad, which contains many miracle stories, is Ibn Ishaq, *The Life of Muhammad: A Translation of Ibn Ishaq's Sirat Rasul Allah*, trans. A. Guillaume (London: Oxford University Press, 1955; repr. 2004).

6. These miracle accounts may have been developed to solidify Muhammad's status in competition with Jesus and other Abrahamic prophets. Logically, if Jesus' status is due, at least in part, to the miraculous circumstances surrounding his conception and birth, which the Qur'an confirms, one might expect to find similar miraculous signs surrounding the conception and birth of Muhammad as God's final Messenger. Some historians have also posited that such accounts were developed as a missionary (*da'wah*) tool for outreach to surrounding Jewish and Christian populations, particularly as the Islamic Empire expanded. Reynolds, e.g., has called for reading the Qur'an as a homily intended for a Christian audience. See Reynolds, *The Qur'an and Its Biblical Subtext*, esp. 230–58.

As an orphan, Muhammad could not depend on family connections alone for social status or financial security. He had to prove himself through character and hard work. From adolescence, he worked to achieve a reputation for honesty, trustworthiness, and fairness. He also demonstrated remarkable arbitration skills.

Marriage to Khadijah

It was Muhammad's reputation for honesty that brought him to the attention of a wealthy—and widowed—businesswoman, Khadijah. In need of a trustworthy man to carry her goods to Syria, sell them, and return with the profits, she hired Muhammad. According to Islamic tradition, he did so well that she proposed marriage. The proposal was unusual in that tradition indicates Khadijah was older than Muhammad; at forty, she was fifteen years his senior.[7] Yet neither the age difference nor the fact that she proposed to him has been a source of criticism or concern within the Islamic tradition.

It could be argued that Muhammad saw his opportunity to become a more prominent member of society and took full advantage of it. However, Islamic tradition records a deep and meaningful relationship, based on love and mutual respect. Khadijah was Muhammad's strongest and most faithful supporter, believing in his call to prophethood even before he did. She was the first convert to Islam and supported his ministry, even through times of persecution and starvation. During their twenty-five year marriage, Muhammad had no other wives. Although he married a number of women after her death, he always upheld Khadijah as an exemplary wife and Companion,[8] referring to her as one of the four perfect women in Islam.[9]

---

7. There are some today who question whether Khadijah was truly forty years old when she married Muhammad as they had six children together—four daughters and two sons.

8. The honorific *Companion* refers to Muhammad's male and female followers during his lifetime.

9. The other three are the Virgin Mary (mother of Jesus), Muhammad and Khadijah's daughter Fatima, and Asiya, the wife of the Egyptian pharaoh, considered perfect because she continued to believe in the One God rather than follow the Egyptian religious practice of worshipping the pharaoh as god.

Leadership before Prophethood

Even before he was called to prophethood, Muhammad was known for his concern for marginalized people. He belonged to an alliance known as Hilf al-Fudul, a pre-Islamic fraternity committed to generosity, hospitality, chivalry, and compassion, helping those in need, including widows, orphans, slaves, poor people, and elderly people.[10] These values transcended tribal lines in favor of thinking of the community holistically. Muhammad carried these values forward into his ministry.

Muhammad had also earned a reputation as a skilled arbitrator, capable of stepping into blood feuds and finding solutions that allowed the quarreling tribes to save face and end the conflict. When Muhammad was thirty-five, repairs were undertaken at the Kaaba, at that time the center of sacrifice, pilgrimage, and worship for many religions. As the repairs reached their conclusion, the tribes began squabbling about which one would have the ultimate honor: putting the central piece—the Black Stone[11]—back into place. As the argument threatened to escalate to bloodshed, Muhammad was called in to calm the situation and find a solution. Rather than choosing a single tribe, Muhammad laid his cloak on the ground and placed the Black Stone in the center. He asked each tribe to choose a representative. Each representative then grasped an edge of the cloak and, together, lifted the Black Stone back into place. Not only did this allow all of the tribes to share in the honor, it engaged them collectively and equally in a visible demonstration of solidarity and community building. This simple gesture set aside notions of nobility and socioeconomic status, allowing each tribe the autonomy to choose their own representative according to their own criteria, but with the intent of working toward a common goal. These themes emerged repeatedly throughout Muhammad's later ministry.

---

10. Asma Afsaruddin, *The First Muslims: History and Memory* (Oxford: Oneworld, 2007), 2–3.

11. According to tradition, the Black Stone is connected to Adam as the first builder of the Kaaba following his expulsion from heaven. It is also believed to be the stone used by Abraham and Ismail (Ishmael) to build the first altar to the One God referenced in Q 2:125–129. The stone therefore serves as a connection to monotheism and to Abrahamic history.

Call to Prophethood[12]

Muslim tradition teaches that Muhammad was called to prophethood in 610 CE at the age of forty. The age carries symbolic importance in the Islamic tradition because forty is considered the age of perfection when a person is believed to receive wisdom.

As with the prophets of old, Muhammad had not expected to become a prophet. Given his background—tribally insignificant, reportedly illiterate, someone who had to earn his way through life rather than rely on privilege, and a man who started his professional career working for a woman—he probably did not appear to the surrounding community as the first choice for prophethood. In fact, many people jeered and mocked the idea that he had received a revelation from God. The early years of Muhammad's prophethood did not produce impressive results in terms of numbers of followers.

Muhammad's call came during one of his spiritual retreats in the cave of Hira, which is about two miles outside of Mecca. Disturbed by the gross inequalities and injustices he perceived in his society—rising materialism and corruption, exploitation of the poor and marginalized by the wealthy and powerful, and an ever-increasing gap between rich and poor—he often took time away from the stresses and pressures of life to contemplate the human condition. These were times of prayer, meditation, and solitude. One day, as he was praying, the angel Gabriel came to him. Gabriel commanded him to recite, but Muhammad said he could not recite. Muhammad described feeling as though he were being squeezed to the point of having difficulty breathing. Three times the angel commanded him to recite and, finally, as he felt he was being squeezed almost beyond endurance, he began to recite the opening words of the Qur'an: "Recite in the Name of thy Lord Who created, created man from a blood clot. Recite! Thy Lord is most noble, Who

---

12. In the Islamic tradition, prophethood is not about receiving a new revelation for a specific group of people, but repeating a message that God has sent before but that humanity has forgotten. That message is universal, so that, in theory, no prophet is considered to be greater than another. The role of the prophet is to convey the message and focus attention on the One who sent it. That said, within the Islamic tradition, Muhammad clearly holds a status above the other prophets as God's final messenger. For further discussion of prophethood in Islam, see Omid Safi, *Memories of Muhammad: Why the Prophet Matters* (New York: HarperOne, 2009), 195–58.

taught by the Pen, taught man that which he knew not" (Q 96:1–5).[13]
Thus began a series of revelations that would continue throughout
the rest of Muhammad's life.

Terrified by the experience, Muhammad ran out of the cave and
home to his wife, Khadijah. Recounting his experience, he asked her
if he was insane or perhaps possessed. Khadijah reassured him he had
received a message from God, believing in his revelation before he
did. For further reassurance, the couple later sought the counsel of
Khadijah's cousin, a Christian monk named Waraqa, who confirmed
Muhammad's message as divine in nature, based on its consistency
with the Torah and the Gospels.[14]

The Meccan Years

Muhammad was so shaken by his experience of the revelation that
he did not talk about it publicly for several years.[15] Yet the revelations
continued to come, verse by verse, compelling him finally to convey their message to his tribe. The initial response was not encouraging. Some members, still considering him a lesser member of the
tribe due to his humble origins, refused to believe him on principle.
Others rejected the message out of concern for its potential negative
impact on their financial and business interests. In fact, only one person pledged support: Muhammad's younger cousin, Ali. At thirteen,
Ali was still a child and thus hardly a powerful ally. Yet Ali became
the first male convert to Islam and went on to lead the entire Muslim
community after Muhammad's death.

The failure of Muhammad's message to resonate in the early
years was due at least in part to the social upheaval it suggested.
Judgment by God in the afterlife was a far cry from the justice
and vengeance tribes were accustomed to claiming for themselves.
Though some saw value in ending blood feuds of retaliation that,

---

13. Translation is from Seyyed Hossein Nasr et al., *The Study Qur'an* (New York: HarperOne, 2015), 1537.

14. Details can be found in Ibn Ishaq, *The Life of Muhammad*, 82–83.

15. This information is recorded by the ninth-century exegete al-Tabari, cited in Reuven Firestone, *Jihad: The Origin of Holy War in Islam* (New York: Oxford University Press, 1999), 51. For details of Muhammad's early prophetic experiences, see Safi, *Memories of Muhammad*, 101–13.

once begun, proved very difficult to end, others nevertheless feared the potential impact on their personal wealth that greater reflection about personal behavior and social responsibility might bring. Even more startling was that, rather than basing the social order on the typical hierarchies, bloodlines, and financial power, Muhammad based his social vision on association by choice, belief in a common set of guidelines and principles for private and public conduct, and, most importantly, the equality of all believers. Like Jesus' message six hundred years earlier, Muhammad's message appealed to the marginal members of society—poor people, women, people from lower-level tribes, outcasts, and racial minorities. Also similar to Jesus' message was Muhammad's consistent message of nonviolence. For the first twelve years of his ministry, violence, even in the case of self-defense, was absolutely and unequivocally prohibited by repeated Qur'an revelations.

Being a Muslim in those early days was not a simple matter of freedom of religious belief or expression. It was personally dangerous. Muhammad's Quraysh tribe, seeing the potential loss of income and prestige they held in Mecca, not only rejected Muhammad and his message, but actively persecuted him and his followers to the point of killing some of them. Muhammad sent some of his early followers to seek asylum in Abyssinia (Ethiopia today). There they were protected by the black Christian ruler identified in Islamic sources as the Negus, even when a delegation sent by the Quraysh in Mecca came to demand their return. This protection set an important precedent for Muslim-Christian, as well as interracial, relations.[16]

Remaining in Mecca, Muhammad was subjected to significant abuse and harassment, ranging from verbal insults to people throwing garbage at him and even an assassination attempt. One story highlights Muhammad's daughter, Fatima, placing herself between him and his opponents, so he could pray in peace. Another story describes Muhammad being harassed daily by a female neighbor who threw rotten food at him. She did this so often that, when a day finally came that she did not, Muhammad asked about it and learned she was sick. Rather than giving in to the all-too-human impulse to

---

16. For details, see chapter 9, "Muslim-Christian Encounters: Conflict and Coexistence." See also Hugh Goddard, *A History of Christian-Muslim Relations* (Chicago: New Amsterdam, 2000), 19–33.

rejoice in payback, Muhammad decided instead to visit her with a gift of food. The woman was reportedly so moved by his kindness and mercy that she converted to Islam.

Yet, for all of the individual stories of conversion, the overall story was one of increasing pressure to silence Muhammad. Even his uncle and protector, Abu Talib, begged him to stop preaching in order to save himself and his followers. Muhammad refused. He told his uncle he had no choice. For whatever reason, God had chosen him to convey this message and convey it he would or he would die trying. Seeing his nephew's conviction, Abu Talib reassured him of his protection.

Meanwhile, the Quraysh remained relentless in their persecution, striking where it would hit the hardest—financially. Muhammad, Khadijah, and the early Muslims were socially boycotted, shut out of business dealings and reduced to poverty. Abu Talib lost everything. Stories recount Muhammad's family eating leaves from the trees, because they could not afford food. Aging and likely weakened from starvation, Khadijah, Muhammad's closest confidant, died in 620 CE, followed by his protector, Abu Talib. Muhammad called it the Year of Sadness and the darkest period of his life.

In the midst of his sorrow, Muhammad had an important experience, which some believe was physical and others believe was mystical.[17] The Night Journey (Miraj) to heaven has been interpreted as God's reassurance to Muhammad of his mission during the greatest losses of his life. One night, in 621, as he was praying in the mosque, the angel Gabriel came to him and hoisted him onto Buraq, the traditional heavenly steed of the prophets of old. Buraq carried Muhammad first to Jerusalem to the Temple Mount, where Muhammad prayed, and then up into the seven stages of heaven where he met Adam, John the Baptist, Jesus, Joseph, Idris (believed to be Enoch), Aaron, Moses, and Abraham, and then finally entered into the Divine presence. During the Night Journey, the direction of prayer was changed from Jerusalem to Mecca and the number of

---

17. The Night Journey has inspired literature, meditation, poetry, music, and art, commemorating this event as a literal journey and a spiritual, mystical one. The journey is said to have occurred in a time beyond time; as the door was swinging when Muhammad departed, so it was still in the same motion when he returned. For discussion and analysis of various understandings of the Night Journey, see Safi, *Memories of Muhammad*, 165–93.

daily prayers was set.[18] Symbolically, the Night Journey placed Islam within the Abrahamic traditions. It connected Islam to Judaism and Christianity, marked Jerusalem as a sacred city in Islam, and further placed Muhammad within the prophetic tradition, albeit at the top as the "seal of the prophets."[19] Muslims today commemorate the Night Journey with popular festivals that include candles, lights, special prayers, offerings, and celebrations.

The Medinan Years

Despite the relative failures of Muhammad's ministry, his reputation as a skilled arbitrator remained. This reputation led the people of the oasis town of Yathrib, known today as Medina, to seek his counsel in 622. For some time, Yathrib had been entrenched in a constantly escalating blood feud that no one seemed able to stop. Muhammad agreed to travel there to arbitrate. Several hundred of his followers also emigrated over the next several months. This event, known as the Hijra, marks the first year of the Muslim calendar and emphasizes the importance of the faith community in Islam.[20] Moving was dangerous, because it meant leaving the collective protection tribal kinship offered and going someplace where they had neither family nor protection. Instead, they had to rely on complete strangers, which was unheard of in Arabia at the time. Those who received them and provided food and shelter have come down across history

---

18. The number of prayers was a topic of some debate between Muhammad and Moses and then between Muhammad and God. God ultimately agreed to reduce the original assignment of fifty daily prayers down to five. One of the most famous accounts was recorded by al-Bukhari and can be found in Jane Dammen McAuliffe, ed., *The Norton Anthology of World Religions: Islam* (New York: Norton, 2015), 167–70.

19. Meaning he was recognized as the last in a line of prophets stretching back to Adam and as the most perfect of all prophets. Some interpreters claim this status was verified by a physical "seal" or defining mark said to have been between Muhammad's shoulders and recognized by a Christian monk. For a discussion of prophethood in the Islamic philosophical tradition, see Frank Griffel, "Muslim Philosophers' Rationalist Explanation of Muhammad's Prophecy," in Jonathan E. Brockopp, ed., *The Cambridge Companion to Muhammad* (New York: Cambridge University Press, 2010), 158–79.

20. Beginning the Islamic calendar with the birth of the community, rather than the birth of Muhammad, helps Muslims focus on living in relationship with God and the *ummah* as outlined in the Qur'an, rather than focusing exclusively on Muhammad.

as the Ansar, or Helpers. They remain an important symbol of the mutual responsibility that Islam teaches people should have for each other, as well as of the obligation Muslims have to welcome refugees and provide for their needs, since they themselves were once refugees with neither home nor sustenance.

Muhammad's successful intervention with the tribes in Yathrib resulted in not only an end to the conflict but also a creative approach to building a new community on the basis of collective security and choice of association, rather than tribal lineage. In this new community, security and social status were not based on an accident of birth, but on a deliberate and free decision to join. Conversion to Islam was not required, although it was allowed. Non-Muslim tribes, including Jews, remained free to practice their own religion and observe their own religious laws.

Critical to community membership was agreement to the Constitution or Pact of Medina, which placed all of these groups in alliance with and responsible for each other. According to the terms of the Constitution, in the event that any signatory was attacked, all signatories would rise to their defense. As long as everyone abided by the terms of the agreement, the community held together. This period, therefore, marked a transition in Muhammad's status. No longer simply a prophet with a divine message, he now also served as the head of a multireligious polity,[21] responsible for the security of Muslims and non-Muslims alike. It further marked the transition of the Muslim community from its prior stance of absolute nonviolence to justifying the use of violence in certain circumstances. Qur'an revelations from this time grant permission for self-defense in the event of an attack or an imminent attack.

The Quraysh of Mecca proved to be a determined enemy that continued to persecute the Muslims even though many had left Mecca for Medina. They sent periodic military expeditions against Medina and engaged in skirmishes. The Muslims also engaged in small attacks, including on trade caravans belonging to the Quraysh, disrupting both trade and the route itself. The first major battle between the Quraysh and Muhammad's forces took place in Badr in 624.

---

21. A polity is a community of people united by a self-selected cohesive force, such as identity or religion, in possession of resources, leadership, and organization, such as institutions.

The Battle of Badr proved a pivotal event in Muslim history for a number of reasons. First, although Muhammad was both a political leader and a prophet, he had relatively little military experience. One follower questioned his proposed battle plan, asking if Muhammad was speaking as a prophet or as a person. When Muhammad replied that he spoke only as a person, the follower proposed an alternative plan that proved successful. Taking such advice highlights an important pattern in Muhammad's leadership—engaging in consultation (*shura*) when making decisions, rather than acting as an all-powerful autocrat. He never claimed to know everything and remained open to advice from all people, women and men alike. Second, it underscored the reality that Muhammad was, at the end of the day, a human being. Not everything he said was a divine revelation and not every thought he had came from a divine source. Not only did he consult with other people, particularly those he considered to have more expertise in a given situation, he also did not think of himself as infallible, reserving that level of authority for God. Third, although the Quraysh outnumbered the Muslims by more than three to one, the Muslims won. Muslims celebrate this victory as evidence of divine intervention on their behalf. Finally, the victory solidified the new social model introduced in Medina as a viable alternative to the tribal model that existed elsewhere in Arabia.

After the battle, Muhammad and his followers returned to Medina, taking with them some seventy prisoners. By tribal custom, they had the right either to put the prisoners to death or sell them into slavery. However, Muhammad chose instead to ransom and release most of them. Those who were literate were ransomed not for money but for teaching ten Muslim children to read and write. The image that emerges from the Battle of Badr, therefore, is not simply one of military victory but also one of conduct after war, in particular of the humane treatment of prisoners and of not creating circumstances that would have called for more blood retaliation under Arab tribal custom.

Nevertheless, the Quraysh were angered by their loss, particularly the deaths of several prominent leaders. They returned in 625 to attack the city of Medina in the Battle of Uhud. Although it looked as though the Muslims would win, a group of archers disobeyed orders and left their posts, allowing for a surprise attack that killed many Muslims and seriously injured Muhammad. The Muslims lost.

Coming on the heels of the victory at Badr, the loss at Uhud had a profound psychological impact. A Qur'an verse revealed shortly after the loss chastised the Muslims for pursuing this battle out of desire for booty and criticized the disobedience of those who had cost the Muslims their advantage. Whereas Muslims see the victory at Badr as proof of God's support, they interpret their loss at Uhud as evidence that God had become frustrated with them for losing focus. Still, the verse offers hope for forgiveness, provided a behavioral change occurs.

The Muslims had their chance for redemption in 627 at the Battle of the Trench—a twenty-seven-day siege of Medina by the Quraysh and allied tribes, which included some of the Medinan Jewish tribes who, by joining with the Quraysh, violated their promise as signatories of the Constitution of Medina. The Battle of the Trench became important for many reasons. First, the Muslims, despite being outnumbered by more than three to one, won the day, in part because of a defensive strategy based on digging a trench around Medina that prevented the enemy cavalry of horses and camels from participating effectively. Second, they won this battle more by wits than by fighting, as Muhammad used diplomacy and other tactics to break up the enemy confederation. Third, their victory marked the decisive military defeat of the Quraysh, costing them prestige and much of their trade. They no longer constituted a serious threat to the Muslims after this battle. Fourth, and most seriously over time, it highlighted the challenge of dealing with those tribes that had broken the collective security agreement of the Constitution by joining the enemy. Muhammad placed the fate of those tribes in the hands of a gravely wounded Muslim. The wounded man ruled that the men of the offending tribes should be killed and the women and children sold into slavery. Muhammad concurred, and the ruling was carried out.

Because some of these tribes were Jewish, there are those on both sides of the conflict who have tried to create an anti-Semitic paradigm from this story—that, on the one hand, Jews cannot be trusted and are always enemies of Muslims and, on the other, that Muslims hate Jews and seek to kill them. Such oversimplifications have had negative consequences for Muslim-Jewish relations, because they assume the conflict was religious in nature, rather than consider the important political dimension of the broken collective security agreement. Interpretations of this battle often highlight either danger to Jews at the hands of Muslims or the need to punish dangerous political enemies. Often overlooked in these debates is that those Jewish tribes that remained faithful to the Constitution continued to live peacefully with the Muslims and continued to practice their faith and religious law freely after this incident.[22]

Return to Mecca

Having defeated the Quraysh, the Muslims had now attained a position of relative power. More tribes from throughout Arabia joined them in alliance, expanding Muhammad's influence in the peninsula. Yet he remained exiled from his original home and the geographic center of Islam: Mecca. In 628, Muhammad led his followers in an attempted pilgrimage. This was a daring move given hostilities with the Quraysh, because, as pilgrims, Muhammad and his followers had to come unarmed. The attempt also put the Quraysh in a difficult position. As the overseers of the Kaaba, they had to allow pilgrims access so they could fulfill their religious obligations. To refuse entry to any religious group would violate their role. Yet allowing the Muslims to enter would result in an unacceptable loss of face. The Quraysh consequently sent emissaries to meet Muhammad and his followers partway to negotiate an agreement.

The negotiation was successful insofar as both sides elected to find a diplomatic, rather than military, solution. The outcome, the Treaty of Hudaybiyyah, established a ten-year truce. The Muslims agreed to return home without completing the pilgrimage in exchange for permission to return the following year. Some of Muhammad's followers were not satisfied with this outcome, feeling they and their Prophet had lost face and were being insulted. Muhammad feared a mutiny was imminent. As he often did when faced with a tense situation, he turned to a trusted Companion for advice—one of his wives, Umm Salama. She recommended

---

22. Muslim history records examples of Jewish tribes that remained faithful to the Constitution, including one rabbi who was killed upholding that obligation. For more detail, see Firestone, *Jihad: The Origins of Holy War in Islam*, esp. 117–24.

sacrificing a camel—normally the last rite of the pilgrimage—to symbolize the end of the pilgrimage. The symbolism had the desired effect and averted a mutiny. Muhammad and his followers returned to Medina and waited until the following year for the full pilgrimage. However, when they tried to return in 629, the Quraysh reneged on the terms of the treaty.

Only in 630 did the Muslims finally reenter Mecca, fulfilling the pilgrimage and giving Muhammad the opportunity to rededicate the Kaaba to the One God and demonstrate his victory over the Quraysh. His destruction of the pagan idols filling the Kaaba is typically presented in parallel to Abraham's similar actions[23] and reminiscent of Jesus' clearing of the Temple, establishing monotheism as the norm. Yet it also symbolized his victory over the Quraysh. Although tribal custom certainly would have permitted Muhammad to have his enemies killed, given the years of persecution he and the Muslims had suffered at their hands, Muhammad chose instead to offer amnesty.

Many important lessons can be drawn from the conquest of Mecca. First, Muhammad's military campaigns were not geared toward annihilation of the enemy but rather to the restoration of a previously broken relationship, which is possible only when both parties are alive to work through the problem. Second, Muhammad was not bent on vengeance. Although he had military objectives, he also had broader, long-term objectives related to community-building and peaceful relations so that people could go about their daily lives. Third, and perhaps most important, Muhammad was not a "one-size-fits-all" leader. He recognized that there is a time and a place for peace, not just war; for forgiveness, not just vengeance; and for diplomacy, not just fighting. The power of his leadership was rooted in his ability to adapt to different circumstances, defuse tensions, and convince people of the value of a long-term vision focused on the good of the community, not just the short-term goals of an individual. Muhammad's example thus offers a full range of options for dealing with enemies.

---

23. The Qur'an portrays Abraham as denouncing and even destroying the idols worshipped by his ancestors, defying his own father in the process. See Q 21:51–70, 26:69–89, and esp. 37:83–98.

Death

Just as Muhammad's life is central to Muslim belief and practice today, so, too, Muhammad's death in 632 holds important lessons. First, many of Muhammad's followers, including some of his closest Companions, refused to believe that he had died. Only when Muhammad's father-in-law, Abu Bakr, reminded people that only God never dies and that Muhammad was strictly a human being, did they accept his mortality. Second, Muhammad chose a peaceful setting for death. He asked to be with his family and for quiet and calm, rather than tears and wailing. He died in his wife Aisha's embrace. Third, Muhammad did not die a wealthy man. Throughout his life, he maintained a practice of living frugally and sharing with those less fortunate. In fact, he owned so little when he died, the community had to chip in to support the family he left behind. Fourth, although Muhammad's community faced challenges after his death, it was strong enough to survive his loss. Stories of his actions and deeds circulated, and the community quickly realized the importance of preserving these for posterity.

Key Events in Muhammad's Life	
570	Birth of Muhammad
610	Muhammad receives first revelation of Qur'an
613/616	Migration to Abyssinia
620	Year of Sadness—deaths of Khadijah and Abu Talib
621	Night Journey
622	Hijra from Mecca to Medina
624	Battle of Badr
625	Battle of Uhud
627	Battle of the Trench
628	Treaty of Hudaybiyyah
630	Muslims enter Mecca
632	Death of Muhammad

Muhammad's Legacy

Any time a respected leader dies, the followers who remain help protect his or her legacy, determining how that leader is remembered and in what capacity. Muhammad's legacy binds his humanity to his religious authority. Emphasizing Muhammad's humanity reminded followers that only God is eternal and that all human beings, even the most perfect, eventually die. Allowing Muhammad to remain human in the memories of Muslims has prevented deification while still calling for deeper investigation into his life example. His authority is therefore mixed. When speaking as a prophet, his word is infallible, but Muhammad was clear that, sometimes, he spoke simply as a person. Indeed, in some instances the Qur'an validated the opinions of his Companions over Muhammad's opinion, even on matters related to military tactics, affairs of state, and governance. This suggests not all aspects of his behavior require obedience or imitation. The challenge for Muslims, then, lies in discerning which aspects one must imitate and which not.[24]

Hadith

Much of what is known about Muhammad's Sunna ("example") is recorded in the hadith, or accounts of Muhammad's sayings and deeds. The hadith were initially oral accounts, transmitted at first by a Companion and then by individuals who had heard a Companion tell the story. Over time, as distance increased between the person hearing the account and the original witness, verification of the chains of transmission (*isnad*) became an important method of authentication.

Historically, preference was given to memorization of hadith and oral transmission from teacher to student. However, by the ninth century, it had become clear that written records were also needed for the sake of long-term preservation. The major hadith collections were thus compiled and authenticated at this time.[25]

---

24. Today, some adhere to even minute details, such as manner of dress or sleeping position, as a matter of caution and supererogatory piety.

25. The two most authoritative hadith for Sunnis are those compiled by al-Bukhari and Muslim, although four others are also considered authentic: the collections of al-Tirmidhi, al-Nasa'i, Abu Dawud al-Sijistani, and Ibn Majah. Authoritative collections for Shia are those collected by al-Tusi, ibn Babawayh, and al-Razi.

Still, the idea of a "living chain of transmission" remained the ideal and continues today, encouraging direct learning of a hadith from a recognized teacher so that the chain of transmission remains theoretically unbroken.[26]

Given that Muhammad lived a full and complete life, it is not surprising there are tens of thousands of hadith covering topics ranging from religious ritual to personal habits, such as how he brushed his teeth. Sometimes a specific event may be recorded in only one hadith, while other events may be recounted in dozens or hundreds of hadith. Different hadith about a single event may exist because more than one person witnessed it. Because different people notice different things, it may be helpful to think about a series of hadith about a single event creating a composite image, taken from different viewpoints. Slight variations in Muhammad's wording often exist, so that hadith are best not taken literally. Instead, it is more appropriate to attend to the overall meaning of the hadith and its intended impact.[27] It is also important to consider the hadith as demonstrating a spectrum of possible responses that depend on context, rather than a "one-size-fits-all" approach.

Hadith transmission served as an equalizer of sorts in the early Muslim community. Anyone who had come into contact with Muhammad could transmit a hadith based on memory. Women, men, slaves, free persons, and even children were accepted as transmitters. Hadith therefore can provide insights not only into Muhammad's life but also into other issues of concern to the Muslim community, including religious authority and gender dynamics. For example, women are responsible for transmitting an estimated 12–20 percent of all hadith in various collections and are portrayed as full participants in the community,

---

26. A parallel can be found in Christianity with apostolic succession, one of the four marks of the church (one, holy, catholic, and apostolic), and the ordination of priests, which began with Saint Peter and continues down through bishops to the present day. Whether such an unbroken chain can be fully proven is beyond the point of the powerful symbolism that an unbroken chain represents.

27. Parallels exist in the four Gospels, particularly when they contain similar but slightly different wording for the same events. Though some scholars argue that such differences in wording "prove" a story was fabricated, it might be more useful to consider that different authors simply found different phrasing to express the same meaning.

bringing their petitions, legal issues, and marital problems to Muhammad for advice.[28]

Curiously, those male Companions who spent the most time with Muhammad rank among the least prolific transmitters. Some scholars speculate that those who served as the Rightly Guided Caliphs after Muhammad's death focused on preserving the spirit of Muhammad's teachings through their actions and methods of reasoning, rather than through simply memorizing what he said.

For all of the attention given to chains of transmission, there are, nevertheless, some hadith that have been declared "weak," either because the chains of transmission are doubtful, as the transmitter was not considered particularly reliable, or because the content of the hadith is suspect. Questions about hadith authenticity constitute a source of ongoing academic inquiry.[29] Today, scholars give more attention to the context of hadith to understand if a given hadith is intended as prescriptive of what believers are expected to do or as simply descriptive of the time and place in which it was recorded.[30] Ultimately, hadith may prove more useful for reconstructing the development of particular attitudes than for assertions as to how, exactly, the Prophet behaved or what he literally said.

---

28. See chapter 8, "Women and Gender," for more detail. For more information on women's roles in hadith transmission, see Asma Sayeed, *Women and the Transmission of Religious Knowledge in Islam* (New York: Cambridge University Press, 2013). On conflicts between hadith transmitted by different parties, see Fatima Mernissi, *The Veil and the Male Elite: A Feminist Interpretation of Women's Rights in Islam*, trans. Mary Jo Lakeland (Cambridge, MA: Perseus, 1992).

29. For more information on a trend in hadith studies that focuses on content rather than chain of transmission, and for comparison with the teachings of the Qur'an, see Natana J. DeLong-Bas, *Wahhabi Islam: From Revival and Reform to Global Jihad*, rev. ed. (New York: Oxford University Press, 2008), 10–11 and 45–54.

30. This is particularly contentious when gender dynamics are concerned, especially when one hadith appears to contradict another. For example, one hadith says, "Women are the twin halves of men," whereas another says, "If I were to command anyone to prostrate before another, I would command women to prostrate themselves before their husbands, because of the special right over them given to husbands by God." The first hadith appears to support gender egalitarianism; the second clearly does not. Such contradictions raise the question of whether such hadith are best understood as historical accounts of what was said or as examples of collective historical memories shaped by the context of the time in which they were recorded and authenticated.

Miracles

Unlike Jesus, Muhammad was not known as a miracle worker—and never claimed to be one. Muslim theologians have consistently pointed to a single miracle attributed to Muhammad: receipt of the revelation of the Qur'an. Insistence on the uniqueness and centrality of the Qur'an as a miracle has maintained focus on God as the singular object of Islamic worship, rather than on Muhammad, who was strictly a Messenger.[31]

A calligraphic representation of Muhammad's name. The consonants M-H-M-D appear bold, right to left. The lighter symbols above and below the consonants are diacritical marks serving as pronunciation cues, including short vowels and a doubling of the second "M."

© Svetlana Prikhnenko / Shutterstock.com

This emphasis on monotheism helps explain why visual depictions of Muhammad are generally discouraged. Fearing people will misunderstand such depictions and use them as icons or objects of worship, Muslims generally avoid portraiture of Muhammad to make clear worship belongs to God alone. There are no known images of Muhammad made during his lifetime. Preference has been given to artistic modes that convey verbal portraits of the prophet, such as the Hilya (the oldest known verbal description of Muhammad's appearance and demeanor); these modes make use of calligraphy, rather than imagery. In those cases in which Muhammad is portrayed, such as in Persian art, he is typically shown with his face covered by a veil or a halo of fire (placing him in the line of prophets who received divine revelation) or with his head or entire body surrounded by a halo.[32]

---

31. Islamic tradition identifies five Messengers—Noah, Abraham, Moses, Jesus, and Muhammad—in confirmation of the Qur'an's recognition of the Torah and Gospels as divine revelations.

32. Depictions of prophetic or divine figures with halos, flames of fire, or other references to light were not unique to Islam. They had a long history in the Roman Empire, where the king was identified with the sun, and in India, where Krishna was known as the "light of the world." Christianity made similar revisions, such as replacing popular imagery of Venus and Cupid with the Virgin Mary and the Infant Jesus. Borrowing artistic forms and imagery that were already familiar to local populations can be viewed as an incorporation of the old with the new, but transformed to new purposes.

Only in the later Ottoman and Mughal empires and among Shia did images of Muhammad and other saintly figures become more commonplace.

Muhammad as a Family Man

Many in the West have criticized Muhammad for his marriages to multiple women,[33] comparing him negatively with Jesus, who never married, and overlooking the examples of other biblical prophets who had more than one wife. Muslims often respond by reminding people many of these marriages were made to form tribal alliances to benefit the community, similar to alliances by marriage in Europe historically.

Muslims also note the importance of Muhammad's example as a husband and a father, arguing that the quality and character of his relationships are more important than the quantity. Knowing that Muhammad faced the joys and tribulations of marriage and raising children—balancing his responsibilities as a prophet and statesman with his role as a family man—makes Muhammad a fully relatable

---

33. The hadith largely agree that Muhammad had fourteen wives over his lifetime, nine of whom were alive at the time of his death. Two of those marriages have come under strong criticism—those to Aisha and Zaynab. Aisha was married to Muhammad when she was only six or seven years old to solidify the alliance between Muhammad and her father, Abu Bakr, who was one of his strongest supporters and ultimately became the first caliph after Muhammad's death. Muhammad did not consummate the marriage until Aisha was nine years old and even then only at her father's insistence. Though Muslims are often careful to emphasize the difference in context (average life expectancy in pre-Islamic Arabia was much shorter than it is today, so people tended to marry at much younger ages), the example of Muhammad with a child bride has generated extensive criticism in the West and ongoing concerns among Muslim women activists working to end the practice of child marriage. Zaynab was originally married to Muhammad's adopted son, Zayd ibn Harithah—a marriage Muhammad himself had arranged and for which he personally paid the dower. However, the couple never got along and Muhammad's efforts to counsel them failed. When they divorced, Muhammad married her. The community considered this marriage to be incestuous. Even when Muhammad received a revelation invalidating adoption, thereby cancelling out accusations of incest, the community remained upset. Even Aisha remarked that such a revelation seemed overly convenient. For details, see Spellberg, *Politics, Gender and the Islamic Past*, and Barbara Stowasser, *Women in the Qur'an, Traditions, and Interpretation* (New York: Oxford University Press, 1996).

figure for Muslims. Even knowing that there were moments of tension within his marriages and that he didn't always get along perfectly with his wives or some of his Companions, that he experienced the devastating loss of several beloved children, as well as a cherished wife, is important for Muslims who look to his example for help in keeping faith in the midst of tragedy.

Muhammad's example set a clear precedent and norm for the marriages of religious leaders after him. There is no tradition of celibacy for Muslim religious leaders. Embracing sex as a normal, important, and mutually fulfilling part of marriage, Muhammad is known to have criticized male followers who were harsh toward their wives, reminding them not to fall on their wives like beasts but rather to approach them with kisses and caresses.[34] Women and men are expected and encouraged to find sexual fulfillment in marriage, regardless of whether children are produced.

Islamic tradition further records Muhammad as a devoted and playful father known to carry his children on his shoulders and back. As a husband, he shared household chores, including cleaning, mending his own clothes, and helping out with cooking. He enjoyed spending time with his family and was known for his laughter, good humor, and treating his wives kindly, with respect, and as full partners, even when they talked back to him and bickered with each other. He sought their counsel on personal and community matters. He never struck any of his wives and berated followers who did. He included women among his followers, listening to and answering their questions, responding to their requests for religious opinions and rulings, and otherwise ensuring they were fully included as members of the religious community, including communal prayer at the mosque and religious instruction. Muslim women activists throughout the world urge more attention to these realities as central to a full understanding of Muhammad as prophet and man, warning against the tendency to focus only on his military and political roles.

---

34. Devin J. Stewart, "Sex and Sexuality," in Jane D. McAuliffe, ed., *Encyclopedia of the Qur'an* (Leiden: Brill, 2006), 4:580–85.

Dr. Omid Safi (b. 1970)

Dr. Omid Safi is an Iranian-American Shia and Sufi Muslim and public intellectual who specializes in medieval mysticism and contemporary Islamic thought, with a focus on diversity, social justice, and gender equality within Islam. A self-defined "progressive Muslim" who claims descent from Muhammad, he was born in the United States but raised in Iran until his family fled in 1985. Safi has made explaining Islam to Westerners and Muslims his life's work. His book, *Memories of Muhammad: Why the Prophet Matters* (HarperOne, 2009), offers a complex portrait of Muhammad's life and memory in response to Westerners' criticisms and to Muslims' questions. *Memories* also offers English translations of many medieval Persian and Arabic texts that provide verbal portraits of Muhammad, as well as twenty visual images, in order to demonstrate the diversity of Islamic thought and practice throughout history. Safi is the author of a regular column of the Religion News Service, "What Would Muhammad Do?" and a weekly show for On Being, a public radio podcast and website. An award-winning teacher, he is the director of the Duke Islamic Studies Center at Duke University and chairs the Islamic Mysticism Group at the American Academy of Religion.

Conclusion

As a person, family member, leader, prophet, and statesman, Muhammad was a complex and multidimensional figure. He did not have a one-size-fits-all, black-and-white approach to interacting with other people, whether friend or foe, Muslim or non-Muslim. Instead, he gave careful consideration to context to produce flexible and nuanced decision-making. Consequently, any method for studying his example (Sunna) in a reductionist fashion by considering only one aspect of his life, whether to praise or condemn, risks not only oversimplification but also, more importantly, a failure to fully grasp what his life and legacy mean to Muslims around the world. Having that broader picture facilitates, for example, a better understanding as to why Muslims express hurt and, in some cases, retaliation over depictions of Muhammad as a terrorist or pedophile. Though some reprisals have taken the form of violence, as occurred in 2015 with the massacre of journalists at *Charlie Hebdo* magazine by extremists, other responses have been more measured, such as the international boycott of Danish products following the publication of offensive cartoons in the daily newspaper *Jylland-Posten* in 2005. Perhaps most importantly, having a broad understanding of Islam also highlights the intellectual and theological bankruptcy of groups like ISIS that select only part of Muhammad's example to follow without considering the full scope of his interactions, particularly when non-Muslims are concerned.

Review Questions

1. Why is Muhammad such a pivotal figure for Muslims? What does it mean to look to his example for inspiration and where can such information be found?
2. What impact did Muhammad's life experiences before the revelation of Islam have on his ministry and leadership?
3. Identify and discuss three ways in which Muhammad brought about changes to his surrounding society.
4. What challenges did Muhammad face to his religious message and why? By whom?
5. How might a Muslim best follow Muhammad's example?

Discussion Questions

1. How can Muslims draw upon Muhammad's example with respect to citizenship and community involvement? Are there parts of his example that are emphasized more than others and, if so, why and what impact does that have for both Muslims and non-Muslims? Are there other parts that should receive more attention and, if so, why?
2. How would you evaluate Muhammad as a religious leader? As a political leader? Is it possible to separate those two roles or must they go together? How would you evaluate the religious and political roles of leaders today? Is it possible to separate the roles?
3. How does Muhammad compare to or contrast with other prophets and religious figures? What might those similarities

and differences indicate about relationships between Muslims and other faith traditions?

For Further Study

Readings

Armstrong, Karen. *Muhammad: A Prophet for Our Time.* New York: HarperOne, 2007.

Brockopp, Jonathan E., ed. *The Cambridge Companion to Muhammad.* New York: Cambridge University Press, 2010.

Brown, Jonathan A. C. *Hadith: Muhammad's Legacy in the Medieval and Modern World.* Oxford: Oneworld, 2009.

Lings, Martin. *Muhammad: His Life Based on the Earliest Sources.* Rochester, VT: Inner Traditions International, 1983.

Mernissi, Fatima. *The Veil and the Male Elite: A Feminist Interpretation of Women's Rights in Islam.* Translated by Mary Jo Lakeland. Cambridge, MA: Perseus Books, 1992.

Ramadan, Tariq. *In the Footsteps of the Prophet: Lessons from the Life of Muhammad.* New York: Oxford University Press, 2009.

Safi, Omid. *Memories of Muhammad: Why the Prophet Matters.* New York: HarperOne, 2009.

Sayeed, Asma. *Women and the Transmission of Religious Knowledge in Islam.* New York: Cambridge University Press, 2013.

Schimmel, Annemarie. *And Muhammad Is His Messenger: The Veneration of the Prophet in Islamic Piety.* Chapel Hill: University of North Carolina Press, 1985.

Stowasser, Barbara. *Women in the Qur'an, Traditions and Interpretation.* New York: Oxford University Press, 1996.

Films

Akkad, Moustapha, et al. *The Message.* [Troy, MI]: Anchor Bay Entertainment, 1976.

An epic historical drama about Muhammad's life told by his uncle, Abu Hamza, played by Anthony Quinn.

Al-Harithy, Muwaffak, et al. *Muhammad: The Last Prophet.* [Bridge-view, IL]: Fine Media Group, 2009.

An accessible, animated portrayal of Muhammad's life.

Gardner, Robert, et al. *Islam: Empire of Faith*, part 1. [Arlington, VA]: PBS.org, 2007.

A three-DVD documentary series covering the birth of Muhammad through the Ottoman empire with attention to developments in art, civilization, and culture, in addition to history and politics.

Kronemer, Alexander, et al. *Muhammad: Legacy of a Prophet.* KQED-TV (San Francisco), 2011.

Documentary film made for PBS about Muhammad's life and legacy as seen by modern American Muslims.

Links

Oxford Islamic Studies Online, *oxfordislamicstudies.com.* The world's largest online database on Islam. Contains more than six thousand articles, including hadith studies and criticism and many perspectives on Muhammad's life and legacy.

The Qur'an

God's Final Message to Humanity

The foundational event and heart of Islam is the revelation of the Qur'an. Muslims believe the Qur'an is a collection of words from God spoken in the Arabic language to the Prophet Muhammad by the angel Gabriel over a period of twenty-two years (610–632 CE) as God's final, complete, and perfect revelation to humanity. Muslims believe, although God created human beings with an innate sense of right and wrong, human beings are capable of being led astray by selfish or sinful desires. Revelation is thus needed to guide human beings back to right behavior. Just as Jews look to the Torah and Christians look to the Bible for divine guidance and inspiration, so Muslims look to the Qur'an to know and follow God's will.

The Historical Qur'an

During Muhammad's lifetime, the Qur'anic revelation was an ongoing process. Muhammad received revelations at any and all times, regardless of what he was doing or whether he was by himself or in the company of his Companions.[1] Sometimes he could hear the words very clearly; at others, the sound reverberated like a bell, and

---

1. Similar to Jesus' disciples in Christianity, Muhammad's Companions hold special status in the memory of Muslims because they personally knew and interacted with Muhammad.

he had to listen very carefully to hear the words.[2] As the revelations progressed, professional memorizers and scribes began to accompany Muhammad to immediately commit revelations to memory and writing.[3] Written records of revelations were then entrusted to different tribes as a point of honor, emphasizing the revelation as a collective holding of the community.

At the same time, written records were of limited use, as the Qur'an was not revealed in chronological order and chapters were not always revealed in their entirety. As long as Muhammad was alive, the text was considered a developing, rather than a finite, text to which additional chapters or verses could be added. This meant that writing down the complete text was not necessarily the most effective means of preserving it, because the text was subject to change. The text only became finite with Muhammad's death. It was then the Muslim community began to pay greater attention to complete written records and to the order of the verses and chapters.

Muhammad's death brought almost immediate concern about gathering all known parts of the revelation to assure the Qur'an would not die with him. The first caliph, Abu Bakr (r. 632–634 CE), ordered the collection of all written records while those most familiar with the revelations were still alive. One of Muhammad's most trusted scribes, Zayd ibn Thabit, was charged with coordinating these efforts. Not only did Zayd investigate and collect as

---

2. There was one occasion when Muhammad thought he had received a revelation but realized that what he had actually heard was Satan's temptation (the so-called Satanic Verses). There are also sayings called *hadith qudsi*, which are in Muhammad's own phrasing but with God's revealed meaning. The chain of transmission is therefore traced directly to God, rather than to Muhammad. There is much debate among scholars and exegetes over the correct number of *hadith qudsi*. See William A. Graham, *Divine Word and Prophetic Word: A Reconsideration of the Sources, with Special Reference to the Divine Saying or Hadith Qudsi* (Berlin: De Gruyter, 1977).

3. In that time, people had greater confidence in the accuracy of oral records than in written ones, which were easier to forge or alter. In an oral society that prized memorization skills, any person could pick out a mistake in an accepted recitation, whereas errors in written documents would be detectable by a much smaller group of literate persons. In addition, paper had not yet been introduced in Arabia, and written records on papyrus were expensive. Sometimes verses were recorded on other materials, such as palm leaves or animal bones, but these were known to decay over time. Oral recitations, on the other hand, were seen as easier to control and certify, particularly given the cultural practice of requiring two witnesses to authenticate an oral record.

many written transcriptions of revelations as he could; he also only accepted as authentic those verses for which two witnesses could verify that Muhammad had recited them or that they personally had been present at their writing. Zayd's collection of verses was transcribed and given to the second caliph, Umar (r. 634–644 CE). Upon his death, they were passed to his daughter, Hafsa, who was one of Muhammad's widows.

Nevertheless, by the time of the third caliph, Uthman (r. 644–656 CE), quarrels broke out among different groups over which group had the "correct" recitation of the Qur'an, as Muslims from different regions had slightly different recitation methods.[4] There was also rising concern about the number of Muslims who had memorized the entire Qur'an being killed or dying. Uthman therefore ordered a second collection, again under the direction of Zayd ibn Thabit. Zayd again consulted all experts with knowledge of the full revelation, including Muhammad's cousin and son-in-law, Ali, in assembling this

---

4. These differences were known during Muhammad's lifetime and were permitted to facilitate learning and recitation by different tribal groups. Any recitation traceable to Muhammad's approval was accepted as authentic. Ultimately, seven recitations were accepted as equally valid, the most prominent of which today is the reading of Asim (d. 744), popularized in the 1924 royal Egyptian edition. See Mahmoud M. Ayoub, updated by Afra Jalabi, "Qur'an: History of the Text," *The Oxford Encyclopedia of The Islamic World*, 6 vols., editor-in-chief John L. Esposito (New York: Oxford University Press, 2009), vol. 4, 464–68. Part of the challenge in standardizing recitations came from the rudimentary nature of Arabic writing in the seventh century. At that time, Arabic was written with a number of homographs—using the same letter to signify different sounds. Later Arabic scripts added dots and dashes to these letters to distinguish those sounds. In addition, short vowels were not originally written into the text—a common phenomenon with Semitic languages. Again, this issue was resolved over time through the addition of other diacritical marks. Some scholars, such as Ingrid Mattson, believe this points to the original nature of the Qur'an as an oral tradition, one intended for memorization. Mattson posits the written version of the Qur'an served as a supplemental memory aid with the expectation that only those who had already memorized the transmission would be reading it. See Mattson, *The Story of the Qur'an*, 90–98, for details. Others scholars, such as Andrew Rippin, argue that the full text of the Qur'an did not take its final form until the eighth century and that the current text is therefore best understood as a reflection by exegetes on a primitive written text, rather than an oral tradition. See Andrew Rippin, *Muslims: Their Religious Beliefs and Practices*, 4th ed. (London: Routledge, 2012), 31–34. Whatever the original nature of the text, the memorization of and ability to recite the text has been a key part of Islamic education and artistic expression throughout Islamic history. Today it is possible to purchase copies of the Qur'an that not only have all of the vowels and diacritics indicated but even specialized coloring and scripts designed to preserve the exact-known pronunciations and rhythms of recitation.

final compilation. During this second collection, any differences in recitation or dialect were resolved in favor of the preferred method of the Quraysh (Muhammad's tribe). The final, authentic, and complete version, known as the Uthmanic Codex, was then read aloud publicly in Medina and copied by scribes. All other versions were reportedly then destroyed.[5] Copies of the Uthmanic Codex were sent to the four major cities of the Islamic world at that time—Mecca, Kufa, Basra, and Damascus—along with Qur'an reciters assigned to teach and propagate the text. Uthman reportedly kept

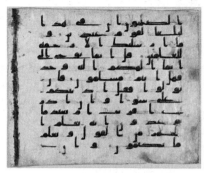

The Metropolitan Museum of Art, New York, Purchase, Lila Acheson Wallace Gift, 2004

A page of the "Tashkent Qur'an" (late eighth-early ninth century), likely from Syria or North Africa. It contains little illumination and is written in Kufic script using only consonants and long vowels; the text omits the diacritical marks that aid pronunciation.

one copy for himself.[6] Those five texts became the basis for the written Qur'an of today. This canonized version of the Qur'an was reproduced by hand in manuscript form thousands of times; many of these are preserved in libraries and museums around the world.

Other Companions, some have suggested, had complete written copies of the Qur'an that they did not surrender to Uthman, leading

---

5. The narrative of the Uthmanic codex is broadly accepted by Muslims. However, some Western scholars, applying methodologies used in biblical studies, have challenged this narrative. For details on the earliest manuscripts of the Qur'an and current Western scholarly theories about the Qur'an's compilation, see the collection of essays in Gabriel Said Reynolds, ed., *The Qur'an in Its Historical Context* (London: Routledge, 2008), and Angelika Neuwirth, "Qur'an and History—A Disputed Relationship: Some Reflections on Qur'anic History and History in the Qur'an," *Journal of Qur'anic Studies* 5 (2003): 1–18.

6. Although there are traditions about specific texts claiming to be Uthman's copy, radiocarbon dating has not supported these traditions. One example is the text variously known as the Samarkand codex, Samarkand manuscript, and Tashkent Qur'an kept in the Hast Imam library in Tashkent, Uzbekistan. Radiocarbon dating showed a 95% probability of dating between 765 and 855 CE, more than a century after Uthman. See E. A. Rezvan, "On the Dating of an 'Uthmanic' Qur'an from St. Petersburg," *Manuscripta Orientalia* 6, no. 3 (2000): 19–22.

some scholars to question whether alternative versions of the Qur'an existed.[7] For example, some polemical accounts claim Ali had a complete version containing certain chapters pointing to him as Muhammad's successor that the Uthmanic version reportedly deleted.[8] However, no such document has been discovered.[9] On the other hand, the oldest known fragments of an official written version of the Qur'an that matches the modern text has been dated to the late first Islamic century, lending credibility to the claim that the Uthmanic Codex did, indeed, serve as a comprehensive master document in the seventh century.[10] Overall, the Qur'anic text has proven to be remarkably consistent over time and space—more so than any other scripture.[11]

---

7. It would not be surprising if Companions had maintained and passed down their personal transcriptions of the Qur'an, as they had written them in Muhammad's presence. One possible such copy was found in an archaeological dig in Yemen in the 1990s.

8. This view is not accepted by mainstream Sunnis and Shiis. The only variance in Qur'ans used by Sunnis and Shiis is a slight difference in the numbering of a few verses.

9. Some Western scholars argue that an earlier master document—the "Ur-Qur'an"—served as a template, similar to the Q document posited by biblical scholars as the original source for the Gospels of Matthew and Luke. However, similar to Q, no "Ur-Qur'an" has been found. See Fred M. Donner, "The Qur'an in Recent Scholarship: Challenges and Desiderata," in Reynolds, ed. *The Qur'an in Its Historical Context*, 29–50, esp. 31–40.

10. These fragments of the Qur'an (Mingana 1572b), written on sheep- or goatskin, were identified in the University of Birmingham library in July 2015. They had gone unnoticed for years, having been misidentified and bound to another seventh-century manuscript. Carbon dating places these fragments between 568–645 CE—a remarkable match to the life span of Muhammad (570–632 CE), with revelation received from 610–632. Other copies dating to the late seventh/early eighth century are held in Istanbul, Turkey, in the Turkish and Islamic Arts Museum. Some scholars have challenged the radiocarbon dating of the Birmingham text, as there are other features that suggest a later date of writing, including chapter separators, dotted verse endings, and other grammatical marks. See Gabriel Said Reynolds, "Variant Readings: The Birmingham Qur'an in the Context of Debate on Islamic Origins," *Times Literary Supplement*, August 2015, 14–15.

11. Seyyed Hossein Nasr, "General Introduction," in Seyyed Hossein Nasr et al., eds., *The Study Qur'an: A New Translation and Commentary* (New York: Harper Collins, 2015), xxxiv. On continuity of the text, see F. E. Peters, *Muhammad and the Origins of Islam* (Albany: State University of New York Press, 1994), 257. Occasionally, minor disagreements have been found with the received texts, likely owing to changes in scripts or human error. Some variations do not affect the text itself, such as the introduction of titles in the second Islamic century and the use of ornamental designs, marks, and blank spaces to indicate beginnings and endings of chapters and verses. In a few places, grammarians have noted the sentence structure appears to be missing something, although this would not appear to change the theological meaning of the passage. See Mattson, *The Story of the Qur'an*, 27.

Important Events in the Qur'an's History	
610–632	Revelation of the Qur'an to Muhammad
632–634	Collection of Qur'an materials by first Rightly Guided Caliph Abu Bakr
644–656	Second collection of Qur'an materials under third Rightly Guided Caliph Uthman—Uthmanic Codex
568–645	Radiocarbon-dating timeframe of oldest known Qur'an fragments
8th through 10th centuries	Asharite-Mutazilite controversy over nature of the Qur'an

The Qur'an: A Structural Overview

Roughly the length of the New Testament, the Qur'an consists of 114 chapters (*suras*) and more than 6,200 verses (*ayat*, or "signs"). The chapters vary in length, with the longest containing 286 verses and the shortest being comprised of only 11 words. In general, the chapters are organized with the longest chapters appearing first and the shortest chapters appearing last.[12]

Unlike the Bible, which is organized as a chronological account of God's interaction with humanity, specifically with the Jewish people in the Old Testament, followed by accounts of the life of Jesus[13]

---

12. Nevertheless, the first chapter, called "al-Fatihah," is not the longest—it holds place of pride owing to its centrality in worship practices, as it is recited at each of the five daily prayers. Although it is not the last, the shortest chapter is 108, al-Kawthar.

13. The Qur'an confirms the Gospel as God's revelation to Jesus, as well as Jesus' miraculous conception and birth through God's Spirit breathing into the Virgin Mary (Q 19:16–26). Jesus' miracles are also recognized, including speaking in his mother's defense as an infant when she is accused of sexual impropriety while presenting him to her family (Q 19:27–34). Muslims nevertheless do not believe in Jesus' crucifixion, death, and Resurrection, although they do believe that Jesus was "raised up" by God directly to heaven (Q 4:157). Muslim scholars vary in interpretation of this phrase, although most recognize this as Jesus' ascension into heaven. Muslims believe in individual accountability for their deeds, alone at the Final Judgment by God. They do not believe that the sins of one person will be counted against another or that one person can atone for the sins of another. Consequently, they do not share the Christian belief in original sin or the idea of an all-atoning savior. For more detail, see Tarif Khalidi, ed. and trans., *The Muslim Jesus: Sayings and Stories in Islamic Literature* (Cambridge, MA: Harvard University Press, 2001).

and the early Christian church in the New Testament, the Qur'an is neither a record of Muhammad's life nor a history of a given community. Rather, it is a collection of verses revealed to a single individual as a universal message of guidance and warning. In some cases, an entire chapter was revealed in a single moment. Other chapters are comprised of verses revealed at many different moments.[14] Because the chapters themselves were not revealed in chronological order, the Qur'an is not designed to be read in a linear, chronological fashion; rather, it can be opened for reading at any point.[15]

Traditionally, the chapters of the Qur'an are designated according to the location where they were revealed—ninety in Mecca (the first twelve years of Muhammad's ministry) and twenty-four in Medina (the last ten years of Muhammad's ministry).[16] Although more chapters date from the Meccan period, the Medinan chapters constitute fully one-third of the text. Scholars have noted certain themes common to each. Meccan chapters tend to be more universal in nature, reflecting their status as early revelations designed to call people to worship the one God and warning of punishment for those who do not. Meccan chapters are generally short, use signs from the natural world to point to God, and present Muhammad's message as consistent with the messages of earlier prophets. Medinan chapters tend to be longer, more specific and regulatory, reflecting the change in Muhammad's status from Prophet to both Prophet and head of a multireligious polity. Medinan chapters give more attention to

---

14. The Qur'an itself says it was sent down in parts, rather than as a whole, so that it could be recited to the people in stages (Q 17:106).

15. A popular Muslim tradition holds that Muhammad specified the order of the verses and chapters and this order was verified twice by the angel Gabriel in the year before his death.

16. This designation was determined by Ibn Abbas (d. 688), a close Companion of Muhammad known for his knowledge of the Qur'an, and has been widely accepted among Muslim exegetes. This places definitive demarcation within fifty years of Muhammad's death, well within the living memory of the earliest Muslim community. Though some Western scholars have questioned the Meccan vs. Medinan designations, as well as the codification process, most scholars continue to find these designations helpful. For discussion of the codification process and the challenge of sources, see Fred McGraw Donner, *Muhammad and the Believers: At the Origins of Islam* (Cambridge, MA: Belknap, 2012), 39–89, and Gerhard Bowering, "Recent Research on the Construction of the Qur'an," in Reynolds, *The Qur'an in Its Historical Context*, 70–87, as well as Rippin, *Muslims: Their Religious Beliefs and Practices*, esp. 20–40.

issues related to the establishment and organization of the expanding Muslim community, such as legal matters, civil society, and collective security. Attention is also given to individual salvation and inner spiritual life.

Each chapter of the Qur'an has a name[17] and opens with the *bismillah*,[18] or phrase, "In the name of God, the Most Merciful, the Most Compassionate."[19] Some chapters also have a series of disconnected letters at the beginning.[20] Although chapters have been assigned numbers by Western scholars to indicate their order, Muslims prefer to identify chapters by their revealed names, such as "al-Fatihah" for chapter 1, "al-Baqarah" for chapter 2, and so on, similar to Christian identification of books of the Bible by their names—Genesis, Exodus, and so on. Finally, although chapters appear in a standard order in printed copies of the Qur'an, there is no requirement that they be recited in a particular order. Worshippers are free to read or recite any combination of passages they choose, in keeping with the examples of Muhammad and his Companions.

Content

The content of the Qur'an can best be described as a universal guide for God's expectations of human beings—toward God through acts

---

17. Muslims believe some of these names were revealed to Muhammad, along with the verses. Some chapters have more than one name. Nasr et al., *The Study Qur'an*, xxxiv.

18. The exception is chapter 9, al-Tawba, which omits the *bismillah*.

19. This phrase plays an important role not only in the Qur'an but also in Muslim daily life and practice. It is used as an invocation, a prayer, and to ward off evil, and is frequently represented in calligraphic artwork, ranging from pen and ink to wood carvings and embroidery.

20. These appear in 29 chapters. Muslim scholars are divided as to their meaning. One opinion is that the letters contain mystical mathematical significance, comparable to the Jewish mystical science of *gematria*, in which each letter is assigned a numerical value. The comparable Islamic science, *al-jafr*, claims the Qur'an's inner teachings are hidden in this mathematical structure and symbolism. Other opinions posit the letters are there either to serve as memory devices or to signal an intended audience that a recitation is about to begin. Supportive historical evidence exists for all three. For a discussion of the exegetical explanations of this feature, see Nasr et al., xxxii and 13–14. For a discussion of mystical interpretations, see Annemarie Schimmel, *Mystical Dimensions of Islam*, 35th ed. (Chapel Hill: University of North Carolina Press, 2011), esp. appendix 1, on "Letter Symbolism in Sufi Literature," 411–25.

of worship (*ibadat*) and toward each other (*muamalat*) in interactions and transactions. As a guide filled with ethical and spiritual lessons, the Qur'an encourages individual virtues and qualities that help to build society, such as justice and generosity, while also helping human beings navigate between good and evil, truth and falsehood. It provides good news and warnings and promises rewards and punishments. Using a combination of invocation, affirmation, and petition, the Qur'an is said to have both outward (*zahir*) and inward (*batin*) meanings, so that messages can be found on many levels beyond the literal meanings of the words. Such polyvalence is understood to reflect the complexity of God.

In the Islamic tradition, God is beyond human ability to comprehend. Therefore, the Qur'an does not fully define who or what God is or specify God's nature. Although images such as God sitting on a throne or God having a face are occasionally used to try to convey concepts that human beings can understand, Muslims are generally careful not to anthropomorphize God, believing God is unique and unlike human beings. What can be known about God is mostly expressed through God's names or attributes, which indicate what God does and the powers God wields, not necessarily what God is. These attributes are often referred to as the "99 names of God"; the most frequently mentioned of these are al-Rahman (the Most Merciful) and al-Rahim (the Most Compassionate).[21] The 99 names have served as important teaching tools for Muslim theologians and mystics (Sufis) for learning about and approaching God. Yet even these attributes do not fully convey the complete reality of God; they permit only glimpses.

In addition to the 99 names, the Qur'an portrays natural phenomena, particularly the sky, trees, water, and weather, as means of perceiving God. It describes these phenomena as signs (*ayat*)[22] that point to the One who created them. Qur'an 30:20–24 particularly highlights the role of creation in pointing to the Creator, repeating "And among His signs" at the beginning of each phrase for a lyrical and rhythmic reminder of the harmony and balance present in God's

---

21. These names appear more than 2,000 times in the Qur'an.

22. This is the same term used for a Qur'an verse, indicating there are multiple "signs" God gives to humanity, both verbal and perceptual, so that human beings can perceive God in every aspect of daily life.

creation while also emphasizing God's majesty and power as Creator of human life and love, the diversity of languages and colors, the heavens and the earth, lightning and water. All of these signs suggest a back-and-forth between perception and realization, hearing God and seeing God's signs. Engaging God's creation thus becomes a means of engaging God. Although God's power is reflected through God's command over all of creation, God nevertheless remains accessible to human beings through worship and prayer.

Although the Qur'an does not specify God's nature, it does specify the nature of human beings—who they are, why they were created, why they are here on earth, what they are supposed to do with their lives, their rights and responsibilities, what they will be held accountable for, what will happen when they die, and the consequences of life on earth for status in the afterlife. It portrays human beings as intelligent and gifted with reason and free will, although God also reserves the option to interfere with human choice when God has a lesson to teach. Perhaps most importantly, the Qur'an always talks about human beings in relationship—to God and to each other, beginning with the first two human beings created as mates for each other from a single soul (Q 4:1). Other verses address sexuality, family life, responsibilities in marriage, and various aspects of community life. The correct relationship between the individual, society, and the rest of God's creation is a central Qur'anic theme.

The Qur'an presents many stories familiar to Christians and Jews, such as the stories of the prophets shared in common with the Bible,[23] although the method of storytelling and theological

---

23. These include Aaron, Abraham, Adam, David, Elijah, Elisha, Ezekiel, Jesus, Job, John the Baptist, Jonah, Joseph, Lot, Moses, Muhammad, Noah, and Solomon, as well as Mary, the mother of Jesus. In some cases, the Qur'an provides more information than the canonical Bible. The most striking example is Mary, the mother of Jesus. Parallel information can be found in the noncanonical gospel of Mary, suggesting that Christians with whom Muhammad came into contact had access to this text. Western scholars have long questioned where the parallels between Qur'anic and biblical material originate. Although nineteenth- and early twentieth-century Western scholars saw this as "evidence" of Muhammad's "borrowing" from other religions to create his own, Muslims counter that the Qur'an refers to a Mother Book that resides with God in heaven (Q 13:39) from which all recognized revelation—specifically naming the Torah, Psalms, and Gospels—is drawn, so that parallel material should be expected and serves as evidence of their common divine origin (Q 10:37). For additional information about parallels to other religious material, see chapter 9, "Muslim-Christian Encounters: Conflict and Coexistence."

emphases differ significantly from the Bible. In the Qur'an, the point of telling a story is to emphasize a lesson God wants humanity to learn; the point is not the exact details, chronology, setting, character, or plot development. Qur'anic stories often begin with the word *remember*, implicitly assuming familiarity with the main parameters of the story. They also frequently discuss themes that run parallel to Muhammad's experiences, placing him at the end of a long line of prophets that began with Adam, as well as reassuring Muhammad that he is not the first to experience challenges and rejection because of his message. In this way, the stories of the prophets present a cyclical approach to history[24] in which each cycle includes God sending a prophet with a message, which, once accepted, is gradually forgotten, resulting in punishment from God, followed by the sending of a new prophet. Muhammad marks a rupture with this cycle, because, although he continues the cycle by receiving and preaching a fresh revelation, the cycle of prophethood nevertheless ends with him and is to be followed by eschatological events marking the end of this world and humanity.

Like the Bible, the Qur'an gives significant attention to eschatological events—those related to death, resurrection, Judgment Day, and final consignment to either paradise or hell. In keeping with the rhyming of ideas throughout the Qur'an (i.e., heaven and hell, good and evil, the heavens and the earth), there is a rhyming of ideas about life[25]—how to live in this life and how to prepare for the afterlife, how to live in justice in this world and be judged according to those deeds in the next world.

---

24. This cyclical approach is not unique to the Qur'an. Arabic literature historically took a cyclical view of history in which certain patterns reoccur. Knowing where one is in a cycle is more important than knowing where one is chronologically. There are biblical parallels in, e.g., 1 and 2 Kings and 1 and 2 Chronicles, in which the Children of Israel and God are in a good relationship until the Children do what is evil in the eyes of God and God gets angry and punishes them. At some point, the Children repent and repair their relationship with God, and the cycle begins again. Just as Muhammad breaks the pattern for Muslims, so Jesus breaks the cycle for Christians. For cyclical understandings of time in Arabic literature, see Esad Durakovic, *The Poetics of Ancient and Classical Arabic Literature: Orientology*, trans. Amila Karahasanovic (London: Routledge, 2015).

25. The rhyming of ideas was commonly used in Semitic literature as a poetic device. See the subheading "Linguistic Features" of the Qur'an in this chapter.

Signs of the End of the World

As in the Bible, the Qur'an lists certain "signs of the end of the world" or warning markers that final judgment is coming. Some of these signs are unnatural events in the natural world, such as changes in the sun, moon, or stars, natural disasters such as earthquakes and floods, and changes in animal or human behavior that suggest an upset of the current order. These signs are reminders of God's ultimate power over all of God's creation, including human beings, who will be held to account for all of their deeds, righteous and unrighteous.

> When the sun is enfolded,
> And when the stars fade away;
> When the mountains are set in motion,
> And when pregnant camels are abandoned;
> When the wild beasts are gathered,
> And when the seas are made to swell over;
> When the souls are coupled,
> And when the female infant buried alive is asked for what sin she was slain;
> When the pages are spread,
> And when heaven is laid bare;
> When hellfire is kindled,
> And when the Garden is brought nigh,
> Each soul shall know what it has made ready. (Q 81:1–14)[26]

Descriptions of paradise and hell in the Qur'an often parallel those in the Bible. Paradise is portrayed as a beautiful garden filled with shade, servants, and plenty of water and food, whereas hell is a place of fire, torment, and physical deprivation.[27]

---

26. Translation is from Nasr et al., *The Study Quran*, 1480–81.

27. Although there are some differences in the descriptions, some of these details have parallels in the Syriac Christian tradition. See Reynolds, *The Qur'an and Its Biblical Subtext*, 251–52.

Although some people understand these descriptions literally, others consider them from a symbolic perspective—namely, that all of the material benefits and comforts one might lack in this life will be provided in the next. Thus true paradise becomes a level of existence in which all needs are met and there is no more pain and suffering, rather than a specific location. Some interpreters suggest this frees believers to focus exclusively on God for eternity.[28]

In the Qur'an, there are many indicators of the "Signs of the Hour," or end of the world. Their common thread is a combination of socio-moral decay, as evinced by rife injustice and oppression, and environmental disaster in the heavens and the earth.[29] These "signs" (*ayat*) point to the One sending them as a warning of impending Final Judgment.

As awe-inspiring as God's displays of ultimate power can be, it is also important to recognize that God never leaves human beings in despair. God always provides choice. Thus the ultimate issue is not what happens in life but how one chooses to respond to it. God does not promise faith will make one's life free from pain and suffering. Rather, God promises reward in the afterlife to one who remains faithful to the values and teachings God has revealed, particularly through ritual, worship, and acts of charity and kindness, even if such faith leads to persecution and death in this life. In this regard, Abraham, the common faith ancestor of Muslims, Christians, and Jews alike, is upheld as a role model for individual struggle, sincere commitment to truth, and humility in asking for God's guidance and forgiveness when he makes mistakes.

---

28. This tends to be a common theme among Sufis and some philosophers.

29. These signs are often raised by apocalyptic groups pointing to current events and claiming the end of the world is near. Searching for signs of the end-times has a long history that continues up to the present with groups such as Al-Qaida and ISIS. For details, see David Cook, *Contemporary Muslim Apocalyptic Literature* (Syracuse, NY: Syracuse University Press, 2008), and William McCants, *The ISIS Apocalypse: The History, Strategy, and Doomsday Vision of the Islamic State* (New York: St. Martin's Press, 2016).

Linguistic Features

From the earliest days of revelation, the exceptional quality and beauty of the Arabic prose of the Qur'an has been considered evidence of its divine nature and origin. The inimitability of its language is a core theological belief.

Muhammad's contemporaries struggled to classify what they heard, questioning whether Muhammad was a soothsayer or sorcerer or perhaps even possessed. Yet the revelation did not fit any of those categories. Soothsayers were known for mumbling, not issuing clear messages; sorcerers used words to accompany other signs, such as blowing on knots;[30] and possession was typically accompanied by choking and spasms. None of these applied in Muhammad's case. Instead, people were mesmerized or spellbound by the beauty of the words themselves. Some of Muhammad's most vehement opponents are said to have been so moved by the beauty and sophisticated linguistic skill of the revelation that they converted to Islam on the spot.[31]

Sophisticated linguistic skill displayed through poetic composition was a prized commodity in the oral society of pre-Islamic Arabia. Long before Muhammad's birth, Mecca had hosted an annual poetry competition. Winning verses were decoratively hung with honor on the Kaaba, the central location of pilgrimage. Although not poetry per se, Muhammad's revelation became the ultimate winner. His opponents frequently hired other poets to try to imitate the language—and convey a different message more suited

---

30. Pre-Islamic Arabs practiced a variety of forms of divination to try to discover the future through supernatural means, believing that spirits could communicate with the human world by manipulating natural elements or objects such as tea leaves, coffee grounds, the dissolution of knots, or selection of lots or arrows from a pile.

31. One case was Umar ibn al-Khattab, initially one of Muhammad's most violent opponents. When Umar learned that his sister, Fatima, and her husband had secretly become Muslims, he was furious. He went to their home and reportedly struck her—and then regretted it. When Fatima begged him to perform ablutions and read the verses for himself, Umar was reportedly so moved by the language that he immediately sought out Muhammad to pledge his conversion and allegiance. He became known forever after as one of Islam's greatest and most powerful defenders who served as the second Rightly Guided Caliph after Muhammad's death. See chapter 4, "Sunnis and Shia."

to their purposes—but none succeeded. The Qur'an itself challenges people to try to produce something like it (Q 2:23, 10:38, 11:13), while predicting failure. The display of Qur'an verses draped over the Kaaba thus symbolizes the victory of the Qur'an as the ultimate winning verses that can be neither improved upon nor surpassed.[32]

Considered the literal Word of God, the Qur'an is always memorized in the original Arabic and is used daily in prayers. Muslims view recitation of the words in the original language as a sacred experience, because it literally allows the Divine to pass through the speaker. Philologists have speculated that the Arabic of the Qur'an is likely the closest among Semitic languages[33] to the original from which they stemmed,[34] bringing full circle the idea of Islam as a reassertion of the "first," rather than the "last" of the Abrahamic traditions.

Much of the power of the Qur'an's language is lost in translation, because translations cannot replicate its multifaceted methods of rhyming, rhythm, and assonance, all of which facilitate memorization. The most common method of rhyming in the Qur'an is the use of similar ending-sounds at the conclusions of phrases, such as -im and -in and -um and -un, although the length of the phrases may vary.[35] Similarly, repetition of an initial word or phrase can be used like a drum beat to hammer home a particular message, generally a warning about human mortality and accountability. Specific patterns of letters can also be used to express messages about God. For example, commands from God often use short syllables and consonants (*jalali* mode), whereas loving and forgiving messages

---

32. Every year, a new drape, or *kiswa*, is produced. Select verses of the Qur'an are embroidered in gold thread onto a background of black silk. Today, financed by the Saudi government as part of its role as "Custodian of the Two Holy Mosques," the *kiswa* weighs nearly one ton and costs about $5 million per year to make.

33. The most important related Semitic languages include Hebrew, Aramaic/Syriac, and Arabic.

34. See Robert Hoyland, "Epigraphy and the Linguistic Background to the Qur'an," in Reynolds, *The Qur'an in Its Historical Context*, 51–69.

35. The opening chapter, "al-Fatihah," is a good example of this kind of rhyming. For an example of recitation by one of the most popular reciters, Mishari al-Afasy, see *https://www.youtube.com/watch?v=xCwtpNgFw5g*.

from God are typically found in longer phrases with gentle rhymes (*jamali* mode).[36]

Another method of "rhyming" consists of deriving multiple words from the same root letters so that the sound of the root letters is repeated, although the words themselves vary.[37] English has no equivalent to this method. One example of the use of common root letters would be **s-l-m**. The name of the religion, **Islam**, is based on these three root letters, as is the word for one who follows the religion of Islam, a **Muslim**. The word for peace, **salaam**, also shares these root letters. Muslims often say "Islam is a religion of peace," a saying that tries to capture in English what is implied through the linguistic connection of words based on these root letters—that the one (Muslim) who submits (Islam) to God achieves peace (salaam) within oneself, with God, and with others.

Another example of common root letters, **w-h-d**, emphasizes Islam's absolute monotheism, or belief in a single God.[38] The Arabic word for "one" is *wahid*. One of the 99 names of God is al-**Wahid**. The word for belief in one God is *tawhid*. Again, the linguistic interconnection of the terms serves to emphasize the importance of monotheism in Islam.[39]

---

36. *Jalali* mode tends to emphasize God's power, majesty, and transcendence, while *jamali* mode is softer in tone and focuses on God's nearness to human beings. For an example of *jalali* rhyming, see the recitation of Q 82 by Hajjah Maria Ulfah (biography appears later in this chapter) at *https://www.youtube.com /watch?v=t8z3np50kbE*.

37. Arabic words are generally formed from three root letters, although occasionally four or, even more rarely, five are used. From those three root letters, ten different verb forms can be derived, which can then be turned into other parts of speech.

38. Muslims do not believe in the Christian doctrine of the Trinity in which there is one God who exists coeternally in three persons: Father, Son, and Holy Spirit. For Muslims, there is only one singular, unique, and eternal God who does not exist or appear in different persons.

39. Sometimes God refers to Godself as "we" in the Qur'an. This is not viewed as evidence of a multiplicity of gods, but rather as a linguistic convention—the "royal we"—in which use of the first person plural is intended to signify the majesty and status of a person holding high office, such as the Queen of England or the Pope. It is comparable to the use of Elohim in Hebrew to refer to the One God, rather than a plurality of deities.

The Nature of the Qur'an

Although Muslims have always agreed the Qur'an is the Word of God revealed to the Prophet Muhammad, what that says about the nature of the Qur'an has been a source of theological debate and controversy.[40] A major question historically was whether God's Word is of the same nature and essence as God and, therefore, coeternal with God, or whether God's Word is specific to a particular moment, implying that it is created at that moment. Those who supported the idea of an uncreated Qur'an (the Asharites) argued that God's Word is an inherent part of God. Those who claimed the Qur'an had to have been created (the Mutazilites) argued that God's Word is not the same as God because God is utterly unique. Therefore, even God's Word could not infringe upon God's uniqueness. This controversy became so important historically that state policy for a time under the Abbasid Empire (750–1258) asserted the created nature of the Qur'an and engaged in an inquisition to ensure that senior religious scholars and judges asserted this belief. This program was relatively short-lived, however. Within a century and a half, the Qur'an was declared to be uncreated and an inherent part of God—and has been considered so by the majority of Muslims ever since.

Interpreting the Qur'an

Muhammad is often referred to as "the living Qur'an," which expresses the belief that his life represents a perfect adherence to the Qur'an's teachings. As long as Muhammad was alive, there was no need for anyone else to interpret the Qur'an's meaning.[41] After his death, the community had to develop methodologies for interpreting the Qur'an.

Diverse methods for Quran interpretation and explanation exist and have varying degrees of authority and popularity. As in other faith traditions, interpretation may be exegetical (*tafsir*, or explaining

---

40. Similar debates over the nature of Jesus—is he divine, human, or a combination of the two—have also occurred historically among Christians. As with the Qur'an, these debates took centuries to resolve.

41. The Qur'an constantly admonishes believers to obey God and His Prophet.

and interpreting what the text says) or eisegetical (examining the text for a predetermined interest). Historically, exegetical approaches to the Qur'an have been preferred, particularly when focused on linguistic analysis. Although eisegetical approaches are popular in many places today, particularly among those calling for a values-based approach to faith, they have long been perceived as running the risk of projecting human agendas onto the Divine Word.[42]

Islam does not have an ordained clergy, thus no institution claims exclusive authority as caretaker or interpreter of the text. After Muhammad's death, a few of his closest Companions served as caliphs to lead the community. Although each of these caliphs had a good sense of the revelation's meaning and context and how Muhammad might have interpreted it, none claimed an exclusive right to interpret the Qur'an. In fact, records of this early time show the caliphs seeking other Companions' opinions.[43]

After this time, a class of scholars (*ulama*) emerged that specialized in certain Islamic studies considered key to the accurate interpretation of the Qur'an. These included Arabic language and grammar; logic; and a thorough knowledge of the hadith, *sira* (Muhammad's biography), and *asbab al-nuzul* (occasions of revelation). Traditionally, knowledge of Muhammad's life, activities, and example has been central to Qur'an interpretation.

Throughout history, interpreters have recognized the import of contextualizing the Qur'an. Knowing the events that precipitated or surrounded the revelation of a given passage, the textual context of a given passage, and its original meaning (what Muhammad's followers would have understood) is crucial to a full grasp of its meaning. This is particularly true in discerning whether a verse is intended as universally applicable or as specific to a certain context. Such

---

42. The Qur'an itself warns against those who speak of God without knowledge (Q 7:33) or preach and teach their own notions of God, thereby misleading others (Q 16:25). Nevertheless, modern interpreters often engage the text eisegetically to explore themes such as social justice, gender relations, and religious pluralism.

43. Over time, Shia came to assign infallibility in Qur'anic interpretation to their Imams. Historians argue this was a later development and did not immediately follow Muhammad's death. For details on the development of Sunni and Shia identities, see chapter 4, "Sunnis and Shia," in this book, as well as Jonathan Berkey, *The Formation of Islam: Religion and Society in the Near East, 600–1800* (New York: Cambridge University Press, 2002).

understanding also allows one to extract the relevant value or lesson when reinterpreting it in a current context. Yet determining the occasion of a revelation is not always straightforward. Although Muslims agree on the text of the Qur'an, opinions vary on the focus of and circumstances in which certain verses were revealed, especially when that context has important political implications.[44]

Interpretations that adhere only to the literal meanings of the Qur'an's words, without any contextual understanding, are generally viewed with suspicion,[45] because the framework for grasping the original meaning has been divorced from the text, making interpretation more liable to error. Studying a verse out of context risks misunderstanding the verse, as well as allowing it to override other clear or more numerous directives or transforming a situation-specific directive into a universal one. Some interpreters single out verses as proof-texts for their predetermined agenda. These approaches say more about the interpreter than the text. Such risks are manifest in current groups such as Al-Qaida and ISIS that cherry-pick their way through scripture to support political and religious agendas and actions that the vast majority of Muslims find abhorrent.

Two key questions regarding Qur'an interpretation are whether the Qur'an can abrogate itself, meaning that a later verse can override earlier ones, and whether the Qur'an as a whole must be considered authoritative because of its status as God's Word. Some scholars uphold abrogation as a legal principle because the Qur'an was sent gradually, rather than all at once, opening the possibility that God might refine the message as people grew into it. Support for this approach typically

---

44. Scholars such as Asma Afsaruddin and Reuven Firestone argue for the importance of contextualizing the contextualizations, noting that political agendas were often introduced into certain passages. Afsaruddin documents changes in extra-Qur'anic literature that came to be applied to Qur'anic interpretation. Firestone argues certain passages in the Qur'an were joined together because of their common thematic material, even though they were revealed at different times, which sometimes obscures their original contexts. He also challenges claims that verses calling for peaceful relations with non-Muslims were limited to the Meccan period, offering evidence of Medinan verses supporting peace. For details, see Asma Afsaruddin, *Striving in the Path of God: Jihad and Martyrdom in Islamic Thought* (New York: Oxford University Press, 2013), and Reuven Firestone, *Jihad: The Origin of Holy War in Islam* (New York: Oxford University Press, 1999).

45. This is one of the strongest criticisms of movements such as the Wahhabis and Salafis.

cites the case of drinking date wine, which was initially permitted, then restricted, and finally prohibited altogether. The argument is that immediate prohibition would have been too difficult at the outset, so God gave people time to adapt to the restriction before prohibition. Some current theologians and jurists have applied this logic to cases such as slavery and polygyny, arguing that the Qur'anic intent over time was acceptance, then restriction, and finally prohibition.

Those opposed to the tenet of abrogation cite discomfort with the idea of God changing God's mind, because this appears to portray God as imperfect, arbitrary, or capable of error, none of which is theologically sustainable. Abrogation further asserts that whatever God said last about an issue is God's final word on the matter. This suggests there is always but one way to approach an issue, robbing Muslims of applying wisdom in considering the full spectrum of options offered by the text for complex situations. It also raises serious questions about why God would take the time to send a variety of solutions if only the last one was to be implemented. For example, the Qur'an offers a multiplicity of options for dealing with non-Muslims, ranging from peaceful coexistence to diplomacy to engaging in collective security arrangements to treaty relations to supporting trade to fighting and warfare. Reducing those options to a single approach would cripple the Muslim community's ability to engage others and potentially harm the community in the long run.

Translating the Qur'an

Translating the Qur'an presents unique challenges, given its status among Muslims as the literal Word of God and the proclaimed inimitability of its language. Part of the challenge lies in linguistic characteristics that cannot be replicated in translation. Similarly, the art of recitation is lost in translation. Other translation concerns focus on meaning, particularly where a single word in Arabic may contain many meanings that do not come across in other languages. For this reason, Muslims prefer to describe translations as commentaries, or as meanings of the Qur'an, rather than as the Qur'an. This allows scholars to include notes on word choices, complexities of the original language, and grammatical choices that explain their methodology and grasp of the text without claiming to be the text itself.

Historically, writing a *tafsir*, or explanation of the Qur'an, was considered a valuable act of scholarship and piety, though not all scholars wrote one.[46] *Tafsir* tended to be written in the order in which the verses appear in the Qur'an, which led to critiques that *tafsir* tend to be segmented, to focus on individual verses, rather than the whole text. In addition, historically, *tafsir* was the product of one individual. Only recently has a team of scholars produced a *tafsir*.[47]

Although translations are widely available today, Muslims prefer to learn the text in its original Arabic to maintain the connection with the Word of God, even if they do not speak Arabic. Some Muslims choose to learn Arabic as a second language both to have a more direct encounter with the Word of God and due to concerns about relying on potentially faulty or politicized translations. Full translations in some languages have appeared only relatively recently, such as that in the Berber language, even though Berbers were among the first non-Arab people to embrace Islam. Similarly, Islam has been practiced in China for twelve hundred years, but the first translation of the Qur'an to Chinese dates only to the nineteenth century, owing to the preference for encountering the Divine Word in its original form.

Reciting the Qur'an

From Islam's earliest times, the most basic Muslim education, whether for females or males,[48] has included memorization of the Qur'an in the original Arabic.[49] Mosque circles and schools were formed to teach correct memorization, with the teacher playing

---

46. Writing a biography of the Prophet (*sira*) was another expression of piety and scholarship.

47. Nasr et al., *The Study Quran*.

48. The purpose is to create a permanent imprint of the Qur'an on the mind as a resource that can be drawn upon throughout one's life.

49. The Qur'an has been memorized in its original language more than any other sacred text, even when Arabic is not the native tongue of the memorizer. Although respect remains for the divine nature of the Arabic, focus on memorization alone has come under criticism in the past century owing to rising concerns about the need to understand the meaning of the text.

a key role in transmitting the text as a lived tradition to the next generation.[50] Although written copies of the Qur'an are often used as memory prompts and to ensure textual accuracy, the focus is on the oral, not the written, text.[51] Memorization of the entire text entitles a person to use the honorific title of *hafiz* for men or *hafiza* for women.

Hafiza Hajjah Maria 'Ulfah

A world-renowned Qur'an reciter, *Hafiza* Hajjah Maria 'Ulfah is an acclaimed artist, educator, and celebrity. Born in 1955 in the East Java province of Indonesia, 'Ulfah received a traditional education in a *pesantren* (private Islamic boarding school), followed by advanced religious studies at the State Institute for Islamic Studies in East Java. She also received a Master of Arts degree from the Institute for Qur'anic Studies in Jakarta. 'Ulfah began performing Qur'an recitation on radio and television in 1977. In 1980, she won first place in the National Competition in Qur'anic Recitation in Jakarta, Indonesia. She also became the first woman to win the International Competition

© Freer Gallery of Art and Arthur M. S Gallery, Photographer: Hutomo Wicaksono

Hafiza Hajja Maria 'Ulfah demonstrates the nuances of Qur'an recitation. Women and men are considered equally capable of teaching and performing.

Continued

---

50. This tradition of personal transmission lives on today, with reciters earning certification (*ijazah*) from certified reciters who trace their genealogy of transmitters (*isnad*) back to Muhammad himself as both recipient and first reciter. These reciters are considered "living texts" and are expected to model apt behavior, such as piety, ethics, learning, discipline, and compassion; their authority lies not only in their knowledge, but in their ability to apply that knowledge in daily life. For a modern story of certification of such a transmission, see Mattson, *The Story of the Qur'an*, chapter 3.

51. This remains true today as certification is given for only for recitation, not the ability to read a written text.

Hafiza Hajjah Maria 'Ulfah *Continued*

in Qur'anic Recitation in Kuala Lumpur, Malaysia. 'Ulfah has since been invited to recite throughout Europe, the United States, and the Islamic world. Reciters of her caliber are said to be one in ten million. She also routinely serves as a judge for national and international competitions. In addition to her scholarly work lecturing at the Institute for Qur'anic Studies and the Islamic State University in Jakarta, 'Ulfah has founded a *pesantren* to continue to teach her art to young girls.

Muslims recite the Qur'an in different ways for different reasons. In the years after Muhammad's death, public recitation was a means of verifying that the text was recited correctly in its official order. It also served continually to solidify the community (*ummah*) and ensure the Qur'an remained central to Muslim identity and practice.

Qur'an recitation is part of the five daily prayers, thus it is a skill every Muslim is expected to engage at a basic level. Some Muslims wish to embrace and internalize the text more fully by learning the art and science of formal Qur'an recitation; others are satisfied with more passive encounters with the text by listening to recitations. Either way, the text is intended to be heard, not read silently, keeping the Word of God eternally articulated and bringing blessings to believers.

Formal recitation of the Qur'an is a complex art involving words and melodic techniques. Such recitation involves rules for pauses, vocalization, and stresses on certain words and syllables. Artistic choices include tempo, volume, and tone. Becoming a certified and skilled reciter takes years of training and practice. It brings prestige to the reciter and the reciter's family and constitutes a form of social capital in many countries. Because of the public demand for excellent Qur'an recitation for events such as openings of buildings and facilities, weddings, funerals, official government events, and even athletic games, it can also be a path to employment. In some countries, such as Indonesia and Malaysia, Qur'an recitation has become an equal opportunity option, as both female and male reciters are renowned and participate in national and international recitation competitions.[52] In some countries, these competitions are so popular, they are held in football stadiums and preceded by parades.[53]

Texts guiding proper recitation have existed since the eleventh century, probably because an Arabic modal system of music was developed and practiced at that time. Recitations passed down through the centuries are believed to preserve the original recitation methods used and approved during Muhammad's lifetime. There are seven accepted recitations, believed to reflect the variations approved by Muhammad. Each method has distinctive characteristics that include tone, points of etiquette, and methods of melodic enhancement. In general, only scholars learn more than one style of recitation.

There are also different formats for Qur'an recitation, depending on the reciter's objective. Some choose passages for specific events. Those wishing to recite the entire Qur'an have several options. Recitation of the entire text takes about thirty hours, traditionally broken up into thirty equal parts. This corresponds to the number of days in the month of Ramadan, when Qur'an recitation is believed to bring special blessings to the reciter and to the listeners and is encouraged as an act of supererogatory worship. Muhammad received his first revelation commanding him to recite during the month of Ramadan.[54] Many Muslims attend the mosque nightly for extra prayers during Ramadan to hear the full recitation. The Qur'an may also be divided into seven equal parts so that recitation can be completed in a week. Division into seven or thirty equal parts is so popular that the Qur'an can be purchased in separately bound portions to facilitate carrying only the portion needed for that day's recitation. Though it is possible to "speed recite" the Qur'an, such as in one day, this is discouraged by some scholars as being too focused on the act of recitation to the detriment of contemplating the text. Typically, the

---

52. In other countries, particularly conservative locations such as Saudi Arabia, there have been major debates among Muslim scholars as to whether a woman's voice should be excluded from public space for fear of exciting male desire. Yet such is the value of excellent Qur'an recitation that *Hafiza* Hajjah Maria Ulfah has recited live on Saudi radio.

53. Prizes are also awarded, ranging from cash and appliances to the Grand Prize, typically an all-expense-paid Hajj trip.

54. Ramadan is also special because the angel Gabriel is believed to have visited Muhammad yearly at this time to verify his memorization and recitation were correct.

completion of the recitation in whatever form it occurs is celebrated as "sealing the Qur'an."

Today, Muslims have many options for learning and hearing the recited Qur'an, including computer and video programs, albums, cassettes, CDs, podcasts, radio and television broadcasts, and apps on portable electronic devices. Reciters can reach global audiences through YouTube videos and websites. Some reciters have become global celebrities with followings in the millions.

The Qur'an in the Lives of Muslims Today

The Qur'an plays a central role in the lives of believers, in formal worship and in cultural practices. When a baby is born, the first sounds recited in the baby's ears are Qur'an verses. The Qur'an is recited at weddings and during holiday celebrations. When a person leaves to travel, it is traditional in many Muslim societies to hold a Qur'an over the person's head as they depart.[55] As death approaches, Muslims listen to Qur'an recitation to ensure its verses are the last earthly sounds they hear. Sura 36 is commonly recited after someone dies, and friends and family will gather to hear Qur'an recitation as they remember the recently departed. Muslims will also greet each other with the phrase from Q 2:156, "To God we belong and to God we return," upon hearing of someone's death.

Sometimes short phrases from Qur'an passages are invoked, such as *bismillah* ("in the name of God") before leaving the house for work, starting a task, eating a meal, or welcoming someone to one's home. Similarly, one might say *al-hamdu lillah* ("thanks be to God") upon completion of a task or in response to inquiries about health and family. A person might recite more extensive verses, such as the last three chapters of the Qur'an, before going to sleep at night or when ill, following Muhammad's example. Consulting the Qur'an for guidance, in combination with prayer, is a common way of making momentous decisions, such as deciding on a career or course of study or choosing a marriage partner.

---

55. This practice was so widespread in the past that some traditional cities in the Islamic world have gates containing the Qur'an so everyone passing beneath them literally passes under the Qur'an.

Al-Fatihah

This is an English translation of the opening chapter of the Qur'an, "al-Fatihah":

> In the Name of God, the Compassionate, the Merciful. Praise be to God, Lord of the worlds, the Compassionate, the Merciful, Master of the Day of Judgment. It is Thee we worship and from Thee we seek help. Guide us upon the straight path, the path of those whom Thou hast blessed, not of those who incur wrath, nor of those who are astray.[56]

Some Muslims believe the Qur'an contains curative powers and carry or wear jewelry with verses as a talisman to promote healing, protection, and blessings. The opening chapter of the Qur'an, "al-Fatihah," is believed to be the most powerful healing prayer and typically opens any healing ritual. Some passages are believed to help with illness, childlessness, marital infidelity, loneliness, insomnia, and the evil eye. The "Throne Verse," Q 2:255, is supposed to protect people from harm.

Qur'an verses are sometimes featured on clothing and battle armor. Passages are also used to bless food and water used in medical treatments. Many homes display Qur'an verses in decorative calligraphy as a statement of faith and as a protection. Various types of buildings, including mosques, shrines, palaces, libraries, and schools, have long included Qur'an verses carved into walls or gates for blessing and art, as well as a statement of the patron's piety.[57] Owning a beautiful copy of the Qur'an for special occasions is a point of pride for a Muslim family. Simpler copies are used for daily study and prayers.

The love and respect Muslims have for the Qur'an is a reflection of their love and respect for God and their appreciation for God's

---

56. Translation from Nasr et al., *The Study Qur'an*, 5.

57. On the use of Qur'anic calligraphy in architecture, see Sheila Blair, *Islamic Calligraphy* (Edinburgh: Edinburgh University Press, 2008), and Mohammad Gharipour and Irvin Cemil Schick, eds., *Calligraphy and Architecture in the Muslim World* (Edinburgh: Edinburgh University Press, 2013).

gift of revelation. Some keep the Qur'an wrapped in fine fabric as a sign of devotion and to keep it protected from the elements. Others will kiss the Qur'an whenever they pick it up or hold it in their right hand over their head to place themselves literally under its blessing. Many Muslims have a special place in their home for the Qur'an, typically up on a shelf so they have to look and reach up to access it and so nothing will be placed on top of it; symbolically, this is a reminder of the superiority of God's Word and that God always watches over them. The Internet, computer programs, CDs, live streaming, and phone apps help to keep the Qur'an always accessible, to read and to hear.[58] But whatever the form, the message remains the same—God is present in all aspects of daily life and constantly speaks to the believer.

Review Questions

1. What do Muslims believe the Qur'an is and why and how is it central to their faith?

2. How was the Qur'an revealed and compiled? Does this history add to or detract from the overall credibility of the Qur'an? Why?

3. Identify and discuss three major themes of the Qur'an. What do these themes indicate about God's overall expectations of human beings in terms of their relationship with God and their relationships with other people?

4. Identify and discuss three methods of interpreting the Qur'an. Who is responsible for interpretation? What qualifications, if any, should an interpreter have? How has this changed over time? What are the contributions and drawbacks of each approach?

5. Why is Qur'an recitation important to Muslims? What role does it play in the lives of individuals and Muslim societies?

---

58. Examples of apps include iQuran and Quran for Android. Live streaming of Qur'an recitation can be found at *http://www.liveonlineradio.net/arabic/al-quran-mp3.htm.*

Discussion Questions

1. How does the Qur'an compare and contrast to the Bible in terms of history and content? What might those comparisons and contrasts indicate about the relationship between the two and between their respective faith communities?
2. What are some of the challenges of translating a sacred text? What risks being lost in translation?
3. What opportunities and challenges are presented by exegetical and eisegetical interpretations of scripture? How should those contributions and drawbacks be weighed? Is there room for both?

For Further Study

Readings

Abdel Haleem, Muhammad. *The Qur'an: A New Translation*. New York: Oxford University Press, 2004.

Abdel Haleem, Muhammad. *Understanding the Qur'an: Themes and Style*. London: I. B. Tauris, 2010.

Kaltner, John. *Introducing the Qur'an: For Today's Reader*. Minneapolis: Fortress, 2011.

Kaltner, John. *Ishmael Instructs Isaac: An Introduction to the Qur'an for Bible Readers*. Collegeville, MN: Liturgical Press, 1999.

Mattson, Ingrid. *The Story of the Qur'an: Its History and Place in Muslim Life*. Malden, MA: Blackwell, 2008.

Nasr, Seyyed Hossein, Caner Karacay Dagli, Maria Massi Dakake, Joseph E. B. Lumbard, and Mohammed Rustom, eds. *The Study Qur'an: A New Translation and Commentary*. New York: HarperCollins, 2015.

Rasmussen, Anne. *Women, the Recited Qur'an, and Islamic Music in Indonesia*. Berkeley: University of California Press, 2010.

Reynolds, Gabriel Said, ed. *The Qur'an in Its Historical Context*. London and New York: Routledge, 2008.

Sells, Michael. *Approaching the Qur'an: The Early Revelations.* Ashland, OR: White Cloud, 1999. Includes CD with recordings of Qur'an recitations.

Van Doorn-Harder, Pieternella. *Women Shaping Islam: Reading the Qur'an in Indonesia.* Urbana and Chicago: University of Illinois Press, 2010.

Films

Thomas, Antony, and Dimitri Tchamouroff. *Inside the Koran.* [New York]: First Run Features, 2009.

Examines the role of the Qur'an in the daily lives of Muslims today, including interviews with male and female reciters, interpreters, and followers from all walks of life and different countries.

Barker, Greg, Julie Goldman, and Claude Chalhoub. *Koran by Heart: One Chance to Remember.* [New York]: HBO Documentary Films, 2011.

Documentary following three ten-year-old children, two boys and one girl, from Tajikistan, Senegal, and the Maldives, as they prepare for an international Qur'an recitation competition in Cairo.

Links

Beliefnet, *beliefnet.com*—A multifaith website that includes daily Qur'an readings.

Oxford Islamic Studies Online, *www.oxfordislamicstudies.com*—Offers multiple translations of and commentaries on the Qur'an, as well as a concordance.

Sunnis and Shia

The Origins and Evolutions of Sectarianism in Islam

Media headlines today are filled with Sunni-Shia tensions, conflict between Iran and Saudi Arabia, and ISIS declaring seemingly everyone an apostate, heretic, or deserving of death. These tensions are rooted in debates and beliefs about the identity and leadership of the Muslim community that arose after Muhammad's death and play out today in politics and religious beliefs and practices.

Background

They say history is written by the victors. In tracing the success of a leader or movement with the benefit of hindsight, it is tempting to see certain historical outcomes as "inevitable." But in the midst of events, who the victor will be or what form that victory will take is rarely clear. Leaders and movements emerge in specific contexts, in response to specific situations. Leaders and ideas always vie to steer society in particular directions. This is as true of Islamic history as of any other.

During Muhammad's lifetime, a strong sense of unity among his followers became rooted in his person. Although he was not God, he was a prophet and the agreed upon leader of the community. When he died, questions arose about the future of the religion and the community built on it.

Although sectarian identities did not instantly form after Muhammad's death, three groups of questions became key to Muslim self-identification and community life:

1. Who would lead the community as political head of state?
2. Who would serve as religious leaders, and what would religious leadership look like post-Muhammad?
3. What role would Muhammad's descendants play in the community?

Different responses to these questions sowed the seeds of sectarian identity. They also led at times to the construction of historical memories supporting a particular answer, sometimes establishing contending memories. These memories and identities hardened over time and space in response to and often in conflict with each other.[1]

Questions of Leadership

After Muhammad's death, the crucial question was who would lead the Muslim community and in what capacity. Equally urgent was the question of whether the Muslim polity could survive his death. Communal identity had become so tied to Muhammad as a person that his death threatened to end the community as it was known. Because Muhammad had not left a clear, widely known, and agreed upon plan of succession, many contenders vied for leadership, claiming Muhammad had named them as his chosen candidate.

The first task of Muhammad's successor was to save the community. Here, pre-Islamic Arabian tribal customs posed a challenge. Tribal political relationships were based on ongoing negotiation, rather than permanency or institutions;[2] thus every time a leader died, relationships and alliances were renegotiated. Therefore, some tribes saw Muhammad's death as the end of their alliance to the

---

1. Numerous academic studies outline the complexities of identity formation in early Islam. See, e.g., Jonathan P. Berkey, *The Formation of Islam: Religion and Society in the Near East, 600–1800* (New York: Cambridge University Press, 2003). For contending memories, see Jonathan Brown, *Hadith: Muhammad's Legacy in the Medieval and Modern World* (Oxford: Oneworld, 2009).

2. This approach allowed flexibility in political relationships but also permitted constant shifts in alliances and federations among tribes and clans. This structure worked well in a desert environment where nomadic life was common, but its lack of centralized authority and long-term institutions and allegiances did not allow for a settled community, let alone a geographically widespread, stable empire.

community. But other tribes believed Islam transcended tribal alliances and favored a greater alliance—to God and to each other. These groups deemed rejection of the communal alliance a rejection of God, which rendered those who left the community apostates. The battles that erupted over the political implications of these differing beliefs came to be known as the Wars of Apostasy (*Ridda*).[3]

Sunni Perspective

Sunnis believe Muslim political leadership passed to Muhammad's close Companion and father-in-law, Abu Bakr.[4] Abu Bakr had accompanied Muhammad on the dangerous *hijra* ("migration") from Mecca to Medina undertaken following rumors of an assassination plot against Muhammad. After Muhammad's death, Abu Bakr claimed the title of caliph, or political successor to God's Messenger and thus head of the community, although not a prophet.[5] His first challenge came when Muslims in Medina tried to separate their community from Muslims in Mecca.[6] Abu Bakr insisted both communities remain united under the umbrella of Islam and his leadership.

Sunni literature portrays Abu Bakr as the "consensus candidate"—the person agreed to by most Muslims, based on his qualifications of public perceptions of trustworthiness, recognized and demonstrated leadership, and knowledge of the Qur'an and Muhammad's example, including his legal rulings. Yet family dynamics, combined with his role as a close friend and loyal follower of Muhammad, also played a role. Some say Abu Bakr came to power in a last-minute sleight of hand, a sign of the turmoil of the time.[7]

---

3. See Berkey, *The Formation of Islam*, 70–73, and Afsaruddin, *The First Muslims*, 27–30, for details.

4. Abu Bakr was the father of Muhammad's wife Aisha.

5. Prophethood ended with Muhammad's death.

6. This move reflected claims of status based on when individuals converted to Islam as well as participation in the *hijra* and pre-Islamic claims to nobility. It made manifest the power struggle between Mecca and Medina for leadership of the community.

7. This is a common claim of Shia, who favored a different candidate. For rivalry over leadership, see Vali Nasr, *The Shia Revival: How Conflicts within Islam Will Shape the Future* (New York: Norton, 2007), 34–43, and Berkey, *The Formation of Islam*, 70–71.

However it happened, portrayals of Abu Bakr as the community consensus (*ijma'*) candidate became pivotal to Sunni theories of and claims to political leadership, community function, and the development of Islamic law. Sunnis often cite a saying of Muhammad (hadith), "My community will never agree in error," to support their view. Current Muslim advocates of democracy point to this tradition of consensus, arrived at via consultation (*shura*) with the community, as the basis for compatibility between Islam and democracy.

Sunnis recognize four "Rightly Guided Caliphs" after Muhammad. They oversaw a period now known as the "Golden Age" because the members of the community as well as its leaders had known and interacted with Muhammad. Because the caliphs had been close Companions of Muhammad, they could best answer the question WWMD, What Would Muhammad Do?[8] They represented rule in the Prophet's spirit and authority, though they were neither prophets, appointed by God, nor infallible. Most Muslims simply judged them as best qualified for leadership because of their proximity to Muhammad and long-standing role in the Muslim community. Other than the fourth caliph, Ali, none were blood relatives of Muhammad, although all were related by marriage.[9]

Four Rightly Guided Caliphs	
NAME	PERIOD OF RULE
Abu Bakr	632–634 CE
Umar	634–644 CE
Uthman	644–656 CE
Ali	656–661 CE

8. The caliphs' knowledge of Muhammad's Sunna, or normative practices, became pivotal to Qur'an interpretation and Muslim beliefs and practices. The idea of Sunna stemming from an individual grew out of pre-Islamic custom, which looked to renowned ancestors as exemplars of behavior to emulate. Sunna for Muhammad's Companions also developed alongside Muhammad's Sunna as a resource for the community. See Asma Afsaruddin, *The First Muslims: History and Memory* (Oxford: Oneworld Publications, 2008), 54.

9. Abu Bakr's daughter, Aisha, was married to Muhammad, as was Umar's daughter, Hafsa. Uthman was married to Muhammad's daughter, Ruqayya.

Being a caliph was dangerous. Abu Bakr died just two years into office after fighting the Wars of Apostasy to hold the fledgling community together; the other three Rightly Guided Caliphs were assassinated, causing even more turmoil in the Muslim community. Not only was there opposition to chosen leaders, but social status within the community was also contentious. The key question was whether all tribes should be treated equally or if some recognition and status were due those who had converted first. This question came to a head under the third caliph, Uthman, who too often gave his clan of Umayya financial and administrative favors. Though such nepotism is not uncommon among rulers, in this case it was especially hurtful as the Umayya clan had been among Muhammad's most vehement enemies until shortly before his death. To some Muslims, it seemed wrong for a late-coming clan to receive such favor in the community when others had a much longer history of loyalty to Muhammad and Islam. This tension ultimately resulted in Uthman's assassination, which sparked an even greater divide in the community. Some believed it marked a moment of justice. Uthman's relatives called for vengeance. The fourth caliph, Ali, came to power in the midst of this crisis.

Ali's failure to find and punish Uthman's assassin led to Ali's assassination in 661 CE. One of Uthman's relatives, Muawiyah ibn Abu Sufyan, then claimed the caliphate and founded the Umayyad Dynasty (661–750).[10] His ascension to power marked two major changes: the passing of political power to people who had not known Muhammad personally, and the creation of the first Islamic state clearly built on the claim of one family (the Umayya clan) to the right to rule. This dynastic approach marked a return to a familiar pre-Islamic pattern, in which certain members of a given lineage were deemed noble based on their military achievements or control of religious sites. Yet it also marked a break with the new tradition, developed since Muhammad's death, of leadership being claimed by a Companion. Because it represented such a rupture—and because of disapproval of the wealthy and often ostentatious lifestyles of its caliphs—the Umayyad Caliphate was not promptly or even

---

10. Muawiyah was governor of Syria at the time and maintained Damascus as his power base.

uniformly recognized. The Umayyads responded to periodic rebellions by formulating a doctrine of obedience to the ruler, as a way to maintain the social goods of order and stability, even if the individual ruler was considered to be impious.[11]

This model of obedience to state and dynastic political power, even if sometimes challenged, has continued in Sunni dynasties ever since. Though Sunni legal and religious literature endorses the ideal of a leader chosen by consensus (*ijma'*), the lived reality rapidly departed from this ideal in favor of dynastic succession. The Umayyad dynasty was short-lived, but the caliphate flourished through the Abbasid Empire (750–1258) under which Islamic civilization reached its peak.[12]

Early Events in Sunni-Shia Identity Formation	
632	Death of Muhammad
632–661	Rightly Guided Caliphs
632–634	Abu Bakr
634–644	Umar ibn al-Khattab
644–656	Uthman ibn Affan
656	Battle of the Camel
656–661	Ali ibn Abi Talib, fourth Rightly Guided Caliph and first Shia Imam
661–750	Umayyad Empire
680	Martyrdom of Husayn in Karbala, Iraq
750–1258	Abbasid Empire

---

11. See Berkey, *The Formation of Islam*, 76–79.

12. The Abbasid Empire was originally based in Kufa, Iraq, but a new capital was built to reflect the grandeur of the empire: Baghdad. For an engaging and accessible history of the Abbasid Empire, see Hugh Kennedy, *When Baghdad Ruled the Muslim World: The Rise and Fall of Islam's Greatest Dynasty* (Cambridge, MA: Da Capo Press, 2004). For the story of the building of Baghdad, see al-Tabari's history in Jack Miles et al., eds., *The Norton Anthology of World Religions: Islam* (New York: Norton, 2015), 2:339–42.

The violent end of the Abbasid Caliphate at the hands of Mongol invaders is a critical event in Sunni historical memory, because it signifies the end of the idealized vision of all Muslims living under the authority of one caliph, even though this vision did not represent reality.[13] Idealized visions of the past are often intended to provide symbolic meaning, spiritual guidance, and a historical ideal toward which to strive in the present, rather than a reflection of lived reality. Movements calling for a "return" to the original Muslim community of Muhammad's lifetime tend to portray past caliphates, particularly the Abbasid Empire, as the "Golden Age" of Islam in which Islam and Islamic law formed the heart of the state and Muslims ruled much of the known world.[14] Often the finer points of history, such as rival caliphates or the poverty and persecution faced by early Muslims, are forgotten or deemed irrelevant to the larger dreams of living in an ideal Muslim community and of Islam as a path to power.[15]

Dismissing such idealized—and often impractical—visions of the past may be tempting. But in the end what matters is the effect of such visions on peoples' worldviews, particularly if their effect is to prompt a desire to make such visions a reality. Part of the power of groups like ISIS comes from their ability to manipulate and effectively use such narratives for their own political purposes.

Today, Sunnis constitute the overwhelming majority—between 80–85 percent—of the world's Muslims. Institutionally based prominent Sunni leaders today include the Grand Shaykh of al-Azhar University Ahmed El-Tayeb, chairman of the International Union of Muslim Scholars Dr. Yusuf al-Qaradawi, and Shaykh Hamza Yusuf, founder of Zaytuna College.[16] In addition,

---

13. There were many rival caliphates to the Umayyads and Abbasids, including that of Ibn al-Zubayr in the Hijaz (Arabia) (681–692), the Shia Fatimid Caliphate in Egypt (909–1171), the Umayyad Caliphate in Cordoba (Spain) (929–1031), and the Almohad Caliphate in North Africa (1147–1269). Even the nominally Sunni Abbasid Caliphate was ruled de facto by the Shia Buyid dynasty from 945 until 1258.

14. Examples include the Salafis (those following the example of *al-salaf al-salih*, literally "the pious ancestors", meaning the earliest Muslims) and ISIS, which calls for restoration of the caliphate that was abolished in 1924 as the last remnant of the Ottoman Empire (1299–1922).

15. For a complete history of caliphates, see Hugh Kennedy, *Caliphate: History of an Idea* (New York: Basic Books, 2016).

16. El-Tayeb and al-Qaradawi are Egyptian, although al-Qaradawi is based in Doha, Qatar. Yusuf is American.

noninstitutionally based[17] preachers have grown in popularity, in large part due to mass followings made possible by television, the Internet, and social media.[18] Prominent Sunni voices of the latter type today include Dr. Salman al-Awda, Dr. Aidh al-Qarni, and Dr. Tariq Ramadan.[19] While these preachers have formal training as religious scholars, other mega-preachers with followings in the tens of millions were trained in secular fields, such as Amr Khaled (accounting) and Dr. Tariq al-Suweidan (petroleum engineering).[20]

Shia Perspective

Shia believe Muhammad, during his final pilgrimage, identified his cousin and son-in-law, Ali, as his presumptive heir. Ali had many sources of perceived legitimacy. He was raised in the same household as Muhammad, was Muhammad's closest living male relative, and was married to Muhammad's daughter, Fatima. Ali thus shared a strong personal connection with Muhammad and deep knowledge of his thoughts and mannerisms. Ali was also the first male convert to Islam.[21] Those who supported Ali's candidacy for leadership after Muhammad's death came to be known as *shi'at Ali*, or the party of Ali, shortened to Shia in common usage.

Shia do not recognize the first three caliphs as legitimate leaders. They also do not recognize their hadith as authentic. This rejection of the caliphs is reflected in the original terms Sunnis used to describe Shia—*rafidah* and *rafidi*—which literally means "rejecters." These terms still appear in anti-Shia literature as pejorative titles. Shia further reject hadith transmitted by Muhammad's wife, Aisha, because she was the symbolic leader of a military campaign challenging Ali's leadership. Shia only consider as authentic those hadith

---

17. The distinction between those who are institutionally based and those who are not became increasingly important in the late twentieth and twenty-first centuries, as questions arose about whether such leaders' loyalty is to Islam or to the institution with which they are affiliated, particularly if that institution receives state funding.

18. For examples from many countries, see *http://themuslim500.com*. The highest-ranking female religious scholar on the list is Dr. Ingrid Mattson of Canada, former (and first female) President of the Islamic Society of North America.

19. Al-Awda and al-Qarni are from Saudi Arabia. Ramadan is Swiss.

20. Khaled is from Egypt. Al-Suweidan is from Kuwait.

21. The first female convert was Muhammad's first wife Khadijah.

directly traceable to either Muhammad or Ali; thus Shia hadith collections differ from those of Sunnis.

Rather than a caliph, Shia follow an Imam, or a direct male descendant of Muhammad believed to have been divinely appointed as a political and religious leader and entrusted with divine inspiration (*ilham*). This divine inspiration, however, is not to be confused with the kind of direct revelation received by Muhammad. Imams, it is believed, also receive special knowledge taught by Muhammad, which has been passed down through the line of Imams and enables them to interpret infallibly the revelation received by Muhammad.[22] Imams do not receive revelation themselves, but their interpretations are considered infallible and they are believed to be sinless (*ma'sum*), which is a concept not known among Sunnis. Shia deem the writings and teachings of their Imams to be a third source of scripture, in addition to the Qur'an and hadith.

In theory, the Imamate is a necessary institution. Shia believe God sends an Imam to every generation so there will always be someone capable of speaking authoritatively on God's behalf. Yet, in practice, keeping a living Imam in their midst was no simple matter for Shia. Doctrinal developments became necessary to explain and cope with lived realities.

The concept of the Imam had a complicated beginning. Although Muhammad had three sons, they all died before they reached toddlerhood. Muhammad's closest living male relative was Ali. Yet it took twenty-four years after Muhammad's death for Ali to come to power.

The circumstances Ali inherited were complex. Two prior caliphs had been assassinated, and relatives of the third caliph were calling for the capture and punishment of those responsible. Ali's first task as caliph was to address that demand. The problem was that some Muslims had been unhappy with Uthman's rule, largely because he tended to favor his relatives with political appointments and wealth. Although this was customary tribal practice, it violated the equality of believers asserted in the Qur'an. Ali was, therefore, caught between relatives of a murder victim demanding justice, if not vengeance, and a community insisting this demand had no weight because of the grave alleged misdeeds of the victim.

---

22. This differs from the Sunni belief in the authority of community consensus (*ijma'*).

Caught between conflicting views, Ali proposed arbitration to settle the dispute, a skill at which Muhammad excelled; yet Ali's arbitration satisfied no one. One group decided to secede from the Muslim community and came to be known as the Kharijites, literally "those who went out."[23]

Another group, feeling Ali was an incompetent leader and leaving him in power would destroy the remaining Muslim community, decided to challenge Ali's authority. This group had Muhammad's wife, Aisha, as its symbolic leader and another of Muhammad's cousins, Zubayr ibn al-Awam, as its military leader.[24] This challenge to Ali eventually led to military conflict.

The Battle of the Camel, fought in 656, marked the first civil war between Muslims and is known as the First Fitna, meaning "chaos."[25] Zubayr was killed and his troops defeated, leaving Ali in power.[26] However, Ali himself was assassinated by a Kharijite in 661, marking the first and last time an Imam effectively held both political and religious power.

---

23. The Kharijites have been portrayed as heretics and the original Muslim extremists, because they left the religion and community over their disagreements and rejected compromise. They declared anyone who did not "go out" with them to be a non-Muslim, even if that person claimed to be Muslim. Such persons were subject to robbery and even killing in the eyes of the Kharijites, because they had compromised with a corrupt regime, thereby demonstrating a lack of commitment to God's will. Not surprisingly, the Kharijites were responsible for a number of rebellions in the first 150 years after Muhammad's death. Even today, governments often describe dissident groups, such as Al-Qaida or ISIS, as "Kharijites," in an effort to delegitimize them and their platforms. There have been attempts in recent years to assert a more positive identity for the Kharijites, focusing on their more constructive ideas, such as the centrality of the Qur'an in Muslim life, rejection of tribal hierarchies in favor of equality of all believers, belief that anyone could potentially serve as caliph if they followed God's will and were righteous, and gender egalitarianism. See Leila Ahmed, *Women and Gender in Islam* (New Haven: Yale University Press, 1992), 70–72.

24. Zubayr was one of the first five male converts to Islam, a close relative and Companion of Muhammad, and a known and trusted political and military figure in the Muslim community. Thus many considered his claim to the caliphate valid.

25. Given the Qur'anic prohibition against fighting between Muslims, this situation should never have occurred. *Fitna* is considered the worst evil that can befall a society, because it leads to weakness and can allow an enemy to take power. It must be avoided at all costs, even if it means leaving an unpopular ruler in power.

26. Aisha was also humiliated in this loss and restricted to her home afterward. Her losing role in the battle became a paradigm for keeping women out of politics. For more on Aisha and her legacy, see D. A. Spellberg, *Politics, Gender and the Islamic Past: The Legacy of A'isha bint Abi Bakr* (New York: Columbia University Press, 1994).

After Ali's assassination, the nominal caliphate passed for a short time to his son, Hasan, who held neither significant territory nor effective power. He also showed little interest in leading the community, preferring to hand the caliphate over to his father's opponent, Muawiyah ibn Sufyan, to keep the peace.[27] Although Muawiyah proved a capable military and political leader and significantly expanded Muslim-controlled territory, some believed Hasan had erred in allowing leadership to leave the hands of Muhammad's descendants and that he compounded this error by doing nothing to reclaim that power. After Hasan's death in 670, reclaiming a role for Muhammad's descendants fell to his younger brother, Husayn.

In keeping with Arab custom, Husayn upheld his brother's peace treaty with Muawiyah until Muawiyah's death in 680. However, he refused to recognize Muawiyah's son, Yazid, as a legitimate successor. Instead, he decided to reclaim leadership of the Muslim community himself. Having received many pledges of allegiance based on his status as Muhammad's grandson and a growing frustration with the Umayyad dynasty's perceived oppression, nepotism, pursuit of luxury, and questionable morals, Husayn and seventy-two men, along with women and children, set out to confront Yazid's forces.

Because he had received pledges of allegiance and was the closest living male descendant of Muhammad, Husayn expected more people would join him on his march. However, the anticipated support never materialized. On the tenth day of the month of Muharram in 680 in Karbala, Iraq, Husayn and his men, vastly outnumbered by Yazid's army, were all killed. The women and children, including Husayn's sister, Zainab, his son, Zayn al-Abidin, and his daughter, Sakina, were captured and held captive. The bodies of the dead, including that of Husayn, were mutilated on the battlefield—an act forbidden in Islam, although known in pre-Islamic times as a means of further humiliating a defeated enemy.

The deaths, desecration, and captivity of members of Muhammad's family—the *ahl al-bayt*, or "people of the House"—as well as the failure of the Muslim community to rise in support, created a paradigm of suffering, sorrow, and regret that have remained central to Shia belief and practice. Husayn's death, which Shia

---

27. Muawiyah ibn Sufyan founded the Umayyad Empire.

consider martyrdom, rendered Karbala a central location of pilgrimage (*ziyarah*).[28] Commemoration of his martyrdom, celebrated on the holy day of Ashura, became a main religious ritual for Shia and can include striking or cutting oneself to participate physically in Husayn's suffering.[29] A symbolic theatrical representation of the tragedy of Husayn, the *taziyeh*, serves as a core component of pilgrimages to Karbala.[30] Commemorations of Husayn's martyrdom are located in *husayiniyyahs*, mourning houses that also serve as important Shia community centers and provide religious instruction.

Husayn's martyrdom was noteworthy not only as a political and, ultimately, religious event but also in shaping Muslim identity. Serious questions arose: How could a descendant of Muhammad meet such a terrible end? What did rejection of their political leadership mean for the community? What role, if any, were Muhammad's descendants to play in Muslim society? What did it mean for Muhammad's descendants to be held as captives by a supposedly Muslim government? These uncomfortable questions and the responses to them helped form nascent sectarian identities and contending visions of leadership.

Branches of Shia

Shia identity has been asserted through the institution of the Imamate. All Shia recognize the same first four Imams—Ali, Hasan, Husayn, and Husayn's son Zayn al-Abidin. After that, Shia split into three different groups—Fivers (known as Zaydis), Seveners (known as Ismailis), and Twelvers (known as Ithna' Ashari or

---

28. This pilgrimage should not be confused with the Hajj, which is one of the Five Pillars. Many Shia seek to go on *ziyarah* as a matter of personal conscience, but it is not required.

29. These celebrations mark a parallel to the passion plays surrounding the crucifixion and death of Jesus in the Christian tradition. As with Shia participation in commemorations ranging from weeping to self-flagellation, so Christians participate to varying degrees, some by observation and others, in some extreme cases, by crucifixion, believing that participation in these foundational events of suffering will influence ultimate redemption. See James A. Bill and John Alden Williams, *Roman Catholics and Shi'i Muslims: Prayer, Passion, and Politics* (Chapel Hill: University of North Carolina Press, 2002), esp. 63–74.

30. For details on *ziyarah* and *taziyeh*, along with other cultural and artistic expressions of mourning among Shia women, see Kamran Scot Aghaie, ed., *The Women of Karbala: Ritual Performance and Symbolic Discourses in Modern Shi'i Islam* (Austin: University of Texas Press, 2006).

Imamis)—depending on how they trace descent and which Imam they count as the last living one.[31]

Fivers, or Zaydis, count Zayd ibn Ali, Zayn al-Abidin's son, as the fifth and final Imam, following his martyrdom in a failed uprising against the Umayyad Caliphate to take back control of the Muslim polity. His martyrdom established a paradigm of revolution against corrupt rulers—the idea that one cannot remain passive in an unjust world—that remains specific to Zaydi Shia. Theologically, of all Shia, the Zaydis are closest to Sunnis: they do not denounce the first two caliphs,[32] they do not recognize the infallibility of Imams after Husayn, and they believe the choice of Imam, though restricted to Muhammad's descendants through Ali, should be based on personal merit, rather than a specific line of descent. Today, Zaydis are the smallest of the Shia sects.[33]

Seveners, or Ismailis, believe succession after Zayn al-Abidin passed to Muhammad al-Baqir (brother of Zayd ibn Ali) as the fifth imam, then his son, Jafar al-Sadiq as sixth, and his son, Ismail ibn Jafar, as seventh.[34] Ismail's son, Muhammad al-Maktum, either died or disappeared in 809 and is expected to return as a messianic figure who will bring in an era of justice.

The Ismailis then split into several branches, including the Fatimids, who founded a major dynasty in Egypt (909–1171) that rivaled the Sunni Abbasid Caliphate; the Qarmatians (894–1078), who have come down through history as heretics;[35] and the

---

31. Although the origins and nature of the Imams go back to Muhammad's death, it is important to recall that Shia identity did not take definitive shape until the first decades of the Abbasid Empire (750–1258). On the development of sectarian identities, see Berkey, *The Formation of Islam,* 130–51.

32. They only denounce the third caliph, Uthman, seeing him as the root of Shiism's tragic history.

33. Zaydis represent only about 0.5% of the global Muslim population today. They are primarily present in Yemen, where they constitute 35–40% of the population and may be more familiar as the Houthis.

34. This marks the point where they split from the Twelvers, who do not recognize Ismail as a legitimate Imam, because he predeceased his father, Jafar.

35. According to historical records, the Qarmatians committed atrocities such as massacring Hajj pilgrims, destroying the well of Zamzam, and carrying off the Black Stone from the Kaaba in Mecca in 930, shocking Muslims everywhere and humiliating the Abbasid caliphs who were supposed to be protecting Mecca. However, the only extant records about the Qarmatians were written by their opponents, so it is possible the descriptions were intended to shock. See Ahmed, *Women and Gender in Islam,* 98–99, for details.

Nizari Ismailis (1094–present),[36] who became notorious as the famous Assassins of Crusader times, even though their main enemy was the Abbasid Empire, not the Crusaders.[37] Today, the Nizari Ismailis are best known as followers of the Aga Khan, whom they consider the forty-ninth Imam.[38]

The Aga Khan, Prince Karim IV (b. 1936)

The spiritual leader of the Nizari Ismaili community, the Aga Khan, Prince Karim IV, is a globally recognized philanthropist. He lives in France and is unique among the world's royalty because he doesn't rule a country. In keeping with the historical Ismaili pattern of redressing social and economic injustices, he actively promotes development, culture, women's education and empowerment, and the end of poverty globally. Born in Geneva, Switzerland, he spent his early childhood in Nairobi, Kenya, before attending boarding school in Switzerland and then earning a bachelor of arts degree with honors in Islamic history from Harvard University in 1959. He acceded to the title of Aga Khan at the age of twenty on the death of his grandfather in 1957, passing over his father and uncle, as his grandfather sought to harness the energy, insight, and lasting power of the younger generation. He is known for his social commitment and interpretation of Islam as a thinking, spiritual faith that highlights tolerance, compassion, and the inherent dignity and worth of all people. One of the world's ten wealthiest royals, he has placed much of his fortune into the Aga Khan Foundation, begun in 1967 as the world's largest private international development agency. Branch institutions spend an estimated $600 million yearly on philanthropic projects largely based

Continued

36. The Nizari Ismailis were founded as the result of a split in the Fatimid dynasty in Egypt over which of two brothers would be the next imam. Nizari Ismailis trace their descent through Nizar, rather than Ismail, and believe in a succession of Imams that contains many "hidden" Imams but ultimately remains unbroken. Descent has been difficult to trace, although specific Imams are identified.

37. Legends of their exploits against injustice continue to inspire fascination, including through the popular video game, Assassin's Creed.

38. The Nizari Ismaili community today has a strong presence in Syria, Iran, Pakistan, India, and in diaspora in the United States and Europe. It has between 25 and 30 million adherents comprising about 20% of the global Shia population.

The Aga Khan, Prince Karim IV (b. 1936) *Continued*

in Africa, Asia, and the Middle East, with special attention to rural areas in Pakistan, India, and Bangladesh. Some of his most famous programs include the Aga Khan Award for Architecture, founded in 1977 to encourage the use of Islamic cultural resources in modern-day built environments, and sponsorship of Yo-Yo Ma's Silk Road Project to preserve and spread the music and culture of Central Asia. The recipient of many honors, awards, and honorary degrees from around the world, he is often accompanied by his daughter, Zahra, as a symbol of his support for women's education and empowerment.

Twelvers, also known as Ithna' Asharis or Imamis, believe there were a total of twelve Imams. Like the Seveners, they recognize Jafar al-Sadiq as the sixth Imam, but then count his son Musa, rather than his son Ismail, as the seventh Imam. Descent then passed from father to son until the twelfth Imam, Muhammad al-Mahdi.[39] Rather than dying, as had been the case for the other imams, Muhammad al-Mahdi is believed to have gone into hiding or occultation (disappearance) and is expected to return at the end of time, along with Jesus, as a messianic figure known as the Mahdi, to bring an era of peace and justice.

Historically, the Twelvers adopted a passive approach to politics, following the example of the sixth Imam, Jafar al-Sadiq, who accepted Abbasid rule as a political reality. This established a model for Twelvers of living as a minority in a political context that does not recognize their Imam, despite the Imam's absolute authority for Shia. This situation was compounded by the tough stance the Abbasid caliphs took toward Shia Imams as potential rivals for political power and legitimacy.[40] So concerned were the Twelvers for their survival,

---

39. Unlike the Fivers, who believe any descendant of Ali willing to take an activist approach can serve as Imam, Twelvers believe the Imam must be a direct descendant of the prior Imam through the line of Husayn.

40. For example, in 850 the Caliph al-Mutawakkil ordered the destruction of Husayn's tomb in Karbala to prevent ritual pilgrimages (*ziyarah*) there. Shia mosques were also destroyed, and those found worshipping there were arrested and imprisoned. To prevent the tenth and eleventh Imams from amassing political influence or large followings, they lived in isolation under virtual house arrest. The Imams were kept under such tight control, midwives were even assigned to their households to detect pregnancies. Berkey, *The Formation of Islam*, 133–34.

they kept the identity and location of the twelfth Imam, Muhammad al-Mahdi, secret, leading some to claim he never existed.[41] Some historians argue that, ironically, these repressive Abbasid state policies, which were intended to eradicate opposition, actually solidified a distinctive Shia identity and leadership opposed to an increasingly authoritarian government.[42]

Comparative Chart of Shia Imams		
FIVER	SEVENER	TWELVER
Ali ibn Abi Talib	Ali ibn Abi Talib	Ali ibn Abi Talib
Hasan bin Ali	Hasan bin Ali	Hasan bin Ali
Husayn bin Ali	Husayn bin Ali	Husayn bin Ali
Zayn al-Abidin	Zayn al-Abidin	Zayn al-Abidin
Zayd ibn Ali	Muhammad al-Baqir	Muhammad al-Baqir
	Jafar al-Sadiq	Jafar al-Sadiq
	Ismail ibn Jafar	Musa ibn Jafar
	Muhammad al-Maktum	Ali ibn Musa
		Muhammad ibn Ali
		Ali ibn Muhammad
		Hasan ibn Ali
		Muhammad al-Mahdi

The occultation of the twelfth Imam, Muhammad al-Mahdi, in 941, marked the end of a living imam's presence in the world, reopening questions about authority and leadership in his absence. Shia theologians argued that, in the absence of the Imam, legal scholars (*faqih*) were most qualified to interpret the Imam's will and, thus,

41. The eleventh Imam died at age twenty-nine, raising questions as to whether he had left a viable heir.

42. On the development of biographies and hagiographies of the Imams, see Matthew Pierce, *Twelve Infallible Men: The Imams and the Making of Shiism* (Cambridge, MA: Harvard University Press, 2016).

to serve as leaders of the community. Certain honorific titles were then given to scholars who had achieved a certain level of acclaim and popularity, including *hojjat al-Islam* ("proof of Islam") and *ayatollah* ("sign of God"). The highest title of acclaim is *marja' al-taqlid* ("reference point for imitation"). Although many *hojjat al-Islam* and *ayatollahs* are expected to exist simultaneously, in theory, there should only be one *marja' al-taqlid* whom all Twelver Shia follow.[43]

Despite their popular acclaim, the authority of scholars is limited. They are not Imams, so their interpretations are not infallible. They cannot legitimately call for an offensive military jihad,[44] though they can call for a defensive jihad as a matter of community self-defense. Historically, their job was simply to preserve the Shia community and religious heritage and encourage patient waiting for the Imam's return. That produced a paradigm of passive acceptance of suffering and persecution that remained intact until the 1970s, when Musa al-Sadr of Lebanon called for the active creation of circumstances conducive to the Imam's return.

The call to activism took on a particularly powerful role through Ayatollah Ruhollah Khomeini's declaration of the doctrine of *vilayat-i faqih*, or "rule of the jurist," which asserts the jurist is to serve as the political leader in the Imam's absence. Khomeini's vision was brought to fruition with the Islamic Revolution in Iran of 1978–79, which overthrew the Shah's secular regime and created an Islamic Republic.

Another type of leadership was introduced in the twenty-first century by leading ayatollahs, including Grand Ayatollah Ali al-Sistani of Iraq and Grand Ayatollah Husayn Fadlallah of Lebanon (d. 2010). These ayatollahs called for a council of leading scholars to redesign the individual position of *marja' al-taqlid* as a collective *marja'iyyah*. Their aim was to include a diversity of voices reflecting a variety of contexts in guiding the global Shia community.[45]

---

43. In reality, many *marja al-taqlid*s (sometimes referred to as Grand Ayatollahs in English) have existed simultaneously. There are now 64 of them, mostly in Najaf, Iraq, and Qom, Iran. One of the most popular and important is Ali al-Sistani.

44. Only an Imam can legitimately call for an offensive jihad.

45. Twelver Shia is the largest group of Shia, constituting about 80% of the global Shia population and 10–13% of the global Muslim population. The biggest populations of Twelver Shia live in Iran, Pakistan, India, and Iraq. Shia are a majority of the population in Iran, Iraq, Bahrain, Azerbaijan, and Yemen. Around 20% of the population in Turkey and Syria are Shia.

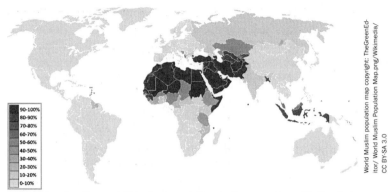

A map showing the world Muslim population. In the countries with the darkest shading, Muslims make up 90–100% of the population. The largest populations are found in Indonesia, Pakistan, India, and Bangladesh, which, combined, account for 44% of the global Muslim population.

A map highlighting the five countries where 50% or more of the Muslim population is Shia: Azerbaijan, Bahrain, Iran, Iraq, Lebanon.

Ongoing Questions of Identity in the Muslim Community

Many today assume Sunnis, as the majority of Muslims and a group that can trace their caliphate to the time of Muhammad's death, have always been the dominant identity. However, some historians argue Shia have an older identity and that Sunni identity was created in response to Shia identity, rather than the reverse. Either way, it was under the Abbasid Empire that Sunni and Shia identities were articulated and solidified theologically, legally, and politically by a class of scholars known as the *ulama*, or "learned ones."[46]

Although they initially came to power through a claim of descent from Muhammad's family,[47] once in power, the Abbasids shifted their vision to a restoration of the ideal Muslim order established by Muhammad. In other words, they focused on the organization of society around Islam, rather than prophetic descent. But they also included elements of Persian imperial tradition, which meant the civilization that developed under them was a composite of elements bound by the Arabic language, rather than by Islam per se.

Incorporating useful elements from nearby empires was not unusual for the time. Historically, conquests of new regions tended to be more lasting when elements of what was familiar to the conquered populations were woven into the new social, political, and religious fabric. Indeed, the ability to adopt and adapt enabled a global spread and localized reinterpretation of Islam, highlighting the importance of Islam as a living faith, rather than one simply known through texts (e.g., see chapter 6 on Sufism).

At the same time, such flexibility raised questions about what defines "true" or "pure" Islam. Is the ability of a faith tradition to be adopted and reinterpreted in new contexts a strength or a weakness? To what degree must new converts accept predetermined interpretations of a faith? If faith cannot be adapted to new circumstances and must be homogenized, standardized, and adhere to a single trajectory, can that faith continue to provide meaning over time and space, as the contexts in which it is lived and experienced change? If a person adapts a practice from another religion or civilization, does that render him or her less Muslim? How is authenticity determined? and by whom? Given the complexity of the historical record in terms of the formation of "Muslim" identity and "Islamic civilization," can anyone truly know what constitutes "pure" Islam? Or who

---

46. Their role will be explored further in chapter 5, "Shariah and Islamic Law: Guiding Principles for Purposeful Living."

47. The Abbasids originally came to power based on their leader's claim to be "the chosen one from the family of Muhammad," drawing from a growing Shia sense of identity. However, once in power, it became clear this leader was descended from Muhammad's uncle, al-Abbas (thus the name "Abbasid"), rather than directly from Muhammad. The Abbasids quickly shifted gear to another claim to legitimacy.

qualifies as a "true" Muslim? And, again, who makes that decision? Are individuals responsible for self-identification as a member of a faith tradition, or can someone else affirm or deny that status? These questions continue to be asked and answered today in different ways in different places. At the heart of all of these questions are the same issues of authority and leadership that first emerged in the aftermath of Muhammad's death.

Sectarian Conflict between Sunnis and Shia

Daily headlines suggest persistent conflict between sectarian groups. There is a tendency to portray conflict in the Middle East, in particular, as occurring along sectarian lines. For example, tensions between Saudi Arabia and Iran are described as a "Sunni-Shia struggle" for regional hegemony. There is some truth to this portrayal, in terms of using religious terminology and symbolism to denounce the enemy and to legitimate fighting those who are nominally Muslim by declaring them apostates or heretics. But it is important to remember these conflicts occur in specific geopolitical and economic contexts and are driven as much, if not more, by claims to power (politics) as to doctrine (religion). Religious rhetoric is an effective means of garnering public support for actions that might otherwise be opposed—namely, destruction of buildings and monuments or killing—but one should not assume that "religion" or "sectarianism" is always at play or constitutes the only driving factor. Although sectarian tensions now dominate news from Iraq, Lebanon, and Bahrain, for example, all three countries also have long histories of sectarian cooperation and even intermarriage.

Nevertheless, the reality of sectarian violence remains a major source of regional instability and international concern, particularly in Iraq and Syria where groups like ISIS and Al-Qaida have specifically targeted Shia for punishment and even death. ISIS is particularly notorious for its destruction of *husayniyya* and attacks on shrines and tombs important to Shia. At the same time, ISIS has also destroyed monuments and buildings with religious and cultural significance to other groups, particularly buildings from the pre-Islamic era. Thus describing ISIS as an "anti-Shia" group misses that other sects, particularly the Yazidis, have also been violently assaulted.[48]

Variations in Lived Practice between Sunnis and Shia

As a living faith, Islam is far more than simply a series of beliefs or texts. As important as differences in doctrine and visions of authority and leadership are, how Sunni and Shia identities are performed as religious practice also merits consideration.

Both Sunnis and Shia believe in the necessity of fulfilling the Five Pillars and agree on the basic details of their performance. However, only Sunnis refer to the Five Pillars as such.

Twelver Shia add to the Five Pillars several more of their own, known as the Ancillaries of Faith. These include paying *khums*, an annual tax of 20 percent, which goes directly to the Imams for redistribution to poor and needy people; jihad;[49] commanding what is right; forbidding what is wrong; expressing love toward good; and expressing disassociation from and hatred of evil.[50] Twelvers also specify the *usul al-din*, or "pillars of belief," which they consider to be basic to Islam; these are *tawhid*, belief in absolute monotheism; belief in God's justice, in prophethood, and in succession to Muhammad through the imams; and belief in Judgment Day and the Resurrection. Thus Twelvers emphasize the importance of belief and practice as central aspects of being Muslim.[51]

---

48. The Yazidis are an ethnically Kurdish group indigenous to northern Iraq that blend elements of Zoroastrianism, Judaism, Christianity, and Islam in their religious beliefs. ISIS has especially targeted this group, killings its men and selling its women and children into slavery.

49. As will be seen in chapter 7, "Jihad: The Struggle to Live Islam and Its Teachings," there are multiple meanings to this term.

50. Many Sunnis also believe in these principles, with the exception of *khums*.

51. Though Sunnis recognize Five Pillars (witnessing, five daily prayers, almsgiving, fasting during Ramadan, and Hajj), Ismailis follow Seven Pillars. In addition to the five daily prayers, almsgiving, fasting during Ramadan, and the Hajj, they add *wilayah* (literally "guardianship," expressed by love and devotion to God, the prophets, the imams, and missionaries), *tawhid* (monotheism, or belief in one God), and jihad (struggle). The necessity of the declaration of faith is assumed by both Ismailis and Twelvers without explicitly stating it.

At the same time, Shia have often been a persecuted minority. Historically, Shia doctrine allows *taqiyya*, or self-protection by concealing one's status as a Shia. Although Sunnis sometimes claim this displays inherent dishonesty on the part of Shia, as they might lie about their faith, Shia say this doctrine as needed when under threat, persecution, or compulsion. In other words, it is intended not as a way of life or an excuse for engaging in blasphemy or heresy but as protection undertaken only in crisis to save one's life.

Although Sunnis and Shia agree on the centrality of the pillars and their general practice, variations developed over time, sometimes with the intent of distinguishing Sunnis from Shia and sometimes as a reflection of specific beliefs. For example, Sunnis generally observe five set times for the five daily prayers. Shia generally consolidate to three time slots. For Sunnis, the Friday noon prayer at the mosque is mandatory for men. Because Shia believe only the Imam can be the true leader of the Friday noon prayer, this prayer has not held the same importance since the last Imam went into occultation. Some Shia nevertheless pray communally on Thursday nights to distinguish themselves from Sunnis. Shia also have additional special prayers, believed to have been revealed by the Imams, that are used either devotionally or during religious holy days; thus prayer is often a private, rather than public, endeavor. Though both Sunnis and Shia pray using a carpet, Shia will touch their heads to the ground or a rock, preferably from Karbala, due to belief that prostration can only be performed on a natural element from the earth that cannot be eaten or worn; by contrast, Sunnis touch their heads to the carpet.

Sunni Call to Prayer

Allahu Akbar (God is the Greatest)—four times
I witness that there is no god but The God—twice
I witness that Muhammad is the Messenger of God—twice
Come (alive) to the prayer—twice
Come (alive) to flourishing—twice
Allahu Akbar (God is the Greatest)—twice
There is no god but The God—once

Shia Call to Prayer

Allahu Akbar (God is the Greatest)—four times
I witness that there is no god but The God—twice
I witness that Muhammad is the Messenger of God—twice
I witness that Ali is the Wali (friend) of God—once
I witness that Ali is the Hujjat (proof) of God—once
Come (alive) to the prayer—twice
Come (alive) to flourishing—twice
Come (alive) to the best work—twice
Allahu Akbar (God is the Greatest)—twice
There is no god but The God—twice

Perhaps the most publicly expressed difference between Sunnis and Shia lies in the text and tone of the *adhan*, or call to prayer. Although both are chanted in a minor key, the Shia call contains an additional tone of longing, mourning, and suffering, reflecting the tragedy of the Imams and waiting for the Imam to return. Most of the text is the same for both calls to prayer (see inserts), but Shia have the option of adding certain phrases, which are considered "commendable" but not "obligatory." These phrases include the assertion of Ali as the *wali* ("friend") and *hujjat* ("proof") of God, and calling the faithful to come alive to the "best work," highlighting the importance of faith and practice. In both cases, the call is intended as an invitation. It is up to the individual to choose to respond.

Other minor distinctions between Sunni and Shia practice include their approaches to the Ramadan fast, with Sunnis breaking the fast as soon as the sun begins to set and Shia waiting until the sun has completely set. Although both Sunnis and Shia celebrate Eid al-Fitr and Eid al-Adha, Shia also have additional holy days commemorating important events in the lives of the Imams, such as Eid al-Ghadir, which celebrates Muhammad's purported announcement of Ali as his successor, Ashura in commemoration of Husayn's martyrdom, and the birthdays of Ali, Fatima, and Muhammad. In addition to the Hajj, Shia go on pilgrimages to the tombs and shrines of the Imams (*ziyarah*).

Outside of these minor variations in religious practice, no visible markers distinguish Sunnis from Shia. Context may provide certain indications, as may names; but, overall, there is no certain method of determining whether a person is Sunni or Shia just by looking at them. Perhaps the most visible sign often associated with Shia is a head covering for men, although such head coverings vary in style and shape and may be worn in different locations as a reflection of local culture. Turbans are typically worn by Shia religious scholars,[52] but turbans are not unique to Shia or even to Islam, as Sunnis wear them in some countries and Sikhs, who are of a different religion altogether, also wear turbans. In addition, Shia men also frequently wear signet rings on their right hands in imitation of Muhammad and the Imams. There are no distinctive modes of appearance for Sunni or Shia women.

Overall, despite their differences of opinion on political and religious leadership, Sunnis and Shia share much in common in terms of basic beliefs and practices. Serious work is being done in some circles to bring Sunnis and Shia into deeper conversation and cooperation with each other in the hope that mutual recognition of legitimacy and shared citizenship will help to bridge their differences.[53]

Review Questions

1. Why did Sunnis and Shia develop different interpretations of Islam and leadership? How important are these differences and what impact have they had on Sunni-Shia relations historically? What about today?

2. What beliefs do Sunnis and Shia share. Where do they differ? Does difference of belief necessarily and inevitably lead to conflict? Why or why not? Are there potential areas for cooperation?

---

52. Only Sayyids, male descendants of Muhammad, are permitted to wear black turbans. Other highly educated Shia men who cannot claim descent may wear white turbans.

53. An example is the Amman Message of 2004, which recognizes the authenticity and validity of both Sunni and Shia law schools. See *ammanmessage.com*.

3. Discuss the significance of the period of the four Rightly-Guided Caliphs and its impact on Muslim history and self-understanding.

4. Discuss the significance of the Imamate and its impact on Muslim history and self-understanding.

5. How have visions of leadership of the Muslim community developed and changed over time?

Discussion Questions

1. Do differences in Sunni and Shia visions of society render Islam a religion with a necessarily political dimension? Why or why not?

2. Why does the caliphate remain an active part of Muslim memory? How has the reality of various caliphates measured up to the original ideals? What might a contemporary caliphate look like? What challenges might it encounter in the contemporary nation-state system?

3. Consider the idealized vision of the Rightly-Guided Caliphs for Sunnis and the example of Husayn's martyrdom for Shia. How do these important symbols impact their broader worldviews?

For Further Study

Readings

Berkey, Jonathan P. *The Formation of Islam: Religion and Society in the Near East, 600–1800*. New York: Cambridge University Press, 2003.

Brown, Jonathan. *Hadith: Muhammad's Legacy in the Medieval and Modern World*. Oxford: Oneworld, 2009.

Marechal, Brigitte, and Sami Zemni, eds. *The Dynamics of Sunni-Shia Relationships: Doctrine, Transnationalism, Intellectuals and the Media*. London: C. Hurst & Co., 2013.

Momen, Moojan. *Introduction to Shi'i Islam*. New Haven: Yale University Press, 1987.

Nasr, Vali. *The Shia Revival: How Conflicts within Islam Will Shape the Future*. New York: W. W. Norton, 2006.

Audio

Sunni call to prayer from Bosnia—*https://www.youtube.com/watch?v=QK1mZs0kCvI*.

Shia call to prayer from Iran—*https://www.youtube.com/watch?v=NVygDpsFyk8*.

Films

Baghdad: City of Walls. Films Media Group, and Journeyman Pictures (Great Britain), 2012.

Examines the impact of a twelve-foot wall built in Baghdad with the intent of separating Sunnis and Shia by keeping them in separate districts.

Pilgrimage to Karbala: Iran, Iraq, and Shia Islam. Films for the Humanities & Sciences; Films Media Group; WNET. New York: Films Media Group, 2007.

Follows the *ziyarah* pilgrimage of a group of Iranian pilgrims—men, women, and children—to Najaf and Karbala, Iraq, after the fall of Saddam Hussein. Includes footage from the Iran–Iraq war of 1980–88.

Shariah and Islamic Law
Guiding Principles for Purposeful Living

As a faith tradition that prizes holistic living, Islam has long nurtured core values and objectives (*maqasid al-Shariah*) that promote righteous living and love of God and neighbor. These values and objectives include the protection of life, family, property, religion, intellect, and the environment; the pursuit of the common good (*maslahah*); collective security; fairness in the marketplace; and justice. Shariah has been elaborated and concretized in Islamic law under many empires, in many countries, and over many centuries in a variety of forms—sometimes as the singular law of the land, sometimes in combination with other legal systems, and sometimes as a matter of personal observance. These varying forms continue to exist today and are the subject of debate in many places.

The core values and objectives of Shariah are prized by Muslims for their guidance in living a God-pleasing life. Yet many in the West have come to fear "Islamic Shariah law" and its perceived potential to creep into Western legal systems. These fears are often stirred by reports of harsh criminal punishments (*hudud*) such as amputation, beheading, and stoning in some countries claiming to follow Islamic law. Critics are rightfully concerned that such punishments are at odds with modernity and international standards of human rights. But it would be a mistake simply to reduce all of Shariah and Islamic law to *hudud* punishments.

Criminal law is only one piece of Islamic law, and Islamic law is not practiced uniformly across Muslim countries or communities. Significant variations in practice and implementation exist, making it important to specify country, region, law school (*madhhab*), and time frame. It is also important to recognize there are many sub-disciplines within Islamic law, such as commercial law, family law, and ritual practices, so that criminal law is but one aspect of Islamic law. In many countries today where Islamic law remains part of the legal system, reforms have been introduced to incorporate current developments, particularly in science, medicine, and technology. That means "Islamic law" is not a static entity set once for all time, but is intended to be living, dynamic, and open to reinterpretation. In addition, just as Muslims vary their adherence to the Five Pillars as a matter of personal choice and recognizance, so Muslims choose the degree to which they follow those aspects of Islamic law that are not enforced by the state.

This chapter provides basic information about Shariah and Islamic law—what they are, what their ideal implementation is expected to achieve, and how they have been practiced in reality, both past and present. Because there is such concern in the West about the status of women and criminal law, particularly the notorious *hudud* punishments, more detail on these important aspects are provided, highlighting how the system was intended to work in theory, how it worked in practice historically, and where it often falls short today. Attention is given both to the impact of Islamic law on the lives of individuals and to how individuals pursue justice under Islamic law.

Historical Foundations of Islamic Law

During Muhammad's lifetime, anyone with a legal question or case could ask him for a ruling. Yet Muhammad did not rule as an auto-crat. He authorized fourteen other people, including those who later became the Rightly Guided Caliphs, to give legal opinions (*fatwas*) while he was alive. After his death, there were many questions as to how the community was to function, given that Muhammad did not leave behind a formal blueprint for the law or government. It fell to the Muslim community (*ummah*), led by the Rightly Guided Caliphs, to rely on their collective knowledge of the Qur'an as well as Muhammad's example and rulings, to develop their own governing systems.

Central to this development was the process of consulting a variety of opinions (*shura*), which ideally led to consensus (*ijma'*). *Shura* and *ijma'* were known and valued parts of Muhammad's example. After his death, continuing that process was both normal and necessary. Because different people sometimes remembered different things or had different perspectives on an issue, moving toward consensus necessarily meant engaging these differences. Sometimes the objective was to determine which memories were most accurate or most likely to be accurate based on knowledge of Muhammad's character and behavior; at other times, the goal was to determine which memories were in the majority, or most likely to benefit the entire community.

Based on Muhammad's saying, "My community (*ummah*) will never agree in error,"[1] authority was rooted in consensus and community, rather than in a single individual. The second caliph, Umar, set up an advisory council to elect a successor after his death so that the choice of leadership would also be subject to community consultation. Although this arrangement changed over time with the expansion of the Islamic Empire and consolidation of power in the hands of the caliphs, the rooting of authority in the community in the earliest days of Islam has become a rallying point in current calls for democratic reform.[2]

The Rightly Guided Caliphs, particularly Umar, played a key role in interpreting and applying Islamic law. Their authority was founded on their close relationship with Muhammad and history of issuing *fatwas* during his lifetime.[3] For example, Umar (r. 634–644) was renowned for his expertise in inheritance shares; abolition of temporary marriages;[4] establishing the office of the *qadi* (Islamic

---

1. By contrast, present-day "Islamist" (a political ideology framed in Islamic terminology) discourse insists sovereignty and authority lie exclusively with God and God's laws. Islamists consider any government deriving its authority from the people un-Islamic and illegitimate. Examples of such discourse range from mainstream organizations, such as the Muslim Brotherhood, to extremists such as Sayyid Qutb and organizations such as Al-Qaida and ISIS.

2. Throughout history, some jurists deemed consultation a pillar of religious law and judicial activity, arguing that any ruler who did not consult with religious scholars and leaders should be removed from office. See Afsaruddin, *The First Muslims*, 45. For a current work that argues democracy is inherent to the Islamic tradition, see Abdulaziz Sachedina, *The Islamic Roots of Democratic Pluralism* (New York: Oxford University Press, 2007).

3. For details on Umar's reign, see Afsaruddin, *The First Muslims*, 35–47.

4. A pre-Islamic custom, temporary marriage (*mu'tah*) (a marriage with set beginning and end dates) is still practiced by some Shia. Sunnis recognize only marriage for which no end date is set.

judge); and carrying out *hudud*[5]—set punishments for certain crimes specified in the Qur'an, including theft, illicit sexual relations, and public drunkenness. However, he also ruled that these punishments could only be carried out when the requirements for evidence were fulfilled and circumstances were appropriate. When mitigating circumstances were present, such as severe drought or famine in the case of theft, Umar suspended harsh sentences because the state had proven incapable of providing a minimum level of subsistence for its subjects. This established a symbiotic relationship between the state's punitive prerogative and the fulfillment of its obligations to those it ruled.

The end of the era of the Rightly Guided Caliphs opened the question of who would now interpret the law. The Umayyad caliphs (661–750) who succeeded them tried to act as both religious and political authorities, but their religious credibility came under frequent fire owing to accusations of immoral behavior, including alcohol consumption and wild partying.

The Abbasid successors (750–1258) tried to maintain the fusion of religion and politics. However, the tradition of rule by community became impractical as the empire expanded geographically and the caliph became increasingly remote and inaccessible. The Abbasids further faced growing rivalry from the Shia community, which called for the Imams, as Muhammad's descendants, to serve as both political and religious leaders. A power struggle for religious authority thus ensued between the caliph and the religious scholars (*ulama*). The *ulama* won owing to their superior knowledge of religion, although political authority was left to the caliphs. Though this did not mark a separation of religion and state per se, it did signify a practical division of religious and political authority.

Foundation and Development of Islamic Law Schools (*Madhhabs*)

Having asserted their religious authority, the *ulama* turned to the elaboration of Islamic law. In the ninth and tenth centuries, certain

---

5. Literally, "fixed" or "boundaries." These punishments apply to specified crimes that hurt public welfare and symbolize a person stepping outside the bounds of acceptable behavior.

scholars known as the "fathers of the law schools" were recognized as pivotal interpreters. They introduced key methods and ideas for examining and interpreting the sources of Islamic law, using them to address current realities. Their interpretations also reflected the common practices of the communities in which they lived and the challenges they faced.

Although the "fathers" were considered high authorities, they were not infallible; their interpretations could always be overridden by another interpretation if it proved more convincing or appropriate for a situation. While a certain level of authority might be held by a law school (*madhhab*) in a particular place,[6] no individual within that law school held absolute authority, including the "father." Nor was there unanimity on a set hierarchy among major interpreters. Ideally, the existence of diverse opinions allowed the judge to select the opinion that best provided justice to the plaintiff and to the broader community while avoiding arbitrariness. Rulings had to be rooted in past precedent and thought, yet flexible enough to address the current situation.[7]

Although a variety of "fathers" and their law schools were established, only those that acquired major followings survived into the present.[8] The most important Sunni schools today are the Hanafi, Maliki, Shafii, and Hanbali. The Hanafi school is the largest and is followed by 33 percent of Muslims. It was the official law school of the Ottoman Empire (1299–1922) and remains dominant in former Ottoman territories throughout the Middle East, Eastern Europe, and the former Soviet republics of Central Asia, as well as throughout

---

6. A law school (*madhhab*) refers to those who followed the methodologies and rulings of a particular "father." The Arabic term implies a journey or path, suggesting a law school is not intended to remain static but is an ongoing experience working toward a goal. Description as a "school" also indicates that such a school represents a process of thought, rather than a body that strictly passes down a set of regulations. All of the schools listed here, along with the minority Ibadi and Zahiri schools, were recognized as legitimate law schools in the Amman Message of 2004. See *ammanmessage.com*.

7. For more on the development of Islamic law and Islamic legal concepts, see John L. Esposito and Natana J. DeLong-Bas, *Shariah: What Everyone Needs to Know* (New York: Oxford University Press, 2018).

8. Those that did not are considered "extinct," although their opinions may still be considered. For example, the Zahiri school is recognized by the remaining Sunni schools. It flourished in Muslim Spain until the fourteenth century.

the Indian subcontinent and China. The Maliki school is the second largest and is followed by 25 percent of Muslims. It was the official law school of several dynasties in North Africa and Spain and remains prominent there, as well as in West Africa and some Gulf states. The Shafii school is followed by 15 percent of Muslims and was the official law school of the Ayyubid (1174–1250) and Mamluk (1250–1517) dynasties in Egypt. It is the exclusive law school in Indonesia today and has significant, although not majority, followings throughout the Middle East and the Indian subcontinent. The Hanbali school is the smallest of the Sunni schools and is followed by 5 percent of Muslims. It is the official law school in Saudi Arabia and Qatar and has a growing number of adherents in parts of the Middle East.

The most important Shia law schools are the Jafari and Zaydi. The Jafari school is the largest and is followed by 10 percent of Muslims. It is the official law school of both Twelver and Ismaili (Sevener) Shia. It is the majority school in Iran, Iraq, Azerbaijan, and Bahrain and is followed by Shia minority populations in Pakistan, Afghanistan, Saudi Arabia, Kuwait, Albania, and Lebanon.[9] The Zaydi school is followed mainly in Yemen today, although it was the official law school of Zaydi states in Iran (864–1126) and Yemen (893–1962) historically.

The diversity of law schools reflects the foundational ideals of consultation of many opinions with the goal of working toward consensus. In addition, there are majority and minority opinions within each school. These differing opinions are regarded as being in conversation, rather than conflict, with each other. Throughout history, unity under the broad umbrella of Islamic law did not mean uniformity. The law was seen as a living, ever evolving body, rather than a fixed or codified entity.

Islamic Law in Multireligious Societies

As a common framework for accepted and expected behaviors, Islamic law was and remains for many Muslims an expression of community identity and belonging, particularly during times of

---

9. Statistics vary as to whether the Shia of Lebanon are a minority or majority today.

increasing contact with non-Muslim cultures, social practices, religions, and legal systems. This contact has been a reality since the initial spread of the Islamic Empire beyond the confines of Arabia into non-Arab and non-Muslim territories in the seventh century, beginning with the Sassanian (Persian, Zoroastrian) and Byzantine (Eastern Orthodox Christian) empires. Although this contact has sometimes led to tensions and even war, there have also been times when adoption of certain ideas or rulings from these conquered cultures was useful to the Muslim community's well-being. This was particularly true as the Islamic Empire grew from a nomadic, tribal society into an urbanized civilization. For example, some of the administrative, bureaucratic, and legal structures of the Sassanid Empire were adopted and adapted by the Abbasids.

At the same time, the expansion of the Islamic Empire throughout the Middle East and into South and Central Asia, North Africa, and Europe by 750, meant Muslim rulers needed to devise effective methods for incorporating newly conquered territories and their people into legal and administrative systems. The earliest historical examples of the Rightly Guided Caliphs (632–661) and the Umayyad (661–750) and Abbasid empires (750–1258) were consistent in allowing members of other faith traditions, such as Christians and Jews, to continue to follow their religious traditions and laws, provided that these did not disrupt public security.[10] Members of non–Muslim religious communities were often able to maintain their own family laws and ritual obligations, although not criminal codes, which were the purview of the state.

Yet there also remained a perceived need for legal coherence within the empire. This led some rulers to expand secular laws alongside religious laws, a practice known as *al-siyasah al-Shariah*. Some religious purists saw such adaptability as evidence of impiety on the part of the ruler and feared its potentially destructive impact on Muslim identity.[11] Others appreciated the strength and stability such an evolving system

---

10. Issues such as religious freedom and freedom of expression are addressed in more detail in chapter 9, "Muslim-Christian Encounters: Conflict and Coexistence." The focus here is on legal matters.

11. For example, the medieval scholar Ibn Taymiyya (d. 1328) denounced mixing cultural practices with Islamic law, fearing dilution of Muslim identity amid the Mongol invasions and Crusades.

provided, particularly for multicultural and multireligious empires seated on the crossroads between Asia, Europe, and Africa, such as the Ottoman (1299–1923) and Mughal (1526–1857) empires.[12]

Concepts and Tools for Interpreting Islamic Law

Central to the ongoing interpretation of Islamic law is the distinction between Shariah (divinely revealed principles) and *fiqh* (jurisprudence or legal reasoning). A hierarchy was created for the main sources for legal reasoning (*usul al-fiqh*) during the foundational era (9th and 10th centuries) that is still in use today. It is important to remember that *fiqh* is a theoretical activity that offers advice on how to think about and frame a case; it does not necessarily tell us how the law is or has been applied in practice.[13]

Although they are interrelated, Shariah and *fiqh* are not the same. Shariah encompasses the values and principles contained in the Qur'an[14] and Sunna (Muhammad's example). Rather than positive law, Shariah is better understood as a broad and wide-ranging behavioral and moral code and system of ethics that addresses human obligations toward God (*ibadat*) and interpersonal relations (*muamalat*).[15] Muslims believe that Shariah comes directly from

---

12. Famous examples include Sulayman the Magnificent (r. 1520–1566) of the Ottoman Empire, known as "the Lawgiver" for his expansion of the *kanunname*, or secular law, alongside Islamic law, and Mughal Emperor Akbar (r. 1556–1605), known for his adoption of multiple religious and legal traditions into the state.

13. Application can only be found through examination of court records. Scholars vary in opinions as to whether *fiqh* or court records are more important for understanding "Islamic law." Analysis of *fiqh* permits understanding of the development of legal thinking over time and space. *Fiqh* is largely recorded in *fatwas*, or legal opinions, which consider hypothetical cases. Court records, on the other hand, provide information about outcomes of real cases. Unfortunately, court records typically record only the facts of the case and the outcome, not the legal reasoning behind it. Both make useful contributions, but neither one alone presents a complete picture.

14. Of roughly 6,200 Qur'an verses, only about 260 deal with legal matters. Nearly three times as many—750 verses—command believers to reflect and to use reason, suggesting the Qur'an encourages the use of human intellect rather than blind obedience.

15. In general, *ibadat* was and is a matter of personal choice. Only *muamalat* have been publicly enforced to varying degrees.

God through the Qur'an and Muhammad's example as the perfect living out of the Qur'an's teachings. *Fiqh*, on the other hand, is the concrete expression of those values and principles produced by human efforts in jurisprudence. Simply put, while Shariah is divine, *fiqh* is not.

The distinction between divine mandate and human effort is important for two reasons. First, while divine revelation is unchanging, interpretations of that revelation are not and should not be. This means that, while the goals (*maqasid*) of Shariah—including protecting life, property, family, religion, and intellect; achieving justice; and fulfilling the common good (*maslahah*)—are fixed for all time, how those principles and values are to be met and lived out is subject to change as the surrounding historical and social context changes.[16] Legal methodologies designed to address changes in context include the concepts of *istihsan* (selecting the most appropriate ruling for a situation, rather than following the majority opinion)[17] and *istislah* (choosing a ruling that is just, equitable, and of public benefit, rather than adhering to the strict letter of the law).[18] These legal tools provide options that consider the impact of a ruling on both the individual and the community, rather than simply matching a specific crime with a specific punishment.

Second, Shariah as divine revelation carries a higher level of authority than the human interpretation of *fiqh*. Making a clear distinction between Shariah and *fiqh* opens the door to reforming the specific content and methodology of *fiqh*, while leaving the principles of Shariah intact. Contemporary reformers often call for greater attention to this distinction, arguing, if the parameters of Islamic law as practiced today no longer result in upholding

---

16. The exception is worship obligations (*ibadat*), which never change.

17. One of the best-known examples of *istihsan* historically was the second Rightly Guided Caliph Umar's suspension of the punishment of amputation for theft during a famine.

18. The guiding principle of consideration of public welfare—*maslahah*—shares the same root letters with *istislah*, indicating the need to consider the impact of a ruling on the community as a whole. Contemporary examples of *istislah* include assigning equal portions of inheritance to both sons and daughters, and considering a woman whose husband divorced her when he was dying a legitimate heir to his estate. In both cases, the goal is to uphold economic justice rather than adhere to a literal interpretation of the law.

Shariah principles and values, then reforming the law to be consistent with these principles is justified. This has proven particularly important with issues related to family law, which is supposed to protect, not persecute, women.

The distinction between Shariah and *fiqh* was carried over into the determination of a hierarchy of sources for legal reasoning. The founders of the major law schools considered four main sources: the Qur'an, Sunna (Muhammad's example), selective use of analogical reasoning (*qiyas*), and consensus (*ijma'*) of a recognized body of religious experts (*ulama*). These sources include both divine revelation (the Qur'an and Sunna, although the latter also required assigning levels of authority to hadith) and human intellect/opinion (analogical reasoning and consensus). All scholars agree upon the ultimate authority of the Qur'an. However, there are differing opinions about the relative weight to be assigned to the Sunna, analogy, and consensus. Among the Sunni schools, for example, Hanafis and Malikis frequently use analogical reasoning, as it allows a ruling from one case to be applied to other similar cases.[19] Shafiis are more limited in their use of analogical reasoning, while Hanbalis permit its use only when deemed absolutely necessary.

There are also pivotal concepts used to interpret Islamic law, the two most important of which are independent reasoning (*ijtihad*) and abrogation (*naskh*). *Ijtihad*, which shares the same root letters with jihad—*j-h-d*—is the personal, intellectual struggle to understand and fulfill the parameters of the law with the intent of serving the common good.[20] Historically, it was understood the practice of *ijtihad* was limited to those with deep knowledge and understanding of the texts and tradition; it was not to be undertaken lightly or by those lacking sufficient knowledge or specialized training.

---

19. The classic example is the use of the ban on drinking date wine as an analogy for banning other alcoholic beverages and recreational drug use. The analogy is based on the effects date wine produces—loss of clear, rational thought; potentially aggressive behavior; and loss of inhibitions that normally limit objectionable behavior. Because these threaten public order, the analogy was carried over to any substance producing similar effects.

20. John Kaltner, *Introducing the Qur'an: For Today's Reader* (Minneapolis: Fortress, 2011), 166, notes there is no inherent association between the struggle of *ijtihad* or jihad with violence.

The degree to which *ijtihad* was practiced after the founding of the major law schools (*madhhab*) has been the subject of considerable scholarly debate.[21] Historically, preference was often given to imitation of scholarship (*taqlid*) after the foundational era, due to a belief that all major questions had already been answered. Thus jurists needed only to examine carefully the record to find an apt response. Limiting responses to those of the past was perceived to provide continuity with tradition while avoiding innovation (*bida*).[22] However, it also risked stagnation and an inability to address new and changing circumstances. Thus, particularly from the eighteenth century on, legal scholars called for a revitalization of *ijtihad* by rejecting *taqlid* and returning to the Qur'an to develop responses that met the needs of modernity.[23] By the twentieth century, some scholars argued returning to the Qur'an meant recovering its fundamental worldview, including calls for justice and liberation, denunciation of oppression, and, in the eyes of many modern Muslim feminists, gender egalitarianism. In addition, some individuals who are not formally trained religious scholars have claimed the right to interpret Islamic law, albeit sometimes with dubious results.[24]

---

21. Some scholars have argued the "gates of *ijtihad*" were closed from the thirteenth through the nineteenth centuries, leading to stagnation in Islamic law. Wael Hallaq has challenged this assertion, arguing that *ijtihad* was ongoing, albeit in a limited way. See Wael Hallaq, "Was the Gate of Ijtihad Closed?," *International Journal of Middle East Studies* 16 (1984): 3–41.

22. Ultraconservative groups, such as the Wahhabis and Salafis, avoid innovation because of its perceived potential to introduce non-Islamic practices or ideas into the tradition.

23. This was one of the hallmark characteristics of the revival and reform movements of the eighteenth and early nineteenth centuries in Arabia, the Indian subcontinent, and Nigeria, as well as Islamic modernism in the nineteenth and twentieth centuries. See John O. Voll, "Hadith Scholars and Tariqahs: An Ulama Group in the 18th Century Haramayn and Their Impact in the Islamic World," *Journal of Asian and African Studies* 15, no. 3–4 (1980): 264–73. Those looking for a Protestant Reformation in Islam often cite these movements because of their focus on returning to the Qur'an and promotion of mass literacy.

24. Examples include Al-Qaida's Osama bin Laden and ISIS's Abu Bakr al-Baghdadi, both of whom have engaged in reductive and combative approaches. Other voices that specialize in other disciplines have criticized those with formal training as being out of touch with young people today. See, e.g., critiques by popular accountant turned tele-preacher Amr Khaled.

Finally, some scholars embraced the concept of abrogation (*naskh*), which argues some early Qur'an verses were overridden by later revelations. Some interpreters take a reductive approach and consider only the last revealed verse as God's literal final word on an issue. While this results in clear and simple decision-making, it also runs the risk of promoting a "one-size-fits-all" solution to issues, such as relations with non-Muslims, which then becomes unnecessarily rigid and even militant. Critics of this methodology note that it robs the community of having many approaches from which to choose based on circumstances, thereby hindering rather than supporting justice.

Critics of abrogation have charged that it is inherently flawed as a concept, because it suggests God has either changed God's mind or made an error that had to be corrected with a later revelation. One alternative approach to abrogation therefore posits that God wanted to change certain deeply rooted behaviors, but realized it would take time to eradicate these behaviors or introduce new ones. Scholars supporting this practice believe in a progressive approach to verses on certain topics, such as slavery and polygyny, that discerns "Qur'anic intent" over time. This opens the possibility of reducing or eliminating certain practices.[25] Although it still means considering the order in which verses were revealed, it does so in a holistic way that considers all verses, not just the last one.

The variety of interpretational tools and concepts shows that Islamic law is intended to be complex, nuanced, and capable of adaptation to and consideration of different and changing circumstances. That complexity is also reflected in how Islamic law has been implemented in practice.

---

25. For a broad historical overview of the issues, see Louay Fatoohi, *Abrogation in the Qur'an and Islamic Law* (London: Routledge, 2014). To date, only Tunisia and Turkey among Muslim-majority countries have formally banned polygyny, although others, such as Malaysia, have introduced laws to limit its practice. Historically, polygyny was limited to elites and was reduced or eliminated in many places. It is making a resurgence today among extremist groups, such as Al-Qaida and ISIS. ISIS has also reintroduced slavery and slave markets, as well as concubinage, despite powerful objections from many religious and legal scholars. See *An Open Letter to Al-Baghdadi* at *www.lettertobaghdadi.com*.

Mechanics of Islamic Law

In many Muslim countries throughout history, Islamic law and secular law have existed in parallel, giving the state an Islamic identity while empowering it to pursue punishment for crimes outside of Shariah court jurisdiction. Islamic law is designed not just to punish criminals but also to give the community a voice in policing itself and making decisions about how public welfare (*maslahah*) might best be served.[26] Historically, the community could demand removal of repeat offenders and individuals who disrupted the social fabric, even if no actual crime had been committed. At the same time, the community could also decide to allow a removed person to return if that person demonstrated remorse and a change in behavior.[27]

In the precolonial era (up through the 17th and 18th centuries), Islamic legal doctrine was enforced by three different agents: (1) judges (*qadis*) who served in the Shariah courts; (2) public security officials, such as political and military figures and police officers, serving in the name of the ruler; and (3) market inspectors, who supervised trade practices, public morals, and observance of religious duties. The separation of jurisdictions and powers established a system of checks and balances that prevented any single individual or agency from exerting disproportionate power. Charges of corruption or abuse by one agency could be investigated by another.[28]

Qadis heard cases brought to the Shariah court by plaintiffs, including law enforcement officials, victims, or a victim's family or heirs. Only Muslims could bring cases to, be tried by, or testify in Shariah courts. Shariah courts were further limited in the types of cases they could hear; cases falling outside of those parameters were

---

26. For a historical analysis of the community's role in implementing Islamic law, see Wael Hallaq, *Shari'a: Theory, Practice, Transformations* (Cambridge, UK: Cambridge University Press, 2009).

27. Rudolph Peters, *Crime and Punishment in Islamic Law: Theory and Practice from the Sixteenth to the Twenty-first Century* (New York: Cambridge University Press, 2005), 87, has found several examples of this type.

28. Ideally, this represented a balance between centralized power and localized governing.

heard in other courts under the ruler's jurisdiction. The *qadi* was expected to review the case, determine what type of crime had been committed, and sentence it appropriately if it fell within his jurisdiction. If the case did not fall within his jurisdiction, the *qadi* referred it to public security officials for trial elsewhere.

The *qadi* was bound by strict rules of procedure and evidence, particularly for testimony and witnessing. Circumstantial evidence and secondhand testimony were not admissible; neither were confessions extracted under torture. Any party to the case, including the *qadi*, could request a legal opinion (*fatwa*) from an external religious scholar (*mufti*), although this was not required. At the same time, the *qadi* was not required to accept any *fatwa*, regardless of who issued it; a *fatwa* became binding only if the *qadi* chose to accept it.[29] Finally, the *qadi*'s ruling was binding and enforceable, and was to be carried out promptly.

Public security officials dealt with crime, carried out assigned punishments, and put down rebellions and disturbances. They also held jurisdiction over homicides. Unlike *qadis*, they could examine circumstantial evidence and the prior convictions and reputation of an accused person to decide whether a charge was probable. They could hear testimonies of people who were not able to testify before a *qadi*, such as non-Muslims. They could send repeat offenders to prison for life, if they were deemed a threat to public security. Most notoriously, they were permitted to use pressure, including torture, to extract confessions from accused persons.[30]

---

29. *Fatwas* by certain scholars may be considered particularly influential, but, because there is no ordained clergy in Islam, there is no one authoritative figure among Muslims comparable to the pope for Roman Catholics. Shia pledge allegiance to an ayatollah of their choice whose *fatwas* they are then obligated to follow, but there is no legal enforcement mechanism. It is a matter of personal conscience.

30. To be legally admissible, the confession must be repeated voluntarily in court without the use of pressure. For details, see Peters, *Crime and Punishment in Islamic Law*, esp. 6–11, and Sadiq Reza, "Torture and Islamic Law," *Chicago Journal of International Law* 8, no. 1, article 4 (Summer 2007): 21–41. In theory, state use of torture was supposed to be limited to the amount "necessary" to obtain a confession. It was not intended to kill the accused. Some Muslim countries today use confessions obtained under torture. Major personalities radicalized by such torture in prison include Ayman al-Zawahiri, the current head of Al-Qaida, and Sayyid Qutb, the godfather of radical jihadist ideology.

Classical Islamic Criminal Law and Punishment

In keeping with Islam's worldview, Islamic criminal law is based on the principles of preserving the social order, serving the public interest (*maslahah*), and individual accountability. As in Western secular law, punishments are intended to provide justice and serve as deterrents. The deterrent factor lies in the public nature of punishment, particularly for *hudud* offenses. Islamic law considers retribution as both redress to the victim and rehabilitation of the offender. Historically, this is why prison sentences generally did not have a fixed term—they ended when the perpetrator demonstrated sufficient remorse and was deemed no longer a present danger to society.[31]

In general, anyone bringing a claim to court was required to prove it. Classical Islamic criminal law generally did not recognize a statute of limitations for bringing charges;[32] however, once charges were brought, justice was to be administered swiftly and efficiently.[33]

Types of Crimes

Classical Islamic criminal law generally divided crimes into three types: (1) crimes against God as outlined in the Qur'an, for which mandatory fixed punishments (*hudud*) were assigned; (2) crimes against persons, including homicide and personal injury, punishable by either financial compensation or retaliation in the form of corporal punishment; and (3) sinful or forbidden behaviors or actions

---

31. This is based on multiple passages in the Qur'an, such as 5:34 and 5:39, where God assigns punishments for certain crimes "unless" or "until" they repent. Only repentance will save a person from punishment in the afterlife, per Q 5:36–37.

32. Only the Hanafi school assigned a statute of limitations for *hudud* offenses, unless there were extenuating circumstances. Peters, *Crime and Punishment in Islamic Law*, 11.

33. Many European observers of Ottoman justice recorded overall favorable impressions of swift justice, efficiency, and effectiveness, compared to European legal proceedings, although they also expressed concerns that certain punishments were cruel or carried out too swiftly. Peters, *Crime and Punishment in Islamic Law*, 81.

presenting a danger to public order or state security, punishable at the *qadi*'s discretion or by public security officials.

In practice, most crimes either fell under discretionary punishment or were left to public security officials to punish. In cases carrying the potential for *hudud* punishments, scrupulous attention was given to the requirements for procedure, specific terminology, witnesses, evidence, confession, and the possibility of mistakes or doubt, whether on the part of the accused or the accuser. If these parameters were not met, the crime could not be convicted as *hudud*. In addition, certain categories of people—minors, insane people, and non-Muslims—could not be convicted of *hudud*. Legal maneuvering around some of these requirements appears throughout court records, suggesting people knew the parameters of the law and how to get around *hudud* punishments.[34] It also seems judges were not particularly keen to convict people of *hudud* crimes and actively looked for alternatives. But this does not mean crimes were not punished. Rather, because they did not meet the strict requirements for a *hudud* punishment, they reverted to discretionary punishment.

Types of Punishments

Historically, justice was supposed to be the driving factor behind the judge's ruling, fitting the punishment to the circumstances of the crime. Classical Islamic criminal law recognized three categories for punishments: (1) fixed penalties (*hudud*) for certain specific crimes; (2) discretionary punishments assigned by the *qadi*; and (3) punishments assigned by law enforcement officials in cases deemed to be matters of public safety or political expediency. State officials were generally responsible for executing the punishment immediately following the sentence, unless there were mitigating circumstances justifying a temporary postponement. Examples include potential harm

---

34. Rhetorical devices to avoid *hudud* punishments appear frequently in court records. Women accused of illicit sexual activity often claimed either to have been asleep or drugged, rendering them incapable of intent. See Elyse Semerdjian, "Gender Violence in Kanunnames and Fetvas of the Sixteenth Century," in *Beyond the Exotic: Women's Histories in Islamic Societies*, ed. Amira El Azhary Sonbol (Syracuse: Syracuse University Press, 2005), 180–97.

to a fetus in the case of a pregnant woman or a preexisting illness or injury that would place the convicted person at risk of death should the punishment be enacted. Death sentences had to be reviewed and approved by the ruler.[35]

Punishments ranged from the more serious corporal punishments[36] associated with *hudud* crimes—flogging,[37] amputation,[38] or the death penalty[39]—to retaliation in the form of corporal punishment, financial compensation, imprisonment, public reprimanding, exposure to public scorn,[40] banishment, and fines. Fines were the most common form of punishment and were paid to the state, as opposed to financial compensation owed to a victim or victim's family or heirs.[41]

Financial compensation could only be assigned in the event of bodily harm or death, whether accidental or deliberate, as a matter of tort (damage caused). Financial liability was considered separate from criminal liability, as criminal liability required proof of deliberate intent. Even in cases where certain people, such as a minor, insane or unconscious person, could not be held criminally liable, they nevertheless remained financially liable for damage caused as a matter of justice to the victim. Financial compensation could be substituted

---

35. Peters, *Crime and Punishment in Islamic Law*, 87, 92.

36. Corporal punishment was intended to be humiliating, but not fatal. It was not permitted to strike the head or the genitals. Some law schools devised methods to lessen the impact, such as issuing two strikes with a bundle of forty thin twigs to apply eighty lashes, as opposed to eighty individual strikes. Practice varied as to instrument and the strength with which it was applied.

37. Flogging of a specified number of strikes is prescribed for proven illicit sexual activity, false accusations of illicit sexual activity, and consumption of alcohol.

38. The fixed punishment for theft is amputation of the right hand for a proven first offense, followed by the left foot for a proven second offense. Some scholars speculate these punishments were introduced at a time when centralized government was weak and long-term imprisonment was impractical. Amputation provided an immediately visible means of identifying someone convicted of serious crime, thereby serving public safety concerns.

39. In the Qur'an, banditry is the only crime punishable by death.

40. Punishments involving public humiliation were considered effective in societies in which honor constituted important cultural capital. The shame of public punishment reduced that capital. Similar measures, such as pillory, were used in Europe and America through the nineteenth century.

41. Peters, *Crime and Punishment in Islamic Law*, 33.

for physical retaliation upon the request of the victim or the victim's family or heirs.

One unusual feature of classical Islamic criminal law for its time was that it was not limited to deterrence and punishment. It also sought the rehabilitation and reform of the perpetrator's soul, so that he would not become a repeat offender. The principle of rehabilitation is outlined in Q 5:33–34.[42] Yet repentance only shielded the perpetrator from a *hudud* punishment. It did not protect the perpetrator from discretionary punishment for homicide, bodily harm, or theft.

Finally, although scholarly literature tends to focus on retributive justice in the form of punishment, the historical record also contains examples of restorative justice.[43] Restorative justice seeks to reintegrate an offender into the community while ensuring the offense is not repeated. Today, restorative justice is most frequently used for juvenile offenders.

Hudud

Of the many headline-generated concerns about "Shariah" and "Islamic law" today, none breeds more fear than *hudud*, with its threats of amputation or death by stoning. Yet for many Muslims, *hudud* are perceived as a public good—not necessarily because of the draconian punishments, to which many today also object,[44] but because of the protection they are supposed to provide to public order, private property, sexual order, and personal honor.

Hudud crimes specified in the Qur'an are theft, banditry, unlawful sexual intercourse (*zina*), false or unproven accusations of

---

42. Rehabilitation could not replace the *hudud* punishment for apostasy, insulting Muhammad, or banditry.

43. See Susan C. Hascall, "Restorative Justice in Islam: Should Qisas Be Considered a Form of Restorative Justice?," *Berkeley Journal of Middle Eastern & Islamic Law* 4, no. 2 (2011): 35–78, and Mutaz M. Qafisheh, "Restorative Justice in the Islamic Penal Law: A Contribution to the Global System," *International Journal of Criminal Justice Sciences* 7, no. 1 (2012): 487–507.

44. For details on Muslim attitudes toward Shariah and corporal punishments by country, see the Pew Research Center poll, "Beliefs about Shariah," at *http:// www.pewforum.org/2013/04/30/the-worlds-muslims-religion-politics-society-beliefs -about-sharia/*.

unlawful sexual intercourse, drinking alcohol, and, according to some law schools, apostasy.[45] These crimes are believed to harm society and individuals.[46]

Although the assigned punishments are severe, the historical record shows *hudud* cases were notoriously difficult to prove. Legal scholars have found few instances of amputation or stoning in practice,[47] although there are many instances of flogging.[48] While neither these crimes nor their punishments were to be taken lightly, their ultimate power seems to have resided in the deterrent factor rather than common application. The record further suggests pressure on judges to find people not guilty of *hudud* crimes. A popular hadith

---

45. The Qur'an does not specify apostasy as a *hudud* crime. There are more than 100 Qur'an verses affirming freedom of conscience and religion and signifying acceptance of a plurality of religions and ways of life. See Afsaruddin, *Contemporary Issues in Islam,* 45–46. Today, only the 1991 Sudanese Penal Code and the Yemeni Penal Code include provisions on apostasy, although other countries occasionally punish such cases. Peters, *Crime and Punishment in Islamic Law,* 161.

46. Briefly, theft represented a threat to private property ownership; banditry was a threat to public security; unlawful sexual intercourse threatened public morality and the social order, as well as personal finances, because of the potential for pregnancy; false or unproven accusations of unlawful sexual intercourse threatened the public order and the personal safety and security of women in particular; drinking alcohol carried the potential for disrupting the social order and public safety due to the potential for aggressive drunken behavior; and apostasy threatened the public order and public safety, because of the potential for unrest.

47. Death by stoning for illicit sexual activity is not mentioned in the Qur'an. Qur'an 4:15 specifies a woman found guilty of illicit sex be confined to her home until she either dies or repents. Qur'an 24:2 specifies flogging with 100 stripes for both parties. Qur'an 24:3 prescribes that any person found guilty of illicit sex be married to another person guilty of the same. Thus, rather than death, the Qur'an provides a mechanism for restoring the offending parties to the community by legitimating their relationship. The death penalty by stoning for illicit sexual activity comes from the hadith and is likely to have been borrowed from other Near East civilizations. See, e.g., Barbara Stowasser's discussion of the incorporation of biblical material into Qur'anic exegesis in *Women in the Qur'an, Traditions and Interpretation* (New York: Oxford University Press, 1994), and Berkey, *Formation of Islam,* 147.

48. These were so rare that Peters, *Crime and Punishment in Islamic Law,* 93, found only one case from the sixteenth through nineteenth centuries in the Ottoman Empire—a woman stoned to death for an affair in 1680. The situation was so unusual that she was brought to Istanbul and executed in the Hippodrome in the Sultan's presence. Peters speculates amputations may have been suspended in favor of sending convicted criminals to the galleys as oarsmen, 98–100.

directs, "Ward off the fixed punishments (*hudud*) from the Muslims on the strength of doubt as much as you can."[49]

Three criteria must be met for a perpetrator to receive the fixed punishment for a *hudud* crime:[50] (1) the perpetrator must have had a choice as to whether to commit the crime, (2) the perpetrator must have committed the act knowing it was a crime, and (3) the perpetrator must have acted with intent. Failure to meet any one of these three criteria indicates lack of criminal intent or lack of awareness of criminal activity, thereby removing the potential for a *hudud* punishment. The criteria also allow for the possibility that a person was coerced into committing a crime, such as killing someone in self-defense or wounding an attacker while protecting one's property or family.[51]

Strict standards of proof, including multiple eyewitnesses, are required in *hudud* cases.[52] For example, in the case of illicit sexual activity (*zina*), testimony of four adult male witnesses to the actual act of penetration was required, as specified in Q 24:4.[53] Circumstantial evidence was generally not admissible in *hudud*

---

49. Cited in Peters, *Crime and Punishment in Islamic Law,* 22.

50. These parameters also apply to homicide, which, as discussed below, is not a *hudud* crime.

51. Peters, *Crime and Punishment in Islamic Law,* 25–26.

52. Under classical Islamic law, the testimony of a woman counted for only half that of a man. This has been adopted in some countries today. Legal reformers argue for contextualization of this practice—namely, in early Islamic Arabia, women were not as experienced in worldly affairs as men, were less likely to be educated, and also were subject to family pressure that could persuade them to tailor testimony in favor of a male family member. These circumstances no longer exist today in many places, so reformers call for focus on personal credibility instead. Otherwise, you could have situations where the testimony of a university-educated female CEO would carry only half the weight of an illiterate, uneducated man.

53. For obvious reasons, this criterion was rarely, if ever, met. Concerns about illicit sexual activity are tied to pre-Islamic concerns about loss of honor related to sexual misconduct. In the case of rape or abduction, the family could recover honor only by taking vengeance against the perpetrator or his tribe. Vengeance could also take the form of killing the woman, if she was believed to have participated consensually. Such so-called honor killings thus have their origins in pre-Islamic and Near Eastern cultural practices, rather than Islam proper, although they remain a reality of tribal practice in some locations, such as Jordan and Pakistan. Honor killings often receive lighter sentences than other murder cases, despite legislative reforms and calls for tougher sentences.

cases.[54] Any testimony or confession had to use the specific terminology related to the offense. Only voluntary confessions made in the courtroom were considered valid; coerced confessions were not admissible. In the case of illicit sex, the confession had to be repeated four separate times to parallel the witness requirement, yet confessions could be retracted up until the moment of execution of the punishment. Finally, the accused could claim doubt as to whether they had committed a crime or about the facts of the case, or could claim they had been coerced. All of this made a *hudud* crime difficult to prove in court.

Accusing someone of a *hudud* offense was also a serious matter. Unlike crimes with discretionary punishments, once investigation into a *hudud* crime began, the victim could not settle with or pardon the accused. As a crime against God, once the sentence was set, it could not be waived, reduced, or commuted.[55] Anyone making an unfounded charge of a *hudud* offense might face punishment for false accusation.[56]

Homicide and Wounding

Westerners are usually surprised that crimes they consider most grievous—homicide and wounding—are not included as *hudud* offenses. Islamic criminal law treated homicide and wounding as private claims because of the direct, personal harm caused to the victim and the victim's family and heirs, not only to the state or community. Retribution was considered a necessary part of justice in Islamic criminal law, based on the Qur'an's assertion in 2:178 that "fair retribution" is a right in the case of murder. The same verse also declares

---

54. This generally includes pregnancy, except in the Maliki school. However, Maliki doctrine recognizes the legal concept of the "sleeping fetus"—the idea that an egg might be fertilized, but remain dormant for up to five years. This argument has been revived successfully today in two cases of divorced women in Nigeria accused of sexual misconduct on the basis of pregnancy.

55. Nevertheless, a confession could be retracted up until the moment of execution of the punishment.

56. A person unable to prove a charge of illicit sexual activity (*zina*) with the requisite four adult male witnesses becomes liable for false accusation of the same, per Q 24:4.

financial compensation as an "alleviation" that provides justice to the victim.[57] The next verse, Q 2:179, specifies the purpose of such "fair retribution"—saving lives and guarding against wrongs. Thus in classical Islamic law, justice to the victim and safeguarding of the community were the primary obligations of the court. For this reason, the victim or the victim's heirs had a voice in the prosecution and sentencing. This process is still followed in some countries today, such as Saudi Arabia and Iran.

Three main principles govern Islamic criminal law on homicide and bodily harm:

1. Generally, the victim or the victim's heirs decided whether to bring a case, although the state reserved the right to pursue discretionary punishment if a case for retaliation could not be proven. The state also reserved the right to demand retaliation if there was no next of kin.[58]

2. If the proven homicide or injury was intentional,[59] the punishment was decided by the victim or the victim's heirs. Options included retaliation[60] (the death penalty in the case of murder or harm for harm in the case of serious wounding, such as loss of a

---

57. This could include financial compensation to a pregnant woman caused to miscarry, based on the stage of fetal development. The more developed and recognizably human the fetus, the higher the amount of compensation, particularly if the sex can be discerned. Classical Shia legal literature even required compensation to a couple interrupted during sex, as coitus interruptus robbed the couple of a potential child. Similarly, a wife was entitled to compensation if her husband practiced coitus interruptus without her consent, because of the loss of a potential child. Peters, *Crime and Punishment in Islamic Law*, 51.

58. Today, decisions about prosecution are made by the state.

59. Intent was determined by the weapon used. If the weapon typically results in death, such as a knife or gun, then intent can be assumed. If the weapon is not normally fatal, then the context in which it was used must be considered to determine intent, such as whether the person wielding it was angry. Lack of intent also mattered, such as if a person lawfully digs a well and someone falls in and is injured or dies. The digger is not liable for intentional killing, because the intent behind digging the well was to gain access to water, not to kill someone. In unintentional cases, only financial compensation could be pursued, not retaliation. See Peters, *Crime and Punishment in Islamic Law*, 44.

60. Retaliation was prominent in Near Eastern cultural practices, when there was no centralized system for justice or law enforcement. The victim's kin had the prerogative of seeking vengeance for murder to restore the family's honor. Ingrid Mattson, *The Story of the Qur'an: Its History and Place in Muslim Life*, 2nd ed. (Malden, MA: Wiley-Blackwell, 2013), 11.

limb or eye),[61] financial compensation payable to the victim or the victim's heirs, or forgiveness of the perpetrator at any point up until the moment of execution of the sentence.[62]

3. If the requirements for retaliation could not be proven, the victim or the victim's heirs could pursue financial compensation. In general, circumstantial evidence was not permitted in cases involving retaliation for homicide or injury, even if the accused was in possession of the instrument used to commit the offense.[63] However, circumstantial evidence could be used in a discretionary case and could include incomplete evidence, such as an accusation by a dying victim (who was thereby unable to provide required direct testimony in court) or testimony that an individual saw someone beating, but not killing, someone later found dead. These strict requirements asserted the primary importance of justice for the victim at the same time that they sought to assure that no person could be unjustly convicted of a serious crime.

Overall, the impression of the historical functioning of classical Islamic law is one of flexibility and a strong role for the judge (*qadi*). Ideally, the judge was to treat cases according to their individual circumstances, assure justice to victims, and protect the public's interests and safety. At the same time, the judge was bound to very specific rules for evidence and witnessing, particularly where *hudud* crimes were concerned. Both victims and the accused had rights and responsibilities in bringing cases to the court's attention.

The Impact of Colonialism on Islamic Law

The onslaught of the colonial era in the eighteenth and nineteenth centuries brought major changes to the Islamic world, particularly in

---

61. Retaliation cannot endanger the life of the person being punished or cause harm to another innocent party. Retaliation is limited to the hands, feet, arms, legs, testicles, nose, ears, eyes, and teeth. Retaliation is not allowed for injuries to the head, spine, or sternum, or injuries that cut through the bone. These latter types of injuries are to be assigned financial compensation. Peters, *Crime and Punishment in Islamic Law*, 48.

62. This right is assigned in Q 2:178, if the victim or victim's heirs so choose.

63. Peters, *Crime and Punishment in Islamic Law*, 15.

the Middle East and North Africa, including the rapid replacement of Islamic criminal law and practice with Western penal codes.[64] These changes were made based on Western perceptions of incoherence in legal practice, uncertainty in legal outcomes, and concerns that too much power lay in the hands of individuals, rather than institutions or the state. In a few places, such as India and Nigeria, colonial rulers tried to revise Islamic criminal law into something closer to Western criminal law, before replacing it with a Western-style penal code. There were also instances of more gradual transitions in Islamic legal systems that reformed Islamic criminal law while leaving Shariah courts intact, although increasingly limited in jurisdiction. Eventually, in many places, such as Egypt and the Ottoman Empire, Shariah courts were abolished.

Faced with expanding urbanization, industrialization, capitalism, and international economies, colonial reforms throughout the Middle East, North Africa, and the Indian subcontinent sought to modernize the state bureaucracy and centralize state power. From the perspective of criminal justice, this meant a shift from deterrence to more efficient policing and punishment as a matter of protecting property and business interests and controlling expanding populations.[65] Westerners believed these new systems were fair, egalitarian, standardized, and professional, and guarded against political and personal abuse.[66] Traditionally, Islamic criminal law had distinguished

---

64. Even countries that maintained their traditional systems, such as Saudi Arabia and Yemen, have been pressed to adapt to global realities, such as international finance and commerce.

65. British administrators, in particular, sought a more efficient and clear method for convicting and punishing criminals, particularly for the death penalty. British administrators often complained convictions were too difficult to obtain under Islamic criminal law and too many people were getting away with crimes they had clearly committed, because the standards of evidence were too rigid. See Peters, *Crime and Punishment in Islamic Law*, 109, 112, and 120–25.

66. In *Shari'a: Theory, Practice, Transformations* (Cambridge, UK: Cambridge University Press, 2009), Wael Hallaq argues the impetus for replacing Islamic law with modern institutions and codified laws was to serve the goals of capital accumulation and state interests through the creation of obedient citizens. By contrast, he argues Islamic law was intended to serve the interest of public welfare. For a critique charging that Hallaq overstates the independence of Islamic law from the state, see Mohammed Fadel, "Review: A Tragedy of Politics or an Apolitical Tragedy?," *Journal of the American Oriental Society* 131, no. 1 (January–March 2011): 109–27.

between Muslims and non-Muslims, males and females, slaves and free, but modern secular law insisted all subjects be treated equally.[67] The state now took on the prosecutorial role, ending the prior practice of victims or their heirs deciding whether to file a case.[68] Practices such as corporal punishment and torture, although not the death penalty, were phased out,[69] laws were rewritten to be more coherent and predictable, and layers of hierarchy were introduced in bureaucracies to ensure colonial standards for fair trials and just outcomes.

However, many Muslims perceived these institutions and regulations as a depersonalized and homogenized approach focused on administration to the benefit of state power and profit rather than justice for people. These policies and procedures removed power and justice from the hands of those personally familiar with and invested in the local community in favor of remote parties with nothing at stake in the outcomes of their decisions, other than fines payable to the state. As centralization led to greater consistency in applying the law countrywide, there was a concomitant loss of discretionary power at the local level. Also lost was the sense of justice having a deep connection to and symbiotic relationship with the grassroots community. Although the aim of Western law was "blind justice," meaning all were to be equal in the eyes of the law, some Muslims charged this new system was blind to justice. They pointed to the winner-takes-all model of litigation in which a case was either entirely won or lost by the accused without considering the impact of the case's outcome on the surrounding community.[70] The privileging of Western law set the stage for conflict and the goal of recovering Islamic identity in many places.

---

67. Yet colonizer and colonized did not have the same status under the law. Peters, *Crime and Punishment in Islamic Law*, 103.

68. The state used this as an opportunity to enrich itself. The British ended financial compensation to crime victims or their heirs in favor of fines being paid to the Crown in 1797. Peters, *Crime and Punishment in Islamic Law*, 117.

69. In theory, the *qadi* retained the right to assign *hudud* punishments, but Peters has found only one case in which amputation was used to punish theft. That sentence was quashed on appeal. Only flogging seems to have continued as a punishment, until it was abolished in 1861 in favor of imprisonment or banishment or both. See Peters, *Crime and Punishment in Islamic Law*, 135–41.

70. Hallaq, *Shari'a*, argues such siloing of justice rendered it a cold, external mechanism, rather than a vital, living part of the community.

Islamic Family Law

As a source of identity politics and, for many Muslims, the heart of Shariah in practice, family law has become a contemporary battleground for reformers of all varieties, ranging from proponents of international standards of human rights to those calling for a greater role for "Islamic law" in the state. Because women are the culture bearers, the legal status of women is often seen as a reflection of the "Islamic" nature of a given state. Yet family law today is frequently a mix of state power; individual, personal conscience; and secular influences. Marriage and divorce most frequently reflect this combination.

Laws and administrative mechanisms related to marriage and divorce vary throughout the Muslim world. Many Muslims seek religious legitimation of marriage and divorce in much the same way that Christians seek church weddings as a supplement to the state marriage license or may apply for an annulment in the Roman Catholic Church in addition to becoming legally divorced.[71] Inviting God to be a part of family life is a reflection of commitment to faith and community.

Marriage

Under Islamic law, marriage is a contract in which both spouses have rights and responsibilities. The husband is responsible for providing his wife and children with maintenance.[72] The wife is responsible for raising the family and caring for the home. Both spouses have a right to sexual fulfillment and children.

The required elements for a legitimate marriage contract include an offer by the groom or his representatives, acceptance by the bride or her representatives, and witnesses to the contract.[73] The husband

---

71. Annulment (*faskh*) under Islamic law must be pronounced by a judge based on a condition that renders the marriage invalid. In some societies, incompatibility of tribal status can be used to justify annulment. See John L. Esposito, with Natana J. DeLong-Bas, *Women in Muslim Family Law*, rev. ed. (Syracuse: Syracuse University Press, 2001), for details. Ahmed, *Women and Gender in Islam*, 89, argues this reflects a pre-Islamic Sassanian custom that was incorporated into Islamic law.

72. This includes housing, food, clothing, health care, and any other needs, based on the standard of living to which the wife is accustomed.

73. Witnesses were required to assure the marriage was valid, legitimate, and a matter of public knowledge.

Solemnization of a marriage contract in a mosque in Kuala Lumpur, Malaysia. The bride and groom are present, but do not sit together. Both men and women are witnesses. In some countries, men and women have separate wedding celebrations and only men witness the signing of the marriage contact.

must also provide a dower, often referred to as the "marriage gift."[74] According to some law schools, the wife may additionally stipulate conditions, such as not moving beyond a certain distance from her family, barring the man from taking another wife, assuring her right to continue her education or work outside of the home, or requiring any wealth acquired during the marriage to be split evenly in the event of divorce.[75] Violation of any these conditions constitutes grounds for divorce.[76]

Traditionally and, in many places, legally, the bride's male guardian is responsible for negotiating the contract, although the bride's consent is required for the marriage to be valid.[77] In theory, requiring the bride's consent should preclude the possibility of forced marriage.

---

74. The marriage gift is intended to provide the bride with financial means in case of divorce or widowhood.

75. Islamic law does not recognize joint property.

76. Some countries now print standardized marriage contracts with proposed conditions that both parties must initial for them to be actionable.

77. The bride's age and status as a virgin or a deflowered woman has an impact on how and when her consent is verified. For details, see Esposito with DeLong-Bas, *Women in Muslim Family Law.*

However, in some places, there is tremendous pressure on women to accept marriages as a matter of respect for the choice of their father or other guardian or because one is expected to follow certain marriage patterns.[78] In some cases, women may feel they do not have any choice in their husband, particularly where the families of the potential spouses have an interest in the marriage. In others, women trust their guardian's choice and are involved in the final selection. Many families today arrange for chaperoned visits with prospective husbands.[79]

It can be difficult for Westerners, raised to think of themselves as independent and autonomous individuals, to find any redemptive value in a woman requiring constant guardianship or approval to marry. It may help to remember marriage brings two families together and is intended to create a new family. Consideration of broader family dynamics beyond the immediate couple carries the hopeful assurance of building a family network of support for the couple and any children born to them. Furthermore, the assumption behind requiring a guardian to contract a woman's marriage was that the bride's guardian, typically her father, would have her best interests at heart and would seek a lasting marriage for her. Many Muslims, both women and men, marry with the hope and expectation of not only a lasting marriage but also love.[80]

Today, some women in even the most traditional societies are finding new ways to involve themselves in the process of screening and interviewing potential husbands. Social media, dating services, and other electronic means allow people looking for a spouse or wishing to get to know a potential suitor to communicate without having to be in the same room or even see each other.[81] This

78. An example would be the traditional preference for first-cousin marriage in the Arabian Gulf.

79. For an often humorous account by an Egyptian woman meeting with prospective marriage partners, see Ghada Abdel Aal and Nora Eltahawy, *I Want to Get Married! One Bride's Misadventures with Handsome Houdinis, Technicolor Grooms, Morality Police, and Other Mr. Not-Quite-Rights* (Austin: University of Texas at Austin Press, 2010).

80. For firsthand accounts by young Muslims on their hopes for romance and love in marriage, see Nura Maznavi and Ayesha Mattu, eds., *Love, InshAllah: The Secret Love Lives of American Muslim Women* (Berkeley: Soft Skull, 2012), and Ayesha Mattu and Nura Maznavi, eds., *Salaam, Love: American Muslim Men on Love, Sex, and Intimacy* (Boston: Beacon, 2014).

81. Popular examples include *https://www.Muslima.com* and *www.shaadi.com*.

is particularly important in societies where gender segregation is observed. Although some conservatives express concerns about the potential for inappropriate relationships, use of such media allows a sense of empowerment for many women. It also allows them to demonstrate their morality and integrity by choosing the type and extent of relationship they pursue, as well as how they represent themselves.[82] Claiming a greater voice in spouse selection and contract negotiation not only reduces the role of the state to one of enforcement of the contract as a legal document but also reflects the role the woman intends to claim throughout the marriage as a partner to the contract rather than an object of it.

Divorce

Fulfillment of the rights and responsibilities outlined in the marriage contract ensures that the marriage continues, while failure to fulfill these provides grounds for divorce, should the offended party opt to pursue one. It is important to note, the right to divorce is not the same as an obligation to divorce. Although divorce is permitted, Muhammad said, of all of the things God permitted, there was none God hated more than divorce.

In the event a couple experiences serious discord, the Qur'an prescribes taking a break and bringing in family members from both sides to help arbitrate, rather than immediate divorce. The Qur'an specifies that a divorce initiated by the husband (*talaq*) requires three separate statements of divorce, which should be made with careful consideration and mediation over a three-month period to be certain differences truly cannot be reconciled.[83] The first two declarations of divorce can be revoked, but the third declaration makes the divorce irrevocable.[84]

---

82. Many women choose something that symbolizes their interests or preferences rather than a profile picture. Creativity and artistry might be shown through the choice of a well-manicured hand or foot or presentation of flowers.

83. The Qur'an specifies a one-month waiting period between each statement of divorce. In practice, however, the "triple *talaq*"—three statements of divorce pronounced simultaneously—has been legally recognized and accepted in some places. Requiring three declarations at three different set times was supposed to ensure the man's intent in divorcing his wife was clear.

84. Even after the third declaration making the divorce irrevocable, remarriage is possible but only if the woman marries and divorces someone else first.

Although the husband can end the marriage at any time without having to provide a reason or justification, there are consequences for doing so. Not only does his former wife become forbidden to him, but he must also pay maintenance to the wife for her "waiting period," which is used to determine whether she is pregnant.[85] Jurists have connected the husband's greater power to initiate divorce to his greater legal responsibility as the family provider.[86]

Women also have the right to initiate divorce (*khul'*), but the grounds for doing so are limited to certain situations. Historically, these were impotence, sterility, or disease on the part of the husband that prevented him from engaging in sexual intercourse.[87] Just as the husband is required to pay maintenance during the waiting period, so the wife must offer financial compensation—traditionally, the amount of the marriage gift—to the husband for initiating divorce. Finally, the husband must consent to the divorce. Historically, jurists have argued that the wife has relatively less power to initiate divorce as she is not obligated to provide financial support for the family.[88]

Ideally, the right of either spouse to initiate divorce is intended to provide a balance of rights in sync with the responsibilities each carry in the marriage. That power is sometimes abused and can lead to instability, uncertainty, and even fear on the part of the wife, who may feel she lives under the constant potential threat of divorce for any or no reason. This is especially true in countries where the wife is owed only the minimum three months of maintenance following

---

85. The waiting period lasts for three months. If the wife is pregnant, the husband owes her child support for as long as she is the custodial parent. The set time frame for maintenance does not take into consideration the length of the marriage or the wife's contributions. Thus some reformers argue the Qur'anic mandate of three months should be understood as a minimum. There is nothing that prevents a man from paying more, as was ruled in the groundbreaking *Shah Bano v. Mohd. Ahmad Khan* case in India in 1985. See Esposito with DeLong-Bas, *Women in Muslim Family Law*, 114–16.

86. This reasoning is also used in the legal literature to explain why men receive twice the inheritance portion of women. Women's rights activists in some places have thus called for reform of inheritance laws to reflect current realities.

87. Infertility does not necessarily result in divorce. Some infertile couples choose to remain married and focus on building their life together.

88. Although the wife is under no legal obligation to contribute to the household financially, the reality today is women often do contribute, particularly where children are concerned, and even serve as head of household. This has led women's rights activists in many places to call for legal reforms to expand women's power to initiate divorce.

divorce, after which she may find herself without a home or provider. Many women additionally fear loss of access to their children, as there is no concept of joint custody in Islamic law—only guardianship, which is exercised by an individual.[89] Reflecting the patriarchal societies in which these legal interpretations were developed, guardianship is generally assigned to the father.[90]

Classical legal limitations for a woman seeking divorce have, at times, placed women in challenging circumstances, as when psychological abuse or physical harm may be taking place.[91] Faced with the reality that some women are in danger in their marriages, some, though not all, countries today have expanded the grounds on which a woman can seek divorce to include harmful disease, such as HIV, on the husband's part, and the wife's personal recognition that she cannot continue in the marriage. Some countries also recognize drug or alcohol abuse or domestic violence[92] on the part of the husband as presenting a real and present danger to the wife and

---

89. Only Morocco recognizes both parents as legal guardians. Such is the fear of loss of access to children that many women remain in a marriage even if it is abusive. Some will give up their financial rights (maintenance and child support) in exchange for guardianship of their children, if they can afford to do so.

90. Although motherhood is revered and praised in Islam, classical Islamic law assigns guardianship of boys at age seven and girls at age nine to the father, regardless of the father's character, circumstances, or ability or willingness to provide for them—or of the mother's. Some countries assign guardianship to the father or the father's extended family at the time of divorce. A mother can only retain custody if she does not remarry. Women's rights activists in many countries are calling for legal reform that considers the character of both parents and the best interests of the child in determining guardianship.

91. Some husbands harass their wives, including by accusing them of cheating, a charge the woman can deny but that is difficult to prove. In such a case, divorce by oath (li'an) can be enacted by a judge if both parties are willing to swear repeatedly they are being truthful.

92. Although Q 30:21 describes the ideal relationship between a husband and wife as one of love and kindness in which spouses find comfort and tranquility in each other, Q 4:34, if read literally, appears to sanction a husband striking his wife, even though Muhammad himself never struck any of his wives and routinely chastised those among his followers who did. For a comprehensive analysis and history, see Ayesha Chaudhry, *Domestic Violence and the Islamic Tradition: Ethics, Law, and the Muslim Discourse on Gender* (New York: Oxford University Press, 2014). Malaysia was the first Muslim-majority country to pass legislation criminalizing domestic violence in 1994. Some countries still have not outlawed domestic violence, including the United Arab Emirates and Lebanon.

children, justifying a judicial divorce (*faskh*). Forced divorces are highly unusual.[93] A minority of women in some countries are now finding ways to fight for custody of their children, particularly where the husband is abusive or has substance abuse issues.

There are also cases of husbands trying to push unhappy wives into initiating divorce by *khul'*, rather than declaring the divorce themselves by *talaq*, so as to avoid paying maintenance during the waiting period. Some women are so desperate to escape their marriages that they agree. In other cases, men are known to use *khul'* to harass their wives and force them to stay in the marriage by constantly changing the parameters by which they would consent to the divorce. Such harassment can consist of demanding a large amount of money that the wife cannot possibly pay or simply not showing up for court proceedings.[94] Some countries have responded to this by legally setting the maximum cost of a *khul'* divorce to the marriage gift and by sending police officers to ensure husbands show up for court proceedings.

As in many places, there is often a disconnect between theory and practice with respect to marriage and divorce laws, largely because laws are based on assumed ideal circumstances, whereas actual people live in realities that often fail to live up to the ideal. This was as true historically as it is today. Simply because a law exists does not mean the courts always enforce it or that those issues left to personal recognizance are always fulfilled. For example, although Islamic law theoretically requires the husband to pay maintenance for the family, in practice this does not always happen. Although it is true women can seek recourse through the courts, doing so requires evidence to prove the case. Historically, some men simply abandoned their wives to escape paying maintenance or left the marriage without fulfilling the legal parameters of divorce. This left women in legal limbo, as not only could they not obtain needed maintenance, but

93. The grounds for an outside party forcing divorce on a couple are extremely rare, although it occasionally happens in cases of apostasy or tribal incompatibility. See William E. Shepard, "Abu Zayd, Nasir Hamid," Oxford Islamic Studies Online, *http://www.oxfordislamicstudies.com*.

94. These methods have become particularly notorious in Egypt and Saudi Arabia. There were so many cases in Egypt, a law was finally passed permitting the police to bring men to court.

they remained legally married because they could not prove they were divorced.[95]

Today, some countries, such as Malaysia, deduct maintenance directly from the husband's paycheck to ensure his financial obligations are met. Many countries require divorces to be recorded with the courts, rather than left to personal arrangement, so any person's legal marital status is thus a matter of public record. Questions have also arisen about indirect statements of divorce, such as whether divorce by text message or changing one's status on Facebook qualifies as a legal divorce. Some jurists do consider these methods to be legally binding, albeit impersonal.

With divorce rates rising among young people throughout the Muslim world today for many reasons, such issues are particularly pressing. Marriage remains the norm and ideal, but, in some cases, young people are pressured to marry before they are ready to assume the responsibilities of marriage and raising a family. Patterns of rapid urbanization in many places have changed the surrounding demographics, which can make finding an appropriate spouse more challenging. Expectations among younger generations for marriage may differ from those of their parents or grandparents owing to rising education levels and the desire to work outside the home. Not only are more young women pursuing graduate degrees and careers, but many young men also see value in an educated and employed wife. Ultimately, social capital is in flux, with education and employability sometimes outweighing more traditional considerations like beauty or social class.[96] While these issues are not related to "Islam" or "Islamic law" per se, they raise questions about the degree to which Islamic law must develop alongside society to remain relevant to current needs. Many women's rights organizations continue to push for changes that bring justice and public welfare back into focus.

---

95. Hanafi law required that a man be gone for ninety years before desertion translated into presumed death. Other schools allowed shorter time periods, recognizing the financial straits in which women and dependent children were left. Some countries, such as Egypt, require an absence of only one year before a wife can request judicial divorce (*faskh*). See Esposito with DeLong-Bas, *Women in Muslim Family Law*, 55–56.

96. The Doha International Family Institute in Qatar studies the impact of modernity and urbanization on families. See *www.difi.org.qa*.

Present-Day Reimplementation of "Shariah"

Countries seeking to reassert their "Islamic identity" often reimplement "Shariah," focusing on selective aspects of *hudud* and restrictions on women.[97] Applying Shariah is seen as a positive assertion of Muslim identity and a means of reconnecting to a proud past in which Islamic empires were the wealthiest and most powerful in the world.[98] For those who believe being a good Muslim requires living in an Islamic state, having Shariah as the law of the land is a necessity, leading to a prosperous and virtuous community.[99] Repealing or abolishing all or parts of Islamic law would be unthinkable; not only would it cost the government its legitimacy but also it would require believers to give up a critical aspect of what they believe God expects of them.

Many Muslims hold justice as a core value and believe Islamic law delivers justice and a voice to the victim in a way that Western law does not. For example, in cases involving homicide, Western states use a prosecutor and judge. Though a victim or a victim's family may offer their personal forgiveness, impact statement, or even oppose prosecution, the state nevertheless must prosecute, regardless of the victim's wishes. Western legal procedures are often criticized for taking longer than Islamic criminal proceedings, which

---

97. The tendency has been to focus on punishments as outcomes, rather than process, including the rules of evidence. Seven countries have reimplemented various aspects of Islamic criminal law, including *hudud*, since 1972—Libya, Pakistan, Iran, Sudan, Northern Nigeria, the Kelantan state of Malaysia, and the United Arab Emirates (UAE), although it has not yet been implemented in the Kelantan state because it has not been approved by the federal government.

98. The Mughal Empire (1526–1857) on the Indian subcontinent was the wealthiest, while the Ottoman Empire was geographically the most widespread and lasted the longest (1299–1922).

99. Not all Muslims want to see Islamic law in power or as the only law applicable to all people. Opinions vary by country, ranging from 8% in support of Shariah as the law of the land in Azerbaijan to 99% in Afghanistan. Those who support the application of Shariah generally call for its use in the domestic sphere, such as in family law, inheritance, and property rights. Opinions vary greatly with respect to corporal punishment. For details, see Pew Research Center poll, "The World's Muslims: Religion, Politics and Society," April 30, 2013, at *www.pewforum.org/2013/04/30 /the-worlds-muslims-religion-politics-society-beliefs-about-sharia/*.

is believed not only to hamper psychological healing but also delay justice to the point that it can seem meaningless by the time it is finally carried out. In addition, many Muslims believe the threat or promise of swifter justice carries a stronger deterrent factor, which is a powerful draw for people living in areas with rampant crime and corruption.[100]

This is not to say that current implementation of Shariah follows the ideals outlined in jurisprudence or is consistent with the historical record. In many cases, the distinction between Shariah and *fiqh* is lost or forgotten in discussions about "implementing Shariah" or "establishing Islamic law." In addition, what, exactly, is meant by "Shariah" and "Islamic law," and whose interpretation is to be used is often unclear, in part because Muslims themselves are often unclear as to the difference.

Some states adhere to literal interpretations of past rulings without attention to the intended function of Islamic law or the underlying principles and values it is supposed to uphold. This results in a "fundamentalist" approach to Islamic law that demands strict adherence to specific rules and regulations assumed to be basic, unchanging, and universally applicable to every time and place. Lost in the process is not only the distinction between Shariah and *fiqh* but also knowledge of how Islamic law formed historically in response to changing community needs and contexts. Ironically, these current interpretations often repeat the mistakes of European colonial authorities, focusing so much on select codifications that they lose the flexibility that formed the heart of justice in the past. Such interpretations also open current practice to charges that Islamic law is applied according to the interests of those in power rather than the interests of the broader public.

One of the greatest dangers that comes with the reassertion of Shariah lies with the *hudud* punishments. Some states have misused capital and corporal punishment to suppress dissent while claiming loyalty to religious law,[101] expanded corporal punishments

---

100. Peters, *Crime and Punishment in Islamic Law*, 146. The twelve states in Northern Nigeria that have adopted Islamic criminal law did so in large part because of the popular belief that doing so would stem crime and corruption. See ibid., 170.

101. Iran became the most notorious example of this after the 1979 revolution, when revolutionary courts were quickly established to quash political opponents.

beyond *hudud* offenses to demonstrate the power of the state,[102] or sentenced children under the age of eighteen to amputation, life imprisonment, or even death. In some cases, the scrupulous safeguards historically applied to evidence and testimony are no longer observed, such as the ban in Shariah courts on confessions obtained through torture and the high standard for witnessing requirements for cases involving illicit sexual activities. Of greatest concern to many are conflicts between Islamic criminal law and standards of universal human rights,[103] particularly in cases where a country is a signatory to international human rights conventions or treaties, yet claims "Shariah reservations" so as to be excluded from certain provisions.[104]

Human rights activists have taken particular issue with *hudud* punishments and retaliations, charging they are, by nature, cruel, inhuman, and degrading, because they involve corporal punishment (flogging, amputation) or the death penalty.[105] Shariah supporters reject characterizing "God's law" in this way, yet their understanding of *hudud* is often essentialized, inflexible, and over-simplified, focusing on the letter of the law rather than its spirit and objectives (*maqasid*). The end result of modern-day Shariah enforcement has been far more convictions and implementations

---

102. Post-revolutionary Iran introduced flogging for driving a car without a license.

103. These include banning cruel, inhuman, or degrading punishments; restricting punishment to situations in which the law and the punishment are clearly spelled out in the law; ensuring equal treatment for all persons before the law; ensuring freedom of religion and religious expression; and ensuring the right of children not to be subjected to cruel, inhuman, or degrading punishment, life imprisonment, or the death penalty.

104. Details of signatories to various conventions and treaties can be found in Nader Hashemi and Emran Qureshi, "Human Rights," in *The Oxford Encyclopedia of Islam and Women*, editor-in-chief Natana J. DeLong-Bas (New York: Oxford University Press, 2013), 1:449–55. These "Shariah reservations" typically focus on family law and inheritance.

105. These charges are often perceived in the Muslim world as hypocritical and embracing a double standard, as violations are only mentioned for certain countries and not others, based on international alliances. Critics charge the United States has little credibility in denouncing countries for human rights violations in light of US prisoner mistreatment and torture at Guantanamo Bay and Abu Ghraib. Similarly, France and Germany have little credibility in denouncing a lack of freedom of religion and expression in other countries, when they themselves restrict what women can wear in public.

of punishments than occurred historically[106]—and often at an alarmingly rapid pace.[107]

Yet simply because laws exist on the books does not mean they are always applied in practice. In Northern Nigeria, for example, the police force is a federal institution, and many police officers are not Muslim. Non-Muslim police officers may not pursue Shariah offenses.[108] Similarly, just because sentences are issued does not mean they are always carried out. They may simply serve as deterrents, which is in keeping with their historical purpose.[109] Despite these cautions, the records of certain states nevertheless remain cause for concern.

Particularly notorious is the twisting of traditional *hudud* parameters for illicit sexual activities. Historically, rape was treated as a separate criminal category from illicit sexual relations because of the lack of consent. Although there was always a possibility that an allegation of rape might be misconstrued as a confession of unlawful intercourse, a woman making the allegation always had recourse to the protective measure of doubt as a defense. In addition, for a confession to a *hudud* offense to be valid, the confession had to be repeated four times in court. Therefore, historically, it was extremely rare to find cases of women receiving *hudud* punishments for making rape accusations.

Today, however, in some places, rape accusations may result not only in imprisonment for the victim but also, in some cases, in the victim's death by stoning. In Pakistan, the 1979 Zina Ordinance

---

106. ISIS serves as a case in point with its draconian interpretations of *hudud* punishments and use of barbarous treatments, such as burning people alive, that were banned historically. See the objections of numerous legal scholars and activists at *www.lettertobaghdadi.com*.

107. In Iran, at least 150 people have been stoned to death since the revolution. Stoning sentences continue to be assigned, most recently in December 2015. Similarly, in the Sudan, between the presidential decree in September 1983 and the overthrow of Nimeiri in April 1985, between 96 and 120 judicial amputations were carried out, including at least twenty cross-amputations.

108. Peters, *Crime and Punishment in Islamic Law*, 172.

109. Some harsh retaliation sentences have been assigned in Nigeria in response to horrific crimes, but it is not known whether these punishments have been carried out. See Gunnar J. Weimann, *Islamic Criminal Law in Northern Nigeria: Politics, Religion, Judicial Practice* (Amsterdam: Amsterdam University Press, 2010), 45–46.

made illicit sex a crime against the state, punishable by death.[110] Under this law, if a woman brings a rape charge to the police, she must be able to prove she was raped via four adult male witnesses or she could face prosecution for illicit sex.[111] Her word alone that the sex was nonconsensual is not considered sufficient proof. Trials therefore focus on proving or disproving her consent, rather than forceful coercion or violation. Not only has this discouraged women from reporting rape, it has also emboldened men to rape without fear of repercussion.

In some places, a victim can be forced to marry her rapist in order to free both parties from charges of sexual misconduct and from the potential embarrassment of a public trial.[112] This has been twisted in Yemen and some Central Asian countries, such as Kazakhstan and Kyrgyzstan, as a license to kidnap and rape a woman as a way of choosing a wife.[113]

Issues related to minority status and rights are also a concern. Although it is sometimes claimed "Islam" commands the annihilation of non-Muslims, this is not faithful to the Qur'an, the historical record of Muhammad's lifetime, the record of the Rightly Guided Caliphs, or examples of multireligious Islamic empires

---

110. The Federal Shariat Court challenged the death penalty on the argument that Q 24:2 only mentions flogging as a punishment for illicit sex. General Zia ul-Haq disapproved of this conclusion, immediately replaced all of the judges, and amended the Constitution to permit a re-hearing of the case, which, not surprisingly, concluded stoning was legal. See Shahnaz Khan, "Locating the Feminist Voice: The Debate on the Zina Ordinance," in *Pakistani Women: Multiple Locations and Competing Narratives*, ed. Sadaf Ahmad (New York: Oxford University Press, 2010), 140–62.

111. Men can also accuse a woman of illicit sexual activity with impunity if they claim they are doing so for the public good. This has been used as a social tool for controlling women or to pressure them into giving a man money. Sometimes the family will kill the woman, if the state does not, to "restore the family honor." More than one million of these cases were filed with police between 1979 and 1995. Available statistics from 1994–1996 for the Women Police Station in Karachi show that 40–45% of women in prison are there on such charges. See Khan, "Locating the Feminist Voice," 149–54, for details.

112. Peters, *Crime and Punishment in Islamic Law*, 114.

113. These practices existed in non-Islamic cultures, so are not attributable to historical Islamic law. See, e.g., Ahmed, *Women and Gender in Islam*, 14, for Assyrian roots, and Anara Tabyshalieva, "Central Asia and the Caucasus: Kazakhstan and Kyrgyzstan," in *The Oxford Encyclopedia of Islam and Women*, ed. DeLong-Bas, 1:122–25.

from the past, such as the Ottoman Empire. Both the Constitution of Medina (622) and the Treaty of al-Hudaybiyya (628) established legal precedents for inclusion of members of other faith traditions within Muslim communities.[114] Poor members of other faith traditions were included in state welfare programs, based on Q 9:60. Jurists declared it the state's responsibility to care for all of the poor, the elderly, and the infirm living in Islamic lands, regardless of religious affiliation.[115] These historical practices stand in marked contrast to state discrimination against and even persecution of certain minority sects today, such as the Ahmadiyya in Pakistan and the Bahais in Iran.[116]

M. Cherif Bassiouni (1937–2017)

Born in Cairo, Egypt, in 1937, Mahmoud Cherif Bassiouni was Professor of Law at DePaul University, where he taught from 1964–2012. He was known for his work on international, domestic, and comparative criminal law and human rights. Bassiouni's interest in government accountability and rule of law began with his service in the Egyptian military in the Suez Crisis of 1956. Although he was wounded and decorated for his service, he was then placed under house arrest for seven months when he protested the torture and disappearance of prisoners under Nasser's regime. Undeterred, he championed the creation of civil society, even amid war, as the long-term solution to peace and justice. Bassiouni served with the United Nations, offering distinguished service to the steering committee for the Crimes Against Humanity Initiative to

Continued

---

114. Rejection of non-Muslims as community members dates to the Umayyad (661–750) and Abbasid (750–1258) empires, which were concerned with state consolidation. Those claiming discrimination against non-Muslims from the outset point to the so-called Pact of Umar. See chapter 9, "Muslim-Christian Encounters: Conflict and Coexistence."

115. Afsaruddin, *The First Muslims*, 42–45.

116. The Bahais are not recognized as a legitimate religion under Iranian law. In Pakistan, the Ahmadis face imprisonment and potentially death if they state their beliefs publicly. Many Ahmadis have been charged and imprisoned and await trial. Peters, *Crime and Punishment in Islamic Law*, 158.

develop comprehensive conventions for prevention and punishment of such crimes and co-chaired the committee that drafted the UN Convention Against Torture. As chairman of a commission documenting war crimes in the former Yugoslavia, he helped detail Serbia's systematic use of torture, rape, prison camps, and killings to engage ethnic cleansing. The report resulted in the formation of the UN International Criminal Tribunal in 1993. Bassiouni served as a United Nations expert on war crimes in Afghanistan, Iraq, Libya, and Bahrain. He won many awards, including the Secretary-General of the Council of Europe's Award (1984), the Special Award of the Council of Europe (1990), UN Association's Adlai E. Stevenson Award (1993), the Defender of Democracy Award from Parliamentarians for Global Action (1998), the Medal of the Commission de Derechos Humanos del Estado de Mexico (2006), the Cesare Beccaria Justice Medal of the International Society for Social Defense (2007), and the Hague Prize for International Law (2007), in addition to receiving many lifetime achievement awards, medals, and honorary degrees from universities in the United States and Europe. In 1999, he was nominated for the Nobel Peace Prize for his work in international criminal justice.

Shariah in the West

Given concerns about *hudud* punishments, women's rights, and the separation of church and state, many in the West worry Muslims will try to implement Shariah in the West. So great is this concern that, since 2010, 120 anti-Shariah bills have been introduced in forty-two states in the United States.[117] Yet no Muslim or Muslim organization has requested implementation of Shariah or Islamic law in the United States. Though there have been cases where Islamic law was mentioned in American courts, these have been related to either commercial or marriage contracts or divorce decrees issued in other countries. The question is whether

---

117. See Swathi Shanmugasundaram, "Anti-Shariah Law Bills in the United States," *Southern Poverty Law Center*, August 8, 2017, at *https://www.splcenter.org/hatewatch/2017/08/08/anti-sharia-law-bills-united-states*.

American legal institutions are bound to recognize these contracts or decrees as a matter of comity.[118]

Because no foreign law can override state or federal law and because American judges are prohibited from interpreting religious law of any kind, concerns about "Shariah creep" are essentially baseless. A judge can only consider provisions in contracts for which no interpretation of religious law is required. For example, a judge could uphold a commercial contract that specifies a beginning and end date, even if written in a Shariah court, because enforcing those dates does not require interpreting Islamic law. Questions related to the marriage gift are more complicated because marriage gifts are not part of American law. If the marriage gift is specified as a condition of an Islamic marriage contract, an American judge could find it enforceable as a condition of that contract. However, an American judge would not be permitted to determine the amount of an unspecified marriage gift or assign one where none is listed, because this would involve legal interpretation.

Finally, American judges are bound by American laws, even in cases involving foreigners. Thus, if a Muslim couple married in another country later divorces in the United States, the judge must consider child custody and division of property based on American law, not the custom of the country of origin. Though some Western countries permit religious courts to exist in parallel to secular courts, the religious courts' jurisdiction is generally limited to family law and their use is a matter of personal choice. Such religious courts have no jurisdiction in criminal matters. Decisions made in these courts cannot override state or federal laws or the US Constitution.[119]

---

118. Asifa Quraishi-Landes and Najeeba Syeed-Miller, "No Altars: A Survey of Islamic Family Law in United States," in *Women's Rights and Islamic Family Law: Perspectives on Reform*, ed. Lynn Welchman (London: Zed Books, 2004), 179–229, *https:// papers.ssrn.com/sol3/papers.cfm?abstract_id=1524246* and Ihsan Ali AlKhatib. "Shariah Law and American Family Courts: Judicial Inconsistency on the Talaq and Mahr Issues in Wayne County, Michigan," *The Journal of Law in Society*, 14 (2013): 83–105.

119. See Asifa Qureshi-Landes, "Rumors of the Sharia Threat Are Greatly Exaggerated: What American Judges Really Do with Islamic Family Law in Their Courtrooms," in *New York Law School Review* 57, no. 245 (2013): 245–57. For more information on Shariah in the West, see Esposito and DeLong-Bas, *Shariah Law*.

Review Questions

1. What is the difference between Shariah and Islamic law (*fiqh*)? Why does making that distinction matter?
2. Identify and discuss some of the values and objectives of the Shariah. How are they intended to shape Muslim lives and societies? Are they best understood as a matter of personal choice or a guide to legislation? What might be the contributions and drawbacks of each position?
3. Why are there different law schools? Does their ability to adapt and change over time and space constitute a strength or a weakness? Why?
4. Identify and discuss three concepts used to interpret Islamic law. What benefit are these concepts or tools intended to fulfill for society?
5. How has the implementation of Islamic law changed over time? What has been gained and lost in the process? Are there any aspects of historical practice that might be worth recovering?
6. What are the hudud? What purpose were they originally intended to fulfill? If the surrounding context changes, should that result in reinterpretation of these crimes and punishments? Why or why not?

Discussion Questions

1. Are the values and objectives outlined in the Shariah compatible with life in Western societies? Why or why not?
2. Is it possible to live as a faithful Muslim in a society that is not ruled by Islamic law? What if the system in place respects Shariah objectives and values without specifically identifying them with Shariah?
3. To what degree is living under Islamic law a requirement or expression of Muslim identity?

For Further Study

Reading

Afsaruddin, Asma. *Contemporary Issues in Islam*. Edinburgh: Edinburgh University Press, 2015.

Bassiouini, M. Cherif. *The Shari'a and Islamic Criminal Justice in Time of War and Peace.* New York: Cambridge University Press, 2013.

Esposito, John L., and Natana J. DeLong-Bas. *Shariah: What Everyone Needs to Know.* New York: Oxford University Press, 2018.

Esposito, John L., with Natana J. DeLong-Bas. *Women in Muslim Family Law,* Revised. Syracuse: Syracuse University Press, 2001.

Hallaq, Wael. *An Introduction to Islamic Law.* New York: Cambridge University Press, 2009.

Hallaq, Wael. *Shari'a: Theory, Practice, Transformations.* Cambridge, UK: Cambridge University Press, 2009.

Peters, Rudolph. *Crime and Punishment in Islamic Law: Theory and Practice from the Sixteenth to the Twenty-First Century.* New York: Cambridge University Press, 2005.

Sonbol, Amira El Azhary, ed. *Women, the Family, and Divorce Laws in Islamic History.* Syracuse: Syracuse University Press, 1996.

Films

Jawad, Mohammad, et al. *Saving Face.* [New York]: HBO Documentary Films, 2013.

Documentary following a group of Pakistani women who were victims of acid attacks in their fight for justice.

Links

DIFI: Research to Advance Family Policies, *www.difi.org.qa*—The Doha International Family Institute in Qatar studies the impact of modernity and urbanization on families.

An Open Letter to Al-Baghdadi: Join Hundreds of Muslim Leaders and Scholars Worldwide in Their Open Letter to Baghdadi, *www.lettertobaghdadi.com*—An letter to Al-Baghdadi critiquing his approach to the interpretation of Islam and Islamic law.

Pew Research Center: The World's Muslims—Religion, Politics and Society, *www.pewforum.org/2013/04/30/the-worlds-muslims -religion-politics-society-beliefs-about-sharia/*—Pew Research Center Poll on Muslim perceptions on a variety of topics, including Shariah (April 30, 2013), as well as American perceptions of Muslims and American Muslim opinions.

CHAPTER

Sufis

Saints and Subversives in the Quest for the Divine

Described as Islam's mystical tradition or "the art of knocking on the door of the Divine," Sufism represents the individual spiritual quest to follow and know God, which requires discipline of mind and body. The emphasis on individual experience, ritual devotion, love of God, and openness to finding meaning in ritual practices, customs, and even faiths outside of Islam has often placed it in disagreement and even conflict with more orthodox understandings of Islam, particularly those more dedicated to the law. Frequently spread by traveling merchants and personal connection, Sufism has been and remains, in many places, the most popular mass expression of Islam.

Rise and Historical Development

Historically, Sufism has been described as a subversive movement that actively encouraged people to break free from traditional hierarchies and authorities in favor of finding individual meaning and spirituality in a personal connection to God.[1] It began as a reactionary response during the Umayyad Empire (661–750).

---

1. Jonathan Berkey insists on the subversive nature of Sufism, as well as its inherent historical connection to Shiism, in *The Formation of Islam: Religion and Society in the Near East, 600–1800* (New York: Cambridge University Press, 2003). Being outside of the formal structures of power became a key distinction between Sufism and Islamic law. Islamic law was strongly connected to the ruling elites and their power structures. Sufism maintained at least the appearance of independence. Yet some rulers, such as many of the Ottoman Sultans, were members of particular Sufi orders, including, most

Although Muhammad and the early Muslim community adopted modest lifestyles and emphasized redistributing wealth to the less fortunate rather than building their own personal fortunes,[2] this focus rapidly changed as Islam transitioned from the religion of the marginalized to the religion of an empire. The Umayyad caliphs assumed the trappings of court life and civilization—the pursuit of wealth, luxury, power, conquest, and often questionable morals. Rising attention to power, prestige, and other earthly pleasures led many to set aside focus on spirituality and the Afterlife, although they retained some aspects of ritual correctness, such as prayer and fasting. Growing perceptions of a disconnect between values and actions set the stage for critique and a "return" to the simpler lifestyle of Muhammad and the early community, as some sought a closer relationship with God.

Though scholars differ on the dates for various trends in Sufism,[3] they agree these trends included individual spiritual devotion and asceticism, borrowing and reinterpretation from other religions and cultures, institutionalization and mass experience of mysticism, and the centrality of charismatic individuals. Overall, Sufism was—and remains—characterized by the individual desire to express devotion to God and achieve spiritual progress. Mechanisms for doing so have varied across time and space.

At the outset, Sufism remained independent of institutional structures. Rather than aiming to escape the world, Sufis aim

---

prominently, the Mevlevis, whether owing to personal spiritual interest or political expediency. Other orders, such as the Bektashis, were associated with the Janissaries (slave military corps) and often critiqued the Ottoman rulers to the point that they, along with the Janissaries, were banned by Sultan Mahmud II in 1826.

2. Muhammad reportedly gave away so much of what he owned his immediate family members often struggled to find sufficient means to survive.

3. J. S. Trimingham identifies four time periods: 700–950 CE as the era of individual asceticism and spirituality; 950–1100 as the accommodationist and eclectic era; 1100–1300 as the era focusing on chains of transmission; and 1300–1700 as the era of institutionalization. See J. S. Trimingham, *The Sufi Orders in Islam*, with a foreword by John O. Voll (New York: Oxford University Press, 1998). Others, such as Berkey, argue institutionalization of the individual mystical experience occurred initially in the Middle Period of the ninth and tenth centuries; see Berkey, *The Formation of Islam*. Still others combine a world historical perspective with a regional focus, analyzing trends and developments specific to particular locations. See Ira Lapidus's magisterial *A History of Islamic Societies*, 3rd ed. (New York: Cambridge University Press, 2014).

to actively participate in it in an ethical way, shunning distractions and renouncing excessive material pleasures. Sufis advocate prayer, fasting, meditation, and following Muhammad's example. Though some level of self-denial, including poverty as indifference to wealth, is encouraged, extremes such as solitude and celibacy are not. Sufis remain connected to the world and its social responsibilities.

The earliest Sufis emphasized individual inner spirituality and asceticism. Rather than rules, regulations, or institutions, which were associated with expanding legal and political systems, Sufism focused on individual attainment of mystical states and spiritual stations on the path (*tariqah*) to God, including "annihilation" or abandonment of the self in God. Constant remembrance of God (*dhikr*) sometimes led to "ecstasy" or "drunkenness." Some early Sufis became so enthusiastic in their pursuit of God they claimed to have achieved union with God.[4] Others became known for weeping—for their sins, the sins of the world, and the torments awaiting those who fail to respond to God's call. Weeping as a devotional exercise became a common trait of Sufis and was frequently mentioned in hagiographical literature.[5]

Central to the debate between Sufis and those with a legalistic or scholarly approach to God is the question of whether God is and must remain utterly unique and separate from human beings or whether God desires a close and strong personal relationship with each believer who then becomes a "friend" (*wali*) of God. Early Sufis did not see an inherent conflict between Sufism and the law. They pursued their individual approaches to devotion to God and the quest for truth within the parameters of both their *tariqah* and Shariah.[6]

---

4. The Persian mystic Mansur al-Hallaj (d. 922) ecstatically proclaimed, "I am the Truth" (one of God's attributes), and was executed for heresy, as some thought he was claiming to be God. He did not, of course, claim this; he was just trying to express his experience of God.

5. See excerpts from various Sufi writers in Jane Dammen McAuliffe, ed., *The Norton Anthology of World Religious: Islam* (New York: Norton, 2015), esp. 382–457. Weeping as a sign of piety is not unique to Islam. It is present in other religious traditions, including Christianity.

6. During the Middle Period, identifying as both a jurist and a Sufi was the norm.

Muhammad's Night Journey

Sufis root their mystical experience in Muhammad's miraculous Night Journey (miraj) from Mecca to Jerusalem and then up to heaven. As he traveled through the seven layers of heaven, he met prophets from the past and ultimately entered into the presence of God. This story, recorded in the hadith collection of al-Bukhari, is a favorite among Sufis, philosophers, and poets alike. The presence of Old and New Testament characters in the story connects Muhammad with Judaism and Christianity. The story also marks Muhammad as not only belonging to the line of prophets beginning with Adam (the first human being) but also as the last prophet—at the pinnacle of that heritage. This solidifies the place of Islam as the first and the last monotheistic faith, as well as the closest to God.

The Metropolitan Museum of Art, New York, Purchase, Louis V. Bell Fund and The Vincent Astor Foundation Gift, 1974

This sixteenth-century manuscript from Afghanistan or Uzbekistan, illustrated in ink, gold, and colors on paper, depicts Muhammad riding Buraq on his Night Journey (Miraj). The flaming halo identifies Muhammad as a Prophet.

The Abbasid Empire (750–1258) marked the "Golden Age" of Islamic civilization, with major achievements in commerce, art, architecture, literature, learning, and the development of Islamic law and Sufism. As the empire rapidly spread and expanded its trade relations into Europe and South and Southeast Asia, some legal and religious scholars expressed concern over what they saw as a growing—and alarming—tendency within Islam toward accommodation, eclecticism, and syncretism, as new cultures and other religions were encountered, particularly at the level of the common people.

The growing popularity of mysticism became apparent with the rise of the first mystical groups (*taifa*) and orders (*tariqahs*). Initially, these groups and orders may have been seen as personality cults, as they were centered on the personal authority and perceptions of blessing (*barakah*) residing in the *shaykh*,[7] who was sometimes referred to as a "saint."[8] Although part of that *barakah* was believed always to remain with the *shaykh*, even in death, it could also be passed on to others, women and men, either by family connection or mystical spiritual connection. The purpose of becoming close to the *shaykh* was thus not only to become close to God but also to access *barakah*.

Because they retained *barakah* even in death, renowned *shaykhs* were buried in shrines that became centers of popular pilgrimage (*ziyarah*)[9] and celebrations.[10] Certain shrines and tombs became known for particular types of assistance, such as finding a spouse, curing disease, or getting pregnant. The popularity of these pilgrimages made control over the shrines an important source of revenue for the order connected to them. Ultimately, popular expressions of Sufism became a major commercial venture with money to be made and spent on the way to, from, and at the shrine. Tombs and shrines also served as important locations for social interaction, particularly for women.

During the Abbasid era, women were often discouraged from attending the mosque and, in many places, were segregated from

---

7. *Shaykhs* were also known as *pirs* or *murshids*.

8. Though often such "saints" were respected and venerated by the masses, they are not an exact parallel to saints in the Christian tradition. Like Christian saints, Sufi saints are believed to serve as mediators and intercessors with God on behalf of human beings and often have miracles attributed to them; they also reflect belief in a hierarchy of believers in which a special individual can help a person become closer to God. That hierarchy is based on individual "god-consciousness" (*taqwa*), which the Qur'an teaches is the only distinction God recognizes between human beings. Sufi saints differ from Christian saints in that Sufi saints were generally countercultural and antiestablishment during their lives, rather than being part of the religious establishment. In some cases, Sufi saints rejected book learning and attention to scripture in favor of focusing on individual experience of the Divine, however achieved. In addition, they were believed to possess *barakah* due to their special position as a "friend of God"(*wali* or *vali*).

9. This term is also used by Shia for pilgrimage to Karbala and other Shia holy sites and shrines.

10. One of the most important historical sources of information about these shrines and tombs was written by the great traveler, Ibn Battuta—often described as the Muslim Marco Polo, even though Ibn Battuta's travels were more extensive. For an account of Ibn Battuta's travels, see Ross E. Dunn, *The Adventures of Ibn Battuta: A Muslim Traveler of the Fourteenth Century*, rev. ed. (Berkeley: University of California Press, 2012).

men and had few "legitimate" reasons for accessing public space or leaving the house. Visiting shrines and tombs became an important way for women to participate in public religious life and to feel a personal connection to God and Islam, whether by petitioning for specific requests or giving thanks for answered prayers. Such visits also became an important way to connect and socialize with other women, thereby making these visits a source of concern for those more orthodox interpreters seeking to control women's movements, interactions, and religious experiences.

Sufism's accessibility to the masses and opportunities for popular celebrations, practices, and sense of community and belonging led to concerns that it might detract from more orthodox rituals of prayer, fasting, almsgiving, and Hajj. A pending crisis was resolved by the work of a pivotal scholar of the period, Muhammad al-Ghazali (d. 1111). He wrote a masterful synthesis of Sufism and orthodox theology, bridging the disciplines of mysticism and the law. He showed each as a meaningful structure for the world it addressed— the law for life in this world and mystical divine service in pursuit of spiritual truth as preparation for the next.[11]

Another moment of crisis for Sufism and the law arose with the Mongol invasions in the thirteenth century, which brought a forcible end to the Abbasid Empire and, with it, the idealized image of the Muslim community (*ummah*) united under a single ruler. There had always been other contenders for power, whether Shia Imams or rival caliphs. But the end of the Abbasid Caliphate led to a leadership vacuum in both political and religious spheres that brought legal scholars, on the one hand, and Sufi masters, on the other, into competition for influence over the masses and institutionalization of religious thought and practice. Some responded with calls for greater orthodoxy and rejection of mysticism. Others became even more mystically inclined, adding elements of eschatology (end-of-the-world scenarios) and veneration of Muhammad's lineage, traced through his cousin and son-in-law, Ali.[12]

---

11. See R. J. McCarthy, SJ, trans., *Al-Ghazali's Path to Sufism and His Deliverance from Error, an Annotated Translation of al-Munqidh min al-Dalal*, with preface by David Durrell, CSC (Louisville: Fons Vitae, 2000).

12. Some scholars, such as Berkey, therefore assert a strong connection between Sufism and Shiism.

Rather than the earlier claim to *barakah*, many *shaykhs* tried to bolster their legitimacy and authority by claiming to be part of an unbroken chain leading back to Muhammad. Like earlier caliphs and Shia Imams who had claimed ties to Muhammad or the Rightly Guided Caliphs, Sufi *shaykhs* presented themselves as alternatives and rivals for religious and political leadership and power. Those seeking personal connection back to Muhammad could obtain it by binding themselves to a *shaykh* who claimed to be part of an unbroken chain connecting followers to secret knowledge passed down by Muhammad and available only to a spiritual elite, namely, the followers of that *shaykh*.

Ibn al-Arabi (d. 1240)

References to Muhammad proliferated in specific rituals and devotional practices, particularly through the influence of Ibn al-Arabi (d. 1240), an Andalusian[13] mystic and legal scholar. Al-Arabi made Muhammad central to understandings of reality (*haqiqa Muhammadiyyah*), light (*nur Muhammadi*),[14] and the concept of the perfect being who reflects God and responds to God's longing to be known to humanity. He was also responsible for the doctrine of unity of being (*wahdat al-wujud*), which asserts that God and God's creation, including human beings, are inseparable. God's creation cannot exist without God, and God's creation is necessary for reflecting God's perfect attributes. The natural world and the cosmos mirror God's creative abilities, order, and beauty. Thus, for Ibn al-Arabi, God and God's creation must exist together.[15] Ibn al-Arabi was considered a heretic by those who believed that God and God's creation are completely separate entities.

---

13. Al-Andalus refers to Spain under Muslim rule (711–1492).

14. This is the belief that light was the preexistent form of Muhammad. Shia further believe that the Imams and Muhammad's daughter and Ali's wife, Fatima, are included in this light, placing Muhammad in Paradise with God prior to Creation. See Mary F. Thurlkill, *Chosen among Women: Mary and Fatima in Medieval Christianity and Shi'ite Islam* (Notre Dame, IN: University of Notre Dame Press, 2007).

15. See William C. Chittick, *The Self-Disclosure of God: Principles of Ibn al-'Arabi's Cosmology* (Albany, NY: State University of New York, 1998).

By the thirteenth century, Sufism was the most popular expression of Muslim belief and identity and had spread throughout North Africa, the Middle East, and South and Southeast Asia among elites and commoners alike. Sufism was characterized by the sheer diversity of its adherents and their experiences. In contrast to the more formally trained legal and religious scholars, who were overwhelmingly male and had come to form a class of their own, Sufis included women and men from a variety of educational backgrounds and social classes. Some orders (*tariqahs*) became associated with specific professional groups and guilds; others were known for distinctive rituals.

Though many orders welcomed women and men, some were more male-oriented, having grown out of the tradition of urban fraternities (*futuwwa*). In others, women not only participated but also rose to positions of leadership.[16] Sufi poetry often praised the positive attributes and imagery of women, such as the loving and tender relationship between mother and child—even using this relationship as a metaphor for the kind of relationship that should exist between the *shaykh* and his followers. Yet Sufism also sometimes portrayed women as "deficient men," so that part of following the path of God for female adherents meant setting aside their femininity in favor of "becoming male."[17]

Organization and Institutions

Originally a social movement, Sufism developed into an array of social institutions that wielded local, regional, and international influence and economic power. Sufi lodges or compounds (*zayiwahs*

---

16. See Camille Adams Helminski, *Women of Sufism: A Hidden Treasure, Writings and Stories of Mystic Poets, Scholars and Saints* (Boston: Shambhala Publications, 2003), and Julia Clancy-Smith, *Rebel and Saint: Muslim Notables, Populist Protest, Colonial Encounters (Algeria and Tunisia, 1800–1904)* (Berkeley: University of California Press, 1997).

17. This is not unique to Sufism. Similar trends can be found in Christianity, including in the apocryphal Gospel of Philip, which describes Mary Magdalene "becoming male" in her pursuit of discipleship. It can be difficult for women to escape patriarchal tendencies in religion when the male is considered a more accurate and genuine reflection of the Divine and the female is thus expected to play a secondary, supportive role.

or *ribat*) began to serve as social and cultural community centers, particularly when they included space not only for worship and education but also for accommodations for full-time adherents, students, and pilgrims, as well as for soup kitchens and hospitals. Institutionalization of a given order tended to coincide with a more "mass produced" experience wherein collective participation in devotional exercises (*dhikr*) came to replace individual spiritual exercises, meditation, or pursuit of the Divine. Although some have criticized such "routinization" of spiritual activities as detracting from individual seeking of the Divine, mass experiences helped guarantee the survival of the tradition by bringing it under some form of control and standardization.[18]

Centralizing the order and tying it to specific locations enhanced the power of a *shaykh*. This was reflected in a shift in emphasis from obedience to God to obedience to a *shaykh* and his spiritual supervision. More complex hierarchies also began to appear within some orders. A *shaykh* determined his successors and heads of various satellite lodges, including the person who would lead the order upon his death. In general, although a *shaykh* could be elected or could simply decide to pass on his blessing (*barakah*) to whomever he wished, the successor was typically his son or relative. This kept an order's lineage both spiritual and genealogical. From a practical standpoint, it also meant one family maintained control over an order and its assets.

Lodges typically included charitable endowments (*waqf*) designed to provide ongoing financial support independent of the government. The relative independence and self-sufficiency of orders and their lodges led to growing authoritarianism among some *shaykhs* while also permitting orders to continue their history of subversion against established political powers.[19] There are also

---

18. This challenge arises in many religious traditions. For example, the Roman Catholic Church has also tried to find balance between producing mass ritual experiences and encouraging individual spiritual practices and disciplines.

19. Parallels between Sufi lodges and Christian monasteries include engagement in worship, spiritual discipline, and caring for poor and needy people. Important differences include that, unlike Christian monks and nuns, most Sufis were married and had families. There is no tradition of celibacy in Islam. Also, unlike the monastic tradition in Christianity, there is no practice of complete withdrawal from the world in

historical instances of political regimes co-opting Sufi practices or claiming connection to a given order's spiritual lineage to bolster their legitimacy.[20]

The combination of subversion, financial independence, and self-sufficiency came to a head in the struggles for independence from European colonial rule in the nineteenth and twentieth centuries, particularly in North Africa.[21] Sufi lodges were financially independent from ruling powers and had an infrastructure that allowed them to hide and move people and materials. Furthermore, Sufi *shaykhs* were acclaimed by the masses and thus able to step into political and religious vacuums left by overtaken or co-opted regimes or colonial administrations. Many jihad movements against European overlords were led by Sufi *shaykhs*,[22] challenging the popular, but misleading, modern

---

Sufism, although it may be done for a short time as a matter of spiritual refocusing and purification of the heart and mind. It is not intended to be a way of life. Sufis must return to the world to engage and transform it. Because Islam is a deliberately community-oriented faith, engagement and fellowship with other people is central to faithful life and practice. Last, there is no history of mortification of the flesh in Sufism such as existed historically in certain Christian denominations, including among Roman Catholics, Lutherans, and Methodists. Although some early Sufis are believed to have worn coarse wool (*suf*) clothing, the purpose was to set aside luxury in favor of focusing on God. Overall, Sufis have tended to focus on spiritual disciplines such as fasting, control of the body and thoughts, breathing techniques, repeating the names and attributes of God, and silence. There are, of course, Christian parallels to these practices, such as the silence practiced by the Benedictine Order, the Spiritual Exercises of silence and solitude for contemplation and discernment of the Jesuits, the fasting of the Franciscans, or the singing of a few words repeatedly as a meditative approach to prayer used by the monks of Taize today.

20. The Mughal Emperor Akbar (d. 1605) is one example of a ruler who was initially orthodox in his thinking but was influenced by Sufism and came to embrace tolerance. He founded the Ibadat Khana, or "House of Worship," to which he invited theologians from different religions, as well as mystics and courtiers known for their spirituality, to seek common ethical and spiritual ground. See Ruby Lal, *Domesticity and Power in the Early Mughal World* (New York: Cambridge University Press, 2005).

21. European colonial administrative records document many frustrations over resistance rooted in Sufi orders.

22. In one of the most famous examples, the Algerian Emir Abd al-Qadir (son of the head of the Qadiriyya Order) led a seventeen-year-long struggle against French colonial rule before he was finally captured. See Clancy-Smith, *Rebel and Saint*. Another famous example was the resistance against Italian colonial rule in Libya led by Sayyid Ahmad al-Sharif al-Sanusi, head of the Sanusiyya Order.

view of Muslims as one of two varieties: peaceful Sufis or violent Wahhabi-Salafi-jihadists.[23]

On Being a Sufi

Just as some Muslims are drawn to legal studies and affiliation with a particular law school (*madhhab*), so others seek connection to a Sufi order (*tariqah*).[24] Membership in an order provides a person with a built-in network of like-minded individuals beyond their neighborhood. Belonging to an order can, for example, facilitate relocation owing to work or to finding a better quality of life. Being admitted to an order also places a member in a chain of spiritual authority that connects the individual back to Muhammad or the order's founder. This offers not only an expanded spiritual genealogy but also a sense of belonging to a history greater than oneself.

Personal connection to a *shaykh* is central to seeking membership. Joining an order begins with meeting a *shaykh* to declare interest in participating in the order's spiritual life and practices. The next step is a training period in which devotional activities are introduced and the would-be member attends the *shaykh's* teaching sessions. When the *shaykh* recognizes a sufficient degree of spiritual progress in the trainee, the *shaykh* initiates the trainee, connecting the new member to the order's lineage. In many cases, the initiation is marked

---

23. This binary is presented in many popular twentieth- and twenty-first-century Western texts on Muslims that sacrifice history and detail for the sake of a clear but oversimplified argument. This binary is a product of debates and conflict dating to the early nineteenth century between the Wahhabis as doctrinal purists and Sufis and Shia, whom the Wahhabis accused of bringing superstitious and non-Islamic beliefs and practices into the Islamic tradition. Points of conflict included not only saint veneration and popular pilgrimages, which the Wahhabis said directed worship to people, rather than to God, but also the use of religious icons. See Natana J. DeLong-Bas, *Wahhabi Islam: From Revival and Reform to Global Jihad*, rev. ed. (New York: Oxford University Press, 2008), esp. 41–92.

24. In the early centuries, just as students went to learn from different religious and legal scholars, so it was possible to belong to multiple Sufi orders simultaneously—the more ways of accessing the Divine, the better. However, as *shaykhs* claimed greater levels of authority and obedience, exclusivity entered the picture and adherence to one order became the norm.

with a ceremony that includes being invested with the distinctive clothing of the order, such as a cloak.[25] Acceptance of the clothing symbolizes the embrace of material poverty and spiritual riches, a pledge of obedience to the *shaykh*, and receiving the *shaykh*'s blessing. The initiation thus marks the beginning of a more formalized and permanent relationship with the order; ongoing spiritual progress and participation in spiritual activities, particularly the order's devotional rituals (*dhikr*), are expected.

There are generally two types of membership in an order: full-time, which means living in a compound,[26] and associate or affiliate (layperson), which provides members with access to the compound and places them under a *shaykh*'s authority, yet permits them to live and work in the outside world. Like full members, associate or affiliate members receive a special cloak symbolizing their association, although it usually differs from the garment given to full members. Associate and affiliate members are crucial to the financial survival of Sufi orders and their provision of community and social services.

Different orders have different devotional rituals (*dhikr*) focused on remembrance of God. These rituals range from chanting religious phrases or the names of God to recitations, ritual devotions, special prayers, music, dancing, and poetry. Some orders worship by performing complex rituals with music or dance known as *sama'*, or spiritual "hearing" or "concert," in order to achieve spiritual "ecstasy." The Chishti order fuses Persian, Arabic, Turkish, and Indian musical traditions into a devotional form of singing called *qawwali*, which today is particularly popular in India and Pakistan. Other orders, such as the Naqshbandis, seek spiritual communion through meditation, repetition of short phrases, concentration on breathing, and mindfulness. Still other orders seek a balance between doctrine and spiritual practice. For example, the Shadhiliyya order focuses

---

25. This ritual is traced back to Ali, Muhammad's cousin and son-in-law. The Sufi master puts the cloak on the person being initiated, signifying their "taking of the path" of the order and marking their completion of spiritual training.

26. The global spread of Sufism has broadened the definitions of what constitutes a "lodge." Though it may be a sprawling complex of buildings, as is often the case for lodges founded long ago, today it may also be as simple as a house or an apartment building.

on public worship, preaching, and pious exhortation; members are also expected to lead socially normal and economically productive lives. They do not engage in ecstatic expressions of poetry or musical production. Culturally oriented approaches to *dhikr* have become particularly popular in Iran, the Indian subcontinent, and Anatolia (modern Turkey).

Perhaps most famous of all is the order associated with Jalal al-Din Rumi—the Mevlevis. Commonly known as the "Whirling Dervishes," the Mevlevi order combines elevation of the soul through poetry with elevation of the spirit through music and freedom from the constraints of the body facilitated by the practice of "whirling" or "turning" as a reflection of the self-emptying necessary to be filled with sweet closeness to the Divine. The "whirlers" move not only individually but also around each other, mirroring the movements of Divine Love in the heavenly spheres and the planets around the sun. The "whirlers" place their rights hands palm-up toward the sky and left hands palm-down toward the ground, receiving and channeling Divine blessing, love, and knowledge from heaven down to the earth.

"Whirlers" of the Mevlevi Order engaged in *dhikr* in an old caravanserai in Nevsehir, Turkey. A celebration of divine love through music and poetry, the spinning of the whirlers reflects the loss of self, mind, and body, to the demands of this world and release to the Divine.

Jalal al-Din Rumi (1207–1273)

Jalal al-Din Rumi has been described as a mystic, poet, teacher, preacher, humanist, visionary, and even saint by people of many different faith traditions. Born in a small town west of Mazar-i-Sharif in what is today Afghanistan, Rumi spent much of his life as a displaced person, living in Samarqand, Tajikistan, Syria, and, ultimately, Turkey. Rumi is the quintessential example of multicultural inclusivity and religious pluralism, counting Muslims, Christians, Jews, Hindus, and Buddhists among his followers who come from all socioeconomic classes. He was fluent in Arabic, Persian, and colloquial Turkish.

Trained as a legal scholar, Rumi grew disenchanted with his studies and turned to mysticism, particularly through music and poetry, seeing them as languages of the heart that allow for intoxication and ecstasy in the Divine. Rumi believed each person needed to find their way to God through lived experience, not just intellectual knowledge. Central to this experience is recognizing the Divine in each person, so that human beings respond to each other not just with tolerance but with full acceptance, embracing and welcoming one another into one's life. By embracing each other, one embraces the Divine in each person. As Rumi said, "The religion of Love is different from all religions—For lovers, religion and denomination is God alone."

Rumi's poetry, which consists of more than sixty-five thousand verses, talks about the devastation of separation from the beloved and the longing the lover experiences for the beloved as a metaphor for the human longing for God, from whom individuals are separated. People long for God because God gives people unconditional and never-ending love, no matter how unworthy people prove themselves, how many mistakes they make, or how many times they reject the love offered to them.

Today, Rumi is the best-selling poet in the United States and has inspired musicians ranging from Richard Strauss and Franz Schubert to the Paul Winter Consort and Phillip Glass. Self-help writers such as Steven Covey and Deepak Chopra draw upon his work. Even entertainment personalities read his poetry, including Goldie Hawn, Demi Moore, and Madonna. His influence ranges from fairy tales (Hans Christian Anderson) to philosophy (George Hegel) to fashion (Donna Karan). Because his message is universal enough to speak to the global human experience, Rumi is a complex mix of pop-culture icon, object of mass consumption, and interfaith phenomenon. His shrine in Konya, Turkey, remains a major site of pilgrimage for people from many religious and cultural backgrounds.

Theological Teachings

Two broad theological trends exist in Sufism. One takes an intellectual and holistic approach to life and spirituality, and considers Sufism a religious and ethical discipline. Based on adherence to the teachings of the Qur'an, hadith, and Islamic law, it embraces spiritual practices designed to cultivate outward conformity with Muslim norms and inner insight into spiritual realities. A more formalized approach, it recognizes authority and holiness as rooted in religious knowledge, ethical discipline, and spiritual insight. The other trend is more popular than intellectual and is based on veneration of saints and holy persons, particularly those believed to possess *barakah*. Holy persons serve as spiritual teachers, mediators between humanity and God, and, in some cases, miracle workers. This trend relies on the relationship to a *shaykh* as an avenue to *barakah*, rather than personal cultivation of particular knowledge or qualities. Although both theologies promise personal and direct experience of God, they offer different paths to achieving it. The former is more elitist, intellectual, and a matter of personal discipline; the latter is tied closely to key personalities and is more widespread and popular.

> "I looked for God. I went to a temple and I didn't find Him there. Then I went to a church and I didn't find Him there. Then I went to a mosque and I didn't find Him there. Then finally I looked in my own heart—and there He was." —Rumi

Sufis believe academic study alone cannot bring true understanding of God. Such insight can only come from spiritual struggle and is considered a gift bestowed by God on those who work toward insight and mastery of spiritual disciplines. Sufis cite a hadith in which the angel Gabriel talks about the importance of faith—belief in God, outward submission to God as shown through performance of rituals and good deeds, and pursuit of perfection. Perfection means living with a constant awareness of God, worshipping God as if God could be seen, because, even if one cannot see God, God sees all.[27]

---

27. The three hadith addressed in this segment—of Gabriel, the Treasure, and Reason—are discussed in Jonathan A. C. Brown, *Hadith: Muhammad's Legacy in the Medieval and Modern World* (Oxford: Oneworld, 2009).

Some Sufis also look to two hadith cited by Ibn al-Arabi—the Hadith of the Hidden Treasure and the Hadith of Reason—that were not spoken by Muhammad, but which Ibn al-Arabi claimed had been "unveiled" to him through experience. In the Hadith of the Hidden Treasure, God says, "I was a hidden treasure, and I wanted to be known. So I created the cosmos so that I might be known." Ibn al-Arabi interpreted this to mean God is the ultimate purpose of creation and creation exists because God wanted creation to know and reflect God. There is a sense of God longing for creation in much the same way human beings long for connection to their Creator. This sense of separation, emotional longing, desire, and seeking intimacy with the Divine are central to the Sufi tradition. Rumi captured that sentiment in his poetic statement, "Every person who has long remained far from his source, longingly seeks the day of his reunion."[28]

The Hadith of Reason teaches that God is the Creator of reason and that God considers reason the pinnacle of God's creation. This places reason in a subordinate position to God, as a created entity. Yet reason proves critical to grasping divine truth. Without reason, one cannot fully know God, and yet reason can only exist where God chooses to create it. Ibn al-Arabi taught that knowledge comes in three forms: prophetic revelation as direct communication from God; inspiration from God, which he referred to as "unveiling" or "tasting," meaning it is indirectly communicated by God and must be sensed or perceived by the human being; and rational investigation, or the use of human experience and reason to know God. Some more orthodox Sunnis considered this hadith problematic because of its insistence that human reason possesses some degree of authority, potentially detracting from God. However, Sufis maintain reason takes nothing away from God, given that reason must always obey God and prophecy.

Ultimately, the Sufi's goal is "annihilation" in God—a symbolic death before physical death. Dying to oneself and the needs and demands of this limited, transient, created world frees one to fully know and experience the limitless Divine. The Sufi's greatest

---

28. Longing is also captured in the haunting sound of the reed flute, the *ney*, used in Sufi music, calling out to the base from which it was cut. Without separation, the flute cannot produce music, yet the music is filled with longing for reunion with its source. Master musician Amir Vehab's website, *tanbour.org*, provides audio clips of various instruments used in Persian, Turkish, and Azeri classical music, including the *ney*.

accomplishment is penetrating the veil of this world to reveal God's beauty, present in every aspect of the world—seeing beyond the material, tangible, and finite signs of this world to the spiritual, eternal, and infinite Divine attributes hidden within these signs. Becoming "dissolved" in God allows the human being to fully connect to the source of all existence, reuniting Creator and created.

The greatest theological theme of Sufism is love of God, expressed joyously, with anticipation and complete loss of self in the Divine. Rather than seeing fear or the quest for justice as motivating factors in the human relationship with the Divine, the Sufi places love at the center. This takes power out of the equation, leaving room for a selfless devotion to the Divine that seeks neither reward nor punishment, only the Divine presence. The earliest Sufi to introduce this concept of selfless love into practice was Rabia al-Adawiyya. In her most famous prayer, she asked, "O Lord, if I worship You out of fear of Hell, then burn me in Hell; if I worship You in hope of Paradise, then exclude me from Paradise; but if I worship You for Your own sake, do not deny me Your beauty."

Rabia's life and teachings reflect four stages guiding Sufis on the path (*tariqah*) to the Divine.[29] The first stage is repentance, defined as remorse for disobedience, determination not to sin again, and immediate abandonment of sin. Rabia viewed sin as a problem, not because it is "evil" or leads to punishment in the Afterlife, but because it causes separation between the believer and God. Repentance, therefore, is a gift, because it provides a way to remove that barrier between the believer and God, restoring that relationship to balance and harmony.

The second stage is patience, which helps a person hold out for greater reward amid adversity. Rabia taught patience through personal example, highlighting where God provided care and sustenance. She also taught that gratitude complemented patience and should be expressed for blessings and chastisements alike because both reflect God's attention to the believer. Rather than focusing on the gift as the outcome, Rabia focused on the Giver, considering constant thanksgiving for God's goodness, regardless of one's life circumstances, as the truest expression of gratitude.

---

29. For a detailed study of Rabia's life and influence, see Margaret Smith, *Rabi'a the Mystic and Her Fellow-Saints in Islam* (New York: Cambridge University Press, 2010).

Rabia al-Adawiyyah, or Rabia the Mystic (c. 717–801)

One of Sufism's most visible female teachers, Rabia al-Adawiyya is widely credited with introducing the selfless love of God into Sufism. Born in poverty in Basra, Iraq, Rabia was soon orphaned in a famine and sold into slavery. Despite her challenging circumstances, Rabia prayed faithfully, asking only to serve God. Legend says her master awoke in the middle of the night to find her praying and surrounded by light. He freed her the next morning.

Rabia's life story brings together many major themes in Sufism: relying solely on God for her provisions and living simply; resisting physical needs such as sleep or illness as distractions from God; viewing sin and hell negatively because of the separation from God both represent; considering death a moment of joy because it marks the moment of eternal joining with God; emphasizing devotional discipline through a lifetime of prayer—reportedly a thousand prostrations every day and night; and seeking closeness to God. Yet her example also contains unique or unusual features, such as celibacy; she feared being a wife and mother would distract her from her singular devotion to God. She also gave little attention to study of the Qur'an and hadith, believing individual experience and a direct relationship with God requires no intermediary, whether human or textual. Her definition of prayer did not include making supplications but served instead to engage in loving conversation and communion with God.

As the greatest of Islam's women mystics and the woman who made the most significant contributions to Sufism, Rabia is held in high esteem and is considered an authoritative teacher of Sufism along with the great male Sufis. Her high status is reflected in the prominence of the writers who mention her. For many Sufis, Rabia was a "second spotless Mary," who exemplified the mystical tradition of Islam. Rabia died in 801 and was buried in Basra.

Rabia identified the third stage as poverty, which she defined as complete self-loss and lack of dependence on material things. Because she considered Paradise a state of contemplation of the Face of God rather than a physical garden of sensual delights, she believed living a life of poverty on earth was preparation for the eternal activity of pure contemplation and adoration of God, undistracted by material or physical needs or desires.

The fourth and final stage is love. Rabia expressed a joyous love, seeing God's beauty and experiencing the satisfaction, longing, and fellowship that result from the mystical union of the believer and God. Thus death, rather than a moment to be feared, was to be embraced, reuniting the lover and the beloved.

Theological Critiques

Sufism has been widely credited with rapid missionary work over a broad geographic range, often through trade. Because it is devotionally and spiritually oriented, rather than focused on orthodoxy, Sufism spread more rapidly than did the Islamic Empire. Sufism's receptivity to and frequent adoption and adaptation of local customs and practices often placed it in conflict with more conservative interpretations of Islam or Islamic law even as it made Islam more palatable to new audiences. Sufism's use of local religious rituals and traditions in its devotional programs resulted in popular perceptions of this "new" religion as culturally appropriate and acceptable to converts, allowing them to maintain a sense of continuity with their past religious traditions.[30] Yet Sufism's openness and acceptance often resulted in harsh critiques and opposition, particularly from religious scholars and jurists, on doctrinal grounds.

One of the most consistent theological critiques of Sufism concerned its possible roots in and cross-pollination with non-Islamic religious traditions, particularly Christianity. Given that mystics from many religions engage in similar devotional activities designed to discipline body and mind, such borrowing and inspiration are neither surprising nor unique.[31] The very name *Sufi*, for example, may be rooted in the rough wool (*suf*) cloaks worn by some early Sufis that were also commonly worn by certain Christian monks

---

30. In this manner, the spread of Sufism is comparable to the spread of early Christianity, particularly in the Roman Catholic tradition, where saint veneration was adopted from local religious practices, emphasizing the ability of certain beings to intervene in individual human lives in God's stead or to serve as intermediaries between the individual believer and God.

31. Parallels include practices such as devotions, prayers, fasting, silence, and meditation.

of the time, symbolizing a setting aside of worldly wealth in favor of spiritual treasures. Early Sufi narratives record Muslim mystics encountering and learning from Christian hermits and ascetics. They also adopted the Christian and Jewish practice of locating spiritual power in specific persons—"friends of God"—who then became objects for veneration, imitation, or intercession. Elements of other traditions are also apparent in certain teachings, such as the annihilation of the self, which was particularly popular among Persian mystics.

Such critiques raise questions about the importance of the origins of various practices. Should the focus be on the desired outcome—closeness to God—or on the mechanism used and whether it was purely "Islamic" in origin? While more orthodox interpreters sought to distinguish and maintain particularity between Islam and other religions, most Sufis have remained adamant that God is not the monopoly of any single religion or even individual experience. Therefore, knowledge and experience of God should be sought wherever they might be found. Sufism's universality and reluctance to claim sectarian labels placed it inside a broad wave of mysticism that swept from Western Europe to South and East Asia. Thus Rumi could ask, "What is to be done, O Muslims? For I do not recognize myself. I am neither Christian, nor Jew, nor Zoroastrian, nor Muslim." Similarly, Ibn al-Arabi could proclaim, "My heart has become capable of every form: it is a pasture for gazelles and a convent for Christian monks, and a temple for idols, and the pilgrim's Kaaba, and the tables of the Torah and the book of the Qur'an."

A second critique of Sufism concerns leadership. Particularly after the early centuries, many Sufis were popular religious leaders rather than formally trained religious scholars (*ulama*). Some leaders said their connection to Muhammad through their spiritual chain provided sufficient legitimacy. Claiming true knowledge of God comes only from the Prophet, through dreams or the heart, rather than through books, some Sufi leaders eschewed book learning. A few even claimed religious scholars (*ulama*) sought only to perpetuate their personal culture and power, not to advance learning about God.

Although this logic was consistent with the Sufi tendency to emphasize esoteric knowledge passed down from Muhammad through the line of *shaykh*s rather than exoteric knowledge obtained through formal study of the Qur'an, hadith, and Islamic law, it nevertheless appeared to deny the centrality of the Qur'an and Muhammad's personal example (Sunna). Thus, while religious scholars (*ulama*) may have acted out of self-interest, seeing their own legitimacy, power bases, and institutions at stake, there was also reason for concern that a lack of formalized training among Sufi *shaykhs* would allow anything and everything to be added into the tradition, diluting, if not potentially eliminating, its Islamic roots and nature. Lack of formal learning credentials also placed great authority and power in the hands of sometimes unscrupulous individuals who located themselves outside of community consensus and institutional control. The most suspect of these were self-proclaimed unlettered Sufi masters from humble backgrounds who made public spectacles of their lack of education and of themselves through extreme demonstrations of purported piety, such as snake charming and fire eating.

Related to criticisms of Sufism's adaptability and leadership was suspicion that popular practices and metaphors for experience of the Divine simply served to cover up unorthodox activities. For example, Sufis often describe the experience of the Divine using the metaphors of "ecstasy" and "drunkenness," which take them to a different plane of feeling, expression, and existence. Critics charged that such imagery opened the door to consuming alcohol or drugs, which were prohibited by Islamic law. Similarly, homoerotic imagery of handsome young boys and other sexual metaphors were criticized as encouraging illicit sexual behaviors. Some orthodox interpreters considered Sufi use of music as suspect, fearing it might stir up lustful feelings or other temptations. Even as broad a thinker as al-Ghazali (d. 1111) recommended against listening to music unless one had learned to control lust.

Some of these critiques were not without substance. Many religious scholars pointed to popular (and fun) celebrations, such as Muhammad's birthday (Mawlid) and the Persian New Year (Nawruz), as objectionable Sufi innovations. They criticized the celebrations' non-Islamic origins and methods of celebration—excessive consumption of food and drink, gift exchanges, masquerades, and purchase of new clothing—which they saw as detracting from the more orthodox celebrations of Eid al-Fitr and Eid al-Adha.[32] Similar critiques were made of other popular practices, such as visitation of saints' tombs and shrines, particularly by women, as detrimental to God's uniqueness (*tawhid*) and not in accord with "proper" worship, ritual, and public behavior. Critics also charged that Sufis emphasized personal fulfillment and spirituality as the center of religious experience, rather than trying to improve society, encourage adherence to higher moral standards, eliminate injustice and oppression, or alleviate human suffering. Though these concerns may have had more to do with the *ulama*'s desire to preserve their authority, the fear of sexual immorality, in particular, struck a chord throughout many Islamic societies, which saw the patriarchal social order as endangered. Polemic against such activities as leading to sexual immorality permeated medieval Islamic legal and religious writings.

One final theological critique of Sufism had to do with its proclaimed capacity to unite the human with the Divine. Orthodox Islam has long insisted on the complete separation between the human and the Divine; nothing and no one can be associated with God. Associationism (*shirk*) is the one sin that God will not forgive.[33] Because only God can create, everything but God is necessarily created. What is created cannot be like God. Thus claiming humans can be united or joined with God, even in a spiritual or mystical way, was considered not only objectionable, but downright heretical by orthodox interpreters.

Conclusion

Despite these critiques, Sufism has continued to expand globally and remains the most popular expression of Islam today, drawing believers into an individual relationship with God. Sufis do not claim to fully "know" or "explain" God, only to experience and respond to the call of their Creator. Relationships by their very nature are complex and require work. They go through different phases, some good and

---

32. Ironically, many of the same means of celebration are used for the Eids, including extensive and often elaborate meals, gift exchanges, and new clothing.

33. This belief comes from Q 4:48 and 116.

others troubling. What matters most is committing to and sticking with the relationship and working through challenges to be able to delight in the overall experience. Rumi wrote, "Let the body dwindle and the soul decisions increase, Diminish what you give your physical self, Your spiritual eye will begin to open." Only when one ceases to focus solely on the self and becomes vulnerable can the Divine enter into one's existence and experience.

Review Questions

1. What is Sufism and how does it differ from other interpretations of Islam?

2. Identify and discuss some of the ritual methods used by Sufis and their purposes. How has this contributed to the development of Islamic civilizations and cultures?

3. What are the stages of development of Sufism? How has this resulted in changes in Sufi beliefs and practices over time? What changes have occurred with respect to leadership?

4. What are some of the theological critiques of Sufism? Why has Sufism sometimes come into conflict with more legalistic interpretations of Islam?

5. What opportunities did Sufism present to women for greater inclusion in religious activities?

6. Identify and discuss the importance of the four stages guiding the Sufi on the path to the Divine.

Discussion Questions

1. As with other faith traditions, Sufism has proven adept at moving into new locations and adopting and adapting cultural practices and religious rituals particular to that location. What are the possibilities and potential drawbacks of this approach? Does the introduction of popular religious practices deepen or weaken a faith?

2. Consider the two broad theological trends in Sufism: the intellectual, approaching Sufism as a religious and ethical discipline,

and the more popular and focused on saints and holy persons. What benefits and perspectives does each offer? Must they necessarily be in conflict? Are there any inherent dangers in either approach?

For Further Study

Readings

Barks, Coleman, with John Moyne. *The Essential Rumi*. New York: HarperCollins Publishers, 1995.

Chittick, William C. *The Self-Disclosure of God: Principles of Ibn al-'Arabi's Cosmology*. Albany, NY: State University of New York, 1998.

Clancy-Smith, Julia. *Rebel and Saint: Muslim Notables, Populist Protest, Colonial Encounters (Algeria and Tunisia, 1800–1904)*. Berkeley: University of California Press, 1997.

Helminski, Camille Adams. *Women of Sufism: A Hidden Treasure, Writings and Stories of Mystic Poets, Scholars and Saints*. Boston: Shambhala, 2003.

Lings, Martin. *What Is Sufism?* Cambridge, UK: Islamic Texts Society, 1993.

McCarthy, R. J., SJ, trans. *Al-Ghazali's Path to Sufism: His Deliverance from Error: An Annotated Translation of al-Munqidh min al-Dalal*. Preface by David Durrell, CSC. Louisville: Fons Vitae, 2000.

Raudvere, Catharina. *The Book and the Roses: Sufi Women, Visibility and Zikr in Contemporary Istanbul*. London: I. B. Tauris, 2002.

Renard, John, ed. *Tales of God's Friends: Islamic Hagiography in Translation*. Berkeley: University of California Press, 2009.

Schimmel, Annemarie. *Mystical Dimensions of Islam*. Thirty-fifth anniversary ed. Chapel Hill: University of North Carolina Press, 2011.

Smith, Margaret. *Rabi'a the Mystic and Her Fellow-Saints in Islam*. New York: Cambridge University Press, 1928; repr. 2010.

Trimingham, J. S. *The Sufi Orders in Islam*. Foreword by John O. Voll. New York: Oxford University Press, 1998.

Films

Friedlander, Shems. *The Circles of Remembrance*. [Delmar, N.Y.?]: Zawiya, Inc., 2007.

A documentary film showing *dhikr* exercises in the United States, Turkey, Egypt, and Morocco, along with commentary by prominent modern Sufis and musicians.

Kearns, Kell, et al. *Rumi Returning: The Triumph of Divine Passion*. American Public Television, 2008.

Biographical documentary on Rumi's life and experiences that also explores the meaning and symbolism of his poetry through contemporary interpreters.

Links

Rumi.org, *Rumi.org.uk*—Website dedicated to the writings of Rumi, including access to poetry by theme and recommended daily quotes and poems for reflection.

Tanbour.org, *tanbour.org*—Website with audio and video clips of Persian, Turkish, and Azeri Sufi music and demonstrations and histories of different instruments, featuring master musician Amir Vahab.

Jihad

The Struggle to Live Islam and Its Teachings

Perhaps no word associated with Islam evokes more fear or is more misunderstood than *jihad*. The media is filled with images associating Islam with violence, killing, and destruction. From the so-called Islamic State in Iraq and Syria to the Palestinian territories and Afghanistan to terrorist attacks in Europe and the United States, extremists claim to be waging jihad, a "holy war," in the name of Islam. Yet conflating jihad with terrorism and violence reduces a central concept of the faith to a purely militant idea, missing out on fuller understandings of the meaning and practice of jihad in the daily life of Muslims around the world.

Jihad Defined

Properly defined, *jihad* means "striving" or "struggle." Muslims throughout history have understood this as the struggle to follow God's path by living a faithful life consistent with the teachings of Islam. Being "on God's path" is a central theme of the Qur'an and Muslim religious life.[1] This theme places God at the heart of all decisions and behaviors and interprets faith as a constant, engaged effort to stay on the right path of obeying God's will and following God's guidance.

---

1. The Fatihah, or opening chapter of the Qur'an, recited seventeen times over the course of the five daily prayers, asks God to guide humanity on this straight path.

Greater and Lesser Jihads

Muslims often speak of two levels of jihad: first, the greater, inner struggle to live a faithful, righteous life in accordance with God's will (jihad of the heart) and by performing good deeds (jihad of the hand); and second, the lesser, outer jihad of defending the Muslim community, which can take a variety of forms, ranging from speech (jihad of the tongue) and writing (jihad of the pen) to physical defense (jihad of the sword). Otherwise stated, while jihad can involve physical violence, it can—and must—be expressed in many other ways.

The greater, inner jihad is about turning inward to overcome and control desires or inclinations that draw a person away from God. A major part of this striving is intentional living, defined as giving thoughtful consideration to the impulses and impacts of one's actions, for oneself and for one's family, community, nation, and world. On an individual level, a person might avoid swearing, gossiping, or having a negative outlook, or he or she might strive to be more compassionate when dealing with others. Another choice might be deciding to eat only halal foods (those permitted by Islamic law) and to read product labels to ensure the ingredients do not include pig products or alcohol. Though initially an individual choice, this decision could have broader impacts, for example, on one's family when buying groceries. Contacting companies that routinely use such ingredients in their products to ask them to make a halal version could have a further national or international impact. In other words, the greater, inner jihad often manifests as a desire to live out a more holistic and interconnected understanding of Islam, in which personal choices are intended to have a larger positive impact and to form consistency between one's beliefs and practices.

The lesser, outer jihad can, but does not have to, involve a physical "struggle." One hadith records that a follower of Muhammad asked the prophet which jihad was best, to which he answered, "A word of justice to a tyrannical ruler." Although jihad may include the use of violence, the Qur'an as well as subsequent developments in Islamic law state that violence must only be used to defend oneself or the Muslim community in response to a direct physical attack or threat of imminent physical attack, specified as one in which the opposing military has gathered and is preparing for battle. This is not the same as a preemptive strike, which attacks an enemy before it has time to prepare. The Qur'an and Islamic legal literature only permit military engagement with a clearly defined military enemy to be fought in a specific location. Neither discusses nor suggests any cosmic conflict between good and evil in which the individual must play a violent role, however much extremists claim otherwise.

The distinction between the inner, greater and outer, lesser jihads connects to a famous hadith in which Muhammad and his followers had returned home from war. The followers were proud of themselves for having fulfilled their duty of jihad with a successful military defense of the Muslim community. Yet Muhammad told them, "We have now returned from the lesser jihad to take up the greater jihad." In essence, although sometimes necessary, violence is the least praiseworthy way to engage in jihad; the more important struggle is the struggle within oneself to live a faithful life in obedience to God's will.[2]

In another hadith in which Muhammad overheard one of his followers wishing that strong men would engage in military service "on the path of God," Muhammad warned,

> Whoever goes out in the world seeking licit work to support his family is on the path of God; whoever goes out in the world seeking licit work to support himself is on the path of God. Whoever goes out seeking worldly increase has gone down the path of the devil.

This hadith clearly shows that being "on the path of God" has more to do with intent and struggling to live a righteous life than with fighting. Other early hadith similarly emphasize the superiority of the Five Pillars as religious obligations over military jihad. Some do not mention military jihad at all.[3]

---

2. For the development of jihad as internal spiritual struggle, particularly in the Sufi tradition, see Richard Bonney, *Jihad: From Qur'an to bin Laden* (New York: Palgrave Macmillan, 2008), 91–107.

3. For details, see Asma Afsaruddin, *Striving in the Path of God: Jihad and Martyrdom in Islamic Thought* (New York: Oxford University Press, 2013), 118–20. Hadith calling for jihad as military adventurism became prominent during the period of the Umayyad Empire (661–750 CE) and were cited by scholars in the Umayyad power bases of Iraq and Syria, reflecting the interests of that empire-building project. The earliest known hadith, however, emphasize traditional religious obligations and were consistently upheld by scholars living in the Arabian home territory of Muhammad

Jihad in the Qur'an

In light of modern-day images associating jihad with violence,[4] some may find it surprising that, for the first twelve years of revelation (610–622 CE), more than seventy Qur'an verses absolutely and repeatedly prohibited violence on the part of Muslims, even in the case of self-defense—despite the presence of violence in the surrounding context.[5] Pre-Islamic Arabian tribes routinely practiced raiding against other tribes, caravans, and settled communities to acquire wealth and material goods. Fighting and even killing were an inherent part of raiding, though not its main purpose.

Early Muslims felt challenged by God's ban on an activity that had been so central to their economy and society; the Qur'an instead encouraged them to respond through prayer, patient forbearance (*sabr*), and forgiveness. This ban became a real test of commitment to the new faith as many early converts faced serious persecution, oppression, and in some cases death. That so many verses say the same thing suggests Muslims not only faced intense violence but also kept asking whether God would allow them to fight back. God repeatedly said, "No."

---

and the early community. Afsaruddin has noted that some hadith popularized under the Umayyads are of questionable origin as the tactics described were not in use during Muhammad's lifetime, particularly those hadith promoting the merits of frontier protection and naval campaigns. She believes the rise by the ninth century of dubious hadith claiming military jihad was 50, 100, 1,000, or more times more meritorious than worship were invented for political purposes. See Afsaruddin, 122–27, 130–43, 155, and 159–60.

4. On the power of images to frame how particular groups are viewed, see Edward Said, *Covering Islam: How the Media and the Experts Determine How We See the Rest of the World* (New York: Vintage Edition, 1997). For statistical information on the differences between media images and majority opinions among Muslims, see John L. Esposito and Dalia Mogahed, *Who Speaks for Islam? What a Billion Muslims Really Think* (New York: Gallup, 2007). The Pew Research Center also conducts ongoing opinion polls of both American Muslims and Muslims in other countries, available at *www.pewresearch.org*.

5. See, e.g., Q 15:94–99 and Q 25:52, 63–67 and 70–77, which describe the appropriate response to harassment as patience and striving even more to remain faithful to God, rather than giving in to the all-too-human inclination toward vengeance. For a chronological approach to the Qur'an on war that highlights the early nonconfrontational stage followed by defensive fighting only, see Reuven Firestone, *Jihad: The Origins of Holy War in Islam* (New York: Oxford University Press, 1999), 51–65, esp. 51–56.

The phrase "holy war" never appears in the Qur'an.[6] In fact, the term *jihad* appears only four times in the entire Qur'an (9:24, 22:78, 25:48–52, and 60:1). It never describes fighting or warfare. Rather, it is most often mentioned in the context of patient forbearance (*sabr*), connecting it to the greater, inner struggle to live a faithful life, fulfilling the Five Pillars, and placing God at the center of all one does and believes.[7] Qur'an 9:24 declares the struggle (jihad) to place God at the center of one's life as the most important priority of the believer, overriding relationships, money, possessions, and business interests. The text does not specify how one is to "struggle," but violence is not inherently implied.

Qur'an 22:78 places jihad in the middle of a series of commands about worship and good deeds. It instructs believers to strive in God's way in a worthy jihad, because Muslims are to be witnesses to all people through prayer, charity, and seeking refuge and protection in God. There is no implication of violence, given that it was revealed during the years when fighting was banned.

Qur'an 25:48–52 discusses God as the source of all that is good, including mercy and water to sustain the earth and all life. Muhammad is told to use the Qur'an in striving (jihad) against unbelief by reminding people of what God has done for them. Again, violence is not a part of this picture.

Finally, Q 60:1 warns against taking enemies, defined as those who have denied the truth and rejected Muhammad and his message, as allies. God also warns against the hypocrisy of claiming to be striving (jihad) in God's path while befriending people who have rejected God. The exegetical literature records that this verse was revealed during a difficult moment for the Muslim community. The early Muslims had emigrated from Mecca to Medina following serious persecution and oppression. One of the Muslims betrayed the safety of the entire community by telling family and friends back in Mecca that Muhammad intended to return, thus

---

6. The term for war (*harb*) appears only four times in the Qur'an (5:64, 8:57, 47:4, and 2:279). It never appears with the phrase "in the path of God," which suggests that war is neither the ultimate purpose of jihad nor necessarily an expression of following in God's path.

7. Examples of verses include Q 16:110 and 47:31. See Afsaruddin, *Striving in the Path of God*, 2–3.

giving them time to prepare an attack. The exegetes believe the revelation of this verse in this context was intended to remind Muslims of their primary loyalty to God and to each other as members of the faith community, rather than to blood relatives. Again, it does not suggest violence but rather serves as a reminder about primary loyalties.

Further evidence for the connection between jihad and patient forbearance is found in the Qur'an's frequent statement that the most morally excellent persons are the *mujahid* (the one who strives) and the *sabir* (the one who is patient and steadfast).[8] Given that those who possess *sabr* embody the attitude and internal discipline necessary for engaging the human struggle on earth, jihad clearly falls within the realms of ethics and social conduct. Historically, Shia remained quiet during tribulations, believing God would reward those who were patient and obedient and avoided sin, rather than those who engaged in military jihad.[9] Sunni commentators associated *sabr* with the internal discipline required for performing religious obligations, such as fasting.[10] The great scholar Muhammad Al-Ghazali (d. 1111) identified the centrality of *sabr* by calling for patience in carrying out God's commands, refraining from what God has forbidden, and exercising self-restraint when faced with misfortune or tragedy. He asserted the superiority of this spiritual and noncombative inner jihad over the physical or combative methods of outer jihad.[11]

Other Qur'an passages use the same root letters of jihad—j-h-d—to describe striving and struggling in a nonviolent way.

---

8. Afsaruddin, *Striving in the Path of God*, 25.

9. This is based on Q 2:153, which commands those who believe to seek help in patience and prayer, and Q 3:200, which calls for patience, perseverance, and reverence of God. See commentary in Nasr et al., *The Study Qur'an*, 67 and 187, and Afsaruddin, *Striving in the Path of God*, 179–80 and 191–94.

10. See Q 90:17 and 103:3, which connect patience to compassion. Commentaries have connected patience to believers encouraging each other in maintaining religious practices, even in the face of difficulties. See commentary in Nasr et al., *The Study Qur'an*, 1517 and 1558, and Afsaruddin, *Striving in the Path of God*, 185.

11. An English translation of Al-Ghazali's most famous work can be found in Walter James Skellie, trans., *The Marvels of the Heart: Science of the Spirit, Ihya Ulum Al-Din/The Revival of the Religious Sciences* (Louisville: Fons Vitae, 2010).

For example, Q 16:110 talks about Muslims persevering even after being persecuted and driven from their homes for their faith, while Q 29:69 assures that God will guide those who strive in God's cause. This striving has no connection to violence or punishment; justice and punishment are the prerogative of God, not human beings.

The elaborate statement in Q 49:13–15, which talks about the common origins of all human beings, also puts jihad in context. Because all descend from a single woman and a single man, God does not recognize distinctions, such as race or tribe. The only distinction God recognizes between people is their piety. Characteristics like tribe and race are accidents of birth and out of one's control, whereas faith is a matter of personal choice. Thus God's assurance that people will not be judged on matters beyond their control, but only on what they choose, is intended to end conflict over things out of people's control and instead favor competition with one another to do good deeds. The passage asserts that God has deliberately created people of different tribes and races so they "might come to know one another." Diversity is, therefore, a divine blessing that opens the door to dialogue and partnership, not conflict. Qur'an 5:48 further states that God sent different scriptures to different groups of people, assigning a law and a path to each, so that these groups might compete with each other in good works. All of this supports the understanding that jihad's place in Muslim belief and practice is not inherently connected to violence or fighting.

Violence and Fighting in the Qur'an

If the Qur'an does not use jihad to describe violence or fighting, then what term does it use? Fighting and violence by Muslims have clearly taken place, including during Muhammad's lifetime, and Muhammad fought in several military campaigns, including the famous battles of Badr, Uhud, and the Trench. The earliest exegetes emphasized obligations, such as prayer and Hajj, as the most important religiously mandated duties and relegated combative jihad to a lesser duty, from which one could abstain if one showed neither inclination nor aptitude for it. Yet, by the eighth century, the juridical and administrative literature reflects a stronger tendency to describe jihad as militant or armed combat.[12] Some groups today refer to themselves as *mujahidin* to emphasize their participation in jihad as violent struggle.[13] Clearly, something happened that changed the ban on fighting into some sort of divine permission.

The turning point on the question of violence came after the emigration (Hijra) to Medina in 622, when Muhammad used his considerable arbitration skills to craft a resolution between warring parties that returned them to a state of peaceful coexistence. His subsequent shaping of the Constitution or Pact of Medina as a collective security arrangement recognized the possibility of legitimately engaging in violence in limited circumstances, although verses supporting nonviolence also continued to be revealed in Medina.[14]

Muslim scholars generally agree the first Qur'an verses permitting Muslims to engage in fighting—Q 22:39–40—date to the period shortly after the Hijra. These verses give those who have been attacked, oppressed, and driven from their homes because of their faith permission to fight back. They also call for the defense of any place where God is worshipped, specifically including churches, synagogues, and temples along with mosques, which reflects the religious pluralism of the community Muhammad served. The term used for fighting is not jihad, but *qital*. This fighting is permitted

---

12. This literature highlights when military engagement is obligatory, who is and is not responsible for engaging it, moral and ethical restrictions on fighting, and the required qualifications of the leader for a declaration of war to be valid, particularly the ruler's personal characteristics. Afsaruddin believes this reflects popular concerns of the time about the often questionable morals of the Umayyad caliphs, and that exegesis became an indirect way of making political critiques. See Afsaruddin, *Striving in the Path of God,* 1 and 117–18. Firestone, *Jihad: The Origin of Holy War*, 47–65, also traces the exegetical interpretations, noting this more militant approach is possible only if one approaches Qur'an verses through the lens of abrogation. He calls instead for recognizing that the plurality of Qur'an verses on "defending the faith" include many approaches that do not always involve violence, 67–91.

13. Groups and organizations referring to themselves as *mujahidin* are typically paramilitary groups engaged in guerrilla warfare or insurgencies that are trying to claim the religious mantle of jihad in their largely political struggles. This includes the struggle of the Afghan mujahidin against the USSR in the 1980s and the insurgency in Iraq in the 2000s.

14. See Firestone, *Jihad: The Origin of Holy War in Islam.*

only for defensive purposes, in the event of prior aggression against people and places associated with God.[15]

The Qur'an always ties acceptable violence in the form of fighting (*qital*) to self-defense in the face of injustice and oppression (*zulm*).[16] Only in the presence of *zulm* is *qital* justified. Qur'anic definitions of *zulm* include being driven unjustly from one's home, desecration of Muslim places of worship, and being prevented from living according to one's faith. Although fighting back is permitted in such cases, it is limited in scope; the Qur'an asserts punishment of the perpetrators as God's prerogative. In addition, although fighting is permitted in these cases, its ultimate purpose is not annihilation of the enemy but rather the reestablishment of peaceful, productive relations. This remains true even with some of the arguably most militant verses of the Qur'an, including the so-called Sword Verse, 9:5,[17] and the oft-cited 2:190–91.

These verses are a challenge because they are frequently cited only in part and out of context. Take, for example, the part of Q 9:5 frequently cited by extremists: "When the [four] forbidden months are over, wherever you encounter the idolaters, kill them, seize them, besiege them, wait for them at every lookout post." This seems to permit abject, unrestricted warfare against any and all enemies. However, such a reading is not faithful to the principles of Qur'an recitation, which do not permit pausing partway through a verse for fear of distorting the verse's meaning.[18] In this example, extremists conveniently leave out the rest of the verse, which states, "But if

---

15. Some scholars use this verse to denounce modern-day groups and organizations that destroy religious sites and execute members of other faith traditions, such as ISIS and Boko Haram.

16. For details on the appearance and frequency of words based on these root letters, see John Kaltner, *Introducing the Qur'an for Today's Reader* (Minneapolis: Fortress, 2011), especially the chapters on "Jihad" and "Violence and War," 165–214.

17. Afsaruddin notes, this verse received little attention in the exegetical literature prior to the thirteenth century as exegetes then understood it to apply only to Muhammad's lifetime. When the scholar al-Qurtubi (d. 1273) reinterpreted the verse as applicable to the circumstances of his time—i.e., ongoing conflict with the Byzantine Empire and the Crusades—and nicknamed it the "Sword Verse," more blanket applications were introduced into the exegetical literature. See Afsaruddin, *Striving in the Path of God*, 275–78, for details. Also see Nasr et al., *The Study Qur'an*, 506–7, for related debates about use of force.

18. Kaltner, *Introducing the Qur'an*, 184.

they turn [to God], maintain the prayer, and pay the prescribed alms, let them go on their way, for God is most forgiving and merciful." Looking at the following verse can also be instructive for the overall meaning. Qur'an 9:6 states, "If any one of the idolaters should seek your protection, grant it to him so that he may hear the word of God, then take him to a safe place for him, for they are people with no knowledge." Placing the selected portion of the verse into the broader context of the full verse and surrounding verses results in a different meaning from that claimed by the extremists—one that is not a blanket prescription for violence, but on the contrary limits the occasions in which violence would be justified and provides parameters for ending a conflict and providing safe haven to a presumed enemy.

A similar situation occurs with respect to Q 2:190–91, also a favorite of extremists. These verses state,

> Fight in God's cause against those who fight you, but do not overstep the limits. God does not love those who overstep the limits. Kill them wherever you encounter them, and drive them out from where they drove you out, for persecution is more serious than killing. Do not fight them at the Sacred Mosque unless they fight you there. If they do fight you, kill them—this is what such disbelievers deserve.

Standing alone, these verses appear to permit vengeance in the form of fighting and killing the disbelievers as just reward for their aggression. However, the verses that immediately follow (Q 2:192–93), state, "But if they stop, then God is most forgiving and merciful. Fight them until there is no more persecution, and worship is devoted to God. If they cease hostilities, there can be no [further] hostility, except toward aggressors." The surrounding verses again offer more nuance than would otherwise appear.

Early exegetes agreed, these verses gave Muslims the right to defend themselves anywhere they came under attack, including inside the Kaaba, a site where fighting had previously been banned. However, defense was only allowed if they were being physically attacked and then only in proportion to the attack being committed.[19] Most

---

19. Afsaruddin, *Striving in the Path of God*, 53. See also Caner K. Dagli, "Conquest and Conversion, War and Peace in the Quran," in Nasr et al., *The Study Quran*, 1805–17, esp. 1807.

important is the command that, if the enemy stops fighting, then the Muslims are also obligated to stop fighting. In the end, both of these passages, rather than supporting abject, total warfare, prescribe limited fighting with a desired end of restoring peace.

Despite this permission finally to fight back, many continued to resist violence, with some seeming to prefer the nonviolent approach to dealing with conflicts and communities, and others simply not wanting to engage in dangerous activities at all.[20] The historical record shows significant disagreement about fighting and war began during Muhammad's lifetime and continued for several centuries afterward.[21]

That so many Qur'an verses record the reluctance to fight implies fatigue with the ongoing fighting and violence of pre-Islamic times, when tribal warfare and raids were common. Indeed, part of the attraction of the early revelations of the Qur'an was likely the nonviolence they taught. These revelations suggested the possibility of communal living that was secured not through military prowess or kinship but through shared values, and commitments to God and each other. The introduction over time of the right to self-defense marks a concession to the past reality of constant violence in which absolute pacifism proved not only impractical but dangerous to the community's survival. Nevertheless, getting Muslims to abandon the pacifist message proved challenging, even for God.[22]

For example, Q 2:216–18 commands Muslims to fight "though you dislike it," because God instructed them to do so. Questions had been raised about fighting during a month when it was normally banned. Although under normal circumstances, fighting during that

20. Qur'an 4:95 notes exceptions were always made for certain community members—typically understood to include women, children, sick people, elderly people, and otherwise incapacitated males.

21. See Dagli, "Conquest and Conversion," 1815. For a full analysis of fighting in the classical period, particularly on the changes in hadith collections on fighting, see Afsaruddin, *Striving in the Path of God*, 116–48.

22. Later rulers often found it challenging, too, as recorded in the earliest exegetical literature and through the Umayyad and Abbasid empires. See Michael Bonner, *Jihad in Islamic History: Documents and Practice* (Princeton: Princeton University Press, 2006), 118–31. Afsaruddin, *Striving in the Path of God*, 149–78, traces a shift in tone over time toward support, encouragement, and even insistence on the necessity of violence as well as promising rewards to those who fight and die in battle. A detailed historical analysis tracing the transformation of jihad from a polyvalent concept to an institutionalized state system can be found in Bonney, *Jihad: From Qur'an to bin Laden*, esp. 21–90.

month would remain banned, the context at the time did not qualify as a normal situation, because Muslims were being barred from the Sacred Mosque in an attempt to force them to renounce their faith. God therefore reassured Muslims of their right to personal security and religious freedom, even if it meant fighting during a time it was normally forbidden.

Similarly, Q 9:38–41 expresses God's frustration with those who are reluctant to fight in permitted situations, questioning whether they focus more on the pleasures of this world than the next. The situation was apparently so dire God threatened those who did not fight with punishment. Much of the Qur'an's chapter 9, which is titled "Repentance," focuses on the challenge presented by those Muslims who wanted all of the trappings and benefits of being community members without contributing to the community's collective security and stability. Indeed, it seems there was considerable whining about weather conditions, health problems, lack of appropriate equipment, and the cost of fighting. Verses 90–93, in particular, chastise those who stayed in the comfort of their homes, rather than engaging the enemy (in this case, the Byzantine Empire) in the face of a looming attack. Faced with such a powerful and well-equipped enemy, the Muslims needed to put up a strong defense, requiring every able-bodied person to participate, in accordance with the collective security terms of the Constitution of Medina. Failure to fulfill that responsibility was not only selfish, it put the entire community at risk. This chapter clarifies, when collective security is in danger, Muslims have the right and responsibility to defend themselves and their community from external aggression.

Some interpreters today use parts of chapter 9 to claim self-defense is needed when Muslims experience Western "neo-colonialism" through the spread of Western culture, values, or trade. They claim chapter 9 offers blanket permission for dealing with "enemies," justifying violence against enemies wherever and whenever possible. They further use verses from this chapter, such as Q 9:14–15, to attribute responsibility to God, claiming God commands violence, absolving Muslims from moral responsibility,

---

23. See Kaltner, *Introducing the Qur'an*, 181.

because they are following orders from God.[23] Extremist groups often toy with individuals' consciences, either pressuring people into taking personal responsibility for avenging injustices experienced by the community or exonerating fighters of individual responsibility for mass killings because of their role in a supposed broad cosmic conflict not of their making. Such decontextualized generalizations often change the nature of the text.

Jihad and the Islamic Empires

Many in the West wrongly believe ancient Islam spread by the sword, based on the growth of the Islamic Empire through wars with the Byzantine and Sassanian empires. Those Arab conquests began as an extension and redirection of the older practice of tribal raiding to unite in a single state the Arabs of the peninsula. Although some have accused the Islamic Empire of expanding via forced conversions to Islam, the historical record does not support this claim.[24] In fact, conversions were discouraged at first, because they would have meant a loss in tax revenues and, in keeping with Islam's egalitarian vision of believers, the creation of equal status for newly conquered converts. Muslim conquerors had a vested interest in *not* pressing conversion but, instead, allowing conquered peoples to follow their own religious beliefs and laws, and offering them security in exchange for paying a special tax called the *jizya*.[25] The historical record also shows, in many places, conquered peoples found their new Muslim rulers more religiously tolerant than prior rulers; this included minority Christian churches that had been persecuted by the Byzantines for their dissenting views. In some cases, people welcomed liberation from Byzantine rule in favor of Muslim rule.[26]

---

24. For details, see Ira M. Lapidus, *A History of Islamic Societies*, 3rd ed. (New York: Cambridge University Press, 2014), esp. 46–53.

25. Jonathan P. Berkey, *The Formation of Islam: Religion and Society in the Near East, 600–1800* (New York: Cambridge University Press, 2003), 72–73. For a broad historical overview, see Hugh Goddard, *A History of Christian-Muslim Relations* (Chicago: New Amsterdam Books, 2000), esp. 34–49, for this early period.

26. See Lapidus, *A History of Islamic Societies*, 58–63.

Perhaps the crucial event fueling a militant spirit for jihad was the Crusades (1095–1291), which marked the Christian invasion and reconquest of lands in Spain, North Africa, and the Middle East. Christian "Soldiers of the Cross" came by land and sea to reclaim land and put "infidels" (not only Muslims but also Jews and Christians from minority churches) to the sword.[27] In the process, they appropriated many Muslim religious structures.[28] Meanwhile, the Mongols invaded from the East, forcibly ending the Abbasid Caliphate in 1258.

The scale of the occupation and ongoing violence accented militant jihad as a religious ideal and individual obligation. Many treatises popular among jihadists today,[29] such as those outlining requirements and merits of jihad and asserting the "otherness" of the enemy, were written and read in public forums during this time.[30] Those trying to stir up popular support for defending against the Crusaders and Mongols used religion and religious language (for example, referring to specific leaders, such as Saladin, as *mujahidin*) to justify their goal.[31]

This period marked a critical change in Qur'an interpretation.[32] Although this change shows a capacity to adapt Islamic thought and practice to new realities, it also highlights the danger this capacity represents in allowing the mobilization of mass support for violence, particularly when amateur interpreters use the

---

27. For a full analysis of the historical relationship between religion, politics, and violence in multiple faith traditions, see Karen Armstrong, *Fields of Blood: Religion and the History of Violence* (New York: Anchor, 2015). Also see chapter 9, "Muslim-Christian Encounters: Conflict and Coexistence."

28. The Dome of the Rock was converted to a church. The Al-Aqsa Mosque became the headquarters of the Templars. There was also an aborted attempt to sack Mecca and Medina.

29. These include a collection of forty hadith by Ibn Asakir (d. 1176) and selective use of treatises by Ibn Taymiyya (d. 1328) and his student Ibn al-Qayyim al-Jawziyyah (d. 1350).

30. See Afsaruddin, *Striving in the Path of God,* 163–78, for details.

31. See Berkey, *The Formation of Islam,* 199–202.

32. Afsaruddin, *Striving in the Path of God,* 174, clearly shows this development with attention shifting from traditional religious duties to declaring the superiority of fighting, to the point of declaring God loves fighters more than others by the late fourteenth and early fifteenth century.

Qur'an to claim power for themselves. This tendency also arises with respect to hadith, as some of these seem to have developed to meet perceived community needs.[33]

Of particular relevance today are hadith discussing Muhammad's premonitions of future military campaigns in Iraq and Persia. These hadith originally appeared when such campaigns needed religious legitimation; but today, ISIS uses these dubious hadith to justify terrorism. No attention is given to the origins or strength or weakness of the chains of transmission or even to contradictions between these hadith and the Qur'an. Instead, such decontextualization of the hadith permits narratives of violence that seemingly cannot be contested, because they claim to be rooted in Muhammad's example. To contend that the example of such hadith interpretations is absolutely, permanently, and fully definitive for Muslims of every time and place ignores that Muhammad's example, taken as a whole, includes many methods for interacting with enemies, many of which do not involve violence.

That Muhammad's example and the Qur'an would present diverse possibilities for interaction between communities should not be surprising. Religion, properly understood, is not intended to be a "one-size-fits-all" approach to life. Just as human experience is wide-ranging, so must a faith tradition offer diverse options for human behavior. The Qur'an often addresses how to deal with members of other faith traditions, suggesting this was a vital issue for the early community and that no one method applied to every situation. The Qur'an was revealed in a pluralistic context and had to be as diverse in dealing with that reality as with the situations it sought to address. Interpreters who employ reductionism, claiming only one "correct" method for dealing with the religious "Other," not only ignore passages in the Qur'an that do not support their argument but rob the Qur'an of its practicality in recognizing the diversity of human experience.

---

33. For the development of the hadith as a body of texts and hadith criticism throughout history, see Jonathan A. C. Brown, *Hadith: Muhammad's Legacy in the Medieval and Modern World* (Oxford: Oneworld, 2009), esp. 46–58, 67–120, and 240–65.

Jihad as an Individual and Collective Duty

Islamic legal literature has identified two levels of responsibility for defense of the Muslim community: individual (*fard 'ayn*) and collective (*fard kifayah*). In general, Muslims understand defense of the community as a collective responsibility that must meet certain parameters to be legal. Only a legitimate ruler can declare a valid jihad as a collective duty (*fard kifayah*) and then only for the purpose of collective defense, not self-aggrandizement. Jihad as a collective duty is supposed to be undertaken once a year, ostensibly to demonstrate the ongoing strength of the state as a deterrent to outside attacks.[34] As long as some community members take part, the requirement of collective duty is fulfilled, which means not everyone has to participate. Finally, those seeking to partake must have parental permission. A famous hadith records a young man who, eager to join the fighting, presented himself to Muhammad. After inquiring about his parents, Muhammad realized their son was their only caretaker. He informed the young man his jihad was to care for his parents, not join the fighting. This established a key precedent for granting that different individuals have different family circumstances and obligations, which may take priority over engaging in collective security. Jihad as military defense was consistently portrayed as a *fard kifayah* through the tenth century.[35]

Engaging in jihad as military defense as an individual duty (*fard 'ayn*), on the other hand, is rare. This occurs only in the event of abject warfare requiring an immediate response to an imminent security threat. Such an urgent situation precludes the requirement for parental permission. Emphasis on jihad as an individual duty became prominent during the Crusades and Mongol invasions, periods of intense violence that presented an immediate security threat.

The distinction between collective and individual duty and their accompanying parameters is vital today because extremist groups, such as Al-Qaida, use new interpretations that do not respect these

---

34. Historically, this kind of "annual jihad" was often undertaken in a token manner as it was considered a legal obligation. Afsaruddin, *Striving in the Path of God,* 10.

35. Berkey, *The Formation of Islam,* 199.

classical parameters.[36] They also tend to use abrogation (*naskh*) to override clear Qur'anic bans on aggression and instead initiate fighting, declaring war without provocation, thereby ignoring Qur'an verses and hadith that support alliances and peacemaking. This reduces the Qur'an to only one approach to dealing with disagreements. Sometimes such interpreters use hadith to undermine the Qur'an, marking a crisis of religious authority; the Qur'an, as the divine word of God, should not be overridden.

These interpreters have asserted the necessity of military jihad as a duty incumbent on all Muslims, citing perceived threats to the physical and spiritual well-being of Muslims, dating from the nineteenth-century European colonial occupation through the twentieth-century postcolonial period of developing states and the post–9/11 era. In many cases, Muslims were responding to things that happened to them. Particularly during the colonial era, military jihad took on renewed importance as a means of legitimate self-defense against Western colonizers and as an expression of authentic religion and culture in countries where Western culture and law had been imposed. In some cases, writers, such as Hasan al-Banna (1906–1949), founder of the Muslim Brotherhood in Egypt, spoke of jihad as a military defense of the truth designed to redress the humiliation, disgrace, and loss of dignity Muslims faced at the hands of superior European military power. He argued that being prepared to fight offered the best means of guaranteeing peace, although he also acknowledged the superiority of the inner, greater jihad.[37]

The most prominent ideologue of jihadism, Egyptian scholar Sayyid Qutb (1906–1966), described jihad in the path of God as a system that recognized worship of only God, thereby eliminating unjust systems and assuring freedom and social justice. His exclusive emphasis on "Islam" in a position of global power did not allow for negotiation or flexibility in dealing with people of different opinions. As the mechanism for putting God's law and authority in power, he

---

36. For a detailed discussion of the disconnect between the classical tradition and Osama bin Laden's interpretation, see Natana J. DeLong-Bas, *Wahhabi Islam: From Revival and Reform to Global Jihad*, rev. ed. (New York: Oxford University Press, 2008), 227–79.

37. For analysis of al-Banna's writings, see Gudrun Kramer, *Hasan al-Banna* (Oxford: Oneworld, 2009).

believed that jihad had to be combative, offensive, and relentless in pursuit of an Islamic state.[38]

Muhammad Abd al–Salam Faraj (1954–1982) carried Qutb's ideas to the next level. Faraj portrayed modern Muslim rulers as apostates comparable to the Mongols. He claimed Muslims faced such extensive internal and external threats that jihad became an individual duty with the end goal of establishing an Islamic state. In his vision, any individual with pure intent was qualified for jihad.[39]

All of these thinkers helped set the stage for Al-Qaida, which began with Abdullah al-Azzam[40] and gained prominence under Osama bin Laden. Both claimed their global jihad was an individual duty because of overwhelming and pervasive Western, specifically American, aggression. Al-Qaida claims it is the duty of every Muslim who has the chance, wherever they are, to kill any and all Americans, whether military combatants or civilians; to liberate Al-Aqsa Mosque in Jerusalem and the Grand Mosque in Mecca; [41] and to force non-Muslim armies to leave what Al-Qaida claims as the "lands of Islam." The goal is not only to defeat America but also render America unable to further threaten Muslims.[42] They argue the United States has engaged in so much aggression against Muslims and Muslim territories that the United States has rendered itself subject to jihad as an individual duty. Claiming jihad as an individual duty seemingly allows Al-Qaida to recruit young male fighters without securing parental

---

38. For samples of Qutb's most pivotal writings, see Albert J. Bergsen, ed., *The Sayyid Qutb Reader: Selected Writings on Politics, Religion and Society* (New York: Routledge, 2008).

39. See Johannes J. G. Jansen, *The Neglected Duty: The Creed of Sadat's Assassins and Islamic Resurgence in the Middle East* (New York: Macmillan, 1986).

40. Abdullah al-Azzam was a Palestinian theologian, founding member and ideologue of Al-Qaida, and Osama bin Laden's mentor. His most pivotal statement, often regarded as the foundation of the global jihad movement, was "Join the Caravan." An English translation is available at *https://archive.org/stream/JoinTheCaravan/JoinThe Caravan_djvu.txt*.

41. The Grand Mosque in Mecca is under control of the Saudi monarchy, which Al-Qaida considers to be an infidel regime. Al-Aqsa Mosque is viewed as a symbol of Israeli occupation.

42. An English translation of the text of this fatwa, issued by the World Islamic Front on February 23, 1998, can be found in Bruce Lawrence, ed., *Messages to the World: The Statements of Osama bin Laden*, trans. James Howarth (London and New York: Verso, 2005), 58–62.

permission.[43] However, because this interpretation fails to respect classical parameters, it has been rejected by the overwhelming majority of the world's Muslims as an abuse of religion and religious imagery in pursuit of questionable political goals.[44]

Suicide Bombings and Martyrdom

Given their prevalence as a tactic used by militant extremists,[45] it is reasonable to ask whether suicide bombings are permissible under Islamic law and what Islam has to say about martyrdom.

Suicide has long been banned under Islamic law, as God is ultimately the one who gives and takes away life. When human beings take matters in their hands, they claim God's powers for themselves, an act classified as *shirk*—association of someone or something other than God with God—the one unforgivable sin in the Qur'an. Although the Qur'an does not directly forbid suicide, it does warn people not to cause their destruction by their own hands (Q 2:195). Furthermore, the hadith record that the one who commits suicide will spend the rest of eternity recommitting that act. Combined with the broad ethic of valuing human life and the obligation to preserve it, logic suggests killing oneself is unacceptable, because of the claim made to God's power and because of the rejection of the life God created. This holds true even if one is seriously or mortally wounded and chooses to end one's life rather than wait to die. Consequently, Muslims are cautioned against not only deliberately seeking out the enemy to fight but also deliberately seeking martyrdom.

Furthermore, the abject killing intended by suicide bombings flies in the face of the values of compassion, mercy, forgiveness, and respect for human life frequently mentioned in the Qur'an. Suicide

---

43. This has become an important point for counterterrorism initiatives. The government of Saudi Arabia, e.g., gives television time to parents of suspected militants to make it clear to their children they have not given permission to them to engage in this "jihad" in the hope that their children will surrender to authorities.

44. Based on findings by Gallup's World Poll. Esposito and Mogahed, *Who Speaks for Islam?*, 65–98.

45. Although today this tactic is often associated with "Islamic" militants, it was developed by the Liberation Tigers of Tamil Eelam (LTTE), a separatist, revolutionary guerilla movement seeking to establish a secular Tamil state in Sri Lanka.

bombings are designed to kill anyone in the immediate vicinity. Given the careful parameters outlined in Islamic law that ban killing civilians, particularly women, children, elderly people, handicapped people, slaves, and religious leaders,[46] all of whom are considered noncombatants, it would be difficult, if not impossible, to justify suicide bombings based on Islamic law.[47] At the popular level, most Muslims globally reject suicide bombings as "never" or "rarely" justified[48] and more Muslim Americans (76%) than the general American public (59%) say that targeting and killing civilians to further a social, political, or religious cause is never justifiable.[49]

The minority of Muslims who claim suicide bombings are appropriate and licit tend to argue that new situations require new methods of warfare or that those who give their lives for the cause show the ultimate expression of faith by dying with purpose (i.e., as martyrs), as opposed to being killed as civilians by the enemy and becoming another meaningless statistic, as is often feared in Palestine. This explains why suicide bombers refer to themselves, not as

---

46. Classical Islamic legal literature specifies rabbis and monks.

47. Many Muslim leaders and groups as well as Muslim statements, including some often cited by extremists as authoritative—such as the current and former Grand Muftis of Saudi Arabia, Abdulaziz bin Baz and Abd al-Aziz Al al-Shaykh; hadith scholar Nasir al-Din al-Albani; Saudi scholar Muhammad al-Uthaymin; umbrella organizations, such as the Fiqh Council of North America; and statements, including the Hyderabad Declaration—have denounced suicide bombings as barred in Islam. The most detailed opposition was provided by Muhammad Tahir-ul-Qadri, *Fatwa on Terrorism and Suicide Bombings* (London: Minhaj-ul-Quran Publications, 2011), a 512-page refutation of terrorist and suicide bombings. A compilation of fatwas and statements by Muslim scholars and groups condemning terrorism and extremism can be found at *theamericanmuslim.org/tam.php/features/articles/muslim_voices_against _extremism_and_terrorism_part_i_fatwas/*, most recently updated May 13, 2015. There are, of course, exceptions, such as Shaykh Yusuf al-Qaradawi, a leading Egyptian preacher and television personality based in Qatar.

48. A Pew Research Center poll conducted in June 2014 of Muslim views on suicide bombings found strong opposition to suicide bombings, seen as "rarely" or "never" justified in Tunisia (93%), Indonesia (89%), Pakistan (87%), and Malaysia (75%). The largest support was in the Palestinian territories with suicide bombings "often" being justified (28%), although this marked a steady drop from a high of 70% in 2007, and far more (45%) said they were "rarely" or "never" justified. See *www.pew global.org/2014/07/01/concerns-about-islamic-extremism-on-the-rise-in-middle-east /pg-2014-07-01-islamic-extremism-10/*.

49. See *http://www.pewresearch.org/fact-tank/2017/08/14/like-most-americans-u-s -muslims-concerned-about-extremism-in-the-name-of-islam/*.

suicide bombers, but as "self-designated martyrs."[50] The difference
is critical because someone who commits suicide is generally seen as
mentally unbalanced and experiencing psychological problems; suicide is an act of desperation. Martyrdom, on the other hand, has long
been respected in many religious traditions as the ultimate expression
of faith and the example every believer should strive for—faithful
and willing to stand up for one's convictions, even at the cost of one's
life. Martyrs face their loss of life with hope and determination, not
despair. They are heroes of the faith. Thus the chosen terminology
is designed to tap into popular respect and admiration for martyrs,
rather than the more negative imagery associated with suicide, in
order to gain support for both the action and the cause.

Although contemporary extremists highlight martyrdom as a positive goal, the Qur'an, notably, never uses the modern term for martyr
(*shahid*)[51] to refer to someone killed in military action. That usage only
appears in external literature, which suggests this view of martyrdom
was a later development.[52] The Qur'an defines *shahid* (pl. *shuhada*) as
"witnesses," those who are declared "the best of companions," along
with prophets, truthful people, and righteous people (Q 4:69).

---

50. See the discussion on Hamas in Mark Juergensmeyer, *Terror in the Mind of
God: The Global Rise of Religious Violence*, 4th ed. (Berkeley: University of California
Press, 2017), 88–98; and on Al-Qaida in Iraq, see Mohammed M. Hafez, *Suicide
Bombers in Iraq: The Strategy and Ideology of Martyrdom* (Washington, DC: United
States Institute of Peace Press, 2007), esp. 117–25.

51. There is a linguistic connection between shahid (martyr), istishhad (self-
designated martyrdom), and shahadah, (the declaration of faith) so that the focus is on
the witness rather than death per se.

52. Afsaruddin has traced this to the ninth century, arguing the cult of martyrdom
was neither central nor inherent to Islam in the beginning but was a later development
connected to the expansion of the Islamic Empire and the need for military recruits to
defend the borders and provide security. Afsaruddin and Firestone argue the historical
literature should be read in that context, not as a blanket statement of law or exegesis
to be universally applied. Similarly, the detailed pleasures purportedly awaiting martyrs killed in battle, including the seventy-two virgins cited by extremists, are outlined
only in later exegetical literature, suggesting ongoing reluctance among Muslims to
engage in warfare and a need to entice them with tangible promises, even if these have
no basis in the Qur'an. Afsaruddin further observes these physical benefits parallel
the rewards a caliph might grant a skilled or loyal military man. Many scholars note
this hadith is not found in the most authoritative hadith collections. See Afsaruddin,
Striving in the Path of God, 3–4, 109, and 124–26, and Firestone, *Jihad: The Origin of
Holy War in Islam*, 100 and 114, for the development of the glories of martyrdom.

The Qur'anic description of those killed in battle—"one who is slain in the path of God"—appears only nine times in the entire Qur'an. In terms of heavenly rewards, the Qur'an makes no distinction between those who are killed and those who simply die in the faith, even if they die in their sleep. The critical issue, according to the Qur'an, is being "in the path of God," not the manner of death.[53] The Qur'an indicates special rewards in the Afterlife for the god-fearing (Q 39:20), patiently forbearing (Q 25:75), and those who believe and do good deeds (Q 29:58), not to those who are killed in battle. Only in the tenth century is emphasis placed on death on the battlefield, suggesting this interpretation was driven by political rather than religious purposes.

Dealing with Disagreements

Although extremist groups claim violence and warfare are the only possible methods for handling opponents, the Qur'an often refers to peaceful coexistence as the ideal relationship between communities and outlines a spectrum of possible behaviors and interactions for dealing with differences of opinion. Just as the Qur'an outlines conduct for warfare, it also talks about when to refrain from and end warfare and make peace with enemies.

Many passages of the Qur'an advocate forgiveness (Q 45:14–15, 2:109), pardon (Q 64:14, 5:13, 7:180, 42:15, 50:39–41), and even ignoring those with whom one disagrees. Judgment and punishment are to be left in God's hands, not the hands of human beings. Coercion is never an acceptable method of interaction (Q 2:256, 50:45, 10:99, 88:21–24).[54] The Qur'an presents peace as the most desirable outcome of interactions with others and calls upon Muslims to respond peacefully to anyone inclined toward peace (Q 8:61). Even in cases warranting retaliation, Q 16:126 reminds Muslims that, if absolutely necessary, it must be undertaken only in proportion to the harm or threat. Nevertheless, showing restraint is always better. Qur'an 60:7–9 calls for peaceful relations with those who are not aggressive, while warning against allying oneself with those who prohibit Muslims from enjoying religious freedom or who drive Muslims from their homes.

---

53. Afsaruddin, *Striving in the Path of God*, 95.

54. See Kaltner, *Introducing the Qur'an*, 196–97, for full details.

All of these passages make it clear that, though sometimes violence was deemed necessary and was an option for handling a problem, it was neither a foregone conclusion nor even necessarily the preferred method. Muhammad's initial reputation rested not on his position as a prophet but as a skilled arbitrator capable of restoring relationships between conflicting parties. He did not abdicate these skills when he became head of state in Medina. When he engaged in violence, the desired end was typically a formalized working relationship with the other party, which highlights the importance of ending conflict rather than seeking it. To reduce Muhammad's example to one method for engaging other parties ignores the broad array of approaches he used.

Contemporary extremists often claim voicing a dissenting opinion threatens the unity of the Muslim community by challenging a uniformity of thought and practice, which they deem essential. However, this denies the reality of Muhammad's example of engaging in consultation (*shura*) and seeking many opinions so that community decisions were truly community decisions. The extremist approach also reduces the reality of a diverse and nuanced Islam to a single authoritative voice in which any difference of opinion becomes sedition. Extremists often overlook the basic rationale for jihad, namely, the removal of injustice and oppression to create a just society. Such a society cannot exist when the rights of one group of people are usurped by another, regardless of religious affiliation. In a truly just society, justice must exist for all, not just for Muslims.[55]

How do extremists justify ignoring the alternatives to violence discussed in the Qur'an? They tend to invoke the principle of abrogation (*naskh*) to claim the last revealed verse on any given topic is God's final word on the matter, privileging a chronological approach to Qur'an interpretation over other methods. Using this approach, one can argue for an "evolution" of thought and directives over time, moving from initial nonviolence and nonconfrontation to defensive fighting, to initiating fighting albeit within standard limitations, to legitimate warfare, and, finally, to unconditional fighting, with the last directive overriding all others.[56] However, this approach fails to allow

55. See the discussion of rights in Tariq Ramadan, *Western Muslims and the Future of Islam* (New York: Oxford University Press, 2004), 153–54.

56. Firestone, *Jihad*, 50–65, gives details on this evolutionary approach and its implications with respect to warfare.

the Qur'an to speak as a complete text or to speak to specific contexts. Extremists tend to ignore the interplay between text and context, often misinterpreting or misapplying passages to dissimilar contexts.

Civilian Jihad

Today, many Muslims around the world continue to believe in the importance of standing up to injustice and oppression and deliberately choose nonviolent means of addressing social ills. Activists consider this the most faithful method of following Muhammad's example, speaking truth to power and engaging in *sabr*, or patient forbearance, along the path of jihad.

© MehmetO/ Shutterstock.com

Poster at an October 2017 #NoMuslim BanEver rally organized by the Council on American Islamic Relations, Jewish Voice for Peace, and the Arab American Action Network in Chicago, calling for solidarity in response to discrimination.

Rather than challenging the state's claimed monopoly on the use of violence, Muslim activists are turning to a range of options, such as social media, public demonstrations, and public awareness campaigns to make their concerns heard and to reclaim the terminology of jihad from extremists. Such "civilian jihads" have taken place in many countries, including Iran's Green Revolution to remove President Ahmedinejad from office; Kuwait's Orange Movement to change voting districts; Egypt's Kefaya ("Enough") movement, which set the stage for the Tahrir Square uprising during the Arab Spring of 2010–12; and Turkey's anticorruption protest initiatives in 2013.[57] Some Muslim women's rights activists talk about

---

57. Details can be found in Maria J. Stephan, ed., *Civilian Jihad: Nonviolent Struggle, Democratization, and Governance in the Middle East* (New York: Palgrave Macmillan, 2009).

engaging a "gender jihad" in their struggle to resist discrimination, injustice, and oppression against women.[58]

In the United States, initiatives for civilian jihad include the public education campaign myjihad.org, which seeks to reclaim Islam from extremists through social media. They have created a Facebook page, produced YouTube videos, and asked ordinary Muslims to tweet about their personal definitions of jihad. The goal is to offer a public presence with a constructive vision of how to engage jihad to improve communities, such as by caring for the less fortunate and struggling against hunger, poverty, domestic violence, and discrimination.

Tawwakol Karman (b. 1979)

Cofounder of the community-based media partnership Women Journalists without Chains and winner of the shared Nobel Peace Prize in 2011, Tawakkol Karman is a Yemeni journalist, politician, and women's and human rights activist. Born in Taiz, Yemen, Karman holds a bachelor's degree in commerce from the University of Science and Technology in Sanaa, Yemen, and a master's degree in political science from the University of Sanaa. She began her career in journalism documenting human rights abuses in Yemen in 2005. Her frustration with systemic government repression, corruption, oppression of women, and social and legal injustice led her to begin organizing weekly protests in Sanaa in 2007. In 2011, with the rise of the Arab Spring, these nonviolent protests picked up popular momentum and ultimately led to the resignation of President Abdullah Ali Saleh in 2011. Karman is recognized within Yemen as the "mother of the revolution" and "the iron woman" for her leading role in the "Jasmine Revolution." She received the Nobel Peace Prize in 2011 for her nonviolent leadership in favor of democracy, women's and human rights, justice, and good governance. She dedicated the prize to the martyrs and wounded of the Arab Spring, particularly youth and women, whom she credited with the struggle for human rights and democracy. She donated the prize money to a fund for those wounded and killed in the uprising in Yemen. The recipient of several honorary degrees in recognition of her work for women's and human rights, she is often considered a controversial voice on the sectarian conflict within Yemen today.

---

58. See Amina Wadud, *Inside the Gender Jihad: Women's Reform in Islam* (Oxford: Oneworld, 2006).

Review Questions

1. What does jihad mean? What is the difference between the greater/inner jihad and the outer/lesser jihad? What, if any, is the role of violence?

2. How are jihad, fighting, and violence discussed in the Qur'an? When and why was permission given to fight and under what circumstances?

3. How are jihad, fighting, and violence reflected in Muhammad's example? Were these the only methods he used to engage people who disagreed with him? If not, what other methods did he use?

4. What role, if any, did militant jihad play in the expansion of Muslim empires? In what situations did military jihad come into play and what was the justification?

5. What is the difference between jihad as an individual duty and jihad as a collective duty? Why does it matter?

6. How have suicide and martyrdom been understood historically in Islam? How and why have these definitions changed today? Are all definitions equally valid? Why or why not?

7. How has the concept of jihad been reinterpreted in contemporary contexts?

Discussion Questions

1. Having encountered a variety of interpretations of jihad, how important is it for discussions of jihad to be more nuanced in public conversations? Are there any interpretations that could be constructive in building relationships between Muslims and non-Muslims?

2. What constitutes self-defense in contemporary society? Is it always and necessarily physical?

For Further Study

Readings

Abu-Nimer, Mohammed. *Nonviolence and Peace Building in Islam*. Gainesville, FL: University Press of Florida, 2003.

Afsaruddin, Asma. *Striving in the Path of God: Jihad and Martyrdom in Islamic Thought*. New York: Oxford University Press, 2013.

Armstrong, Karen. *Fields of Blood: Religion and the History of Violence*. New York: Anchor, 2015.

DeLong-Bas, Natana J. *Wahhabi Islam: From Revival and Reform to Global Jihad*, Revised. New York: Oxford University Press, 2008.

Firestone, Reuven. *Jihad: The Origin of Holy War in Islam*. New York: Oxford University Press, 1999.

Kaltner, John. *Introducing the Qur'an for Today's Reader*. Minneapolis: Fortress, 2011.

Said, Abdul Aziz, Nathan C. Funk, and Ayse Kadayifci, eds. *Peace and Conflict Resolution in Islam*. Lanham, MD: University Press of America, 2001.

Stephan, Maria J., ed. *Civilian Jihad: Nonviolent Struggle, Democratization, and Governance in the Middle East*. New York: Palgrave Macmillan, 2009.

Wadud, Amina. *Inside the Gender Jihad: Women's Reform in Islam*. Oxford: Oneworld Publications, 2006.

Films

Kronemer, Alexander, et al. *Muhammad: Legacy of a Prophet*. KQED, 2002.

Produced in the aftermath of 9/11, *Muhammad* presents historical and modern understandings of the prophet and his legacy, including jihad and the events of 9/11.

Noujaim, Jehane, et al. *Al-Maydān = The Square*. Pottstown, PA: MVD Visual, 2015.

Observational documentary on the events of the Arab Spring in Egypt through the experiences of six protesters, both female and male.

CHAPTER

Women and Gender
Discerning the Divine Will

Perhaps no stronger stereotype of oppression or object of fear and pity exists than the "Muslim woman," shrouded in mystery, secluded, veiled, subject to male authority and sexual appetite, and restricted to the twin roles of wife and mother. Most public conversations discuss Muslim women as subjects of men or governments or objects of state policy or religious teachings as interpreted by men. Despite their participation in public life during Muhammad's lifetime, Muslim women have long been excluded from formal policy conversations about themselves—how they should be defined, what rights they have, what status they hold before the law and the state, and if and how they need to be "rescued" or "saved," whether from their families, men, governments, or religion.

Today, largely due to a shrinking gender gap in education and expanded access to public space via the Internet and social media,[1] Muslim women are increasingly inserting their voices and agency in many fields, including politics, the workforce, cultural production, and interpretation of scripture and Islamic law. In making these changes, women often reference strong, capable, and educated Muslim women of past and present. They serve as CEOs, business owners, muftis,[2] religious scholars, and

---

1. For details on educational progress among Muslim women globally, see Caryle Murphy, "The Muslim Gender Gap in Educational Achievement Is Shrinking," Pew Research Center, December 27, 2016, at *http://www.pewresearch.org/fact-tank/2016/12/27/the-muslim-gender-gap-in-educational-attainment-is-shrinking/*.

2. *Muftis* are religious experts who offer fatwas (legal opinions). Female muftis are formally recognized in India, Syria, and Egypt, although only for issues related to women.

judges[3] and have been elected as members of parliaments and congresses and served as presidents and prime ministers in Pakistan, Bangladesh, Indonesia, and Turkey.

The contrasting images of the oppressed, suppressed, and repressed Muslim woman stands in marked contrast to the achievements of Muslim women in many places, highlighting the importance of distinguishing between Islam the religious tradition and the patriarchal culture often associated with it. Rather than blaming "Islam" for the challenges Muslim women often face, such women today often point to the authoritarianism and patriarchal culture of many Muslim-majority countries as the root of their limited public freedoms. They note that they share many of these hardships with the men who live with them in authoritarian and often underdeveloped societies, suggesting that "women's" problems in Muslim societies are ultimately societies' problems.

Muslim women contend their Islamic faith provides them with strength, purpose, meaning, and empowerment in confronting these challenges. Muslim women are as likely as Muslim men to cite religion as "very important" to them and are slightly more likely than men to maintain observance of daily prayers.[4] Some have joined with Muslim men in calling for reforms and reinterpretations of Islam that implement its core values of justice, human dignity, and working for the common good in the modern era.

The Advent of Islam

Pre-Islamic Arabia was a challenging environment for survival, particularly for women. Rather than an asset, daughters were often seen as a liability. Though needed for survival, women were seen as losses to the tribe; the children they produced belonged to the husband's family. Women were also the honor bearers. Any sexual misconduct

3. Though they are barred from these positions in some Muslim-majority countries, Muslim women serve as judges in Indonesia, Malaysia, Pakistan, Syria, Egypt, Libya, Tunisia, and Morocco. See Nadia Sonneveld and Monika Lindbekk, eds., *Women Judges in the Muslim World* (Leiden: Brill, 2017).

4. For details on the religious gender gap across religious traditions globally, see "The Gender Gap in Religion around the World," Pew Research Center, Religion and Public Life, March 22, 2016, at *http://www.pewforum.org/2016/03/22/the-gender-gap-in-religion-around-the-world/*.

by a woman, whether real or perceived, brought shame to the entire tribe. Families sometimes buried female babies alive to avoid financial hardship and the shame associated with the birth of a daughter, rather than a prized son.[5]

Given this context, Muslims often point to the major improvements Islam brought for women. With respect to their persons, these included the right to life through the ban on female infanticide and the right to consent to marriage and initiate divorce. Financially, women were assured rights in marriage and after divorce, as well as the right to own and manage property, engage in business, and inherit.[6] Their bodies were also protected from male sexual aggression, including rape and prostitution.

Yet many scholars remain cautious about blanket assertions that Islam improved women's status, noting the guarantee of certain rights was not necessarily new and the power dynamic largely continued to favor men.[7] Scholars and women's rights activists also note that raising women's status at one point in history has not guaranteed these rights and the values and principles underlying them across time and space.

Scholarly debates on this improvement in the status of early Muslim women often focus on Muhammad's first wife, Khadijah, whom he married before becoming a prophet. Prior to their marriage, Khadijah was a businesswoman and Muhammad's employer. That she proposed to him indicates she exercised autonomy and some degree of independence in choosing her spouse. Whether Khadijah's agency was because of her status as a wealthy and influential widow or if such freedom was generally available to women of the time is unclear. Although pre-Islamic poetry celebrates individual women engaged in business, military action, and political maneuvers, these women seem to be exceptional. Thus, despite the potential for

---

5. This practice also existed among ancient Greeks and Romans, although not Egyptians or Jews. Roman law required a father to raise all sons, but only one daughter. Leila Ahmed, *Women and Gender in Islam: Historical Roots of a Modern Debate* (New Haven: Yale University Press, 1992), 35.

6. In Western Europe, women did not have the right to own or inherit property until the nineteenth century.

7. Property ownership and engaging in business for women was already part of the pre-Islamic landscape, but men continued to hold a disproportionate amount of power in the family and in inheritance customs.

women's autonomy, it is uncertain how widespread such autonomy was. Many scholars therefore find it prudent to note the Qur'an and Muhammad's example supported these activities and freedoms and likely opened them to a broader group of women but avoid making sweeping, absolute claims about women's status.

Likewise, scholarly opinion varies on whether marriage practices described in the Qur'an represent an expansion or a limitation of women's rights. Those who argue for expansion cite the Islamic legal requirements of witnesses to the marriage; the wife's inheritance of a portion of her husband's wealth on his death; receipt of a dower, also known as a marriage gift (*mahr*), at the time of marriage; provision of maintenance in marriage and in the waiting period after divorce; and the wife's right to sexual satisfaction from her husband. Not only did these legal measures guarantee women certain rights, they also made these rights a matter of public record and hence enforceable.[8]

Other scholars look at the same legal measures and see the incorporation of existing patriarchal customs that put men in a stronger legal position with greater rights in marriage and divorce.[9] For example, though women theoretically had the right to consent to marriage, this did not necessarily translate into having an active voice in the choice of a spouse.[10] By contrast, as the initiator of the marriage contract, a man had choice, unless he was a minor or a slave. Similarly, although Muslim legal literature tends to portray the dower as an assertion of the woman's right to property, the legal and cultural practices that developed allowed for payment of at least half of the dower to the bride's father for "safekeeping" or "guarding."[11]

---

8. Details can be found in John L. Esposito, with Natana J. DeLong-Bas, *Women in Muslim Family Law*, rev. ed. (Syracuse: Syracuse University Press, 2001).

9. Barbara Stowasser argues in *Women in the Qur'an, Hadith and Interpretations* (New York: Oxford University Press, 1994), 102, that the Qur'anic progression with respect to Muhammad's wives is one of increasing restraint rather than liberation, placing the well-being of the community and perfection of Muhammad's household as a higher priority than individual aspirations.

10. The practice of consent varied by law school based on the woman's age and status.

11. Other mechanisms granting male guardians access to the woman's dower have been introduced by custom, such as in modern Saudi Arabia, where a woman often "gifts" her dower to her father or male guardian, or in India, where high nominal dowers are often set in the contract but not paid. See Esposito with DeLong-Bas, *Women in Muslim Family Law*, 113–16.

In addition, women were restricted on the grounds for which they could file for divorce, whereas men did not have to provide any justification. Finally, no sexual relations outside of marriage were considered licit for women after the Qur'anic revelation. Women were restricted to a single husband in order to determine paternity in the event of pregnancy [12] Men, however, retained the right to multiple wives, albeit restricted to a maximum of four at once, provided he could treat them all equally.[13]

Women in the Qur'an

To make a singular sweeping argument about how the Qur'an treats and addresses women would be an oversimplification and inaccurate. Qur'anic discussions of women are generally one of three types: (1) broad passages addressing God's expectations of people, such as worship and adherence to the Five Pillars; (2) interactions with other people, particularly within the family; and (3) portrayals of characters in specific stories, such as the mother of Moses, the wife of the Egyptian official in the story of Joseph, and Mary, the mother of Jesus, who is the only woman named in the Qur'an and the only one for whom a chapter (Surah 19) is named.[14]

Similar to male characters, portrayals of females serve a didactic purpose. They demonstrate ideal qualities, such as submission to God's will, purity, motherly love, prayer, and almsgiving, as well as behaviors to avoid, such as disobedience to God and sexual misconduct. The inclusion of positive and negative female and male

---

12. There are indications in pre-Islamic poetry and other sources that polyandry (multiple husbands) existed in pre-Islamic Arabia, although it is not known how widespread the practice was. See Ahmed, *Women and Gender in Islam*, 41–44.

13. The ability to maintain one's wives equally is a Qur'anic requirement (Q 4:3) and is legally enforceable in some countries. But the Qur'an also states men will never be able to treat multiple wives equally (Q 4:129), no matter how hard they try. This is often overlooked in favor of preserving a man's right to multiple wives.

14. Reminiscent of biblical and extra-biblical sources, the Qur'an says Mary was "chosen by God above all other women" (Q 3:42). For more information, see Stowasser, *Women in the Qur'an*. For more information on theology surrounding Mary as well as Muhammad's daughter Fatima, see Mary F. Thurlkill, *Chosen among Women: Mary and Fatima in Medieval Christianity and Shi'ite Islam* (Notre Dame, IN: University of Notre Dame Press, 2007).

characters demonstrates the broad human, rather than gendered, capacity for agency and choice. It also underscores the Qur'anic teaching that each individual will be held accountable only for their own choices and actions, not those of others. Thus it is the woman's faith and righteousness—or lack thereof—that determine her ultimate destiny, not her relationship to a man.[15] This raises the question of why God would give women autonomy in religious and moral matters, yet place them in a position of subordination in human affairs.

Debates on women's status in the Qur'an typically focus on this perceived disconnect. Although women are considered equal to men in religious and moral matters, there emerge some gender-based differences in human relations, most notably in family dynamics. Some scholars believe the divine intent overall is to consider women and men equal, but social and family relations reflect the complementary roles women and men typically play based on biology.[16]

Historically, this perspective has been used to claim that gender-specific roles—placing men in the public sphere and with a more powerful role in the family as heads of households and breadwinners, and placing women in the privacy of the home as wives and mothers—are ordained by God and, therefore, immutable. However, modern developments, particularly rising levels of literacy, education, and work experience among women, have brought a reexamination of these roles and their connection to a specific cultural and historical context. Reformists argue changes in context require revision of these roles in light of modern-day realities. Circumstances such as dual-income households and women serving as de facto heads of households have led to calls for rebalancing the power equation in the family, expanded rights for women, and, in some cases, equality between women and men.

---

15. Natana J. DeLong-Bas, "Gender Construction: Early Islam," in *The Oxford Encyclopedia of Islam and Women*, ed. Natana J. DeLong-Bas (New York: Oxford University Press, 2013), 1:351–55.

16. Amina Wadud has pushed back against this model of social construction, arguing that "Woman is not just Biology," and that the Qur'an does not propose a single possibility for each gender. She believes greater attention should be given to women and men as moral beings. See Amina Wadud, *Qur'an and Woman: Rereading the Sacred Text from a Woman's Perspective* (New York: Oxford University Press, 1999), 64–65.

Arguments for equality frequently cite Q 4:1, which teaches the first pair of spouses was created from a single soul without giving preference to either sex.[17] Creation as a pair means both parts are needed to have a complete soul, and neither can exist without the other. Nowhere does the verse say man and woman were created from different substances; they come from the same origin. Furthermore, neither is deemed more important than or superior to the other. In fact, the Arabic term for spouse (*zawj*) is gender-neutral.[18] Consequently, woman and man are on equal footing in creation in the Qur'an.[19] Both are created with autonomy, and both are assured no righteous act will be lost, regardless of the acting person's gender (Q 4:124, 3:195, 40:40, and 33:35).

Similarly, the Qur'an asserts the creation of both female and male as part of God's divine plan for humanity, so that they might get to know and compete with each other in righteousness (Q 49:13). Nowhere does it say or even suggest that men in their biological or social capacity are more capable or better able to fulfill this righteousness than women.[20]

Other passages assert the equality of men and women in terms of God's expectations and promises of rewards. For example, Q 9:71–72 places female and male believers in relationship to each other, calling on both to protect each other, behave morally and ethically, and maintain the requirements of worship. In return, God promises equal reward and approval. Similarly, Q 3:195 assures God accepts the work of both women and men and is equally aware when they experience oppression or injustice, promising both rewards for faithful living.

---

17. This stands in contrast to the biblical creation story, in which the man is created first and the woman is created much later from a piece of the man, placing women in an inferior and subservient position to men according to classical theological interpretations. Although there is no basis for this argumentation in the Qur'an, biblical traditions and theology on creation were introduced into the Islamic tradition in the eighth and ninth centuries. See Stowasser, *Women in the Qur'an,* esp. 3–24, for details.

18. See Wadud, *Qur'an and Woman,* esp. 15–27.

19. Asma Barlas, *"Believing Women" in Islam: Unreading Patriarchal Interpretations of the Qur'an* (Austin: University of Texas Press, 2002), esp. 133–36. The Qur'an includes no suggestion of the Christian doctrine of original sin passed down to the rest of humanity. Rather, Adam and Eve are created as equals. Together, they disobey God's commands, receive punishment, repent, and are forgiven. See also Ahmed, *Women and Gender in Islam,* 4.

20. Barlas, *"Believing Women" in Islam,* 142–43.

Ultimately, lawful and unlawful acts are connected to specific actions and their associated morality, not gender. The Qur'an does not sexualize moral agency. Instead, it appoints women and men as each other's guides and protectors. The purpose of such equal accountability and responsibility is to establish a relationship of partnership rather than one of competition or of an imbalance of power. In addition, Q 30:21 states, "Among His signs is that He created spouses for you from among yourselves so that you might find comfort in them. He put love and compassion between you. There truly are signs in this for a people who reflect." The phrase "find comfort" includes the meanings of relying upon, being reassured by, trusting in, and feeling at home in, all of which imply a mutual relationship of security and support between spouses. The verse does not say the wife alone is responsible for providing this to her husband. Rather, the wording makes mutuality clear, suggesting an equal partnership in which domestic harmony can be achieved only if both spouses treat each other with dignity and respect.[21]

Perhaps most striking in many verses is the deliberate linguistic inclusion of both women and men, rather than the use of the ambiguous third person masculine plural, which can refer either to men alone or to both men and women. That ambiguity was not lost on female members of the early Muslim community. When a woman asked Muhammad whether women were always or only sometimes included in these revelations and, therefore, God's plan for humanity, Q 33:35 was revealed in response. This verse offers parallel and identical expectations and rewards for women and men:

> The submitting men and the submitting women, the believing men and the believing women, the obedient men and the obedient women, the truthful men and the truthful women, the patient men and the patient women, the reverent men and the reverent women, the charitable men and the charitable women, the fasting men and the fasting women, the chaste men and the chaste women, and the men and women who remember God frequently—God has prepared for them forgiveness and a great reward.

---

21. John Kaltner, *Introducing the Qur'an: For Today's Reader* (Minneapolis: Fortress, 2011), 111.

Such open and specific declarations of equality in responsibilities and rewards suggest a far more egalitarian vision of men and women than often plays out in practice.[22]

Ultimately, simply looking at what the Qur'an or Islamic law says about women and their status does not provide a full picture of the Islamic revelation's influence on society or how women and men responded to it. Given that women and men converted and remained dedicated to Islam, sometimes in opposition to their own tribes and families, and that Muhammad's earliest followers were mostly women, it is important to look at other sources of information for a fuller understanding of the impact of Islam on women's lives.

Women during Muhammad's Lifetime

Much of our knowledge of Muhammad's life and interactions with women comes from orally transmitted memories about him (hadith) from his wives and Companions, both women and men.[23] Part of the hadith's value is they include women as questioners, subjects and objects of various incidents, making women's voices part of the canonical texts, legal sources, and official history.[24]

The hadith provide a multifaceted picture of Muhammad's interactions with his often outspoken wives, who sometimes enjoyed their time with him and sometimes quarreled with him.[25] Despite

22. This is not the only case in which a Qur'an verse was revealed in response to a woman's question or circumstance. For example, when Muhammad's wife Aisha was falsely accused of adultery, she was exonerated through the revelation of Q 24:11–15.

23. For details on the impact of hadith on women and the manipulation of hadith by male scholars to solidify their own public power and position, see Fatima Mernissi's pioneering work, *The Veil and the Male Elite: A Feminist Interpretation of Women's Rights in Islam*, trans. Mary Jo Lakeland (New York: Perseus Books, 1992), and Wiebke Walther, *Women in Islam: From Medieval to Modern Times* (Princeton: Markus Wiener Publishers, 1993). There are indications that cultural norms and ideals were incorporated into the hadith by male scholars with the aim of limiting women's roles to the domestic sphere and of promoting a patrilineal, patriarchal order, instead of the egalitarian vision of the Qur'an. See DeLong-Bas, "Gender Construction: Early Islam."

24. Kristina Benson, "Hadith: Women and Gender in the," in *The Oxford Encyclopedia of Islam and Women*, ed. DeLong-Bas, 1:405–7.

25. In the one instance in which the bickering became too much for even Muhammad to handle, he took a one-month break from all of his wives to let them decide for themselves whether they wished to continue in the marriage or divorce. Stowasser, *Women in the Qur'an*, esp. 96–97.

the historical tendency in many places to reduce women to the biological roles of wife and mother,[26] Muhammad's wives were clearly
not limited to motherhood. In fact, Muhammad had children with
only two of his wives.[27] Although his other marriages produced no
children, Muhammad neither divorced nor rebuked his wives for this
"failure." Instead, he gave them the honorific title of "Mothers of the
Believers,"[28] charging them with caring for the Muslim community at large. His wives served as confidantes, advisors, and sources
of various kinds of expertise and information, ranging from medicine, history, and poetry in Aisha's case, to political advice and savvy
from Umm Salama. Sawda was known for her leatherwork, Zaynab
bint Khuzayma for her charity.[29] Aisha and Umm Salama became
important sources of hadith after Muhammad's death, and both
served as prayer leaders for other women before and after his death.

Some hadith portray Muhammad's wives as models and
enforcers of newly imposed norms, including modesty, seclusion,
and veiling, which were intended to cement Muhammad's social
status and honor. Although the Qur'an set these requirements only
for Muhammad's wives, over time Islamic tradition made them the
norm for all Muslim women. Ostensibly, this was done to protect
women, but it also solidified a powerful role for the patriarchal

---

26. Reduction of women to biology is not unique to Islam but ranges across religious traditions and civilizations. One of the many critiques of such reductionism is
that it considers a given period of a woman's life—between the ages of 15 and 45—as
normative and formative of her entire life. It does not take into consideration the years
prior to or after child-bearing and rearing.

27. He and his first wife, Khadijah, had four daughters (Zainab, Ruqayya, Umm
Kulthum, and Fatima) and two sons (Qasim and Abd Allah). He also had a son (Ibrahim) with Maryam the Copt. The sons all died as infants.

28. This moniker placed these women in a familial relationship with the community, discouraging sexualized thinking about them.

29. Stowasser, *Women in the Qur'an*, 106–18, has identified and analyzed three
types of hadith material on Muhammad's wives: (1) hadith portraying them as "ordinary" women largely motivated by emotionalism, irrationality, and petty jealousies of
each other, and who, therefore, need to be restricted and controlled by men to maintain the social order; (2) hadith presenting hagiographic images of them in the context
of miracles; and (3) hadith portraying them as blameless, saintly paragons of virtue
that all Muslim women should emulate, particularly in their charity, frugality, and
piety. Muhammad is portrayed as the perfect husband, treating his wives equitably,
visiting each one daily, and showing each one affection. Emulation of Muhammad's
example in this way does not seem to be required of men in the same way as following
the pious examples of his wives is required for women.

male in controlling women as domesticity came to define the core of female social righteousness. This affected Muslim women's status in the faith community, increasing pressure for them to remain within the home rather than continue as active participants in the public sphere.

Some hadith give a negative impression of women; one characterizes women as the most harmful temptation left to the Muslim community and another says angels weep when a woman leaves her husband sexually frustrated. Furthermore, some hadith portray women as morally or religiously defective, ritually unclean, intellectually unfit for political rule, and required to obey their husbands. Although such hadith make up a very small portion of the roughly seventy thousand total hadith believed to be authentic, they are often given disproportionate attention and weight. As a result, they ultimately override more numerous hadith that call on men to treat their wives with gentleness, affirm that Muhammad accepted women's testimony as equal to men's, portray unveiled women as a normal and accepted part of the early Muslim community, and exalt motherhood.[30] The existence of contradictory hadith suggests they may be more useful for gleaning information about the development of particular attitudes, an idealized image of Muhammad, and what people in the first two centuries believed Muhammad said or did, than for referencing Muhammad's exact words or actions.[31]

The primary female hadith transmitter was Aisha.[32] As a beloved wife, Aisha had a deep connection with Muhammad and knew his personal and domestic habits. She also had insight into his private religious observances, because the two often prayed together.

---

30. See Benson, "Hadith: Women and Gender in the," 405–7.

31. Stowasser, *Women in the Qur'an,* 104, makes this argument. See also Asma Sayeed, *Women and the Transmission of Religious Knowledge in Islam* (New York: Cambridge University Press, 2013), ch. 1, esp. 22; Sayeed argues that before the tenth century, it was understood the hadith were more appropriately seen as preserving the meaning of what Muhammad said, rather than his exact words. After this time, classical Sunni orthodoxy promoted the view that the hadith preserved the exact words of Muhammad.

32. Between 1,500 and 2,400 authentic hadith (about 15 percent of the total canonical Sunni collections) are attributed to Aisha—more than the number attributed to Ali, Muhammad's cousin and son-in-law. For a history of Aisha's life and legacy, see D. A. Spellberg, *Politics, Gender and the Islamic Past: The Legacy of 'A'isha bint Abi Bakr* (New York: Columbia University Press, 1994).

Aisha alone among Muhammad's wives was sometimes present when Muhammad received Qur'anic revelations. Aisha's hadith transmissions went beyond reporting the mere content of particular traditions to offering insight into their meanings and legal implications, particularly on issues related to inheritance. Other topics of her hadith included not only the expected categories of conjugal relations, ritual purity, and supererogatory worship practices but also fasting, pilgrimage, and eschatology. She was known to have corrected and even contradicted hadith by male Companions.[33] Women and men alike sought her out for spiritual and medical advice and as a source of knowledge. She was frequently consulted about correct recitation of Qur'an verses and is the only woman from the early Islamic period whose legal thinking has been documented and analyzed from the eleventh century onward.[34] Aisha often transcended limitations placed on other women because of her status as Muhammad's favorite wife and "Mother of the Believers," her strong personality, and her exceptionally important role as a source of religious knowledge.[35]

The second most important female hadith transmitter was another of Muhammad's wives, Umm Salama.[36] Her hadith largely focused on ritual purity, prayer, and marriage. Although Aisha was

---

33. This included the second caliph, Umar, and the Companion Abu Hurayrah. Umar tried to confine Muhammad's wives to their homes and domestic roles, even barring them from going on Hajj and banning women in general from attending prayers at the mosque. The women collectively rebelled and won restoration of these rights under the third caliph, Uthman. See Stowasser, *Women in the Qur'an*, 90. Abu Hurayrah, despite having converted only three years prior to Muhammad's death, became one of the most prolific hadith transmitters, largely because he outlived Muhammad by fifty years. Yet his recollections were frequently challenged by other Companions, including Aisha. See Benson, "Hadith: Women and Gender in the," 405–7. His misogynistic outlook came to be privileged with the adoption of empire culture. His views seem to have been more palatable to hadith scholars than those of the independent and strong-willed Aisha. See Mernissi, *The Veil and the Male Elite*, esp. 49–84.

34. See Sayeed, *Women and the Transmission of Religious Knowledge*, 26–29, for details.

35. Sayeed, *Women and the Transmission of Religious Knowledge*, 44. Some contemporaries blamed Aisha's loss at the Battle of the Camel on her disobedience to Muhammad's command that his wives stay home. The expectation that a woman's proper place is in the home thus came to be emphasized from that time forward.

36. She is credited with between 175 and 375 hadith. Sayeed, *Women and the Transmission of Religious Knowledge*, 25.

generally considered a greater authority and was more involved in the daily life of the Muslim community, Umm Salama's counsel was frequently sought. She was also considered a legal authority and is portrayed in biographical sources and hadith as an influential woman who counterbalanced Aisha in temperament as well as in the household. Yet, like Aisha, she did not always observe the purported requirements of veiling and seclusion.[37] Umm Salama sometimes served as a spokesperson for Muhammad's other wives, including when criticizing Muhammad's preference for Aisha, as he was supposed to treat his wives equally. Shiis view Umm Salama, not Aisha, as the most revered of Muhammad's wives after Khadijah. Thus there are political dimensions to the portrayals of Muhammad's wives.[38]

Yet simply sharing kinship with Muhammad was not a guarantee of becoming a hadith transmitter. His daughter, Fatima,[39] narrated few hadith and his granddaughters, none. However, some early female converts are represented among transmitters, particularly those known for their service to the community, who had been the subjects of legal decisions, or who had personally pledged their allegiance to Muhammad. Of this mixed group, the most important was Asma bint Abi Bakr, Aisha's sister, daughter of the first caliph, and wife of a close Companion. Her hadith focused on prayer, ritual purity, and charity.[40]

---

37. For example, most of the eighty men listed as narrating hadith on her authority were not part of her kinship or cliental circles, yet mention entering her quarters. Sayeed, *Women and the Transmission of Religious Knowledge,* 42.

38. See Sayeed, *Women and the Transmission of Religious Knowledge,* esp. 35–38. This point is further bolstered by Umm Salama's support for Ali, rather than Aisha, in the Battle of the Camel. Umm Salama is credited with several hadith expressing preference for Ali, Fatima, and their children.

39. Fatima, mother of Muhammad's grandsons, Hasan and Husayn, and wife of Muhammad's cousin, Ali, is central to the Shiite doctrine of the imamate. Known for her compassion and nurturing, Fatima was an eminently relatable figure—the ideal mother, daughter, and wife—although she was also reportedly capable of condemning enemies to hell. Parallel to Christian belief about the Virgin Mary, Shiites believe Fatima was chosen and purified above all women by God and was a perpetual virgin. For details, see Thurlkill, *Chosen among Women,* 41–65.

40. Portrayed as an assertive, courageous woman, she is credited with fifty-five hadith and is the third most prolific female transmitter. She lived to be 100 years old and was one of the longest-surviving Companions. See Sayeed, *Women and the Transmission of Religious Knowledge,* 47–52.

Although some crafting of the hadith to provide prescriptive, idealized images of specific women has taken place, it is nevertheless clear women were active members of the early Muslim community and played a role in deliberations and decision-making. Women attended prayer and teaching sessions in the mosque; worshipped in the same space as men; participated in celebrations of religious holy days; decided for themselves whether to convert, often in opposition to their families; pledged oaths of loyalty to Muhammad; oversaw, organized, supervised, and shopped in markets; served as business and trade leaders; and had direct access to Muhammad for counsel and legal advice on a range of issues. Some women accompanied men to their battles and military engagements, providing encouragement with words, songs, and poetry, tending to the wounded, carrying water, and participating in the fighting.[41] One woman saved Muhammad's life by fighting off his attackers after he was wounded.[42]

The hadith offer an extensive record of the many and varied roles played by women during Muhammad's lifetime, roles that were viewed as normal aspects of daily life in the early Muslim community. Muhammad welcomed and responded to women's requests and questions just as he did men's. He sometimes ruled in favor of women, demonstrating that justice, not gender, was the driving concern in his rulings.

Beginning in the eighth century, the elaboration of Islamic law and theology was increasingly marked by the marginalization of women as hadith transmitters in favor of viewing women as subjects and objects of legal rulings. Women generally did not possess the requisite Arabic linguistic and grammar skills or legal discernment that had become important among accomplished hadith transmitters.

---

41. Muhammad's aunt, Safiyya bint Abd al-Muttalib, was celebrated for her courage in the Battle of Uhud. Even when her brother, Hamza, lay dying on the battlefield, she did not give up her spear. She was also commended for her bravery in fighting off a prowler near a fortress sheltering women and children when the male protector failed to defend them. See Sayeed, *Women and the Transmission of Religious Knowledge,* 46.

42. The woman, Nusaybah bint Kaab, was wounded thirteen times defending Muhammad. She later lost her hand fighting in another battle. She was the questioner for whom Q 33:35 was revealed, assuring the community that women were included in God's expectations and rewards. See Sayeed, *Women and the Transmission of Religious Knowledge,* 55.

Those who did memorize hadith generally did so to understand what was expected of them as Muslim women, not only domestically and in terms of family issues but also with respect to worship and religious obligations. Only a few gained reputations for learning and piety.[43]

Veiling

As a Muslim woman's most visible mark of identity, the veil is one of the most contested, debated, reverenced, and vilified symbols of Islam. Many in the West view the veil as a symbol of the oppression of Muslim women, a barrier between women and society and a sign of backwardness, inequality, and male superiority and control. Yet in many parts of the Muslim world the veil is reverenced as a sign of female modesty, piety, and cultural and religious authenticity. Although some Muslim-majority countries mandate a form of veil in public space, others consider it a matter of personal choice or even ban it altogether.[44] In some cases, women are pressured by family members to wear the veil, though other women may choose to veil as an expression of personal religiosity, pride in being Muslim, to ward off unwanted male attention and sexual aggression, or even to oppose family members. Ultimately, the veil carries many layers of meaning, suggesting caution in assuming what veiling means or who has determined the veil be worn. As noted by Muslim American scholar Amina Wadud, "In reality, the hijab of coercion and the hijab of choice look the same. The hijab of oppression and the hijab of liberation look the same. The hijab of deception and the hijab of integrity look the same."[45]

Because the veil is strongly associated with Islamic religion and culture today, many assume a strong Qur'anic and historical basis for veiling. But the veil originates neither in Islam nor the Qur'an. Many

---

43. Sayeed, *Women and the Transmission of Religious Knowledge*, 65–66.

44. For example, Saudi Arabia, Afghanistan, and Iran all require women to veil in public space, whereas Egypt and Lebanon do not. Veiling was banned in public places in Turkey until 2013.

45. Amina Wadud, *Inside the Gender Jihad: Women's Reform in Islam* (Oxford: Oneworld, 2006), 219.

of the societies in and surrounding pre-Islamic and early Islamic Arabia used veils for free women as a symbol of elite status as well as male power and prerogative.[46] The veil served as a visible, public marker for classifying women according to their sexual status and relationship to men.

During Muhammad's lifetime, his wives were the only Muslim women required to veil and seclude themselves. Some scholars argue these measures sent a message about Muhammad's social status and power that would have been understood by and compared favorably with other rulers in the region. Though it is uncertain when veiling and seclusion became widespread, indications point to the seventh- and eighth-century conquests by the Rightly-Guided Caliphs and the Umayyad Empire into parts of the Byzantine and Sasanian empires, where these practices carried social capital, marking urban upper- and upper-middle-class status. They were then assumed into the "Islamic way of life," making them normative by the Abbasid era.[47]

The Qur'an says little about women's dress. *Hijab*, the word typically used today for the veil, appears only seven times in the Qur'an— and never in reference to an article of clothing. In the Qur'an, *hijab* refers to a barrier or partition separating or standing between two things, such as gods and mortals (42:51), wrongdoers and righteous persons (7:46), believers and unbelievers (41:5, 17:45), and light and darkness (38:32). This meaning carried over into popular uses, such as for amulets that were supposed to protect a person from harm or the official who served as a barrier between petitioners and the caliph. Thus the term *hijab* carries a connotation of protection.[48]

The three Qur'an passages frequently cited in reference to veiling (Q 33:53, 33:59–60, and 24:30–31) use three different terms: *hijab*, *jilbab*, and *khimar*. Who is asked to veil, for what reasons, and in front of whom also differs, suggesting there is no single Qur'anic norm.

---

46. Assyrian law stipulated wives and daughters of "seignors" must veil, as must concubines accompanying their mistresses and former "sacred prostitutes" who had married. Harlots and slaves, on the other hand, were forbidden from veiling under penalty of being flogged, having pitch poured over their heads, or even having their ears cut off. See Ahmed, *Women and Gender in Islam*, 11–37, for details.

47. See Ahmed, *Women and Gender in Islam*, 79–91, for details.

48. For more information on the Qur'an verses and their terminology, see Elizabeth Bucar, *The Islamic Veil: A Beginner's Guide* (Oxford: Oneworld, 2012). My summary draws in part on her analysis.

The verse that uses the term *hijab* (Q 33:53) was revealed in Medina after Muhammad took over as head of state and refers specifically to his wives. The occasion of revelation was Muhammad's wedding celebration to a woman named Zaynab. Some of the guests lingered after the meal, delaying the wedding night. Others used the occasion to ask his other wives to intercede with Muhammad on their behalf, creating unrest among some attendees who expressed concern these men were overstepping the boundaries of respectability. The verse therefore established three precedents: (1) guests should do their visiting with each other before the meal, not after;[49] (2) those making requests of Muhammad's wives were to do so with a curtain or screen (*hijab*) between them so as to avoid the potential for lust and gossip;[50] and (3) Muhammad's wives were not available as marriage partners to other men, even in the event of divorce or widowhood. The meaning of *hijab* in this verse thus follows the usage throughout the Qur'an of referring to a barrier or partition, not a clothing item.

The second passage, Q 33:59–60, uses the term *jilbab* to offer guidance on how female Muslims should dress in public—having their *jilbab* hang low over them—so they will not be harassed. The *jilbab* seems to be a kind of garment, but the Qur'an does not tell us what it looked like, how it fit, or what color it was.[51] It clearly does not function as a veil; it simply seems to cover the upper part of the body. It is what the *jilbab* symbolizes that is important—making female autonomy and presence in public space visible and legitimate rather than limited or invisible. It served as a warning to men not to approach. Using the *jilbab* to indicate a woman's faith rather than her sexual status imbued a known pre-Islamic symbol with new meaning rooted in the woman's status before God rather than her status in relationship to men.[52]

---

49. This cultural habit still exists in the Islamic world today. When invited to someone's home for a meal, guests are expected to visit before the meal and leave promptly at its end.

50. The only other place the Qur'an mentions the term *hijab* with respect to a woman is Q 19:17, which describes Mary, the mother of Jesus, as secluding herself from her family before the angel appears to her to announce the pending conception and birth of Jesus.

51. The term does not appear anywhere else in the Qur'an for cross-referencing.

52. Although the exegetical literature varied in terms of descriptions of what parts of the woman's body should be covered by the *jilbab*, commentators from the ninth through the fifteenth centuries were remarkably consistent in asserting its purpose was to prevent harassment.

The final passage, Q 24:30–31, uses the term *khimar* to refer to a garment Muslim women should pull over their bosoms as a matter of modesty. It also instructs them not to show their "adornments" other than what is normally visible to men who could be potential marriage partners. These instructions occur in the context of commands to women and men to lower their glances and guard their private parts[53] when meeting each other. Clearly, then, the *khimar* did not function as a veil; if the woman's face were covered, the man would not need to lower his gaze. The verse only mentions drawing the *khimar* over the bosom, not the face, hair, or head. Furthermore, the passage does not require men to be responsible for ensuring women cover up, nor does it command women to try to control male sexual desire, nor prohibit unrelated and unmarried men and women from meeting. Rather, the passage provides guidelines for such encounters, suggesting, although modest dress and behavior are required, seclusion and gender segregation are not. The Qur'anic vision of society appears to be one in which women and men might meet for legitimate purposes and in which both are expected to guard themselves against sexual impropriety. Nowhere does the burden fall solely on women.

Overall, these passages aim to protect the privacy of the home, the bodily integrity of women, women's access to public space free from harassment and assault, and the modesty of women and men in public encounters. This raises the question of what to do when the purpose of wearing the veil is no longer met, such as when wearing it actually makes harassment more likely. Some women's rights activists in Western countries have set aside the veil as an unnecessary burden on women and an invitation to be harassed in the post–9/11 era. Others insist on an ongoing need and desire for modest dress, particularly in a Hollywood-driven culture that encourages, if not pressures or even forces, women to strip down rather than cover up; they argue for their bodies and beauty as something precious and deserving of protection over which they alone should have autonomy. The driving question is whether women have a constitutional right to dress as they please or whether men have a right to engage in thinly disguised voyeurism.

---

53. Private parts are generally defined as falling between the navel and the knees.

Nowhere has this controversy about women's dress been more pointed than in Western debates about the headscarf commonly termed *hijab*, the more extreme, black, face-covering *niqab*, and other forms of modest dress deemed to be excessive by Western standards, such as the *burkini* (bathing attire that covers a woman from head to foot). The headscarf covers only the hair, can be worn in a variety of ways, and can be as plain or colorful as the woman chooses, making it an expression of individual creativity and identity. The *niqab* leaves only the eyes visible and is culturally associated with the conservative countries of the Gulf. Some countries, such as Germany and France, have banned *niqab* and *burkinis* as symbols of rejection of local culture or security concerns.[54] Muslim women point to the challenges they face to maintain their modesty in these situations, noting that a woman in France can be fined thousands of Euros for wearing a *niqab*, but can strip down to only a tiny pair of bikini bottoms on a public beach and not be fined a cent. They argue this standard essentially requires the female body to be publically available for the male gaze on public beaches, sexualizing women against their will.[55]

Sex and Sexuality

Although the Qur'an condemns illicit sexual behavior, whether voluntary or involuntary, Islam does not stigmatize sex. The Qur'an recognizes sexual desire and attraction as gifts from God to be fulfilled within marriage as an expression of mutual love. Sex is not limited to a procreative role but is seen as leading to a deeper level of intimacy and peace (*sukun*) between the spouses. The Qur'an recognizes women and men have sexual desires and needs, as well as the right to fulfill them. Unlike other faith traditions that sometimes stigmatize

---

54. In the 2002 *Freeman vs. Florida* case, a woman's driver's license was revoked on the grounds that wearing the *niqab* obscured her face, defeating the purpose of the license as a form of identification and creating a public safety concern. The court determined that, although a woman has the right to veil, the license is a privilege with certain accompanying requirements, including a full-face photograph. Failure to meet those requirements leads to either revocation of the license or refusal to grant it. For a discussion of security concerns focused on the veil, see Robin Lee Riley, *Depicting the Veil: Transnational Sexism and the War on Terror* (London: Zed, 2012).

55. For more on this controversy, see Hilal Elver, *The Headscarf Controversy: Secularism and Freedom of Religion* (New York: Oxford University Press, 2012).

sex and sexual desire,[56] the Qur'an describes sex as a divine instrument for creating harmonious relationships of mutuality, love, peace, and mercy.[57]

Licit sexual activity can only occur within marriage in Islam.[58] Regulation of sexual activity is considered critical to the social order and a matter of public concern and record. Although tied in part to the need to determine legitimate heirs in property-owning societies, it is also connected to understandings of chastity and fidelity in the marital relationship.

The Qur'an describes chastity and purity in terms of conduct and moral choices. The defining characteristic of a human being is morally purposeful action, rather than sexual identity.[59] The Qur'an makes clear that women and men are expected to be chaste and both are capable of being either pure or impure (Q 24:26).[60] Chastity is not an absence of sexual activity but an absence of illicit sexual activity, such as adultery, fornication, or lewd or sexually violent behavior.[61] Women and men are considered equally capable of such behavior.

---

56. Islam generally has a more positive view of human sexuality than Christianity, for example, which has tended to favor spirituality accompanied by chastity as a "higher calling" than sexual fulfillment.

57. See, for example, the discussion in Barlas, *"Believing Women" in Islam,* esp. 151–53.

58. Islamic legal literature defines marriage as between a man and a woman.

59. Barlas, *"Believing Women" in Islam,* 130.

60. Ibid., 154.

61. Opinions vary as to whether Islam considers same-sex love illicit. Although there is significant historical and literary evidence of its existence and practice, it has been the frequent target of legal denunciations and punishments, because it falls outside of the legal definition of marriage. This means there is no licit means of fulfilling same-sex desire. Many Muslims struggle to address the reality of same-sex love, seeing it as a behavior and thus a matter of choice, rather than an inherent identity, as it is understood in the West. See Scott Siraj al-Haqq Kugle, *Homosexuality in Islam: Critical Reflection on Gay, Lesbian, and Transgender Muslims* (Oxford: Oneworld, 2010). Those Muslims who identify as gay or lesbian are often faced with heart-wrenching choices about country of residence and how openly they can or cannot live their identity as some countries, such as Iran and Egypt, consider homosexual activity (specifically male-to-male) as crimes punishable by fines, jail sentences, or even the death penalty. Reconciling faith and sexuality has proven challenging to many, as documented in the film *A Jihad for Love,* Parvez Sharma and Sandi Dubowski, [San Francisco]: Kanopy Streaming, 2015.

Although, historically, a woman's status as either a virgin or deflowered woman received much attention, the Qur'an does not particularly prize female virginity. Only one of Muhammad's wives, Aisha, was a virgin when he married her. No shame, stigma, or dishonor was attached to his marriages to widowed or divorced women. Valorization of female virginity was connected to the later spread of the Islamic Empire, when elite cultural habits of the Sasanian and Byzantine empires were adopted and absorbed into Islamic culture and civilization. Similar to the adoption of veiling and seclusion as expressions of wealth and social status, so female virginity in marriage came to be prized.

Education

In light of modern flashpoint issues such as Boko Haram's violent opposition to girls' education in Nigeria and the Taliban's attempt to assassinate Nobel Peace Prize winner Malala Yousefzai of Pakistan for her pursuit and support of education, many people have the impression "Islam" opposes girls' education. However, the historical record contains many examples of Muslim women who were encouraged to pursue education precisely because of their faith, not despite it. Although it would be overly simplistic, in light of the sheer breadth of Islamic empires throughout history, to claim Muslim women have "always" or "never" had access to education, Muslim scholars assert Islam encourages religious literacy and education in general.

The first revealed word of the Qur'an was *Iqra*, which can mean either read or recite. In more than five hundred verses of the Qur'an, the importance and pursuit of knowledge is highlighted both directly and indirectly. The Qur'an commands all Muslims, irrespective of sex, to read, think, contemplate, and learn, and it encourages women to speak their minds and not be silent.[62]

Muhammad urged his followers to seek knowledge from cradle to grave and to pursue it everywhere, including as far away as China, the end of the known ancient world. He referred to education as the "best ornament of a woman" and encouraged women to be present

---

62. Dina Sijamhodzic-Nadarevic, "Education and Women: Contemporary Discourse," in *The Oxford Encyclopedia of Islam and Women*, ed. DeLong-Bas, 1:251–56.

in the mosque alongside men.[63] He also said those who raise and educate their daughters will go to Paradise.[64] He personally set the example by setting a day of the week to provide religious instruction to women.[65] Including women in education was important because, as Muhammad himself noted, "Half of the population are women, and the other half are born, brought up and educated by women."

In the earliest years of Islam, Muslim women made contributions in religious studies, literature, mysticism, medicine, history, jurisprudence, arts, and artistic crafts. Most importantly, Muslim women played a strong role in the transmission of hadith. The historical record documents many Sunni female religious scholars, particularly in hadith transmission to female and male students.[66] Access to and possession of religious knowledge became an important venue for Muslim women, serving as cultural capital that conferred social status and upward mobility. It also kept alive the memory of women's contributions as transmitters of religious knowledge, forming a connection back to Muhammad's lifetime. Pursuit of knowledge of the hadith served as much as an act of piety as it did a path to relative power and prestige. At the same time, it is important to acknowledge female scholars were generally restricted to hadith transmission based on memorization and rarely participated in the male-dominated analytical pursuits of law or theology.[67]

Although it is unclear what kinds of schools for religious instruction existed in the early centuries of Islam, access to religious education was considered a matter of piety and prestige, even with a private tutor in the home. The more formalized school known as the madrasah dates to the eleventh century, but mosque complexes with inns to house travelers, including students, existed before this time, with more than three thousand spread throughout the Islamic

---

63. Soudeh Olahi, "Education and Women: Educational Reform," in *The Oxford Encyclopedia of Islam and Women*, ed. DeLong-Bas, 1:256–58.

64. Sijamhodzic-Nadarevic, "Education and Women," in *The Oxford Encyclopedia of Islam and Women*, ed. DeLong-Bas, 1:251–56.

65. Sariya Cheruvallil-Contractor, "Qur'anic Schools for Girls," in *The Oxford Encyclopedia of Islam and Women*, ed. DeLong-Bas, 2:145–48.

66. A detailed historical analysis can be found in Sayeed, *Women and the Transmission of Religious Knowledge*, esp. the introduction.

67. Ibid., 18.

world by the tenth century.[68] Many schools were connected to either mosques or charitable endowments and included female instructors as well as female students.[69] The proportion of female lecturers in many classical Islamic colleges was higher than it is today.[70] By the end of the Mamluk period in the fourteenth century, it has been claimed, it was hard to find a woman without a teaching license.[71]

The first official Islamic public educational system dates to the eleventh century Seljuq Empire: the Madrasah Nizamiyyah.[72] The world's oldest university, the University of al-Karaouine in Fez, Morocco, was founded in 859 by a woman, Fatimah al-Fihri, and included facilities for women to listen to scholars. A second branch of the university, al-Andalus Mosque, for female and male students, was founded in Fez by Fatimah's sister, Maryam.[73] Another important school for girls was Ribat al-Baghdadiyya, founded in the fourteenth century in Cairo, Egypt. Religious seminaries for girls, known as *khalwah*, have existed in the Sudan since the fifteenth century, providing instruction in Qu'ran memorization and recitation as well as Islamic law.[74]

In some places, movements calling for women's education established schools or study circles for girls. Islamic boarding schools (*pondok pesantren*) for both girls and boys have been maintained in Indonesia since at least the sixteenth century. Since the seventeenth century, the Nu Ahong (female spiritual leaders) of China have worked to educate women, establishing Qur'an schools in Shanxi

---

68. Cheruvallil-Contractor, "Qur'anic Schools for Girls," 145–48.

69. For example, the twelfth-century scholar Ibn Asakir wrote he had studied with eighty different female teachers. Rebecca McLain Hodges, "Education and Women: Historical Discourse," in *The Oxford Encyclopedia of Islam and Women*, ed. DeLong-Bas, 1:246–51.

70. Ruth Roded, *Women in Islamic Biographical Collections: From Ibn Sa'd to Who's Who* (Boulder, CO: L. Rienner, 1994). The percentage of women Islamic scholars rose from 1 percent in the twelfth century to 15% by the fifteenth century. Hodges, "Education and Women," in *The Oxford Encyclopedia of Islam and Women*, ed. DeLong-Bas, 1:246–51.

71. Olahi, "Education and Women," in *The Oxford Encyclopedia of Islam and Women*, ed. DeLong-Bas, 1:256–58.

72. Ibid.

73. Cheruvallil-Contractor, "Qur'anic Schools for Girls," 145–48.

74. Laura Lohman, "Qur'anic Recitation Schools for Girls," in *The Oxford Encyclopedia of Islam and Women*, ed. DeLong-Bas, 2:143–45.

and Shandong provinces, which ultimately developed into women's mosques.[75] The eighteenth-century Wahhabi movement of Saudi Arabia emphasized Qur'an education and literacy for both girls and boys and included women among the teachers, as did Qur'an schools in nineteenth-century Russia. Women's education was similarly encouraged by the nineteenth-century Sokoto Caliphate in Nigeria. Study circles for girls continue today through Al-Huda International, located in Pakistan and in Canada, and in study groups for Qur'an meaning and recitation in Bangladesh and Indonesia. All of these groups serve to build a sense of female community and solidarity.

Although some express concerns about potential radicalization of students in madrasahs, particularly where traditional gender roles for girls are emphasized and curricula are gender-specific, some activists have pushed back, observing that such organizations may be the only avenues to literacy for poor girls from rural areas. They may, therefore, offer routes out of poverty or at least toward better marriage prospects, thereby rendering them agents of change rather than replicators of tradition. This controversy has been pointed out with respect to the Jamia Hafza affiliated with the Red Mosque in Islamabad, Pakistan, for example.[76]

Current debates about women's education are often rooted in negative memories of colonialism. Under colonial rule, education was given in often racist, xenophobic, and religiously insensitive ways as "enlightened" Western, secular values displaced those of native cultures. Hostile attitudes toward local practices, such as gender segregation and veiling, often limited the appeal of such education for girls to only those who were upper-class, Westernized elites who had accepted colonial policies and administrations. In addition, the frequent connection of schools to Christian missionary activities made many families suspicious of education in general, rendering girls' education a particular flashpoint in the subsequent struggles for independence and assertions of national sovereignty and "authentic" cultural

---

75. Lohman, "Qur'anic Recitation Schools,"143–45.

76. Cheruvallil-Contractor, "Qur'anic Schools for Girls," 145–48. On the one hand, this school has become controversial for its students' activism, including the use of violence, in pursuit of a "purer" society. On the other hand, it is the largest school in the Islamic world providing girls' education. Although education is provided in many subjects, including math, female students are only tested on knowledge of Islam.

and religious identities.[77] Yet, today, in most places, mass public education is knowledge-based and rooted in European models. In addition, many women and men travel abroad for Western-style higher education and training. Some very conservative countries, such as the Gulf states, have brought satellite campuses of prestigious universities onto their own territory, thereby eliminating the need for women to leave their home countries for quality education.

Muslim Women's Religious Leadership

Advances in women's education and women's public presence in the modern era have been accompanied by an increase in women's religious leadership in many Muslim communities around the world, from the Middle East to South and Southeast Asia, Europe, and the United States.[78] Particularly with the expansion of religious expression into mass communications technologies, such as radio, television, cassettes, CDs, DVDs, and the Internet, women have gained access to physical and virtual audiences as revivalist teachers, speakers, advisors, and interpreters of scripture and Islamic law. Although the use of unconventional spaces has enabled women to circumvent, to some extent, constraints imposed by the state or male authority, nevertheless, many women find it a challenge to be recognized and to work for change in a system dominated by male interpreters.[79]

---

77. Sijamhodzic-Nadarevic, "Education and Women," in *The Oxford Encyclopedia of Islam and Women*, ed. DeLong-Bas, 1:251–56.

78. Data on women's access to public space, education, health, etc., can be found on a country-by-country basis in the World Economic Forum's Global Gender Gap Report, issued annually: *https://www.weforum.org/reports*. Some Muslim-majority countries continue to make poor showings, such as Pakistan, and a few, such as Afghanistan, are in such poor shape that no quantitative information is available, although some improvement is being made. In other countries, such as in the Gulf, girls outnumber boys in higher education and are more likely to finish their degrees. Perhaps surprisingly, given poverty rates, Bangladesh holds the highest score for any Muslim-majority country.

79. For an overview of the issues, see Hilary Kalmbach, "Introduction: Islamic Authority and the Study of Female Religious Leaders," in *Women, Leadership, and Mosques: Changes in Contemporary Islamic Authority*, ed. Masooda Bano and Hilary Kalmbach (Leiden: Brill, 2012), 1–28.

Muslim women craft their religious leadership through a variety of sources, including knowledge, personal reputation for piety, charity and volunteer work, ability to teach and preach, family connections, and capacity to work with a variety of communities, both Muslim and non-Muslim and ranging from local to national and international. Though they often work in traditional religious spaces, such as mosques and Islamic or Qur'anic schools, Muslim women religious leaders are also increasingly present in nontraditional spaces, such as private homes, rented premises, community and university facilities, and virtual space, particularly on the Internet and social media.[80] Some are even being recognized by traditionally male-led organizations, such as Dr. Ingrid Mattson, the first woman and first convert to be elected president of the Islamic Society of North America in 2006.[81]

Ways in which Muslim women demonstrate religious leadership and authority include Qur'an recitation, instruction, and interpretation; serving as prayer leaders (*imamahs*); interpreting Islamic law as *mujtahidahs* (those engaged in *ijtihad*) and *muftiyahs* (those issuing fatwas); and leading and working in Sufi orders. Although broad documentation of women's roles as master Qur'an reciters can be found throughout the historical record, there is little documentation of their Qur'an interpretation before the nineteenth century outside of anecdotal information. Historically, women most likely served as unofficial interpreters for other women, maintaining reputations through oral tradition rather than written documentation.[82] This began to change in the late nineteenth century with rising levels of education and literacy among women in certain locations, such as Egypt, where Bint al-Shati (Aishah Abd al-Shati Rahman) was one of the first women to publish her exegesis. By the late 1980s, Muslim women were actively participating in interpretation, calling for the deliberate reading of male-female and social equality into the

---

80. Hilary Kalmbach, "Religious Authority of Women," in *The Oxford Encyclopedia of Islam and Women*, ed. DeLong-Bas, 2:177–79.

81. Laleh Bakhtiar, "Ingrid Mattson," in *The Oxford Encyclopedia of Islam and Women*, ed. DeLong-Bas, 1:634–35, and her biography in chapter 9 of this book, "Muslim-Christian Encounters: Conflict and Coexistence."

82. Zahra Ayubi, "Qur'an: Women's Exegesis," in *The Oxford Encyclopedia of Islam and Women*, ed. DeLong-Bas, 2:136–40.

text, particularly where traditional readings of the Qur'an have been used to justify the abuse and degradation of women.[83] Today, women can study exegesis in prominent schools such as Egypt's Al-Azhar University and Qom Seminary in Tehran, Iran.

Most female leaders seeking to reinterpret texts, engage in activist work, or expand possibilities for female religious leadership are working in North America, Europe, Indonesia, and Malaysia.[84] In Malaysia, women's activist groups such as Sisters-in-Islam and Musawah work toward social and religious reform through woman-friendly, egalitarian interpretation of the Qur'an.[85] Women's branches of major Muslim organizations in Indonesia, such as Aisiyah and Fatayat Nahdlatul Ulama, also work to maintain their own conservative, non-Western interpretations of Islamic texts, pushing back against the increasing influence of foreign extremist (particularly Salafi and Wahhabi) and misogynist or patriarchal interpretations that discourage legal reforms related to women's status within the family. Women in Java, in particular, direct prayer circles, write exegetical studies, and call for more egalitarian readings of the Qur'an in the *pesantren* curriculum.[86]

In other cases, state agencies have opened training programs for female religious leaders in order to better respond to women's needs and interests, as well as to counteract extremism. For example, the Diyanet in Turkey certifies women as assistant muftis (legal experts), while the Moroccan Ministry of Habous (Religious Endowments) trains women to serve as religious counselors (*murshidat*)[87] working

---

83. See Barlas, *"Believing Women" in Islam,* esp. 4–7, and 24–25.

84. In the United States, Dr. Kecia Ali became the first American Muslim woman to officiate at a Muslim wedding in 2004. See Kecia Ali, "Acting on a Frontier of Religious Ceremony: With Questions and Quiet Resolve, a Woman Officiates at a Muslim Wedding," Harvard Divinity Bulletin (Jan. 4, 2005), *http://www.hds.harvard.edu/news/bulletin/articles/ali_ceremony.html.*

85. See Zainah Anwar, "Musawah," in *The Oxford Encyclopedia of Islam and Women,* ed. DeLong-Bas, 1:702–3.

86. For details, see Pieternella van Doorn-Harder, *Women Shaping Islam: Reading the Qur'an in Indonesia* (Chicago: University of Illinois Press, 2006).

87. For more information on Morocco, see Doris Gray, "Murshidah," in *The Oxford Encyclopedia of Islam and Women,* ed. DeLong-Bas, 1:701. The program began in 2006 following a major change to the personal status code (Mudawwana) in 2004. Though expected to play a role in preventing radicalization, particularly in poor and marginalized areas, the Murshidah's main job is to communicate legal reforms and rights with respect to family planning, domestic violence, and raising children.

out of government mosques.[88] Other female religious leaders and teachers, such as Nu Ahong of China, have operated in opposition to state communist policies that seek to limit, if not suppress, religious expression and identity, although their main task is to support and promote women's spirituality and education.[89] Finally, some female religious leaders seek fame and fortune on reality TV shows, such as Malaysia's *Solehah*, which crowns the best female preacher among candidates competing in religious knowledge, oratory skills, and personality.[90]

One of the most contested and important roles for women religious leaders has been inserting their voices into Islamic legal interpretation, especially family law. Shiite female legal scholars, known as *mujtahidahs*, often study at the Jamiat al-Zahra, the women's Shiite seminary in Qom, Iran, which teaches an estimated twelve thousand students from around the world. Two graduates, Nosrat Amin Esfahani (d. 1983)[91] and Zohreh Sefati (b. 1948),[92] have been declared ayatollahs, the highest level of scholar, owing to their levels

---

88. Roja Fazaeli, "Education and Women: Women's Religious Education," in *Islam and Women*, ed. Natana J. DeLong-Bas (New York: Oxford University Press, 2013), 1:258–61.

89. China has the longest history of female imams. Today, the Islamic Association of China, a state-controlled body, issues licenses to male and female imams. For details and historical development, see Maria Jaschok, "Nu Ahong," in *The Oxford Encyclopedia of Islam and Women*, ed. DeLong-Bas (New York: Oxford University Press, 2013), 2:15–17, and Louisa Lim, "Female Imams Blaze Trail amid China's Muslims," *http://www.npr.org/2010/07/21/128628514/female-imams-blaze-trail-amid-chinas-muslims*.

90. Angie Teo, "Malaysia Islamic TV Show Crowns Best Woman Preacher," *Arab News*, December 19, 2011. The grand prize is a certificate, an all-expense paid Hajj, $10,000 in cash, and a new car.

91. Amin published extensively in law, ethics, and philosophy, in addition to a widely studied fifteen–volume exegetical study of the Qur'an. She was considered the most outstanding female *mujtahidah* of the twentieth century, on a par with leading male Shiite scholars. In addition to establishing her own all-girls Qur'an school in the 1960s and a women's Islamic seminary, she also taught male students and is included in the chains of teachers of some male ayatollahs. Mirjam Kunkler, "Nosrat Amin," in *The Oxford Encyclopedia of Islam and Women*, ed. DeLong-Bas, 1:37–38.

92. Sefati is considered the most prominent female religious authority in Iran today, having studied with multiple ayatollahs. She is particularly recognized for her work on marriage and has worked with the parliament, Guardian Council, and Expediency Councils on these issues, successfully arguing for raising the minimum age for girls for marriage. Mirjam Kunkler, "Zohreh Sefati," in *The Oxford Encyclopedia of Islam and Women*, ed. DeLong-Bas, 2:217–18.

of learning, popular acclaim, and recognition of their scholarship by male ayatollahs.[93]

Sunni female scholars who issue legal opinions (fatwas) are called *muftiyahs*. Only a few early historical examples of women fulfilling this function exist,[94] beginning with Muhammad's favorite wife, Aisha. One famous *muftiyah*, who was also renowned as an ascetic, was Umm Darda (d. 652). She issued fatwas on Hajj rituals, commerce, and permitting women to pray in the same position as men.[95] In the modern-day era, two Egyptian women, Dr. Su'ad Saleh[96] and Dr. Abla Al-Kahlawy,[97] have been approved by Al-Azhar University to issue fatwas. Both host popular call-in TV shows for on-the-spot fatwas. Both also hold doctorates in comparative jurisprudence from al-Azhar and have served as deans of Islamic Studies in the Women's Faculty there. In other places, such as India and Syria, women work as deputy muftis focusing on women's issues. Women serve as judges (*qadiyahs*) in Palestine and in the family courts of Java, Indonesia.[98] There is also an all-female fatwa council in Hyderabad, India.[99]

93. Roja Fazaeli, "Ayatollah," in *The Oxford Encyclopedia of Islam and Women*, ed. DeLong-Bas, 1:70–72, and Roja Fazaeli, "Mujtahidah," in *The Oxford Encyclopedia of Islam and Women*, ed. DeLong-Bas, 1:698–701.

94. This may be because the record has not been thoroughly investigated. Biographical dictionaries point to the existence of hundreds of female jurists qualified to issue fatwas. See Mirjam Kunkler, "Muftiyah," in *The Oxford Encyclopedia of Islam and Women*, ed. DeLong-Bas, 1:689–90.

95. She was known for her lectures on hadith and *fiqh* in the men's and women's sections of the mosque and for instructing the caliph of Damascus, Abd al-Malik b. Marwan. Her legal advice was sought by many jurists. Sayeed, *Women and the Transmission of Religious Knowledge*, 70–72.

96. Saleh has taken on a number of socially contentious issues, including challenging a man's unilateral right to divorce and, most famously, a 2006 fatwa against the *niqab*, which she declared to be a pre-Islamic custom with no Islamic merit. Although many formal complaints and death threats were issued against her, Egypt's Grand Mufti upheld the fatwa and toured women's sections of Egyptian universities to spread the message. See Shuruq Naguib, "Su'ad Saleh," in *The Oxford Encyclopedia of Islam and Women*, ed. DeLong-Bas, 2:206–8. Saleh is featured in the documentary film *Veiled Voices*, directed by Brigid Maher ([Seattle:] Typecast Releasing, [2010]).

97. Al-Kahlawy is known for critiques of misogynist interpretations of Islamic texts and extremism and has been a strong advocate for women's equal access to divorce and gender equality. Nermin Allam, "Abla Al-Kahlawy," in *The Oxford Encyclopedia of Islam and Women*, ed. DeLong-Bas, 1:558–59.

98. Kalmbach, "Religious Authority of Women," 177–79.

99. Roja Fazaeli, "Education and Women: Women's Religious Education," 258–61.

Finally, Muslim women serve as leaders in many Sufi orders globally, particularly in the United States and Europe. Their most important involvement is in grassroots women's organizations focused on gender, educational, health, environmental, and political issues, as well as provision of relief efforts and human and social services. This is in keeping with a long history of wealthy women being Sufi patrons, benefactresses, and educated commentators on Sufi treatises.[100]

Striving for Gender Justice

Gender justice, defined as resistance to all forms of dominance and oppression based on gender, is one of the main aims for Muslim women's religious leadership. Without the freedom of agency and choice, women are robbed of their ability to be responsible before God for their own moral actions and judgments and their accompanying rewards and punishments.

Dr. Amina Wadud (b. 1952)

An African American convert to Islam, Dr. Amina Wadud (b. 1952) is best known for her progressive focus on gender equality rooted in the teachings of the Qur'an. Her book *Qur'an and Woman: Rereading the Sacred Text from a Woman's Perspective* (1999) calls for reforms rooted in divine intent rather than socially constructed gender roles

Continued

---

100. Between the ninth and eleventh centuries, between 4 and 23% of entries in Sufi biographical dictionaries were women. For details, see Melinda Krokus, "Sufism and Women: Historical Overview," in *The Oxford Encyclopedia of Islam and Women*, ed. DeLong-Bas, 2:285–90. For coverage of contemporary women's involvement in specific Sufi orders in South Asia, see Kelly Pemberton, *Women Mystics and Sufi Shrines in India* (Columbia: University of South Carolina Press, 2010). For Central Asia, see Razia Sultanova, *From Shamanism to Sufism: Women, Islam, and Culture in Central Asia* (London: I. B. Tauris, 2011). For Turkey, see Catharina Raudvere, *The Book and the Roses: Sufi Women, Visibility, and Zikir in Contemporary Istanbul* (London: I. B. Tauris, 2002). For global coverage of the Naqshbandi order, including in Great Britain, see Pnina Werbner, *Pilgrims of Love: The Anthropology of a Global Sufi Cult* (London: Hurst, 2003). For translation of the Qur'an into English by a Sufi woman, see Laleh Bakhtiar's *The Sublime Qur'an* (Chicago: Kazi Publications, 2009).

Dr. Amina Wadud (b. 1952) *Continued*

that reduce men and women to a small number of functions, typically biological. Wadud has been a leading voice in Muslim women's activism in Malaysia, the United States, South Africa, and Indonesia and is a founding member of Sisters-in-Islam, a women's rights NGO (nongovernmental organization). In *Inside the Gender Jihad: Women's Reform in Islam* (2006), she recounts her experiences as a "Muslim woman in the trenches." Recalling her family's ancestry as American slaves, she views dress and modesty as expressions of historical identity, personal dignity, and sexual integrity. She was the first modern Muslim woman to lead a mixed-gender prayer service in Cape Town, South Africa, in 1994 and then again in New York City in 2005, both of which earned her death threats. Wadud was awarded the Danish Democracy Prize in 2007 and was also the subject of a documentary that year, *The Noble Struggle of Amina Wadud*, directed by Elli Safari.

Amina Wadud leads a mixed-gender prayer session at the Synod House in New York City in 2005. Muslim women are on opposite sides of the room but are present in the same space, following the example set during Muhammad's lifetime.

The implications of gender justice extend far beyond "women's rights." Leading Islamic activist Amina Wadud argues that to fully humanize women, gender justice requires the inclusion of women at all levels of Muslim practice, performance, policy construction, and political and religious leadership.[101] A similarly inclusive approach could be applied to any group of marginalized persons, making it clear the central goal of justice can only be pursued in a context of choice. This raises key questions about broader needs for freedom of choice and agency across the board.

With respect to women, activists argue gender justice must begin at home, because women's roles in the family are the birth-place of inequalities in the name of the "ideal" family.[102] Muslim women activists seek to answer questions like the following: Does "Islam" require Muslim women to live only as wives and mothers? What happens when they don't, whether due to divorce, widowhood, infertility, or living as a single person? What happens when Muslim women feel they must adhere to marriage, even when this would endanger their health and well-being, such as in the case of domestic violence, sexual abuse, an unfaithful husband, or a husband infected with HIV? Must a woman always submit to her husband, or are there times when being a faithful Muslim woman means preserving one's own life and that of one's children as a priority?[103] Ultimately, the questions focus on whether there is more than one way to live as a faithful Muslim woman and whether one can only live as a faithful Muslim woman in the context of a nuclear family. Similar questions might be raised regarding men: Must they always fulfill the roles of breadwinner and disciplinarian? What happens in the case of stay-at-home dads? Are they less "Muslim" because they choose to be more involved in child-rearing?

Organizations working toward gender justice generally take a collaborative and consultative approach to their work, reaching across boundaries of class, the rural-urban divide, and, often, inter-national borders, as their goals are not limited to a single group of women. For example, WISE (Women's Islamic Initiative in Spiritu-ality and Equality) is a social network and a grassroots social justice

---

101. Wadud, *Inside the Gender Jihad*, 10.

102. Ibid., 12.

103. Wadud, Ibid., 236, poignantly asks, "The consequences for the *muhsinat*, married virtuous women, and the *qaanitat*, the religious and morally devout Muslim women, are the same—they will die because they did what they had been taught was 'good' . . . How does 'Islam' resolve this problem?"

movement. With strong religious credentials and legitimacy, it has attracted thousands of members in more than one hundred countries. The combination of a global presence with local projects aims for a cohesive approach to redressing women's grievances. Seeing a need for solid interpretations of religious texts that support gender justice, some members of WISE founded the International Shura Council of Muslim Women to articulate and uphold holistic strategies, rooted in Islam, to address social issues that include Female Genital Cutting, adoption, orphans, women's religious leadership, honor crimes and killings, stigmatization and criminalization of rape victims, child marriage, and girls' education. The council is the first composed entirely of women and includes experts in Islamic law, the humanities, and social sciences.[104]

Islamic Feminism

Islamic feminists also work to redress inequities resulting from patriarchy. These feminists denounce the use of "Islam" to justify patriarchal structures and practices, and push back against those who claim "Islam" can only be legitimately and authentically practiced through control over women with veiling, seclusion, and male power over the family unit. Although they have drawn lessons and inspiration from secular feminists, critiques of secular feminism as yet another Western colonial enterprise have led Islamic feminists to distance themselves from Western secular feminists. Islamic feminists believe genuine and lasting change for women's equality will only be widely accepted if presented as an Islamic ideal within an Islamic framework. They seek to achieve modernization, equated with technology, science, and a higher living standard, while avoiding Westernization's association with sexual promiscuity, erosion of the family and community, and drug and alcohol abuse.[105] Thus,

104. For details, see Samaneh Oladi Ghadikolei, "Women's Islamic Initiative in Spirituality and Equality (WISE)," in *The Oxford Encyclopedia of Islam and Women*, ed. DeLong-Bas, 2:497–98. The official website is *http://www.wisemuslimwomen.org*. Information on the Shura Council can be found at *http://www.wisemuslimwomen.org /about/shuracouncil/*.

105. Margot Badran, updated by Natana J. DeLong-Bas, "Feminism: Concept and Debates," in *The Oxford Encyclopedia of Islam and Women*, ed. DeLong-Bas, 1:312–17.

though their goals are "feminist" in aspiration, they present them as "Islamic" in terms of language and sources of legitimacy, rendering these goals inherent to the understanding and practice of the Muslim faith.[106]

The term *Islamic feminism* first appeared in Iran, but quickly spread to other places, particularly countries in which patriarchal political Islam had become popular, such as Turkey, Egypt, and Malaysia.[107] In South Africa, antiapartheid Muslim activists used the liberation of their country as a springboard for liberating its Muslim community from injustices. This turned into a broader struggle for eliminating discrimination of all varieties, including that against women.[108] Islamic feminism has also been active in the United States and disseminated on the Internet.

Goals of Islamic feminists around the world include legal reforms; the right of women to attend congregational prayers in the mosque; access to all areas of education and work; universal health

---

106. Margot Badran, updated by Natana J. DeLong-Bas, "Nature of Islamic Feminism," in *The Oxford Encyclopedia of Islam and Women*, ed. DeLong-Bas, 1:317–21. Not included in this discussion are figures such as Irshad Manji or Ayaan Hirsi Ali, who claim the mantle of "Islam," having been born or raised Muslim, but who have either directly or indirectly left the faith owing to their criticisms of its practices. However legitimate some of their points may be, such as raising concerns about religious freedom, freedom of expression, or breaking away from authoritarianism, their methods for doing so are often reductive, oversimplified, and external to the scriptural sources. They present their arguments in the form of exposés of atrocities allegedly committed in the name of Islam, rather than working for change within the faith tradition; they believe problems are inherent to the faith and so it cannot be reformed. This is similar to the position taken by post-Christian feminists such as Mary Daly, who call for a revolution in the form of complete rejection of the faith rather than reform. Ali even goes so far as to call for getting rid of the Qur'an and hadith altogether. Thus the impact of figures such as Manji or Ali within Islamic discourse is limited, if not nonexistent, despite non-Muslim supporters in the West. Geoffrey Nash refers to this phenomenon as the "native informant" approach to postcolonial theory in which a person writes about Islamic societies with the goal of producing representations of female subjugation by patriarchal oppression as "representative" of Islam. The implication is that all one must do to resolve a given society's problems is to free it from "Islam." Although this makes a good sound bite, the issues at stake are far more complex. See Geoffrey Nash, *Writing Muslim Identity* (London: Continuum, 2011).

107. For details, see Ziba Mir-Hosseini, *Islam and Gender: The Religious Debate in Contemporary Iran* (Princeton: Princeton University Press, 1999).

108. See, for example, Farid Esack, *On Being a Muslim: Finding a Religious Path in the World Today* (Oxford: Oneworld, 1999), 111–36.

care; freedom from violence, abuse, and sexual exploitation; and greater control over their own bodies, including access to birth control, the discontinuation of Female Genital Cutting (FGC),[109] and an end to the obsession with female virginity and the rooting of male honor in women's sexual purity, particularly as a justification for controlling women's movements and activities.

At the same time, many Muslim women believe what some dismiss as merely cultural interpretations of Islam are actually requirements of the faith. Rather than seeking to change parameters such as gender segregation in the mosque or covering their hair, these women look for empowerment within these perceived obligations, such as by creating fashionable and designer-label veils and viewing gender segregation as an opportunity for safeguarding their modesty and avoiding harassment.[110]

"Saving" Muslim Women[111]—By Whom and for What?

Although academic discussions try to identify voices and effective methods for change, and work to rebalance the historical record, the reality remains that, in many places, Muslim women do not have the luxury of intellectualizing about issues affecting their lives. The media remains flooded with what are often terrifying images of Muslim women: Muslim women who have had acid thrown in their faces,

---

109. Although FGC or FGM is not an "Islamic" practice (it is an African cultural practice that remains widespread among Christian and Muslim Africans alike), it remains widespread in thirty countries in Africa, the Middle East, and Asia. Although it is illegal in some countries, such as Indonesia, it nevertheless remains broadly practiced; it is believed that 97.5% of Muslim women in Indonesia are affected. The practice has spread to the United States and Europe, largely through immigration. For more information, see the World Health Organization's website at *http://www.who .int/mediacentre/factsheets/fs241/en/*.

110. For a variety of voices from young (under forty) American Muslim women on these issues, see the collection of essays edited by Maria M. Ebrahimji and Zahra T. Suratwala, *I Speak for Myself: American Women on Being Muslim* (Ashland, OR: White Cloud, 2011).

111. This issue was famously raised in the aftermath of 9/11 by Lila Abu-Lughod, "Do Muslim Women Really Need Saving? Anthropological Reflections on Cultural Relativism and Its Others," *American Anthropology* 104, no. 3 (2002): 783–90.

Muslim women being stoned to death because they were accused of adultery while reporting rape, Muslim women draped from head to toe in black sitting in the back of a donkey cart, Muslim child brides who haven't even reached puberty being married off to much older men, Muslim women suspected of having a boyfriend or even just dancing in the rain being killed to restore their family's honor, and the list goes on. In light of the challenges and opportunities facing Muslim women, many people ask, what can we do? Where do our responsibilities lie? Do Muslim women need to be rescued and, if so, where, from whom, by whom, and how?

These questions have been raised many times since the colonial era, beginning with issues of veiling and education and then expanding to questions about human rights and justice. Today's questions might be rephrased, Who is responsible for ensuring justice for Muslim women, and how can this be achieved without practicing cultural or religious imperialism? How best to address and redress injustices without essentializing[112] or sexualizing "Muslim women" or falling into the trap of fighting for the emancipation of women while assuming this will also free women and society from their backwardness? At the same time, there is a need to acknowledge and critically engage the reality of Western interventions and presence in Muslim-majority countries, whether this is overt in a colonial regime or military presence or covert in business holdings and economic influence. There is also a need to acknowledge and engage the reality of Western support for repressive, authoritarian regimes. Rather than simply viewing the West as a potential source of liberation for Muslim women, the West must take responsibility for its role in adding to their oppression.

There are four ways Westerners could work to change their approach to Muslim women, to shift from "saving" them to working with and supporting them. The first consists of recognizing there is no single category of "Muslim women." Taking a one-size-fits-all approach does not work. The experiences of Muslim women are affected by many circumstances, including colonialism, war, immigration, access to education, and business opportunities, to name but

---

112. *Essentializing* means to reduce "Muslim women" to a single category with the assumption that all Muslim women's experiences, needs, and interests are the same.

a few. In some cases, they have been victims of circumstances and decisions beyond their control, whether in matters of marriage, the eyes of the law, or a political system that does not include their voices. In others, they serve as parliamentarians, prime ministers, ambassadors, CEOs of multinational corporations, and heads of NGOs. Understanding the specific context, local and national, in which a particular Muslim woman lives and works is key to understanding the particular challenges and opportunities she may encounter and how she might best engage them.

The second entails realizing that perceptions of Muslim women are really just that—perceptions, not necessarily realities. It may be tempting and even comforting to think of Muslim women as passive victims, perpetual objects of male desire, subjects of Islamic law and religion, and women who sit at home, raise children, and fulfill men's sexual needs. Such perceptions, however, come across as patronizing and pitying, if not colonial and even Orientalist.[113] They also assume Muslim women want to be liberated and that liberation means becoming more like Western women, an assumption Muslim women do not necessarily support.[114] As one African American Muslim woman put it, "I've been told that, as a Muslim woman, I'm oppressed, repressed, suppressed, depressed, and every other kind of 'pressed' there is, but no one ever asks me what *my* understanding of Islam is or how *I* feel Islam treats women. And ain't I a Muslim?!"[115]

Rather than seeking to become like Western women, Muslim women often pity Western women as overly sexualized in demeanor and appearance; failing to see their exploitation by men, because they are trapped in a language of "empowerment" that often focuses on appearance and wearing scant, if any, clothing. Muslim women sometimes find Western women are insufficiently focused on their personalities, achievements, or individuality. Rather than living in

---

113. Nash, *Writing Muslim Identity*, 53, expresses *Orientalism* as First World women claiming sisterhood with Third World women, but retaining a sense of superiority because of the level of deprivation in the Third World. The equation is unbalanced, despite good intentions. For more on Orientalism as the exoticization of the East, see Edward Said, *Orientalism* (New York: Vintage Books, 1979).

114. Abu-Lughod, "Do Muslim Women Really Need Saving?," 787, warns against this tendency.

115. Personal communication to the author by phone, April 2005.

relationships with family, friends, and neighbors, Muslim women often see Western women as overly stressed by the double burden of working full-time and caring for children and the home; indeed, they are often depressed, anxious, and unhappy. Although Western women might respond that this is a false impression or at least not applicable to every Western woman, the point is that perceptions go in both directions, making it critical to move beyond generalized perceptions to personalized realities.

A third change would be to acknowledge that focusing on "women's issues" risks losing sight of the bigger picture. For example, in the aftermath of 9/11, saving the women of Afghanistan became a mantra for the Bush administration as it worked to generate support for American intervention. The sad reality of Afghanistan at that time was that women were not the only ones in need of being saved. Men and children needed saving too—from foreign interventions that had resulted in twenty-two years of warfare, battling warlords, and the decimation of the people and the landscape. In addition, Afghanistan was then home to the highest per capita concentration of landmines in the world. The majority of its population lived in poverty, malnutrition, and personal insecurity, while the education and public health systems were almost completely defunct. Afghanistan's issues went far beyond worrying about women needing to wear a burqa in public.[116] Similarly, though many in the West have focused on required veiling and the prior ban on women driving in Saudi Arabia, Saudi women generally have been far more concerned about the overriding issue of male guardianship that controls everything from when and if they can leave the house to whether, where, and under what conditions they can get a job. Driving was only a small piece of the picture.

Recognition of these broader issues could productively lead to a fourth change, namely recognition that Muslim women can be active agents with a voice in their own lives, goals, and aspirations,

---

116. Abu-Lughod, "Do Muslim Women Really Need Saving?," 784–86, further notes that Western assumptions about the burqa do not match Afghan perceptions of it. The burqa predates the Taliban and is known among the Pashtuns as a symbol of good, respectable women who were from strong families and not reduced to making a living selling on the street. Rather than a sign of oppression or lack of agency, Abu-Lughod argues for understanding the burqa as a "mobile home" of sorts that indicates respectability, honor, and morality. Again, perception lies in the eye of the beholder.

regardless of their level of education, socioeconomic background, or level of religious commitment. What many seek is the opportunity to make their own choices—about marriage, divorce, property management, education, work, whether to have children, how many, and how to retain custody of them—rather than having choices imposed on them, whether by religious leaders, the state, or other countries. This would shift the focus from trying to save Muslim women to working together with Muslim women to save families and communities torn apart by war, violence, famine, poverty, and other inequalities rooted in conflicts over power and money, and hopefully to bring the world to a more peaceful and mutually beneficial place of constructive cooperation for the common good.[117]

Review Questions

1. What benefits and challenges do Muslim women find in their faith tradition? Are there any areas in which their ability to make their own decisions is limited?

2. Identify and discuss three ways in which the Qur'an addresses women and women's rights.

3. How does the Qur'an describe the nature of women? Of men? Are women and men to be evaluated on their gender or as human beings or moral agents? How are they supposed to interact with each other?

4. What can we learn about women's status and rights from Muhammad's example?

5. What was the original intended purpose of veiling and how has that developed over time? Does veiling today still fulfill that purpose?

6. What is gender justice? What, if any, resources exist within Islam that support gender justice?

---

117. Abu-Lughod, "Do Muslim Women Really Need Saving?," 789, has recommended working to make the world a more just place by organizing it according to values that lead to peace and social transformation rather than strategic military and economic demands, such as oil interests, the arms industry, and the international drug trade.

Discussion Questions

1. How might the status of women in Islam be characterized? According to what criteria? Is more than one characterization possible?
2. To what degree should religion evolve and adapt to changing circumstances, particularly where family dynamics are concerned?
3. Is Islam an inherently patriarchal tradition?
4. What opportunities exist for Muslim women's leadership and participation in public life and how might these best be supported and encouraged?

For Further Study

Reading

Ahmed, Leila. *Women and Gender in Islam: Historical Roots of a Modern Debate*. New Haven: Yale University Press, 1992.

Bano, Masooda, and Hilary Kalmbach, eds. *Women, Leadership, and Mosques: Changes in Contemporary Islamic Authority*. Leiden: Brill, 2012.

Barlas, Asma. *"Believing Women" in Islam: Unreading Patriarchal Interpretations of the Qur'an*. Austin: University of Texas Press, 2002.

Bucar, Elizabeth. *The Islamic Veil: A Beginner's Guide*. Oxford: Oneworld, 2012.

DeLong-Bas, Natana J., ed. *The Oxford Encyclopedia of Islam and Women*. 2 vols. New York: Oxford University Press, 2013.

Esposito, John L., with Natana J. DeLong-Bas. *Women in Muslim Family Law*. Rev. ed. Syracuse: Syracuse University Press, 2001.

Kugle, Scott Siraj al-Haqq. *Homosexuality in Islam: Critical Reflection on Gay, Lesbian, and Transgender Muslims*. Oxford: Oneworld, 2010.

Mernissi, Fatima. *The Veil and the Male Elite: A Feminist Interpretation of Women's Rights in Islam*. Translated by Mary Jo Lakeland. New York: Perseus, 1992.

Sayeed, Asma. *Women and the Transmission of Religious Knowledge in Islam*. New York: Cambridge University Press, 2013.

Wadud, Amina. *Inside the Gender Jihad: Women's Reform in Islam*. Oxford: Oneworld, 2006.

Films

Sharma, Parvez, and Sandi Dubowski. *A Jihad for Love*. [San Francisco]: Kanopy Streaming, 2015.

Documentary following the challenges faced by gay and lesbian Muslims in their struggles to reconcile their faith and sexuality amid public and government opposition.

Maher, Brigid, Karen Bauer, Sarah Hassaine, and Paul A. Oehlers. *Veiled Voices*. [Seattle]: Typecast Releasing, 2010.

Documentary about the work of and social challenges faced by three female Muslim religious leaders in Syria, Egypt, and Lebanon.

Links

Yuna, *www.yunamusic.com/*—Yuna is a Malaysian singer, song-writer, and businesswoman and is not only one of Malaysia's most popular and successful pop musicians but also has broken into Billboard's Best R&B Albums of 2016: Critic's Pick for her album, *Chapters*. See especially her song "Rescue."

Muslim-Christian Encounters
Conflict and Coexistence

Muslim-Christian encounters are often framed in conflict. Whether in the past or today, it is often assumed that contending truth claims necessarily lead to conflict. Examples such as the Crusades, the Spanish Inquisition, assaults on Christian minorities in the Middle East and Southeast Asia, and postulations of an inherent and inevitable "clash of civilizations" have led many to conclude peaceful coexistence between Muslims and Christians is impossible.

But the historical record is more complex. Though there have been moments of conflict and intolerance, there have also been moments of mutually beneficial exchange—theological, cultural, intellectual, diplomatic, and commercial. Given that Muslims and Christians combined represent more than half of today's global population, it is crucial to find a path forward that involves working together rather than against each other to address concerns common to all people, such as poverty, food and water security, and environmental challenges.

Muslim-Christian Encounters during Muhammad's Lifetime

Initial encounters between Muslims and Christians are recorded in biographical literature about Muhammad. Some encounters were theological in nature; others occurred during daily activities and in his personal life. Six of these encounters stand out.

Muhammad's first encounter with a Christian reportedly occurred during his adolescence when he was traveling with a caravan through Syria. A Christian monk named Bahira dreamt that a future prophet would be in the caravan's company. Bahira identified Muhammad as this future prophet by a mark between his shoulders, declared as the "seal of prophethood." Fearing harm to Muhammad should his identity as a prophet become known, Bahira advised the caravan to take a different route home.[1]

A second important encounter occurred after Muhammad received his first revelation. After this revelation, Muhammad and his wife, Khadijah, sought counsel from her cousin, a Christian monk named Waraqa. A scholar of Jewish and Christian scripture, Waraqa confirmed Muhammad's prophethood, noting continuity of the message he carried with previous scripture. Waraqa also reportedly claimed his studies of scripture indicated another prophet was to come after Jesus, specifically to the Arabs.[2] Although Waraqa's recognition reassured Muhammad and Khadijah of the validity of his message, it won Muhammad neither widespread acclaim nor followers.

---

1. This "miracle story," recorded in the oldest biography of Muhammad, Ibn Ishaq's *The Life of Muhammad*, trans. A. Guillaume (New York: Oxford University Press, 1997), 79–81, placed Muhammad as a direct heir to Jewish and Christian prophetic traditions. As miracles did not figure prominently in Muhammad's life and ministry, some scholars believe the miracle stories in this text may have been intended for surrounding Christian populations familiar with miracle stories from the Bible. These stories are thus appropriately understood as a theological topos, or common theme in theological literature with symbolic value, rather than a historical record. Christian Syriac Orthodox sources also mention this encounter. Though this could be evidence the encounter actually occurred, it is also possible it was recorded to allow Syrian Orthodox Christians to claim special status under Muslim rule as the first Christians to recognize Muhammad. See Michael Philip Penn, *Envisioning Islam: Syriac Christians and the Early Muslim World* (Philadelphia: University of Pennsylvania Press, 2015), 86–90.

2. Also recorded in Ibn Ishaq's *The Life of Muhammad*, 83, this story is appropriately understood as a topos highlighting Muhammad as the logical culmination of biblical promises. Many Muslims believe Jesus foretells the coming of Muhammad in John 16:7–13, when Jesus declares the coming of the "Counselor." Though Christians understand the Counselor to be the Holy Spirit, Muslims believe this refers to Muhammad. According to the biblical passage, the Counselor comes to convict the world of guilt regarding sin, righteousness, and judgment—all messages contained in the Qur'an. Verse 13 specifies this Counselor "will not speak on his own; he will speak only what he hears, and he will tell you what is yet to come." Muslims see this as a description of how Muhammad received revelations—by hearing them spoken by the angel Gabriel. Muhammad's title of "Messenger" reflects that Muhammad simply conveyed God's message; he did not compose it.

The third encounter involved the early Muslim community, rather than Muhammad directly. Between 613 and 616 CE, persecution of the Muslims by the Quraysh tribe of Mecca had become so brutal Muhammad sent a group of Muslims to the Christian kingdom of Abyssinia (present-day Ethiopia)[3] to seek asylum.[4] The Abyssinian king, called the Negus, was known for his friendliness and opposition to injustice. When the Quraysh followed the Muslims and demanded the Negus hand them over, the Negus asked the Muslims to explain their faith. The Muslims spoke of the spiritual and community transformation they had experienced through Muhammad's message: to be honest and faithful to their word and contracts, refrain from violence and crime, practice hospitality and charity, respect the property of orphans and the chastity of women, and expand their notion of kinship beyond close blood ties. All of this, they said, was rooted in belief in the One God. When the Negus asked for an example of this message from God, the Muslim spokesperson read from Surah 19, the chapter named for Mary, the Mother of Jesus. Hearing the parallel description to the biblical story of Jesus' conception and birth and assertion of Jesus as a Word and a Spirit from God, the Negus wept, recognized the truth of the Islamic message and declared that Islam and Christianity differ only as much as a twig. He refused to hand the Muslims over and sent the Quraysh away, assuring the Muslims they would be safe with him.[5] Many of these migrants remained in Abyssinia until 622, when they returned to Mecca and made the Hijra (migration to Medina) with Muhammad. The rest returned directly to Medina in 628.

The fourth Muslim-Christian encounter was the most personal of Muhammad's life. In 628, the Coptic Christian ruler of Egypt, in response to a letter Muhammad had sent him, gifted Muhammad with a Coptic Christian slave named Marya. Though sources differ

---

3. The Abyssinians are believed to have been Monophysites, members of a branch of Christianity that holds Jesus has but one divine nature after the Incarnation rather than two (human and divine). The mainstream belief was determined by the Council of Chalcedon in 451 CE.

4. At this time, the use of violence, even in the case of self-defense, was prohibited to Muslims; thus leaving was critical to their survival.

5. Recorded in Ibn Ishaq's *The Life of Muhammad*, 146–54. The details, including names and relationships of those who emigrated, lend credence to the historical veracity of the story.

© Edinburgh University Library, Scotland/With kind permission of the University of Edinburgh/ Bridgeman Images

This fourteenth-century vellum miniature from Rashid al-Din's history of the world shows the Negus of Abyssinia receiving Muslim refugees in his court. Because of their shared religious beliefs, particularly about the Virgin Mary and Jesus, the Negus offered the refugees asylum from persecution by the Quraysh.

as to whether Marya remained a slave or became a wife and whether she converted to Islam, Marya was given the same honorific title— "Mother of the Believers"—as Muhammad's other wives. Marya was also the mother of the only child Muhammad had with any wife other than Khadijah, bringing Muhammad and Marya close together as parents and bringing Muhammad into close contact with Marya's beliefs and practices. Yet this son, Ibrahim,[6] died at only eighteen months old. The death of this son was particularly hard on Muhammad, now in the twilight of his life. Even as a prophet, there was nothing he could do to save his son from illness and death. Ibrahim's death reminded Muhammad's followers of Muhammad's humanity. He was not a divine figure.

The fifth encounter marked the first deliberately theological meeting between Christians and Muslims. About ten years after the Hijra, a Christian delegation from Najran in southern Arabia arrived in Medina, seeking a peace treaty with Muhammad.[7] Muhammad

---

6. *Ibrahim* is Arabic for Abraham, the common faith ancestor of Muslims, Christians, and Jews. The name was likely chosen for its symbolic importance and possibly to connect these faith traditions through a child born to a Muslim father and a Christian mother.

7. These Christians were also Monophysites. Some current research on Muslim-Christian relations and Christians and Christianity in the Qur'an focuses on identifying the kinds of Christians Muhammad met. See, e.g., Gabriel Said Reynolds, *The Qur'an and Its Biblical Subtext* (London: Routledge, 2010); Gabriel Said Reynolds, ed., *The Qur'an in Its Historical Context* (London: Routledge, 2008); and Sidney H. Griffith, *The Church in the Shadow of the Mosque: Christians and Muslims in the World of Islam* (Princeton: Princeton University Press, 2008), esp. 6–22.

was inside the mosque praying when the delegation arrived, so the delegates were sent to the mosque. After praying in the mosque, the Christians and Muhammad engaged in a lengthy discussion of Christology. Both sides explained their views and sought to sway the other. The result was a draw—they agreed to disagree about the status of Jesus—whether he was strictly a prophet and a messenger (Muslim belief) or whether he was also God's Son (Christian belief).[8] The Christians returned home and continued practicing their faith in peace, and Muhammad and the Muslims did the same. The exchange apparently normalized relations between them to the point that the Christians asked that a Muslim arbitrator return home with them to resolve some financial disputes.

The encounter between Muhammad and the early Muslim community and the Christians of Najran is remarkable for the equal opportunity given to each side to present their views. Both sides recognized the validity of each other's religious beliefs. Neither side cursed nor invoked God's wrath on the other. Instead, a civil, in-depth, and frank exchange of ideas, beliefs, and perceptions occurred in which all were free to participate according to their consciences. Dialogue and debate, not violence, governed this theological encounter.

Finally, in the last years of Muhammad's life, between 628 and 632, he engaged in interreligious diplomacy, inviting rulers of neighboring states to Islam.[9] He sent letters to Christian and non-Christian rulers.[10] Some rulers responded positively; others not. In cases in which territory was ultimately conquered by the Muslims, populations were given two options: they could convert or, if they were Christians or Jews, they could retain their faith and pay a tax known as the *jizya* in exchange for submitting to Muslim rule and placing themselves under Muslim protection. These options remained intact as the Islamic Empire grew after Muhammad's death.

The many types of encounters between Muslims and Christians—from the personal in marriage to the political in seeking asylum, forging relationships between communities, sending help to arbitrate disputes,

---

8. This story and the dialogue about Jesus are recorded in Ibn Ishaq's *The Life of Muhammad*, 270–77.

9. Details are recorded in Ibn Ishaq's *The Life of Muhammad*, 652–59.

10. Recipients included the Byzantine Emperor Heraclius, the Negus of Axum, and the Sassanian Chosroes.

and engaging in respectful theological dialogue—suggests modern-day assumptions of only violent encounters between Muslims and Christians are inaccurate. Muhammad's life and times provide many models for meeting, interacting with, and building relationships between faith traditions. Because these are rooted in Muhammad's life, they are part of the Sunna, Muhammad's example, that Muslims are supposed to follow.

Christians in the Qur'an

As with Muhammad's example, the Qur'an offers plentiful models of interaction with Christians. In some verses, Christians are honored for upholding their beliefs and obeying their religion; in others, they are denounced for "mistaken" or "corrupted" beliefs that have led them astray. The Qur'an is thus posited as a corrective to "mistaken" or "corrupted" beliefs, calling for a positive relationship between Muslims and Christians.

Many different Christian groups lived in and around Arabia during Muhammad's lifetime.[11] Evidence of Muslim contact with a variety of Christian groups is found in words borrowed from different languages used by Christians—Greek, Syriac, Coptic, and Ethiopic—as well as Qur'anic descriptions of some beliefs. The Qur'an uses different terms to refer to Christians, including *masihi* (those following the Messiah, from Q 3:67), *nasrani* (Nazarenes, or those from Nazareth, who are Jesus' "helpers," Q 61:14), *ahl al-injil* (people of the Gospel, Q 5:46–7), and as part of the *ahl al-kitab* (People of the Book, Q 3:64), along with Muslims, Jews, and others with a divinely revealed scripture.

Muhammad expected Christians to accept his message as divine revelation, given the similarities of many of the teachings. These similarities are referred to in verses that speak positively of Christians,

---

11. These groups included Eastern Orthodox (also called Byzantines or Greek Orthodox), Melkites (Greek Catholics), various Monophysites, including Syrian Orthodox (sometimes called Jacobites) and Copts, and Assyrians (Church of the East, Nestorians). The term *Nestorian* is considered pejorative today because of its reference to an interpreter (Nestorius), rather than God. Nestorians were dyophysites who believed the two natures of Christ remained distinct within Jesus. The various terms included here all appear in the historical literature. Monophysites in their many forms were likely the most numerous. See Goddard, *A History of Christian-Muslim Relations*, 15. Notably missing among these groups are Roman Catholics.

such as Q 2:62, which lists Christians and Jews among those who
will be rewarded by God; Q 3:199, which reasserts reward for People of the Book; and Q 57:27, which repeats reward for Christians.
Qur'an 5:82 cites Christians as those closest in affection toward
Muslims because of their priests and mystics and lack of arrogance.
Qur'an 3:55 assures that Christians are superior to unbelievers.
Qur'an 28:54 promises that those who received revelations before
Islam (assumed to be Christians and Jews) will be doubly rewarded
for their perseverance in following those revelations by avoiding evil
and giving charitably.

Yet there are also other Qur'an verses that criticize Christians,
often along with Jews, for certain behaviors, such as claiming only
Jews and Christians will go to heaven (Q 2:111), claiming God
loves Jews and Christians more than others (Q 5:18), hiding or forgetting God's revelation (Q 2:140 and 5:14), and claiming to study
the same divinely revealed Book but not respecting one another
(Q 2:113). Monasticism is also criticized (Q 57:27),[12] although
monks are respected as religious men, provided they do not claim
too much power or money for themselves (Q 9:31, 34). Particularly problematic for Muslims were ongoing efforts by Christians
and Jews to convert Muslims rather than recognizing the truth of
the Muslim revelation (Q 2:120, 135). In fact, Q 5:51 warns Muslims not to take Christians or Jews as allies given their refusal to
admit Muhammad's prophethood. Because of concerns that Jews
and Christians would join together against Muslims, Muslims were
commanded to bond with each other. Though some interpret Q
5:51 as a blanket order against taking Jews or Christians as allies
or protectors, other scholars interpret this verse as an order only
applying to that context.[13]

The Qur'an praises Christians for belief in God and the Last
Day, faithful adherence to revelation, doing good works, and giving
charitably, but criticizes Christian belief in the Trinity (Q 5:73) and

---

12. The Qur'an teaches that people are to live in relationships and that marriage
is the expected norm. A famous hadith from Muhammad sums it up, "There shall be
no monkery in Islam."

13. For a detailed discussion of these issues and Qur'anic discussions of Christians,
Jews, and other religious groups, see John Kaltner, *Introducing the Qur'an for Today's
Reader* (Minneapolis: Fortress, 2011), 136–63, esp. 145–52 for Christians.

the Incarnation (Q 5:17).[14] For Muslims, God is utterly unique and cannot take on human form; the Creator is separate from all that is created. The Qur'an teaches absolute monotheism (*tawhid*) and rejects the idea of God being multiple persons or having a son, as offspring is a characteristic of the created, not the Creator. For Muslims, Jesus is comparable to Adam: both are created by God, but neither are God.

One of the most complex discussions of Muslim-Christian relations in the Qur'an can be found in Q 5:65–77. This passage opens with concern that People of the Book might not enter Paradise because they have failed to live righteously. That failure is specified in verse 66 as not upholding the law, the Gospel, or all of God's revelation, though some remain on the right course. In other words, claiming to be People of the Book is not enough to win God's favor; action aligned with stated beliefs is needed. Verses 67–76 lament the rejections of faith and various failures of People of the Book, which include worshipping something other than God, rebellion against God, blasphemy, belief in the Trinity and deification of Jesus, failure to follow scripture and believe in God, the Last Day, and divine punishment, and not turning to God for forgiveness. The failures of Christians to abide by their own teachings prompt questions about the sincerity of their faith. The passage concludes by commanding People of the Book not to be excessive in religion but to heed what is proper and true in their scriptures' teachings and remain on God's path. Ultimately, what matters most is the relationship each person has to God and to their faith tradition.

Although there are many criticisms of Christians' failure to live their teachings, notably, certain negative terms in the Qur'an are **never** used for Christians, specifically *mushrikun* (associationists) and *kuffar* (unbelievers), however much certain groups past and present

---

14. There are also criticisms of beliefs that the Qur'an associates with Christianity but which Christians do not hold. One example is the idea that the Trinity consists of God, Jesus, and the Virgin Mary (Q 5:116). Scholars continue to research minority Christian groups in search of an explanation for this assertion, but, so far, no evidence of this ever having been a Christian belief has been found. It may have reflected common Arabian beliefs about Christianity rather than Christian beliefs per se. It may also have reflected mistaken assumptions about the role of Mary in Christian tradition based on perceptions that considering Mary as the Mother of God connected her to God in the same way as considering Jesus to be the Son of God.

claim otherwise.[15] Verses that imply some Christians might be guilty of acts of associationism or unbelief specify beliefs that are not held by most Christians, such as God being the third of three gods. Overall, the Qur'an acknowledges the essential beliefs Muslims and Christians share—belief in God and the Last Day and the importance of loving God and caring for other people. These themes form the heart of Muslim-Christian dialogue today.

Muslim-Christian Encounters in the Early Islamic Empire

On his deathbed, Muhammad reportedly said two religions could not exist together in Arabia, legitimating Muslim pursuit of territorial conquest.[16] The Islamic Empire spread rapidly, growing by 750 CE into the largest state in history, stretching from North Africa and Spain through the Middle East and Central Asia. Many living in the conquered territories were Christian.

Most accounts of the Muslim conquests focus on conflicts with the Byzantine and Sassanian empires, which surrounded Arabia and were in conflict with Muslims at the time of Muhammad's death. Encounters with Western Christianity occurred later with the Muslim invasion of Spain in 711 CE and the conquest of the Iberian Peninsula and southern France by 714. Muslim expansion was blocked by the Frankish statesman and military leader, Charles Martel, at Tours, France, in 732. Because these encounters were military invasions, it is not surprising Western Christians saw Muslims as threatening, barbaric, and dangerous invaders, comparable to the Vikings who raided northwest Europe in the ninth and tenth centuries.

---

15. *Shirk* (associating anyone or anything other than God with God) and *kufr* (unbelief after receiving proper instruction) are the two unforgivable sins in Islam. Groups charging Christians as unbelievers or associationists include Al-Qaida and ISIS.

16. Many have challenged the authenticity of this hadith, noting that it justified political machinations that came later in time, such as reported pressure by the second caliph, Umar, on the Christians of Najran to migrate to Iraq. Some extremist groups today, including Al-Qaida, uphold this hadith as a divine directive. It figured prominently in arguments against Saudi Arabia bringing in American support to fend off Saddam Hussein in the first Gulf War (1990–91), leading to charges of heresy against the Saudi monarchy. For details on Osama bin Laden's use of this hadith, see Natana J. DeLong-Bas, *Wahhabi Islam: From Revival and Reform to Global Jihad*, rev. ed. (New York: Oxford University Press, 2008), 272–78.

Muslim conquests focused on cities, whose populations were given the choice of resisting militarily or surrendering and paying the *jizya* tax in exchange for protecting their lives, properties, and places of worship.[17] If they resisted and lost, the conquerors did not protect houses of worship and warned they might be repurposed as mosques. In many cases, cities, including Damascus, decided to surrender peacefully. Jerusalem, on the other hand, chose to resist and was ultimately pressed to surrender in 637. Though the Church of the Holy Sepulchre remained in Christian hands, the site of the Jewish Second Temple, which had been destroyed by the Roman Empire centuries before, was cleaned and established as a site for Muslim prayer.[18] Yet the Muslim rulers promised the safety of other holy sites and allowed Jews to return to live and worship in Jerusalem for the first time in five hundred years. Jerusalem remained under Muslim control until 1099.

Initially, Christians living in conquered territories likely thought Muslims were descendants of Hagar and Ishmael, referring to them as "Hagarenes" or "Ishmaelites."[19] Many of these Christians belonged to minority groups persecuted by the Byzantines. In the early period, Muslim conquest often represented relief as it did not mean forced conversion and generally allowed Christian communal rule.[20] Limitations were placed on these freedoms by the Abbasid Caliph al-Mutawakkil in 850. He decreed that Christians and other *dhimmi* (protected people) wear distinctive dress, making their religious status visible, and he also restricted social and educational positions allowed to Christians.[21]

---

17. Symbolically, payment of the *jizya* placed Christians in a "protected" (*dhimmi*) relationship, shifting their status from People of the Book (*ahl al-kitab*) to People of the Covenant (*ahl al-dhimmah*).

18. The Dome of the Rock was built there fifty years later. See Oleg Grabar, *The Dome of the Rock* (Cambridge, MA: Harvard University Press, 2006), esp. 59–120, for the original construction.

19. Such reference can be found in the works of John of Damascus.

20. Jonathan Berkey, *The Formation of Islam: Religion and Society in the Near East, 600–1800* (New York: Cambridge University Press, 2003), 161; for details, see 159–75.

21. Distinctive dress by religious affiliation had previously been used by other empires, including the Sassanians for Christian and Jewish minorities in Iraq, and was continued by both Muslims and Christians through the Muslim Covenant of Umar and the Christian Decree of the Fourth Lateran Council of 1215. See F. E. Peters. *Judaism, Christianity, Islam: The Classical Texts and Their Interpretation* (Princeton: Princeton University Press, 1990), 2:380–82.

Christianity was the majority religion in many conquered territories, but many became majority Muslim over time. In some cases, this change was fairly rapid. For example, North Africa became majority Muslim by the eighth century, even though it had produced some of the great early Christian theologians, including Tertullian (d. 220), Cyprian (d. 258), and Augustine (d. 430).[22] In other cases, the process was much slower, such as in Syria, where Christianity has remained a strong presence until today.[23] The only major center of Christianity in the conquered region that did not convert to Islam at the time was Turkey, which remained part of the Byzantine Empire until the 1071 CE Battle of Manzikert, when it came under Seljuk Turk control. Under Seljuk and later Ottoman rule, Turkey remained fairly tolerant toward religious minorities.

Despite conflicts between the Muslims and the Byzantine Empire, which lost about half of its territory (mainly Egypt and Syria) to the Muslims, the frontier between these empires quickly stabilized and cultural and intellectual exchanges emerged. Eighth-century examples include Byzantine craftsmen helping with decorations on the Great Mosque of Damascus, the Prophet's Mosque in Medina, and the Great Mosque in Mecca.[24]

Among the most valuable were exchanges of information, particularly translations of ancient texts. The Abbasid caliphs (r. 750–1258 CE) became known for their sponsorship of translations, beginning with al-Mansur (r. 754–775) and Harun al-Rashid (r. 786–809). Caliph al-Ma'mun (r. 813–833) expanded these efforts, founding the House of Wisdom (*Bayt al-Hikmah*) in 832 CE in Baghdad as a center for gathering and disseminating the world's known information.[25]

---

22. For more information on possible causes and conditions, see Robert Hoyland, *In God's Path: The Arab Conquests and the Creation of an Islamic Empire* (New York: Oxford University Press, 2014).

23. Goddard observes that although the church was fragmented in Syria, so, too, was Islam; no group could really claim a majority. See Goddard, *A History of Christian-Muslim Relations*, 71–72.

24. Ibid., 47.

25. For a history of the House of Wisdom, see Jim Al-Khalili, *The House of Wisdom: How Arabic Science Saved Ancient Knowledge and Gave Us the Renaissance* (New York: Penguin, 2012). The House of Wisdom survived until the sacking of Baghdad by the Mongol invasions in 1258 CE, which also brought an end to the Abbasid Empire.

The 99

The symbolic power of the House of Wisdom remained alive in Muslim memory and has been revived today in the first Muslim superhero comic book series, *The 99*, created by Kuwaiti psychologist Naif al-Mutawa in response to the 9/11 attacks. Al-Mutawa sought to counter growing religious and political extremism by promoting values of tolerance, cooperation, pursuit of social justice, and respect for knowledge across religions. The series proved so popular, it inspired an amusement park in Kuwait as well as the documentary *Wham! Bam! Islam!*, which was first broadcast in 2011 for PBS's *Independent Lens* season premiere.[26]

Emissaries were sent throughout Byzantium to gather scientific and philosophical works in particular, thereby preserving the heritage of the ancient Greeks. Texts were then translated into Arabic, largely by Christians. Christian participation was key because some of the Greek texts were only available in Syriac translation.[27] Christians also translated Christian material into Arabic, including the Bible,[28] and wrote new texts in Arabic to reach Muslim audiences.[29]

---

26. The official website is available at *http://www.aardman.com/work/the-99 -website/*. A TED talk by al-Mutawa can be found at *https://www.ted.com/talks /naif_al_mutawa_superheroes_inspired_by_islam*.

27. Scholars note, the translation of these Syriac translations into Arabic is likely to blame for confusion over authorship of some works, particularly those of Aristotle.

28. The translation of the Bible took considerable time. Though the Old Testament was fairly easily translated from Hebrew into Judeo-Arabic (Arabic written in Hebrew letters), the translation of the New Testament was more complex. Because the entire New Testament text wasn't available in Greek, the language it was written in, it had to be translated from many languages, including Greek, Latin, Syriac, and Coptic. The earliest translations were likely done in Palestine by Melkite (Greek Catholic) Christians in the eighth century. See Sidney H. Griffith. "The Gospel in Arabic: An Inquiry into Its Appearance in the First Abbasid Century," *Oriens Christianus* 69 (1985): 126–67.

29. The oldest such text was a theological work entitled "On the Triune Nature of God," composed around 755 CE in a Greek Orthodox monastery in Palestine. Other translations followed over time, including the Lord's Prayer in the twelfth century in Egypt and the Coptic liturgy by the fourteenth century, also in Egypt. Details of specific manuscripts can be found in Sidney H. Griffith, *The Church in the Shadow of the Mosque: Christians and Muslims in the World of Islam* (Princeton: Princeton University Press, 2008), 45–74.

Slightly later, a comingling of civilizations and cultures took place in Sicily, particularly under King Roger II (d. 1154). Sicily was a medley of cultures, lost by the Byzantines to Muslim invaders in the ninth century and taken again by Norman raiders in the eleventh century. Roger II surrounded himself with learned men from many countries and religions and issued court documents in Latin, Greek, and Arabic.[30]

Exchanges also took place between Western Europe and the Abbasid Caliphate. The Frankish King Pepin opened diplomatic channels with the Abbasid Empire in 765 CE, sending an embassy to Baghdad. In 800, the Holy Roman Emperor Charlemagne and Abbasid Caliph Harun al-Rashid exchanged gifts, among the most memorable and important of which was a water clock sent by the Abbasid caliph.[31] The impetus for good diplomatic relations was likely the presence of a rival Umayyad Caliphate in Spain, founded in 756, an invasion by which was feared by both parties.[32]

The caliphate in Spain (756–1492)[33] was a brilliant and flourishing civilization in which Muslims, Christians, and Jews lived together. At times this took the form of *convivencia*, a level of tolerant and peaceful coexistence that constituted part of Islam's Golden Age.[34] The caliphate produced many great thinkers, including the Jewish philosopher Maimonides (1135–1205) and the Muslim philosopher

---

30. See Donald Matthew, *The Norman Kingdom of Sicily* (New York: Cambridge University Press, 1992), and Graham Loud, *Roger II and the Creation of the Kingdom of Sicily* (Manchester: Manchester University Press, 2012).

31. Harun al-Rashid also sent an elephant, which caused quite a stir in the court. Charlemagne reciprocated with hunting dogs, horses, and Frisian cloaks, which were used as currency. For more on the role of clocks as a form of technology transfer, see Carlo M. Cippola, *Clocks and Culture: 1300–1700* (New York: Norton, 1978).

32. The retreat from one invasion was immortalized in the epic poem *The Song of Roland (La Chanson de Roland)*, which recorded the attack and slaughter of Charlemagne's troops as they returned to France following the Battle of Roncevaux Pass in 778. The tale became popular and helped demonize the "Saracen" enemy, even though the attackers were actually Basque.

33. There were many fluctuations in territory and names of changing dynasties. This time span embraces the foundation of the original Umayyad dynasty through the fall of Granada to the Catholic monarchs Ferdinand and Isabella in 1492 CE.

34. The Golden Age of Islam is broadly considered to have occurred between the eighth and thirteenth centuries, including both the Abbasid and Spanish Umayyad empires.

Averroes (1126–1198). It also produced valued mathematical, scientific, and medical advances in trigonometry, architecture, astronomy, surgery, pharmacology, and more.[35]

Despite profuse achievements, there were rumblings of discord that portrayed Muslims as the enemy, named Santiago Matamoros (St. James the Moorslayer) as patron saint of Spain, and ultimately led to the Reconquista. Some Christians protested the *jizya* tax and restrictions on their freedom to worship publicly. Christians living in the capital city of Cordoba were isolated from the rest of the Christian world. Two of these Christians, a priest named Eulogius and a layman named Paul Alvarus, became convinced Islam was the precursor to the Antichrist predicted in the Old Testament book of Daniel and the New Testament Johannine literature and the book of Revelation. Believing the return of Christ was near, they called Christians from the luxurious distractions of Umayyad culture and civilization and launched deliberately provocative public declarations of piety, including publicly insulting Muhammad and calling on Muslim officials to convert to Christianity. Their goal was to achieve martyrdom. This so-called Spanish Martyrs Movement (850–860 CE) ultimately led to the execution of fifty Christians, including Eulogius. Muslim authorities warned that indiscriminate execution of Christians would follow if the provocation did not stop.[36] Though the Spanish Martyrs Movement died out, in part because its dire predictions never came true, its historical memory lived on as the first militant apocalyptic Christian reaction against Islam. This memory of the "Muslim threat to Christianity" was revived and reinforced in the central historical effort of militant Christianity, the Crusades.

The Crusades (1095–1291)

The Crusades began at a moment of conflict and opportunity. Although the Great Schism of 1054 had definitively split the Western and Eastern Churches, Christians nevertheless retained a sense of duty to stand together against a common enemy, broadly identified as "the

---

35. For details, see Chris Lowney, *A Vanished World: Medieval Spain's Golden Age of Enlightenment* (New York: Free Press, 2005).

36. For details, see Goddard, *A History of Christian-Muslim Relations*, 81–84.

Muslims."[37] Stunned by his defeat by the Seljuk Turks at the Battle of Manzikert in 1071 and the resulting loss of most of his Asian territory, Eastern Christian Byzantine Emperor Alexius I (r. 1081–1118) turned to Pope Urban II for help in confronting "the Muslims."

The Pope responded in 1095 at the Council of Clermont by calling for a Crusade to recapture the Holy Land, particularly Jerusalem, which had been under Muslim control since 637. He charged Christians with the religious obligation literally to take up the cross, recover the land, and facilitate and even expedite the second coming of Christ.[38] In reward, he promised to all who responded not only release from penance but also eternal salvation.

Carrying the banner *Deus Vult* ("God Wills It"), the Crusaders set out for Jerusalem, even though there is no historical record of Jerusalem's population requesting help. Under Muslim rule, Jews and Christians, including Christians belonging to minority groups persecuted by the Western and Eastern Churches, lived in Jerusalem with more freedom of worship and greater access to holy sites than had been the case under prior Christian rule.[39] Their "rescue" by the Crusaders seems to have come as somewhat of a surprise.

Scholars contend at least some of those who joined the Crusades also had more earthly goals, such as acquisition of land, wealth, fame, and adventure. But the historical record is clear that religious motivations, including the desire to make a pilgrimage to the Holy Land, played an equally important role in raising support for the Crusades. Itinerant preachers such as Peter the Hermit (1050–1115) stirred popular enthusiasm, playing upon medieval obsessions with prophecies that the second coming of Christ was imminent, a claim made more credible by a meteorite shower in 1095. Peter gathered about twenty

---

37. Although "Muslims" were not a single, united force at this time, they are portrayed this way in Christian writings and speeches from this period.

38. The idea that human beings have a preparatory role to play in the second coming of Christ has a long history that continues today. Some American Evangelical Christians today, e.g., believe Jesus cannot return until every Jew has been returned to the land of ancient Israel. This idea, which combines dispensationalism and premillennialism, raises questions about agency and sovereignty as it suggests that God's action is bound by and can be influenced by human choices and actions.

39. For a full account of the Crusades, the importance of Jerusalem, and the ongoing impact of the Crusades, see Karen Armstrong, *Holy War: The Crusades and Their Impact on Today's World*, 2nd ed. (New York: Anchor, 2001).

thousand women and men—called the People's Expedition—and set out for Jerusalem. This expedition proved disastrous, with thousands dying along the way. More successful was the 1096 departure of five armies, totaling about sixty thousand men, from throughout Western Europe, aiming to unite in Constantinople and march on Jerusalem. They crossed into Asia Minor in 1097 and captured Antioch in 1098 and Jerusalem in 1099.[40]

The Christian conquest of Jerusalem was followed by a blood-bath. In two days, about forty thousand men, women, and children were slaughtered, Muslims and Jews alike. One eyewitness and chronicler, Raymond of Aguilers, described picking his way through streets filled with corpses, in which blood ran up to his knees.[41] Many Christians had previously been given safe conduct from the city; those who remained were mostly Eastern-rite priests responsi-ble for liturgies at and upkeep of the Church of the Holy Sepulchre. The Crusaders refused to recognize the legitimacy of their office and cast them from the Church, making it clear Jerusalem was now a Western and Latin-rite-controlled city. The conquest of Jerusalem set the stage for centuries of cycles of vengeance, retaliation, fanat-icism, and demands for justice against the Crusaders. It also estab-lished a fearful image of violent, bloodthirsty "Franks" from whom Muslims must defend themselves.

The Crusades continued on and off for the next two hun-dred years with a total of nine formal Crusades. Up until the thirteenth century, Crusader focus was largely on conflict with Muslims. After the Crusaders' sack of Constantinople during the Fourth Crusade in 1204, however, Christian kings and princes increasingly came into conflict with each other.[42] Emphasis then shifted to expanding Christendom in Spain and the Baltics and

---

40. Details on the first Crusades can be found in Jonathan Riley-Smith, *The Cru-sades: A History*, 2nd ed. (New Haven: Yale University Press, 2005), 1–49.

41. For an English translation of his account, see Raymond D'Aguilers, *Historia Francorum Qui Ceperunt Iherusalem*, trans. John Hugh Hill (Philadelphia: American Philosophical Society, 1968).

42. Goddard, *A History of Christian-Muslim Relations*, 89, notes that this Crusade against Eastern Christianity included killing women and children and destroying monasteries, churches, and libraries. Such inter-Christian conflict reflected more than concerns about heresies within the church; it cast Eastern Christianity outside of the church, with not even houses of worship serving as sanctuaries.

combatting internal heresies, including the Cathars in France and the Hussites in Bohemia.

The Crusades offer key insights into visions of the religious "Other."[43] Heroes on one side were often seen as villains by the other. For example, the Christian saint Bernard de Clairvaux is remembered by Christians today as a contemplative mystic who preached God's infinite love and mercy. He issued the call to take up the cross for the Second Crusade. Crusading was depicted as an act of religious devotion and love—for God and for non-Christians who would thereby have the opportunity to hear the Gospel. It does not appear that Muslims found the Crusaders loving, however, as their chronicles express horror at the Crusaders' bloodshed and violence.[44]

Other figures, such as Richard the Lionheart, were feared for their violence and ruthlessness at the same time their fighting skill was respected. Immortalized in the stories of Robin Hood, Good King Richard, for the English, was brave, steadfast, and courageous, leading his troops into battle to rescue the oppressed and dispense justice. Richard's example stood in contrast to his brother, John, who was blamed for corruption, high rates of taxation, and abuse of power during Richard's absence.[45] Although Muslims admired Richard's bravery and prowess in war, they feared his ruthlessness in slaughtering prisoners of war and residents of towns and cities he conquered, men, women, and children alike. Richard's cold-heartedness lives on in Muslim memories.[46]

---

43. For a full set of documents from both sides, see S. J. Allen and Emilie Amt, eds., *The Crusades: A Reader*, 2nd ed. (North York, Ontario: University of Toronto Press, 2014).

44. The tendency to view battles, skirmishes, raids, pillage, slaughter, and one-upmanship through a religious lens, claiming God's favor for the warriors or God's punishment of the other side, occurs in accounts on both sides. Much like today's media maxim "If it bleeds, it leads," chroniclers on both sides reported violence as the driving force of politics and power. Although trade, social encounters, and cultural and intellectual exchanges happened and occasionally appeared in peripheral remarks, they were not as exciting to report, unless they could be used to demonstrate how different the Other was.

45. In reality, although John collected the taxes, they were largely spent on Richard's expeditions.

46. Richard is a figure of derision for the French, who insultingly nicknamed him "the Lionheart," seeing male lions as lazy, ineffective, and cowardly, leaving hunting to the females. Richard was also arrogant. When he was captured and turned over to the Holy Roman Emperor, Richard demanded his ransom be worthy of a king of his stature, to the tune of nearly three times the annual Crown revenues when the Crown was already overstretched from the cost of war. His mother, Eleanor of Aquitaine, had to confiscate gold and silver items from churches to pay it.

It is important to recognize that histories at this time were not written simply to record facts; they were also expected to have literary merit and set ideals. Biographies of great men were often used as a foil to other great men. Thus, in Muslim writings, the record of what happened during the Crusades was only one part of the picture; another important part was to establish Richard—the most powerful and admired figure among the Franks—as a foil for an even greater character—the Muslim Sultan Saladin. Richard, "a man of wisdom, experience, courage and energy" who put fear in the hearts of Muslims, could only be met and challenged by a man of even higher character, who applied justice with the greater quality of mercy.[47] One Muslim historian who wrote about Richard also wrote a long, complex portrait of Saladin from his vantage point as a member of Saladin's camp, emphasizing his courage, strength, wisdom, and exalted character.[48] Richard is portrayed as a strong man of war who mastered the power of creating illusions, and a brilliant strategist.[49] Saladin is described as a man of exemplary religious character, surpassed only by his dedication to Holy War, leaving behind his family and possessions to win merit in God's eyes by fighting God's enemies.[50]

Though both men had admirable qualities, Saladin emerged as more meritorious because of his deeper devotion to religion and his attention to justice and humane treatment of prisoners of war and members of the enemy camp. For example, when the Crusader Prince

---

47. Francesco Gabrieli, *Arab Historians of the Crusades*, trans. E. J. Costello (New York: Dorset Press, 1969), 213–14, citing the Muslim historian Baha al-Din.

48. Details can be found in Gabrieli, *Arab Historians of the Crusades*, 87–113.

49. Although power politics is typically considered a man's game, the record mentions a few women who were capable players, including Shajarat al-Durr (d. 1257), often called the Muslim Joan of Arc. A slave who rose to become the Egyptian Sultan's wife, she took over the military after her husband was killed in battle. Keeping his death a secret, she rallied the troops and captured the French king Louis IX (Saint Louis) and oversaw his ransoming, along with 12,000 prisoners. When the Abbasid Caliph learned a woman was ruling Egypt, he refused to recognize her. She was murdered by dissenters. See Natana J. DeLong-Bas, *Notable Muslims: Muslim Builders of World Civilization and Culture* (Oxford: Oneworld, 2008), 78–80.

50. Historian Baha al-Din described Saladin as a man who put his whole faith and confidence in God, loved to hear the Qur'an recited, studied the biography of the Prophet, kept the fast of Ramadan, intended to go on Hajj, generously gave away most of what he had, regularly performed his five daily prayers, and more. See Gabrieli, *Arab Historians of the Crusades*, 87–93.

of Antioch asked to see him following a truce in November 1192, Saladin not only received him, but honored him with a gift—namely, the territory he had taken from him in Palestine in 1188–1189.[51] In another case, a Frankish woman begged for Saladin's mercy in recovering the baby who had been taken from her. Saladin ordered one of his knights to find the child and return her to her mother. Mother and daughter were returned to their camp.[52] When Saladin reconquered Jerusalem in 1187, he insisted on law and order among his soldiers and did not permit massacres or looting. Instead, his guards patrolled the streets and gates to assure no vengeance or harm came to the Christians. Though he ordered the cross removed from the Muslim Dome of the Rock, he permitted Christians to continue making pilgrimages to the Church of the Holy Sepulchre, for a fee.

What is powerful for Muslims in these stories is the example of a man who was capable of wielding power through coercion yet chose to respond in mercy. At times, Saladin's mercy seemed to contradict military strategy. Unlike Richard, who slaughtered prisoners of war when they became too costly or impractical to move, Saladin often set them free. For example, following the conquest of Acre, he not only freed all four thousand prisoners but also gave each money to return home. Though some of Saladin's followers criticized this move, noting these men could simply take the money and return to fight him again, Saladin believed mercy was a more powerful symbol of his faith than killing and hoped the mercy he showed that day would be remembered. That deed did, in fact, become part of his legacy not only in the Muslim world but also in the West, where he is often portrayed as a saintlike figure and the ultimate chivalrous knight.[53]

The record of Richard and Saladin is not just one of power politics, violence, and warfare, for they engaged in dialogue in

---

51. Recorded in Gabrieli, *Arab Historians of the Crusades*, 109.

52. Ibid., 111.

53. See, e.g., the recent biography by John Man, *Saladin: The Sultan Who Vanquished the Crusaders and Built an Islamic Empire* (Philadelphia: Da Capo, 2016). Nevertheless, Saladin was also capable of administering harsh justice, particularly when a treaty had been broken by the other side, as in the case of Prince Arnat al-Karak, or when treachery occurred. Saladin reportedly executed all members of Frankish military orders, Templars, and Hospitallers that he captured. Recorded in Gabrieli, *Arab Historians of the Crusades*, 111–12 and 123–24.

search of peace. Even amid the worst fighting, emissaries were sent between the camps to work toward terms of truce, amnesty, prisoner exchanges, compensation for losses, and potential alliances. Emissaries were received with hospitality and honor as a reflection of the good will, honorable character, and conduct of the leaders. Though many treaties and alliances were discussed and often agreed upon, many were later broken, often with deadly consequences.

One alliance was proposed after Richard besieged the city of Acre. The Muslims held out for as long as they could but ultimately surrendered. In exchange for safe conduct for themselves, their families, and their possessions, they agreed to hand over the city along with the city's equipment, munitions, and ships, two hundred thousand dinars in cash, five hundred ordinary prisoners, one hundred important prisoners to be chosen by the Franks, and the ultimate prize for the Crusaders—the True Cross on which Jesus was reportedly crucified.[54] Saladin was dissatisfied with the treaty and delayed carrying out its terms. Richard, furious at the delay, despite having already received the money and the prisoners, massacred all three thousand Muslim prisoners he held. In response, Saladin massacred all Frankish prisoners he held. Thus even an agreed-upon treaty was no guarantee that both parties would faithfully follow it. This also showed that, once violence began, cycles of retaliation rapidly followed.

The broken treaty and massacres on both sides led to more peace negotiations between Saladin and Richard. Richard demanded an end to the fighting, noting that Muslims and Franks were bleeding to death, the country was utterly ruined, and goods and lives had been sacrificed on both sides. However, his three key demands—control over Jerusalem, the True Cross, and the land between Jerusalem and the Jordan River—were not accepted by Saladin. Saladin considered Jerusalem the rightful possession of Muslims as well as Christians because it was the site of Muhammad's Night Journey. He was not willing to give up the True Cross, because its symbolic value to Christians made it a good bargaining chip. And he refused to give up the land because of its long history of Muslim rule. Despite goodwill going into the negotiations, Richard and Saladin found themselves at a stalemate.

---

54. The True Cross had been a much sought after object throughout the Crusades.

Faced with cycles of violence doomed to continue, Richard offered a daring solution for the time: he proposed the hand of his sister, Joanna, in marriage to Saladin's brother, al-Adil. The alliance would have united Palestine, with Joanna ruling those portions controlled by Richard and al-Adil maintaining control over his own territories. It also would have helped end hostilities between Richard and Saladin. Although Richard, Saladin, and al-Adil favored the marriage, high-ranking Church officials and Joanna objected on religious grounds; Richard was threatened with excommunication if the marriage went through.[55] The fighting continued.

Another attempt to change the dynamics of violence occurred in 1219 CE with the arrival of Saint Francis of Assisi. Francis brought with him hope of presenting the Gospel to Saladin's nephew, the Egyptian Sultan Malik al-Kamil, as well as hope of transforming the overall conflict through the power of love. Though Francis knew military victory served the political interests of Christendom, he doubted violence would help Muslims learn anything valuable about Christ. It was Francis's love for God and humanity that led him to intervene in the Crusades.[56]

Saint Francis and the sultan reportedly met in September 1219. After a yearlong stalemate, the Crusaders had attacked al-Kamil's camp outside of Damietta, Egypt. Al-Kamil's army faked retreat and then cut off and captured a large group of Crusaders. Al-Kamil then sent a prisoner to the Crusader camp with a proposal to negotiate peace. The sultan offered to give Jerusalem to the Crusaders, with money to rebuild it and also several castles, if they left Egypt. Because Jerusalem had from the start been the main Crusader goal, al-Kamil expected the Crusaders to jump at the opportunity. However, the Crusader camp had mixed reactions. Some apparently felt that control over Egypt was now a higher priority than Jerusalem and refused the terms. It was at

---

55. At that time, marrying a high-ranking Christian woman to a Muslim man was unthinkable, even though the practice of using marriage to form alliances and consolidate territories was well-known in Europe. Armstrong, *Holy War*, 267–68.

56. Francis was shocked and repulsed by the violence of the Crusades. He was deeply disappointed to find many Crusaders, who were supposed to be holy men driven to serve God, more interested in obtaining personal gain. For Francis's mission and the history of its telling, see John Tolan, *Saint Francis and the Sultan: The Curious History of a Christian-Muslim Encounter* (New York: Oxford University Press, 2009).

this point that Francis crossed enemy lines to speak with the Sultan. The Crusaders did not expect him to return alive.

Francis received a gracious audience from al-Kamil. Like his uncle Saladin, al-Kamil had a reputation for hospitality and treating prisoners of war well. He was also known for presiding over religious debates between Muslims and Christians, including one in which two Christian patriarchs of Egypt, the Monophysite Cyril III and the Melkite Nicholas, participated.[57] Though al-Kamil politely declined Francis's offer to convert to Christianity, he treated Francis with respect, refused to allow any harm to come to him, and sent him safely back to his own camp. Many scholars and religious leaders today look to this example of encounter and dialogue between enemies as a model for a path to peace and mutual understanding during conflict.[58]

The Crusades offer a far more layered example of Muslim-Christian interactions than just violence. Though the Crusades created and left negative images of the religious Other on both sides, remarkable individuals and gestures also made it into the historical record. Neither side was solely heroic, self-sacrificial, or dedicated to serving God, just as neither side was solely evil, barbaric, or dedicated to annihilating the other. Both sides felt their cause was just, that they had suffered harm at the hands of the other, that the other side was guilty, that they had reason to demand vengeance, and that they were owed compensation for harms suffered. Both sides used power through coercion, and both offered treaties, alliances, asylum, and creative gestures to seek peace. On both sides, the Crusades remain a part of modern debates. In the West, the term *crusade* is still used when some abject evil is being fought, such as poverty, tyranny, drugs, or illiteracy. Meanwhile, those in the Muslim world hear the term and fear abject evil, such as invasion, massacre, and intolerance.[59]

---

57. Ibid., 6.

58. Then Cardinal Joseph Ratzinger, later Pope Benedict XVI, affirmed this encounter, using peaceful dialogue rather than violence, as a model for the church in seeking a solution to differences between Islam and Christianity. Tolan, *Saint Francis and the Sultan*, 4.

59. President George W. Bush's use of *crusade* to describe the pending war on terrorism in response to the 9/11 attacks reverberated quite negatively in the Muslim world and caused consternation in Europe. See *https://georgewbush-whitehouse.archives.gov/news/releases/2001/09/20010916-2.html*.

In the end, one of the greatest ironies of the Crusades was their result: although originally begun to take Jerusalem from Muslim rule and protect Christians, the Crusades ended with not only Jerusalem still under Muslim rule but also with previously Christian-controlled lands added to Muslim territory. Further, the status of Christians in Muslim-ruled territory was lowered owing to concerns that they could no longer be trusted as loyal subjects.

Muslim-Christian Encounters in the Age of Empires

Amid the ongoing warfare of the Crusades, the Muslim world faced a second, greater threat: Mongol invasions (1206–1337) from the East. These invasions ultimately forced the end of the Abbasid Caliphate in 1258. Many Christian subjects were initially enthusiastic about the Mongol presence, believing the Mongols might convert to Christianity; indeed, one of Hulagu Khan's wives was Christian, and Christians were in the inner circles of Mongol rulers. But the Mongols converted to Islam instead, causing consternation among Christians, whose hopes for political power were now dashed, as well as Muslims, who found themselves under foreign rule by nominal converts who nevertheless maintained their own, non-Arab customs and laws.[60]

By the fourteenth century, the Muslim world had fragmented into numerous rival dynasties and empires. The most important of these from the perspective of European Christians was the Ottoman Empire, with its incursions into Eastern Europe beginning in 1354, followed by the surrender of Edirne (Adrianople) in 1361 and the Battle of Kosovo in 1389. The Battle of Kosovo proved pivotal in opening the Balkans to the Ottomans, who conquered Constantinople in 1453, besieged Vienna in 1529 and 1683 (both times unsuccessfully), and Hungary, which fell to Ottoman control in the 1540s. So powerful were the Ottomans that Martin Luther (1483–1546),

---

60. Many doubted the Mongols' commitment to Islam. In the thirteenth and fourteenth centuries, the respected religious and legal scholar Ibn Taymiyya (1263–1328) declared the Mongols unfit for rule because of their failure to abide strictly by Islamic law. He justified their overthrow as a legitimate jihad.

a leader of the Reformation, assumed they would conquer all of Christendom. His theological response sought to build up Christians' faith so they could keep it under Ottoman rule.[61] Some of this effort was made by making fearful claims that alarmed Catholics and Protestants alike, including accusing Muslims of replacing Jesus with Muhammad and charges of sexual perversity, particularly among the Turks. At the same time, there were signs of rising tolerance between the faith traditions, particularly as trade, and thus financial interests, grew.

Though the Ottomans were militarily and economically powerful, by the end of the fifteenth century the balance of power had begun to shift toward Europe. Exploration of the navigable world, including discovery of the Americas in 1492 and Vasco da Gama's navigation of the Cape of Good Hope in 1497, opened new markets and direct contact between Europe and Asia without involving the Muslim world.[62] The last stronghold of Muslim Spain was "reconquered" (*reconquista*) for Christianity by the Catholic monarchs Ferdinand and Isabella in 1492, marking the end of Muslim rule in Western Europe and opening the door to persecution of religious Others, both Muslims and Jews.[63] The destruction of the Ottoman fleet by an alliance between Spain, Venice, and Genoa at the Battle of Lepanto in 1571 completed the European rise to power.

Yet trade between Christian and Muslim countries continued, offering opportunities to build relationships and personal connections. England often led the way. Despite ongoing conflict between the Ottomans and Europeans, by the end of the seventeenth century, fully one-quarter of English overseas trade was with the Ottomans.[64] India, then ruled by Muslims, was opened to the British Crown

---

61. For a thorough study of Martin Luther's writings on Islam, see Adam S. Francisco, *Martin Luther and Islam: A Study in Sixteenth-Century Polemics and Apologetics* (Leiden: Brill, 2007).

62. Demand in England for rugs from the Islamic world dates to as early as the sixteenth century. Portraits of King Henry VIII show him standing near curtains with arabesque designs.

63. For more on the impact on Muslims, see Ingrid Mattson, *The Story of the Qur'an: Its History and Place in Muslim Life*, 2nd ed. (Malden, MA: Blackwell, 2008), 119–24.

64. The English also established a consulate presence in Aleppo, Syria, in 1580, followed by the founding of the English Levant Company in 1581.

when Sir Thomas Roe became ambassador to the Mughal court in Ajmir in 1614, seeking trade privileges on behalf of King James I.[65]

Christian Missionary Activity in the Muslim World

As military rivalries and trade ties grew, Western Christians began missionary work among Muslims, particularly after the fall of Cordoba to Christian rule in 1236. A major voice in early Christian missionary work was Ramon Lull (1232–1316), born in Majorca after the Christian reconquest. Lull combined the legacies of Francis of Assisi and Peter the Venerable through peaceful work toward conversion, writing a book to explain Christianity to non-Christians and training Christian missionaries. He consistently denounced Islam as a false religion, but may have drawn on Sufi writings in his contemplative writings. He was so confrontational in his public denunciations of Islam, it is believed he was stoned to death near Algiers in 1314.

Christian missionary work began in earnest with the founding of the Mendicant orders (Dominicans and Franciscans) in the early thirteenth century.[66] The Dominicans used a combination of preaching and teaching to establish ties with universities in Europe and became intimately involved in the study of Arabic and Islam. Some Dominicans undertook diplomatic missions to Muslim rulers, as well as to other parts of the world, including to the Mongols.[67] They were the first order to establish residences throughout the Muslim world.

---

65. Roe later served as ambassador to the Ottoman Empire from 1621–1628. The scene of Thomas Roe arriving at the Court of Ajmir is portrayed in an eight-painting series "The Building of Britain," hanging in the lobby between the House of Lords and House of Commons. Other scenes include Richard the Lionheart leaving for the Crusades.

66. For more on medieval Muslim-Christian relations, see John Tolan, *Saracens: Islam in the Medieval European Imagination* (New York: Columbia University Press, 2002), and Benjamin Z. Kedar, *Crusade and Mission: European Approaches toward the Muslims* (Princeton: Princeton University Press, 1984).

67. Examples include Andrew of Longjumeau, who led the expedition to the Mongol court in 1248. William of Tripoli is reported by some to have accompanied Marco Polo through Syria in 1271, although other medieval scholars have questioned the connection.

Following the example of Saint Francis, who had founded the Province of the Holy Land in Jerusalem in 1217, some Francisans were also sent on diplomatic missions, including to the Khanates of Central Asia, and charged with caring for Christian sites in the Holy Land.[68] The Franciscan Order was the first religious order to mention Muslims specifically.[69]

Some rulers also engaged in diplomacy, albeit for political purposes, such as the alliance between Francis I of France (r. 1515–1547) and Sultan Sulayman the Magnificent of the Ottoman Empire (r. 1520–1566) against the Holy Roman Emperor Charles V (r. 1519–1556). This alliance marked the first formal alliance between a Christian and a Muslim ruler of their stature and the beginning of Muslim powers becoming entwined in rivalries between European rulers.

In the seventeenth century, Pope Clement VIII (r. 1592–1605) sent a Carmelite mission to Iran to make the Christian faith known and to discover whether Iran could serve as a political ally against the Ottomans. During the mission, theological debates occurred between the friars and Shah Abbas I (r. 1588–1629) as well as among English merchants and their Protestant chaplain. The debate[70] was remarkable for its breadth and the participation of Catholics and Protestants, who sometimes agreed and at other times disagreed, and because the advantage went to the Catholics who could communicate directly with the Persian interlocutors, whereas the Protestants had to rely on a translator to make their points. Nevertheless, language skills alone did not suffice to win the debate. The Shah spoke for forty-five minutes against the idea of predestination supported by the Protestants and criticized their claim to follow the earliest form of Christianity while rejecting the papacy they had formerly accepted. Yet the Shah considered the Protestants to be superior partners because they kept their promises and made themselves useful, whereas he charged the Catholics with lying, as the

---

68. Examples include John de Carpini, who was sent by Pope Innocent IV to the Mongol court in 1245, and William of Rubroek, who was sent to the same place by French King Louis IX in 1252.

69. See J. Hoeberichts, *Francis and Islam* (Cincinatti: Franciscan Press, 1997), chapter 16.

70. The topics were preselected: fasting and good works, religious imagery, free will and predestination, and questions surrounding authority.

kings of Spain and Portugal had vowed to make war on the Turks and had yet to follow through. In the end, rather than siding solely with the Catholics or the Protestants, the Shah angled for the best diplomatic outcome for himself and his country.[71]

One of the most important orders for missionary work, particularly in challenging locations, was the Order of the Society of Jesus, known as the Jesuits. Founded in 1534 by Saint Ignatius of Loyola, the Jesuits were involved in major Christian missions to countries including India, Japan, and China. A key figure in Christian-Muslim relations was Jerome Xavier, who was stationed at the Muslim Mughal court in India from 1595–1614 under the reigns of Akbar (r. 1556–1605) and Jahangir (r. 1605–1627).

As the Muslim ruler of a multireligious society in which Muslims comprised only a quarter of the population, Emperor Akbar was concerned about the potential for religious rivalry to undermine the cohesion of his empire. Rather than favoring a single religion, he created a framework for rule within a shared Indo-Persian culture that celebrated and embraced religious difference rather than ignoring or igniting it. A patron of art and literature who collected a library of more than twenty-four thousand manuscripts in Persian, Greek, Latin, Arabic, Sanskrit, Kashmiri, and

Illustrated manuscript of watercolor and ink on gold paper showing Mughal Emperor Akbar receiving guests in his court in India. Differences in dress and head coverings among the guests indicate the varied ethnic groups and religions represented.

The Metropolitan Museum of Art, New York, Rogers Fund, 1908

Urdu, Akbar brought artists, literary men, and representatives of different faith traditions into his court. He developed his own hybrid monotheistic religion—Din-i Ilahi—combining teachings from

---

71. For more, see Goddard, *A History of Christian-Muslim Relations*, 118–20.

Islam, Hinduism, Zoroastrianism, and Christianity, with himself at the center.

Akbar invited the Jesuits to send representatives to his court in 1579. These first three Jesuits engaged in debates with both the emperor and Muslim scholars. So compelling was their performance that Akbar entrusted his second son, Murad, to them to be educated in the Portuguese language and Christianity. However, when it became apparent there were certain Christian convictions that even the most open-minded Muslim could not accept—especially that Jesus is the Son of God—the Jesuits returned home in 1583. A second mission was requested in 1593, but its participants stayed less than a year. The third mission included Jerome Xavier. Known for his sensitivity to local language, culture, and religion, and his gift for making Christian ideas comprehensible according to local idioms, Jerome learned Persian and produced Persian-language Christian literature, including a life of Christ and several works presented in the traditional format of conversations taking place between a Jesuit, a Muslim, and a philosopher. Neither Akbar nor his successor, Jahangir, converted to Christianity, but Jahangir ordered his three nephews to be instructed and baptized into Christianity. When the nephews rejected the faith several years later, the Jesuits ultimately withdrew, leaving the Mughal court open for English Protestant influence.[72]

English Protestants first arrived at the Mughal court in 1614 with Sir Thomas Roe, but no Protestant missionary activity occurred until the emergence of the pietist movement in the eighteenth century.[73] The impetus for English missionary activity came through Baptist preachers, such as William Carey of Nottingham, who argued Christians were accountable to God for assuring that people throughout the world had the opportunity to hear the gospel. The Baptist Missionary Society, founded in 1792, was the first such missionary group seeking to build up the global church of Christ.

---

72. For more on Jesuit-Mughal encounters, see ibid., 120–21, and James W. Laine, *Meta-Religion: Religion and Power in World History* (Oakland: University of California Press, 2014), 144–52.

73. Prior English Protestants were preoccupied with the struggle against Catholicism.

The most important Protestant mission to the Muslim world was led by Henry Martyn (1781–1812). During his travels to India, the Persian Gulf, Iran, and Turkey, Martyn translated the New Testament into Urdu and revised Arabic and Persian translations of the New Testament. Unlike the Jesuits who took a top-down approach to Muslim-Christian relations by working with the emperor, Martyn worked with ordinary folk. Although he formed personal connections, he had little impact on policy.

The main period of Christian missionary work coincided with the European colonial era, from about 1789 until the beginning of World War I.[74] Europeans interpreted their military and territorial successes as proof of God's favor and the righteousness of their cause, fueling desire for further conquests. Although some missionary activity focused on building church congregations, much of it was tied to charity, particularly founding orphanages and medical and educational bodies.[75] This often left a legacy of suspicion of ulterior motives.[76] Like many of their predecessors, some mission groups understood the value of communicating in local languages through a variety of media. The main objective, though, was conversion. The Anglican Church Missionary Society in Egypt used common ground between Islam and Christianity to build relationships encouraging conversion to Christianity. Dutch-American Samuel Zwemer's Arabian Mission of the Reformed Church of

---

74. This period marked the greatest expansion of the church since the era of the first apostles. This time, the main impact was in the Americas and parts of Asia and Africa rather than in the Muslim world. Goddard, *A History of Christian-Muslim Relations*, 123–24.

75. See, e.g., Ussama Makdisi, *Artillery of Heaven: American Missionaries and the Failed Conversion of the Middle East* (Ithaca, NY: Cornell University Press, 2009); Beth Baron, *The Orphan Scandal: Christian Missionaries and the Rise of the Muslim Brotherhood* (Stanford, CA: Stanford University Press, 2014); and Melanie E. Trexler, *Evangelizing Lebanon: Baptists, Missions, and the Question of Cultures* (Waco: Baylor University Press, 2016).

76. Such suspicions continue today. Ayatollah Khomeini's Little Green Book accused Christian missionaries of founding religious schools in Muslim countries to turn children into Christians or atheists. Conservative evangelical groups such as World Witness, Evangelistic International Ministries, Operation Blessing, and Samaritan's Purse, which work throughout the Muslim world and sub-Saharan Africa, combine the functions of hospitals and health centers with proselytizing by medical personnel and staff, Bible verses and tracts, and showing *The Jesus Film*. Lee Marsden, *For God's Sake: The Christian Right and US Foreign Policy* (London: Zed, 2008), 129.

America took a harder, confrontational line, seeing Islam's only value as preparation for Christianity.[77]

Though many Muslims worried about Muslims converting to Christianity, statistically this remained the exception, not the rule. Even so, some were so concerned about cultural and religious imperialism they called for resistance against the British, French, Russians, Dutch, and Italians throughout the Muslim world, often referring to such resistance as jihad.[78]

Others, however, found much to admire in Western civilization, particularly in art, architecture, music, and other cultural ventures, even if there was little interest in Christianity. European architecture and opera houses were constructed in Cairo and Istanbul. The Ottoman Empire adopted institutional, bureaucratic, and civic reforms through the Tanzimat reforms of the nineteenth century, including freedom to convert from Islam to other religions. In British-ruled India, Sir Sayyid Ahmad Khan (1817–1898) borrowed Western educational models and scholarly methods and reinterpreted them for an Islamic context. He particularly encouraged use of Western scholarly methods critically to reexamine the Islamic tradition in comparison with other religions, including Christianity, potentially for positive inspiration.

A similar approach of folding modern knowledge into the Islamic tradition was taken by Muhammad Abduh (1849–1905) in Egypt. Abduh engaged in a comparative analysis of Christianity and Islam intended to rebalance Christian views of Islam. Abduh's analysis still asserted the superiority of Islam to Christianity, claiming stronger rationality, evidenced by lack of praise for Christianity's merits. Despite admiration for certain qualities of the West, both Khan and Abduh expressed concern about Christian missionary activities.[79]

---

77. Zwemer's (1867–1952) work was a precursor to the more developed theology of "anonymous Christianity" of Catholic theologian Karl Rahner. For more on Zwemer, see Goddard, *A History of Christian-Muslim Relations*, 124–25.

78. These movements were often led by Sufis. Examples include the twenty-year resistance in Algeria led by the Qadariyya Sufi Emir Abd al-Qadir, the Rahmaniyya resistance to French occupation in Tunisia and Algeria, the Tijaniyya resistance to French expansion in Central and West Africa, the Sanusiyya resistance to the Italian occupation of Libya, and the Naqshbandi resistance to Russian expansion in the Caucasus. See Ira Lapidus, *A History of Islamic Societies*, 2nd ed. (New York: Cambridge University Press, 2002), 464.

79. For a masterful account of Islam from a world historical perspective with special attention to the modern period, see John O. Voll, *Islam: Continuity and Change in the Modern World*, 2nd ed. (Syracuse: Syracuse University Press, 1994).

The end of the colonial era and successful wars for independence following World War II resulted in different levels of engagement between the Muslim world and the West and Christianity. Though a minority on both sides call for rejection of the Other altogether, others seek limited engagement in the cultural and commercial realms, leaving theological issues to personal discretion. Yet others on both sides believe a constructive relationship between Christians and Muslims is central to global stability and resolution of problems with a global impact. This has led to renewed interest in dialogue and relationships.

A History of Muslim-Christian Theological Dialogue

Early Theological Dialogue

The historical record contains many instances of Muslim-Christian dialogue. Theological treatises addressing Islam and Christianity can be helpful for discerning attitudes, understandings of God, and degrees of familiarity with the religious Other. However, treatises must be read with the caution that they tend to represent deep thinking about theological matters rather than descriptions of lived realities or accurate portrayals of the Other's beliefs. There are diverse approaches to dialogue: education, denunciation of "incorrect" teachings, engagement in polemics, addressing heresies within a tradition, and expanding ties between religions and empires. This diversity highlights the importance of contextualizing dialogue and theological treatises.

Early Christian responses to Islam often describe it as a Christian heresy, generally focusing on issues related to the status of Jesus.[80] This assertion paradoxically denied Islam legitimacy by labeling it a heresy while also placing it in the realm of Christianity. When Islam arose in the seventh century, the Christian church

---

80. One of the first to describe Islam as a Christian heresy was John of Damascus (d. 749), regarded as the last of the Fathers of the Eastern Church. John accused Muhammad of deliberately constructing his own heresy based on the Old and New Testaments with the help of a renegade monk. John is credited with writing a guidebook for Christians on how to engage in theological discussions with Muslims, particularly on the challenging topics of free will and Jesus' status as the "Word of God." See Goddard, *A History of Christian-Muslim Relations*, 39–40.

was already deeply divided over questions related to authority, decision-making, and Christology.[81] The early church had four major centers, known as patriarchates, located in Rome, Jerusalem, Antioch, and Alexandria—three in the East and one in the West. When a fifth patriarchate was added in 324—Constantinople— this resulted in four centers in the East and still only one in the West. The church in the West thus formed around a single authority— the Pope—while the church in the East was divided between four authorities, none of which could claim authority over the others. This resulted in a conciliar approach to authority in which consultation, compromise, and ultimately consensus were sought. These differences in authority and decision-making impacted not only the inner workings of the church but also Christian approaches to other religions.[82]

Western Christianity formed in the Latin-speaking half of the Roman Empire. It focused on the separation, distinction, and defense of the Christian community from surrounding religions and, especially, philosophies. Western Christianity emphasized the distinctiveness of the Christian message and worked to separate Christianity from other intellectual influences. Eastern Christianity, on the other hand, was Greek-speaking and emphasized an inclusive, universal message, reflecting its position as the state religion of a multireligious empire. Justin Martyr (100–165 CE) could thus proclaim that all who strive to do the good enjoined upon Christians shared in God; and Clement of Alexandria (155–220 CE) could thus recognize that all who philosophized accurately could see God and that Jesus' salvation could be universal. These different perspectives came into play in Christian encounters with Islam.

The earliest known Christian text to explicitly mention the Qur'an dates to the 720s. This text was written as a theological refutation of the Qur'an's teachings about Christology, the Trinity, and the origins of the Qur'an.[83] The first dialogue between Muslims and

---

81. *Christology* refers to teachings on the nature of the person of Jesus as the Christ.

82. For details, see Goddard, *A History of Christian-Muslim Relations*, esp. 5–16.

83. Michael Philip Penn, *When Christians First Met Muslims: A Sourcebook of the Earliest Syriac Writings on Islam* (Oakland: University of California Press, 2015), 212–15.

Christians also dates to this time. It was initiated with the Eastern Church because of its geographical proximity and because the Byzantine and Islamic empires had been in conflict with each other.

One of the earliest invitations to formal dialogue was sent by the Umayyad caliph Umar bin Abd al-Aziz (r. 717–720) to the Byzantine emperor Leo III (r. 717–741) following a decline in military hostilities. Umar requested an explanation of the Christian faith, asserting that Muslims and Christians believe in the same God, and invited the emperor to Islam. Leo III declined the invitation to Islam but responded with an explanation of Christianity that he hoped would be helpful to Umar. In particular, he tried to explain the use of icons in Eastern Orthodox tradition, comparing the symbolism of the cross and other icons to the symbolism of Muslims turning to the Kaaba to pray.[84]

The Abbasid caliphs furthered the dialogue by sponsoring debates between representatives of different religious communities on religious and intellectual questions. The debates began under Caliph al-Mahdi (r. 775–785) with an invitation to the head of the church in Iraq, the Catholicos Timothy, likely in 781. Debates continued and grew under Caliph Harun al-Rashid, who invited the Greek Orthodox bishop of northern Syria, Theodore Abu Qurra, in 799, and Caliph al-Ma'mun, who invited a number of representatives, likely in 829. These debates were remarkably honest, open, and informed for their time and shared the purpose of mutual education.[85]

The debate with Abu Qurra was particularly notable, because the Muslim and Christian participants agreed that Jesus is a Word of God and a Spirit from God, as stated in Q 4:171. Yet disagreement as to whether Jesus was created or uncreated remained. When one of the Muslim participants complained to the caliph about certain Christian statements, the caliph reportedly told the Christian bishop that all were free to advance their own arguments and answer without fear in demonstrating the truth of their religion.[86]

---

84. This explanation apparently ultimately fell flat as Leo III later issued a decree banning icons. Goddard, *A History of Christian-Muslim Relations*, 58–59.

85. Goddard, *A History of Christian-Muslim Relations*, 52–54. The historical record cites the Christian Abu Qurra quoting the Qur'an and one of the Muslim representatives quoting the New Testament.

86. A. Guillaume, "Theodore Abu Qurra as Apologist," *Muslim World* 15 (1925): 46.

Unfortunately, by the end of al-Ma'mun's reign, the nature of these religious debates had changed. Rather than an opportunity to seek common ground on truth claims or to educate each other, the focus shifted to attacks on one another's beliefs and mutual attempts at conversion. The debates thus became more polemical. In some cases, invited participants declined to debate altogether because of doctrinal differences.[87]

Antagonism toward Islam is explained in part by the ongoing military confrontations between the Byzantines and the Abbasids throughout Asia Minor and Syria in the ninth century. Byzantine historians such as Theophanes the Confessor described the coming of Islam as a Christian heresy and personally attacked Muhammad, describing him as a false prophet, claiming he had epilepsy and had been influenced by a heretical Christian monk. Particularly offensive to Theophanes were the purported teachings of Islam that heaven was a sensual paradise available only to those who killed or were killed by an enemy and that Islam was mainly a call to military warfare, particularly against Christians, and to hedonistic living. Nevertheless, he acknowledged Islam also preached helping the oppressed.[88]

The trend of rejection and accusation was continued in the mid-ninth century by Nicetas of Byzantium, who responded to two letters from Muslims inviting him to Islam. Although Nicetas's response demonstrated detailed familiarity with the Qur'an, he nevertheless took a harsh tone against Islam. He denounced Muhammad as an assassin and charlatan, claimed the Qur'an was demonic in origin, and asserted that Muslims worshipped Satan rather than God. In his eyes, all of this justified military action against Muslims whenever and wherever the opportunity arose.[89]

Similar Muslim approaches to dealing with Christians can be found. Although Muhammad's example and the Qur'an contain

---

87. One example was the invitation sent to the Arab Christian al-Kindi. Al-Kindi declined to debate, instead attacking Muhammad's prophethood and the authenticity of the Qur'an. For more, see Griffith, *The Church in the Shadow of the Mosque*, 86–88.

88. See Michael Philip Penn, *Envisioning Islam: Syriac Christians and the Early Muslim World* (Philadelphia: University of Pennsylvania Press, 2015), 76. Penn notes that Theophanes's work was based on an earlier, no longer extant, *Chronicle* by Theophilus.

89. For more, see Goddard, *A History of Christian-Muslim Relations*, 56–58.

many instances of fruitful relations and exchanges, the spread of the Islamic Empire and ongoing conflict with the Byzantines led to the rise of anti-Christian polemic among Muslims. In some cases, this polemic borrowed from and expanded upon earlier Jewish anti-Christian polemic. In others, particularly during times of economic stagnation, Muslims borrowed from Christian anti-Jewish writings.

Muslim use of polemic reflects some of the contextual concerns of Muslims who, despite conquering and ruling over vast territories, nevertheless remained a minority within them.[90] Preservation of the community depended on forming a distinct identity. One way of authenticating and legitimizing that identity was to use prophecies and proof texts from other religions to show the foretelling and truth of Islam while also highlighting where these other religions fell short. It also served to prevent syncretism or borrowing from other religions and reframing those borrowings in Islamic terminology and meaning.[91] In some cases, polemic was a response to personal experiences of humiliation.[92] In other cases, Muslim theologians were puzzled by the variety of Christian claims regarding key doctrines, for example, the status of Jesus and the doctrine of the Trinity; these theologians wondered how people with such disparate beliefs about Jesus could belong to the same religion, much less claim religious truth.[93]

---

90. Christians were a minority in Central Asia. Anti-Christian polemic was less present in theological writings there, largely because there was not as much of a political investment in denouncing Christianity. This heritage was reclaimed in Turkey in the late twentieth century, opening the door to teaching and studying Christianity at universities.

91. Abdelmajid Charfi, "La fonction historique de la polemique islamochretienne a l'epoque Abbasside," in *Christian Arabic Apologetics during the Abbasid Period (750–1258)*, ed., S. K. Samir and J. S. Nielsen (Leiden: Brill, 1994), esp. 44–56.

92. One prominent polemicist, al-Baqillani (d. 1013), wrote a strong rejection of Christian beliefs on the nature of God, the Incarnation, and the Trinity after a visit to Byzantium in which he was forced to enter into the emperor's presence through a door so low he had to go through backwards as a demonstration of humility.

93. Many of these theologians had come into contact with Christian minorities. Although Roman Catholic and Orthodox Christians considered these groups heretical and actively persecuted them, Muslims took at face value the claim of all of these groups to be Christian. For a detailed discussion, see Goddard, *A History of Christian-Muslim Relations*, 60–62.

Medieval Theological Dialogue

Despite the mutual polemic, there were also positive Christian-Muslim interactions during the medieval period. Sometime between 1140 and 1180, the Greek Orthodox Bishop of Sidon, Paul of Antioch, composed a work entitled "Letter to a Muslim," which was framed as a response to a Muslim's question about Christian opinions of Muhammad. Its tone is polite, offering positive observations about Muhammad, the legitimacy of his religious mission to the Arabs, and Qur'an verses on Christians. Two later Muslims replied to this letter—Ahmad bin Idris al-Qarafi (d. 1285) and the great medieval theologian and legal scholar Ibn Taymiyya (d. 1328).[94]

Ibn Taymiyya was already involved in Muslim-Christian dialogue in his native Damascus, having engaged the King of Cyprus on behalf of Muslim prisoners of war. His response to Paul's letter, entitled "The Correct Answer to Those who Changed the Religion of Jesus," is considered the fullest Muslim theological critique of Christianity ever written.[95] Because it contains critiques not only of Christianity but also of philosophy, certain styles of theology, extreme Shiism, certain Sufi practices, and Ibn al-Arabi's doctrine of the unity of existence, many scholars believe the work was written for Muslims as a guide to maintaining correct belief in the face of "innovations" introduced by a variety of parties, not just Christianity, even if it took the form of anti-Christian polemic.[96]

Ibn Taymiyya's primary concerns with respect to Christianity were the purported departure of Christians from the original monotheistic message of Jesus by deifying Jesus as the Son of God. He used verses from the Qur'an praising Christians and the truth of Christian revelation as proof texts, arguing that Jesus and Muhammad were both sent by God to call people to monotheism at times when many had departed from it. Ideally, the universality of the message and belief in

---

94. Ibn Taymiyya's response is particularly important, given his ongoing impact in Salafi, Wahhabi, and jihadist circles today.

95. For a sense of scale, the original letter was a twenty-six-page pamphlet. Ibn Taymiyya's response was nearly 1,000 pages long.

96. For a detailed analysis of the intent of the work, see David Thomas, "Apologetic and Polemic in the *Letter from Cyprus* and Ibn Taymiyya's *Jawab al-sahih li-man baddala din al-Masih*," in *Ibn Taymiyya and His Times*, ed. Yossef Rappaport and Shahab Ahmed (Karachi: Oxford University Press, 2010), 247–65.

God should unite people. Nevertheless, he concluded, Muhammad's interpretation of the message was more correct than Christian interpretations. Thus he called on Christians to accept the truth of Islam.

In the West, distance from and lack of contact with Muslims resulted in views of Islam focused on colorful stereotypes with little or no historical basis. Muhammad was portrayed as a licentious epileptic who used sexual license to undermine Christianity and was killed by pigs during one of his seizures. He was also said to be a magician who had destroyed the church in Africa. Popular *chansons de geste* claimed Muslims were polytheists who worshipped three gods—Mahound (Muhammad), Apollyon (Apollo), and Termagent (an unknown deity).[97] More positive and accurate views of Islam did not emerge among Western Christians until the twelfth century, when Christian scholars began to study Muslim scripture and came into more frequent contact with Muslims, particularly in Spain. Corrective observations included recognition of Islam's monotheistic teachings and a revised classification of Muhammad as a human prophet rather than God.

A crucial voice in changing the image of Islam and how it was approached was Peter the Venerable (1092–1156), a friend of Bernard de Clairvaux, who encouraged the Crusades. Believing religions must be studied on their own terms, according to their own sources, Peter formed a translation program in Toledo to make Muslim sources accessible to Christians; the program was comparable to that of Baghdad's House of Wisdom, which translated materials into Arabic. The Toledo project translated much of the knowledge of ancient Greece from Arabic into Latin, including logic, philosophy, science, mathematics, geography, medicine, astronomy, politics, and physics. Additional material from Muslim scholars was also translated.

Though the chief translator of the Toledo project was Gerard of Cremona (1114–1187), with more than eighty works to his credit, the most important work translated into Latin was the Qur'an, completed by Robert of Ketton (d. 1157) in 1143. This translation made the Qur'an available for the first time to the West, enabling serious scholarly study of Islam. Peter himself contributed two important theological works, the first summarized Islamic doctrine and the

---

97. See Goddard, *A History of Christian-Muslim Relations*, 92, for details.

second refuted it. Peter's study concluded Islam was a Christian heresy, because it denied the sacramental system of the Christian church and the Incarnation. Although the work followed the standard apologetic and polemical tone of the time, it was designed to inform Christians of Islamic teachings before stating why they should be considered false. Peter cited both the Bible (1 Peter 3:15) and the Qur'an (Q 3:18–19, 3:61, and 29:46) and called upon Christians to approach Muslims with love and words rather than hatred and weapons in order to bring them to salvation. Though he rejected the Qur'an overall, Peter nevertheless demonstrated knowledge of and respect for similarities between Islam and Christianity.[98] His scholarly approach, grounded in sources rather than the popular imagination, laid the groundwork for later scholars, such as Roger Bacon (d. 1292) and Thomas Aquinas (d. 1274).

Commissioned by Pope Clement IV, Bacon wrote a treatise arguing Christianity had abandoned its efforts toward conversion in favor of domination. He called for renewed attention to learning other languages and religious beliefs in order to refute them more effectively and thereby gain converts. Fluent in Latin, Greek, Hebrew, and Arabic, and the knowledge of science and religion accessible in all four, he taught that philosophy, rather than violence, was the key to responding to unbelief. Bacon made major contributions in bringing Arabic learning in science, particularly astronomy, geography, and optics, into the European curriculum.

Aquinas was arguably the greatest Christian theologian of the medieval era. He cited two major influences on his work—the Greek philosopher Aristotle and the Muslim philosopher Ibn Sina. Aquinas's theological masterpiece, the four volume *Summa contra Gentiles*, was written as a guide for Dominicans working to make the truth of Christianity evident to those not holding it, citing both human intellect and revelation as necessary sources of knowledge.

Although smaller in scope, a popular anti-Islamic tract, *Contra legem sarracenorum*, was written by Dominican Riccoldo da Monte di Croce (d. 1320). The work was later translated into German by Martin Luther and included in Theodore Bibliander's 1543 compendium of Islamic texts, which also included the first copy of the Qur'an printed on a printing press.

---

98. For details, see ibid., 92–95.

In the fifteenth century, efforts to engage in formal dialogue between Christians and Muslims were made by John of Segovia (d. 1458) and Nicholas of Cusa (d. 1464). John of Segovia wrote a refutation of the Qur'an, but also translated it into Castilian. Nicholas wrote a fictionalized work imagining various religions, including Islam, at a summit meeting in heaven, with Christianity being declared superior by all participants. Like John, he also wrote a review of the Qur'an. Though he found complete truth in Christianity, Nicholas credited Islam and Judaism with containing partial truth. These efforts were important in laying the groundwork for other future endeavors by encouraging serious study of other scriptures and the potential for recognizing truth in at least other Abrahamic traditions.

Modern Theological Dialogue

In the eighteenth century, the study of religion took a more historical and factual turn with attention to origins, philological and linguistic concerns, authentication of documents, cross-checking archaeological discoveries against historical records, and searching for evidence of editing and crafting of religious texts over time. Although such academic study claims theological neutrality, preconceived ideas and stereotypes remain in the background, whether consciously or unconsciously.[99] The first serious attempts to engage the textual sources of Islam and translate the Qur'an during this time were Alexander Ross's 1649 translation into English, the first such translation ever, and Louis Maracci's 1698 translation into Latin, the first such translation in over 500 years. Yet these translations were not entirely accurate. A more accurate translation of the Qur'an into English by George Sale was published in 1734. Other major eighteenth-century works include a description of Islam written exclusively according to Muslim sources by Adriaan Reland in 1705, and *History of the Saracens* written by Simon Ockley from 1708–1718.[100]

---

99. Edward Said addressed this issue in *Orientalism* (New York: Vintage Books, 1979).

100. Goddard, *A History of Christian-Muslim Relations*, 143–44. There were also lighter-hearted attempts to bring the Muslim world to Western audiences, such as the translation of *The Arabian Nights* into French by Antoine Galland in the early eighteenth century, followed by translations into German and English in the nineteenth century. The French translation was so popular that it became a best-seller, second only to the Bible in eighteenth-century Europe.

A key outcome from these translations was a demystification of Muslims as the enemy. Muslims became more relatable as their texts became more available for individual study. This effort was bolstered by a rise in travel literature written by European men and women traveling through or living in Muslim countries.[101] A second outcome was the rise of university centers focusing on study of the Islamic world, particularly in Paris and Leiden. At the same time, new myths began to form, often using Muhammad as a foil to church leaders; certain Enlightenment thinkers saw the church as intolerant and demanding obedience and conformity rather than critical thinking, but saw Muhammad as a tolerant ruler and Islam as a rational faith closer to their own deism.[102]

Muslim-Christian Dialogue Today

In the nineteenth and twentieth centuries, changes in Muslim-Christian dialogue came from new Christian learning about Islam and from changes within Christian theology. Central questions about the nature of Christianity came to the fore: Was it best understood as an exclusivist religion holding belief in Christ and membership in the Christian community as necessary for salvation? Could it embrace a more inclusive approach that recognized the potential for Christ to work for salvation through other religions? Did it dare engage pluralism or a belief that there are many paths to salvation through faith traditions without Christ necessarily at the center? At the heart of these questions was the question of how best to interact with other faith traditions.[103]

---

101. Examples include Lady Mary Wortley Montagu, who lived in Istanbul from 1717–18 while her husband served as British ambassador. Her account is unique for its vantage point on the otherwise hidden world of Muslim women. Charles Doughty was the first European to record travels to central Arabia. Accounts of Mecca were written by Italian Ludovico di Barthema in 1503, Englishman Joseph Pitts in 1680, Catalan Domingo Badia y Leblich—"Ali Bey al-Abbasi"—in 1897, Swiss convert to Islam John Louis Burckhardt in 1814, and Sir Richard Burton of England, who visited Mecca in 1853. Dutch scholar Snouck Hurgronje lived in Mecca for more than eight months in 1885 while writing his doctoral thesis on the Hajj.

102. Goddard, *A History of Christian-Muslim Relations*, 144.

103. For an excellent overview of Christian models for approaching other religions, from replacement (one true religion) to fulfillment (one religion fulfills many) to mutuality (many true religions called to dialogue with each other) to acceptance (many true religions), see Paul F. Knitter, *Introducing Theologies of Religions* (Maryknoll, NY: Orbis, 2004).

Part of the challenge lay in the scriptural support in both traditions for exclusivist and inclusive approaches. Exclusivist texts for Christians include the Old Testament example of the Children of Israel holding a special covenant relationship with God that at times places them in confrontation with surrounding nations and religions, even to the point of claiming God commanded genocide.[104] In the New Testament, verses such as John 14:6, "Jesus said to him, 'I am the way, and the truth, and the life. No one comes to the Father except through me,'" and Acts 4:12, "There is salvation in no one else, for there is no other name under heaven . . . by which we must be saved," have been used to assert exclusivist stances that only Christians will be saved.[105] Though some contemporary scholars believe placing these verses in context particularizes their application, others assert literal interpretations, which render these verses universal and nonnegotiable, dividing humanity into those who are saved through Jesus and those who are not.

Muslim interpreters make parallel arguments with respect to passages such as Q 2:190–1, 9:5, and 9:29, which command Muslims to kill idolaters. Though some people insist this means Muslims cannot peacefully coexist with other religions and that non-Muslims must either convert or be killed, others argue for contextualized interpretations, noting that at the time "idolaters" referred to the Quraysh of Mecca who were warring with Muslims, preventing them from fulfilling their religious duties.

Contextual interpretations in both cases are bolstered by solid scriptural support for an inclusive approach to religious Others, recognizing their capacity for knowing and reverencing God and accepting them in community. Among the many Biblical examples are Ruth and Naaman in the Old Testament and Jesus' ministry to the outcasts of society, such as the Samaritan woman at the well in the New Testament. Qur'anic examples of inclusivity include many verses, such as 2:62 and 58:22, which affirm reward for all who believe in God, the Last Day, and the value of righteous deeds.

Because exclusivist and inclusive elements are both present in these scriptures, the assertion of one absolute approach to dealing

---

104. Examples include the book of Joshua, in which God commands Israel to slaughter the Canaanites and take possession of the Holy Land.

105. Scriptural quotations are from the New Revised Standard Version of the Bible. Copyright © 1993 and 1989 by the Division of Christian Education of the National Council of the Churches of Christ in the United States of America.

with the Other is misleading, robbing believers of options for encounter that can only be determined by context and specific circumstances. Both faith traditions today grapple with whether absolute truth claims can be inclusive by inviting people to join the faith tradition or by recognizing the truth in other traditions.

Christianity long had an exclusivist approach to other faith traditions, denying the possibility of salvation outside the church. However, the Second Vatican Council of the Roman Catholic Church (1962–1965) called on Roman Catholics to engage in inter-religious dialogue based on recognition of the "profound religious sense" animating other religions.[106] Regarding Islam, the council's document, *Nostra Aetate* (*Declaration on the Relationship of the Church to Non-Christian Religions*), highlighted central Muslim doctrines, such as belief in the one almighty and all-merciful God, the Creator of heaven and earth, who has spoken repeatedly to humanity and who will judge all of humanity at the end of time. It praised Muslim submission to God, prayer, fasting, almsgiving, common faith descent from Abraham, and veneration of the Virgin Mary and Jesus, despite not recognizing Jesus as Son of God.[107] The council concluded, "If in the course of the centuries there has arisen not infrequent discussion and hostility between Christian and Muslim, this sacred Council now urges everyone to forget the past, to make sincere efforts at mutual understanding and to work together in protecting and promoting for the good and benefit of all men, social justice, good morals as well as peace and freedom."[108]

Similarly, Orthodox leaders called for recognition that modern theology must progress from concerns about salvation to rediscovering the meaning of *oikonomia* (ecumenical relationship) and developing broader appreciation of the movement and activities of the Holy

---

106. John L. Esposito, "Pluralism in Muslim-Christian Relations," *ACMCU Occasional Papers* (April 2008): 11. This revisioning marked a pivotal moment in the Roman Catholic Church. Debates continue as to whether this was a radical break with the past or a refinement of doctrine already present but not fully explored.

107. *Lumen Gentium* also asserts the Islamic connection to Abraham. French Catholic scholar Louis Massignon is credited with recognizing that connection.

108. Second Vatican Council, *Nostra Aetate*, 3, *http://www.usccb.org/beliefs-and -teachings/ecumenical-and-interreligious/interreligious/islam/vatican-council-and-papal -statements-on-islam.cfm.*

Spirit throughout the world.[109] Pope John Paul II made a comparable statement in *Redemptoris Missio*, in which he reminded Catholics that the Holy Spirit sows the seeds of the Word in various customs, cultures, and religions, so that every authentic prayer is prompted by the Holy Spirit who is present in every human heart.[110] This means the Church must seriously encounter and engage in dialogue with all people to discover, foster, and receive the gifts given by Christ through the Spirit to Others.[111]

A major Christian theologian taking this challenge is Miroslav Volf (b. 1956). The son of a Pentecostal minister, Volf was born and raised in the former Yugoslavia and witnessed its destruction, along with the religious hatred and massacre of Bosnian Muslims by Christians, in the 1990s. Questioning what it means to be a Christian in today's multireligious world and how to address hatred of the religious Other, which has so often stained the past, Volf engaged the question of Christology in his work, *Exclusion and Embrace*, asserting that following the example of Christ means reaching out to and embracing the enemy, just as Jesus reaches out to all from the cross.[112] Much of Volf's work has been dedicated to finding common ground between Muslims and Christians, with the goal of building a more just and peaceful society for all.[113]

Muslims began seriously pondering how better to engage Christians in the 1970s. One pioneer in this effort was Dr. Ismail al-Faruqi (d. 1986). Al-Faruqi argued the original message of Jesus was acceptable to Muslims in its challenge to racism, legalism, and interiorization of ethics, but that Jesus' followers had forgotten these challenges and become too focused on matters of sin and salvation.

---

109. For a history of Orthodox-Muslim interactions and modern developments, see George C. Papademetriou, ed., *Two Traditions, One Space: Orthodox Christians and Muslims in Dialogue* (Boston: Somerset Hall, 2011).

110. This was not a new teaching. Discussion of "seeds of the word" dates to the patristic era.

111. See *http://w2.vatican.va/content/john-paul-ii/en/encyclicals/documents/hf_jp-ii_enc_07121990_redemptoris-missio.html*.

112. Miroslav Volf, *Exclusion and Embrace: A Theological Exploration of Identity, Otherness, and Reconciliation* (Nashville: Abingdon, 1996).

113. See especially Miroslav Volf, *Allah: A Christian Response* (New York: HarperOne, 2011).

Recovery of Jesus' original message was, to al-Faruqi, critical in moving Christian-Muslim dialogue forward in the quest for truth.[114]

Tunisian scholar Muhammad al-Talbi (1921–2017) also stressed the import of building dialogue, but without polemics or attempts at conversion. He called for restoring God as judge rather than human beings. He pointed to the example of differences of opinion (*ikhtilaf*)

Dr. Ingrid Mattson (b. 1963)

A Canadian convert to Islam, renowned academic, and the first woman to serve as the elected head of a major international Muslim organization, Dr. Ingrid Mattson is one of the most accomplished female interpreters of Islam today. As Professor of Islamic Studies and Christian-Muslim relations at Hartford Seminary in Connecticut (1998–2012), she founded the first accredited graduate program in the United States for training Muslim chaplains and served as the Director of the MacDonald Center for the Study of Islam and Christian-Muslim relations. An advocate for interfaith engagement and multifaith activism, she was elected first as vice-president (2001–2006) and then president (2006–2010) of the Islamic Society of North America. During her tenure, she founded a national office for interfaith relations in Washington, DC, and helped create programs in tandem with Jewish organizations to promote relationship-building activities between Islam and Judaism. An original signatory of the *Amman Message*, in which the various Sunni and Shia law schools recognized each other's legitimacy, she has spoken out against terrorism and extremism in all forms, including domestic violence. She is a Senior Fellow of the Royal Aal al-Bayt Institute in Jordan and has served on the Interfaith Task Force of the White House Office of Faith-Based and Neighborhood Partnerships (2009–2010). She was also a member of the Faith-based Advisory Council for the US Department of Homeland Security (2012). She has been recognized as one of the world's "500 Most Influential Muslims" by Jordan's Royal Institute for Strategic Studies in 2009, 2010, and 2011, and was named one of Time Magazine's "100 Most Influential People" in 2007. Her book *The Story of the Qur'an* was selected for the Bridging Cultures program of the National Endowment of the Humanities in 2012.

---

114. See Charles Fletcher, *Muslim-Christian Engagement in the Twentieth Century: The Principles of Interfaith Dialogue and the Work of Isma'il al-Faruqi* (London: I. B. Tauris, 2015).

among jurisprudents in interpreting the law as a model for engaging religious difference. He interpreted the Qur'an's message of confirming and guarding what had come before (Q 5:48) as parallel to Jesus' claim to complete and fulfill the law, not to refute or abolish it (Matthew 5:17).[115]

Another prominent Muslim voice addressing interreligious dialogue today is Swiss theologian Tariq Ramadan (b. 1961). Ramadan argues for focusing on the central belief in God the Creator of all humanity and the sender of every revelation, so that God is at the center of the lives of believers, not human power plays. He reminds Muslims God deliberately created human beings in diversity so they might come to know one another (Q 5:48) and God has barred coercion in religious matters (Q 2:256). Therefore, rather than fighting over which religion is superior, he reminds Muslims that God asks people of faith to compete in doing good works (Q 2:148) and to undertake the challenging work of getting to know each other.[116]

Since the 1970s, numerous formal dialogues have been engaged between Muslims and Christians, encouraging critical study of religion—one's own and the other's. These dialogues show willingness to listen and allow each religion to define and speak for itself. In 1989, the Vatican renamed its Secretariat for non-Christians the Pontifical Council for Inter-Religious Dialogue. The Protestant organization, the World Council of Churches, also has an Office on Inter-Religious Relations and works to build trust and respect across religions.[117] Among the most important Muslim organizations calling for dialogue is the Royal Aal Al-Bayt Institute for Islamic Thought in Jordan, which works to find common ground, moderation, and tolerance between Muslims and Christians and facilitate encounters between scholars, research centers, institutes, academic entities, and universities to correct misconceptions about Islam and improve understanding of Islam among Christians as well as other Muslims.[118] Aal Al-Bayt's key initiatives have been sponsorship of

---

115. See Ataullah Siddiqui, *Christian-Muslim Dialogue in the Twentieth Century* (New York: Palgrave Macmillan, 1997), 136–48.

116. See Tariq Ramadan, *Islam: The Essentials* (London: Pelican, 2017). See also Ramadan's website at *https://tariqramadan.com*.

117. See their website and activities at *https://www.oikoumene.org/en/what-we-do /inter-religious-trust-and-respect*.

118. See *http://aalalbayt.org/en/index.html*.

His Excellency Grand Mufti of Egypt Sheikh Ali Gomaa (left) and Archbishop of Canterbury Rowan Williams (right) share a smile at a press conference concluding "A Common Word and Future of Christian-Muslim Engagement" at Lambeth Palace, England, October 2008.

the *Amman Message*[119] and the 2007 open letter, *A Common Word between Us and You*,[120] sent from 138 Muslim leaders to Christian leaders, calling for expanded dialogue on the basis of the shared beliefs of love of God and love of neighbor. As a collective work by many prominent Muslim leaders and scholars, its impact has been profound and has resulted in positive, engaged responses from many Christian denominations.

These initiatives are particularly important today in light of rising Islamophobia,[121] extremist violence, political populism, and other global developments, including large-scale Muslim migration and questions of how to assimilate into—and be received by—new societies without either side losing its identity. As news headlines report violence between Muslims and Christians in Nigeria and other places, intensified persecution of Christians in Egypt, Indonesia, and Pakistan, and rising hate crimes against Muslims in Europe

---

119. See *http://ammanmessage.com*.

120. For full text and list of signatories, as well as ongoing activities, see *http://www.acommonword.com*.

121. For details, see Georgetown University's Bridge Initiative at *http://bridge.georgetown.edu*.

Prince Ghazi bin Muhammad of Jordan (b. 1966)

Professor of Islamic philosophy with expertise on love in the Qur'an, Prince Ghazi bin Muhammad is known for his work promoting interreligious dialogue, particularly between Muslims and Christians, in his native Jordan and throughout the world. He has held the Chair of the Royal Aal al-Bayt Institute for Islamic Thought since 2000, promoting a tolerant and moderate interpretation of Islam. Since 2005, he has served as Chairman of the Royal Steering Committee for the *Amman Message*. He is the author of and coordinator for the *Common Word* initiative, launched in 2008 and called the most successful Muslim-Christian interfaith initiative to date. He was also the architect of the 2010 proposal to the United Nations for what is now called World Interfaith Harmony Week to bring people together in harmony, regardless of religious affiliation. Prince Ghazi has been a consistent voice in calling for dialogue as well as collective action. This work has been recognized nationally in Jordan and internationally by Muslims and Christians. Prince Ghazi has received many international awards from both Muslims and Christians, including the Eugene Biser Award (Germany) in 2008, the Medal of Peace from Greek Orthodox Patriarch of Jerusalem and the Holy Land Theophilos III in 2009, the St. Augustine Award for Interreligious Dialogue (Italy) in 2012, the Grand Cordon of the Order of Al-Hussein bin Ali (Jordan's highest medal, usually reserved for heads of state) in 2013, and the International Interfaith Harmony Award from the International Islamic University in Malaysia in 2014. He has been nominated for the Nobel Peace Prize four times since 2013.

and the United States,[122] the need for dialogue and better mutual understanding has never been greater.

Neither faith tradition lives in a vacuum; both affect and are affected by events and developments in the other, particularly in this age of global communication and travel. Increasingly, Muslims and Christians are neighbors, business partners, coworkers, friends—and sometimes enemies—particularly where conflicts exist over resources, power, or territory. Many of the challenges Muslims and Christians share are not unique to religion. Poverty, natural disasters, rising food and water insecurity, and climate change affect everyone, suggesting

---

122. See *http://www.pewresearch.org/fact-tank/2016/11/21/anti-muslim-assaults-reach-911-era-levels-fbi-data-show/*.

that finding common ground for working together is crucial if there is to be hope for a better future.[123]

As humans step toward that future, it is essential to consider our past and find those historical memories and precedents to guide us toward the world we want to live in. Hurtful moments must be acknowledged—and then used as an opportunity for reflection and amending the behaviors and attitudes that led to them, so that the mistakes and injuries of the past do not determine our future. Rather than love of power or exclusive truth claims leading to Othering and division, perhaps it is time, as a *Common Word* suggests, to make the love of God and love of neighbor at the heart of Islam and Christianity our core vision now and in our future.

Review Questions

1. Identify and discuss Muhammad's encounters with Christians. What models do they offer for Muslim-Christian relations today?

2. The Qur'an contains both praise and criticism for Christians. What opportunities and obstacles do these passages present for Muslim-Christian dialogue?

3. In the past, Muslims and Christians worked together in different places to preserve the world's knowledge, translate each other's works, and engage in diplomacy and trade. There are also instances in which they mutually denounced each other. How might contemporary Muslims and Christians learn from and draw upon this history?

4. Identify and discuss methods of theological dialogue between Muslims and Christians. Which methods appear to be the most and least successful and why? What kinds of outcomes did they hope to produce? How might such dialogue be approached most effectively today?

---

123. One opportunity may lie in responses to two documents addressing environmental concerns and the human condition: Pope Francis' Encyclical "On Care for Our Common Home," May 24, 2015, *http://w2.vatican.va/content/francesco/en/encyclicals /documents/papa-francesco_20150524_enciclica-laudato-si.html*, and the Islamic Declaration on Global Climate Change issued in response by the Islamic Foundation for Ecology and Environmental Sciences, August 18, 2015, *http://www.ifees.org.uk /declaration/*.

Discussion Questions

1. What, if any, common ground exists between Muslims and Christians for working toward common goals?
2. The Crusades provide a complex array of figures, events and interactions between Muslims and Christians. What, if any, resources do they provide for finding potential solutions to military conflicts?
3. How might Muslims and Christians most effectively approach dialogue today?

For Further Study

Readings

Borelli, John, ed. *A Common Word and the Future of Christian-Muslim Relations*. ACMCU Occasional Papers. Georgetown University, Washington, DC: Prince Alwaleed bin Talal Center for Muslim-Christian Understanding, 2009.

Goddard, Hugh. *A History of Christian-Muslim Relations*. Chicago: New Amsterdam, 2000.

Green, Joey, ed. *Jesus and Muhammad: The Parallel Sayings*. Berkeley: Seastone, 2003.

Idliby, Raniya, Suzanne Oliver, and Priscilla Warner. *The Faith Club: A Muslim, A Christian, A Jew—Three Women Search for Understanding*. New York: Atria, 2006.

Merad, Ali. *Christian Hermit in an Islamic World: A Muslim's View of Charles de Foucauld*. Translated by Zoe Hersov. New York: Paulist Press, 1999.

Peters, F. E. *Jesus and Muhammad: Parallel Tracks, Parallel Lives*. New York: Oxford University Press, 2011.

Tolan, John. *Saint Francis and the Sultan: The Curious History of a Christian-Muslim Encounter*. New York: Oxford University Press, 2009.

Volf, Miroslav. *Exclusion and Embrace: A Theological Exploration of Identity, Otherness, and Reconciliation*. Nashville: Abingdon, 1996.

Film

Kronemer, Alexander, Jeremy Irons, Alexander McPherson, et al. *The Sultan and the Saint.* [Arlington, VA]: PBS, 2017. *https://www.sultanandthesaintfilm.com.*

Profiles the famous meeting between Saint Francis and Malik al-Kamil. Website includes a variety of resources.

Hanon, Jim, Mart Green, Sami Awad, Ahmad Al-Azzeh, Yonatan Shapiro, Kirk Whalun, Mike Galloway, Mark Arnom. *Little Town of Bethlehem.* Oklahoma City: EthnoGraphic Media, 2010. *http://littletownofbethlehem.org.*

Documentary film about a Muslim, a Christian, and a Jew who choose nonviolence amid the overwhelming violence in Israel and Palestine.

INDEX

Note: An italicized *i, m, n, s,* or *t* indicates an illustration, map, footnote, sidebar, or table, respectively.

A

al-Tirmidhi, 54n25
Torah, 44, 57n31, 64, 73n23
torture, 132, 143, 154, 157Is, 158s
trade, 278–279
tradition, 129
translations, 265, 266nn28,29, 283,
    291–292
    of Qur'an, 78, 83–84, 291–292,
        293–294
transmission, chains of (isnad),
    54–56, 65n2, 85, 163n3, 201,
    241n91
transmission , 55–56, 224–228
Treaty of Hudaybiyyah (628), 51,
    53t, 157
tribal incompatibility, 14–15,
    144n71, 150n93. see also
    diversity; equality
tribalism. see pre-Islamic Arabia,
    tribal
Trinity, 79n38, 261, 262, 286, 289
Tunisia, 130n25, 215n3, 284n78
turban colors, 116n42
Turkey, 109n45, 130n25, 174, 210,
    215, 228n44, 240, 247, 265, 283,
    289n90, 294n101
al-Tusi, 54n25
Twelvers (Ithna' Ashari or Imamis),
    104–105, 107–109, 108t, 113,
    124

U
'Ulfah, Maria, 79n36, 85s–86s,
    87n52
ul-Haq, Zia, 156n110
Umar ibn al-Khattab, 66, 77n31, 96,
    96t, 97, 98t, 121–122, 127n17,
    225n33, 263n16. see also Pact of
    Umar; Rightly Guided Caliphs
Umayyad Empire (661-750 CE)
    Christians and, 268, 287
    ethics and, 194n12

Fivers and, 105
founding of, 97–98, 103n27
Islamic law and, 122
military conflict and, 189n3
non-Muslims and, 125, 157n114
oppression and, 103
pacifism and, 197n22
rivals to, 99n13, 267
in Spain, 267–268
Sufis and, 162
timeline and, 98t
veiling and, 229
wealth and, 163
Umm Darda, 242
Umm Salama, 51–52, 223,
    225–226
Umm Waraqa, 19–20, 44, 256
unbelievers (kuffar), 262–263. see
    also non-Muslims
United Arab Emerates (UAE),
    149n92, 152n97
United States. see also Wadud,
    Amina and other Americans;
    the West
    Al-Qaida and, 204
    civilian jihad and, 211
    Female Genital Cutting and,
        248n109
    feminism and, 247, 248n110
    gender justice and, 244s
    hate crimes and, 299–300
    human rights and, 154n105
    Islamic Law and, 158–159
    media and, 187
    Muslim feminism and, 247
    Muslim women and, 19n14,
        240n84, 243, 244s, 298s
    Nizari Ismailis and, 106n38
    personal contact with Muslims
        and, 8
    punishments and, 135n40
    terrorist attacks compared to
        other countries and, 9–10